Judges
and
Ruth

TEACH THE TEXT COMMENTARY

John H. Walton
Old Testament General Editor

Mark L. Strauss
New Testament General Editor

Volumes now available:

Old Testament Volumes

New Testament Volumes

Visit the series website at www.teachthetextseries.com.

TEACH the TEXT
COMMENTARY SERIES

Judges
and
Ruth

Kenneth C. Way

Mark L. Strauss and John H. Walton
GENERAL EDITORS

ILLUSTRATING THE TEXT

Kevin and Sherry Harney
ASSOCIATE EDITORS

Joshua Blunt
CONTRIBUTING WRITER

BakerBooks

a division of Baker Publishing Group
Grand Rapids, Michigan

Published by Baker Books
a division of Baker Publishing Group
P.O. Box 6287, Grand Rapids, MI 49516-6287
www.bakerbooks.com

Printed in the United States of America

Library of Congress Cataloging-in-Publication Data
Names: Way, Kenneth C., author.
Title: Judges and Ruth / Kenneth C. Way.
Other titles: Ruth
Description: Grand Rapids : Baker Books, 2016. | Series: Teach the text commentary series | Includes bibliographical references and index.
Identifiers: LCCN 2016009295 | ISBN 9780801092152 (pbk.)
Subjects: LCSH: Bible. Judges—Commentaries. | Bible. Ruth—Commentaries.
Classification: LCC BS1305.53 .W39 2016 | DDC 222/.307—dc23
LC record available at http://lccn.loc.gov/2016009295

16   17   18   19   20   21   22   7   6   5   4   3   2   1

To my precious children: Schuyler, Bradford, and Lila.
May you and your generation do what is right in the eyes of the Lord.

Contents

Welcome to the Teach the Text Commentary Series

Why another commentary series? That was the question the general editors posed when Baker Books asked us to produce this series. Is there something that we can offer to pastors and teachers that is not currently being offered by other commentary series, or that can be offered in a more helpful way? After carefully researching the needs of pastors who teach the text on a weekly basis, we concluded that yes, more can be done; the Teach the Text Commentary Series (TTCS) is carefully designed to fill an important gap.

The technicality of modern commentaries often overwhelms readers with details that are tangential to the main purpose of the text. Discussions of source and redaction criticism, as well as detailed surveys of secondary literature, seem far removed from preaching and teaching the Word. Rather than wade through technical discussions, pastors often turn to devotional commentaries, which may contain exegetical weaknesses, misuse the Greek and Hebrew languages, and lack hermeneutical sophistication. There is a need for a commentary that utilizes the best of biblical scholarship but also presents the material in a clear, concise, attractive, and user-friendly format.

This commentary is designed for that purpose—to provide a ready reference for the exposition of the biblical text, giving easy access to information that a pastor needs to communicate the text effectively. To that end, the commentary is divided into carefully selected preaching units (with carefully regulated word counts both in the passage as a whole and in each subsection). Pastors and teachers engaged in weekly preparation thus know that they will be reading approximately the same amount of material on a week-by-week basis.

Each passage begins with a concise summary of the central message, or "Big Idea," of the passage and a list of its main themes. This is followed by a more detailed interpretation of the text, including the literary context of the passage, historical background material, and interpretive insights. While drawing on the best of biblical scholarship, this material is clear, concise, and to the point. Technical material is kept to a minimum, with endnotes pointing the reader to more detailed discussion and additional resources.

A second major focus of this commentary is on the preaching and teaching process itself. Few commentaries today help the pastor/teacher move from the meaning of the text to its effective communication. Our goal is to bridge this gap. In addition to interpreting the text in the "Understanding the Text" section, each unit contains a "Teaching the Text" section and an "Illustrating the Text" section. The teaching section points to the key theological themes of the passage and ways to communicate these themes to today's audiences. The illustration section provides ideas and examples for retaining the interest of hearers and connecting the message to daily life.

The creative format of this commentary arises from our belief that the Bible is not just a record of God's dealings in the past but is the living Word of God, "alive and active" and "sharper than any double-edged sword" (Heb. 4:12). Our prayer is that this commentary will help to unleash that transforming power for the glory of God.

The General Editors

Introduction to the Teach the Text Commentary Series

This series is designed to provide a ready reference for teaching the biblical text, giving easy access to information that is needed to communicate a passage effectively. To that end, the commentary is carefully divided into units that are faithful to the biblical authors' ideas and of an appropriate length for teaching or preaching.

The following standard sections are offered in each unit.

1. *Big Idea*. For each unit the commentary identifies the primary theme, or "Big Idea," that drives both the passage and the commentary.
2. *Key Themes*. Together with the Big Idea, the commentary addresses in bullet-point fashion the key ideas presented in the passage.
3. *Understanding the Text*. This section focuses on the exegesis of the text and includes several sections.
   a. The Text in Context. Here the author gives a brief explanation of how the unit fits into the flow of the text around it, including reference to the rhetorical strategy of the book and the unit's contribution to the purpose of the book.
   b. Outline/Structure. For some literary genres (e.g., epistles), a brief exegetical outline may be provided to guide the reader through the structure and flow of the passage.

   c. Historical and Cultural Background. This section addresses historical and cultural background information that may illuminate a verse or passage.

   d. Interpretive Insights. This section provides information needed for a clear understanding of the passage. The intention of the author is to be highly selective and concise rather than exhaustive and expansive.

   e. Theological Insights. In this very brief section the commentary identifies a few carefully selected theological insights about the passage.

4. *Teaching the Text*. Under this second main heading the commentary offers guidance for teaching the text. In this section the author lays out the main themes and applications of the passage. These are linked carefully to the Big Idea and are represented in the Key Themes.

5. *Illustrating the Text*. At this point in the commentary the writers partner with a team of pastor/teachers to provide suggestions for relevant and contemporary illustrations from current culture, entertainment, history, the Bible, news, literature, ethics, biography, daily life, medicine, and over forty other categories. They are designed to spark creative thinking for preachers and teachers and to help them design illustrations that bring alive the passage's key themes and message.

Preface

What a pleasure and a privilege to write this commentary on the books of Judges and Ruth! I pray that, despite any shortcomings, it would make known and bring honor to the "Judge of all the earth," who ultimately brings justice and deliverance to his people. I must also express deep gratitude to many colleagues and their communities for contributing to this work on multiple levels.

First, Lori Way has lived with the books of Judges and Ruth by virtue of being married to me, and her influence is represented in every pericope. For her ongoing logistical support, theological conversations, editorial feedback, emotional inspiration, and love, I am immeasurably indebted.

Second, my first mentor in Old Testament studies and the general editor of this unique series, John Walton, took a risk by inviting this young scholar to contribute a volume. He generously offered wise guidance and warm support throughout the writing process, and he helped me to clarify and refine many remarks. He also introduced me to the expert team at Baker Publishing Group, especially Brian Vos and James Korsmo.

Third, my local Christian family at Granada Heights Friends Church in La Mirada, California, provided a rare environment of nurture for this commentary. Pastors Ed Morsey and Michael Sanborn preached masterfully through every section of Judges. They also spent time in weekly study on Judges with me alongside my colleagues Mark Saucy and Tom Finley.

Fourth, Talbot School of Theology, Biola University, generously contributed funds and granted me both a research leave (fall 2010) and a sabbatical (spring 2014) so that I could write this commentary. Special thanks must be expressed to my deans (formerly Dennis Dirks and Mike Wilkins; presently Clint Arnold and Scott Rae) and my department chair (John Hutchison).

Fifth, I had the personal privilege of presenting this material in a variety of settings. These included teaching elective courses at Talbot (spring 2010; 2013), presenting papers at a Biola faculty integration seminar (summer 2011) and at the Society of Biblical Literature (fall 2011; 2014), teaching Sunday school lessons at La Habra Hills Presbyterian Church (January 2011; 2012), and preaching sermons at Granada Heights Friends Church and Biola University (chapel, spring 2010; 2015). Many people at these diverse venues offered constructive feedback and raised helpful questions that facilitated my writing and research.

Finally, I must thank some additional colleagues for their various forms of influence. Stephen Kaufman, about fifteen years ago, guided my reading of Judges and Ruth in a Hebrew prose course at Hebrew Union College–Jewish Institute of Religion. More recently Ed Curtis, Ron Pierce, and Moyer Hubbard, authors of other Teach the Text volumes, offered encouragement, accountability, and advice during the writing process. Garry DeWeese, Gary Manning, Bruce Seymour, and Mark Hansard also offered wise feedback in numerous conversations over parts of the manuscript.

For all these fellow laborers I am deeply grateful.

Abbreviations

Old Testament

Gen.	Genesis	2 Chron.	2 Chronicles	Dan.	Daniel
Exod.	Exodus	Ezra	Ezra	Hosea	Hosea
Lev.	Leviticus	Neh.	Nehemiah	Joel	Joel
Num.	Numbers	Esther	Esther	Amos	Amos
Deut.	Deuteronomy	Job	Job	Obad.	Obadiah
Josh.	Joshua	Ps(s).	Psalm(s)	Jon.	Jonah
Judg.	Judges	Prov.	Proverbs	Mic.	Micah
Ruth	Ruth	Eccles.	Ecclesiastes	Nah.	Nahum
1 Sam.	1 Samuel	Song	Song of Songs	Hab.	Habakkuk
2 Sam.	2 Samuel	Isa.	Isaiah	Zeph.	Zephaniah
1 Kings	1 Kings	Jer.	Jeremiah	Hag.	Haggai
2 Kings	2 Kings	Lam.	Lamentations	Zech.	Zechariah
1 Chron.	1 Chronicles	Ezek.	Ezekiel	Mal.	Malachi

New Testament

Matt.	Matthew	Eph.	Ephesians	Heb.	Hebrews
Mark	Mark	Phil.	Philippians	James	James
Luke	Luke	Col.	Colossians	1 Pet.	1 Peter
John	John	1 Thess.	1 Thessalonians	2 Pet.	2 Peter
Acts	Acts	2 Thess.	2 Thessalonians	1 John	1 John
Rom.	Romans	1 Tim.	1 Timothy	2 John	2 John
1 Cor.	1 Corinthians	2 Tim.	2 Timothy	3 John	3 John
2 Cor.	2 Corinthians	Titus	Titus	Jude	Jude
Gal.	Galatians	Philem.	Philemon	Rev.	Revelation

General

ASOR	American Schools of Oriental Research	ca.	*circa*, about
		cf.	*confer*, compare
b.	Babylonian Talmud	chap(s).	chapter(s)
BC	Before Christ (= BCE, Before Common Era)	e.g.	*exempli gratia*, for example

esp.	especially	kg	kilogram(s)
etc.	*et cetera*, and others	lb.	pound(s)
ft.	foot/feet	v(v).	verse(s)
Heb.	Hebrew	vol(s).	volume(s)
ibid.	*ibidem*, there the same	//	parallel passages
i.e.	*id est*, that is		

Ancient Versions and Manuscripts

BHS	*Biblia Hebraica Stuttgartensia*	4QJudg^a	Judges manuscript A from Qumran Cave 4
LXX	Septuagint	Vulg.	Vulgate
MT	Masoretic Text		

Modern English Versions

CEB	Common English Bible
ESV	English Standard Version
HCSB	Holman Christian Standard Bible
JPS	· *The Holy Scriptures according to the Masoretic Text*. Philadelphia: Jewish Publication Society of America, 1917.
KJV	King James Version
MSG	*The Message*
NASB	New American Standard Bible
NET	The NET Bible (New English Translation)
NIV	New International Version
NJB	New Jerusalem Bible
NJPS	*The Tanakh: The Holy Scriptures: The New JPS Translation according to the Traditional Hebrew Text*. Philadelphia: The Jewish Publication Society of America, 1985.
NKJV	New King James Version
NLT	New Living Translation
NRSV	New Revised Standard Version

Modern Reference Works

ABD	D. N. Freedman, ed. *The Anchor Bible Dictionary*. 6 vols. New York: Doubleday, 1992.
ANEP	J. B. Pritchard, ed. *The Ancient Near East in Pictures Relating to the Old Testament*. Princeton: Princeton University Press, 1969.
ANET	J. B. Pritchard, ed. *Ancient Near Eastern Texts Relating to the Old Testament*. Third edition with Supplement. Princeton: Princeton University Press, 1969.
ARM	*Archives Royales de Mari* (Mari Royal Archives)
COS	W. W. Hallo and K. L. Younger Jr., eds. *The Context of Scripture*. 3 vols. Leiden: Brill, 1997–2002.
DCH	D. J. A. Clines, ed. *The Dictionary of Classical Hebrew*. 8 vols. Sheffield: Sheffield Academic Press, 1993–2011.

DDD	K. van der Toorn, B. Becking, and P. van der Horst, eds. *Dictionary of Deities and Demons in the Bible*. Leiden: Brill, 1999.
IVPBBCOT	J. H. Walton, V. H. Matthews, and M. W. Chavalas. *The IVP Bible Background Commentary: Old Testament*. Downers Grove, IL: InterVarsity, 2000.
JETS	*Journal of the Evangelical Theological Society*
NIDOTTE	W. A. VanGemeren, ed. *New International Dictionary of Old Testament Theology and Exegesis*. 5 vols. Grand Rapids: Zondervan, 1997.

Introduction to Judges

Have you ever watched a movie that was rated PG-13 or even R? Have you ever felt slightly sick or disturbed after viewing a depiction of intense violence or behavior that was immoral or illicit? I raise this question because I believe such movie experiences are in some ways analogous to what a Bible reader experiences when he or she encounters the biblical book of Judges.

In fact, one could debate whether Judges should be assigned a PG-13 or an R rating. The Motion Picture Association of America explains that "a PG-13 motion picture may go beyond the PG rating in theme, violence, nudity, sensuality, language, adult activities or other elements." Furthermore, "There may be depictions of violence in a PG-13 movie, but generally not both realistic and extreme or persistent violence." On the other hand, the R rating is reserved for those movies that include "intense or persistent violence."[1] The book of Judges certainly depicts intense violence (sometimes of an "adult" nature), which is, relatively speaking, most palatable at the beginning of the book and most repulsive at the end. Perhaps one should assign a PG rating to the opening chapters, a PG-13 rating to the midsection, and an R rating to the concluding narratives. As the book unfolds, Israel's illicit behaviors continue to increase, and by the end the reader is left with that disturbed or sick feeling.

Judges is in fact a dark and disturbing book. It was meant to be so. It is a book that is preoccupied with inverted accounts—stories of reversal where the teachings of Deuteronomy are often unknown or ignored altogether by the characters.[2] The stories of Israel's so-called heroes are mostly stories of scandal presented with billowing intensity.

I often remind my students that it is helpful to ask strategic questions of the book of Judges, such as "What is wrong with this picture?" and "Where is God in this story?" These two interpretive questions are the keys that will be employed in this commentary to unlock the big ideas and the theological themes of each pericope (i.e., the passage or coherent literary unit). But before unpacking the meaning of the respective pericopae (which is the aim in the rest of this commentary) it is necessary to briefly introduce the literary structure, theological contribution, and historical setting of the book of Judges.

Literary Structure

There is a virtual consensus in recent scholarship that Judges has a tripartite structure. There is clearly an introduction (1:1–3:6), body (3:7–16:31), and conclusion (17:1–21:25). Since the early 1980s many scholars have observed thematic and semantic connections between the introduction and the conclusion. For example, Gooding demonstrates that there is a two-part introduction that corresponds to a two-part conclusion, together forming the pattern A-B-B′-A′ (1:1–2:5; 2:6–3:6; 17:1–18:31; 19:1–21:25).[3] Gooding also suggests that the Gideon narrative (6:1–8:32) is the central pivot (F) of a chiasm that accounts for the arrangement of the entire book (A-B-C-D-E-F-E′-D′-C′-B′-A′).[4]

Recently, anthropologist Mary Douglas has made a significant contribution to our understanding of complex chiastic devices in eastern Mediterranean literature, and she calls these patterns "ring compositions."[5] While she has identified ring structures in many short biblical passages, she is most known for theorizing that the entire book of Numbers is arranged in a ring.[6] Based on her exposition of the essential components of a ring composition, I suggest that the entire book of Judges also follows the same pattern (see the figure).[7]

According to Douglas, there are seven characteristics of a ring.

(1) *Exposition or prologue* (1:1–3:6): This section "states the theme and introduces the main characters. . . . It is laid out so as to anticipate the mid-turn and the ending that will eventually respond to it."[8] The primary concepts that are introduced in the prologue of Judges are Israel's military and religious failures with respect to the tribes, leadership, and covenant and the cyclical pattern of apostasy, oppression, and God's deliverance through a leader. The relationships between the prologue, mid-turn, and ending are specifically treated under characteristics 5 and 7 below.

(2) *Split into two halves* (1:1–7:25 and 8:1–21:25): "If the end is going to join the beginning the composition will at some point need to make a turn toward the start. . . . An imaginary line . . . divides the work into two halves, the first, outgoing, the second, returning."[9] The deliverer stories in the first half of the book (Othniel, Ehud, Deborah/Barak) are depicted in a relatively positive light, whereas those of the second half are decidedly negative (Abimelek, Jephthah, Samson). The transitional account of Gideon is a mixed portrayal

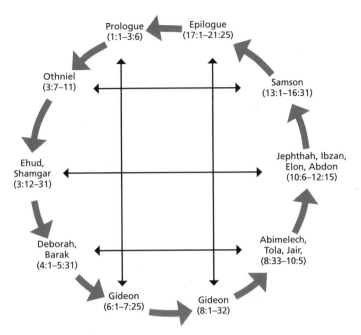

Figure 1. The Ring Structure of the Book of Judges

of both positive/ambiguous and negative elements. It is rightly observed that the body of Judges moves from triumph (3:7–7:25) to tragedy (8:1–16:31), with the shift occurring in the middle of the Gideon narrative.[10] Also, in the first half of the book (including the transitional account of Gideon) the land is said to have rested *x* number of years (3:11, 30; 5:31; 8:28), whereas in the second half leaders are merely said to rule/judge *x* number of years (9:22; 12:7; 16:31), and the land apparently has no rest.

(3) *Parallel sections* (3:7–11 // 13:1–16:31; 3:12–31 // 10:6–12:15; 4:1–5:31 // 9:1–10:5): "Each section on one side has to be matched by its corresponding pair on the other side."[11] Interesting semantic and thematic correspondences will be explored in the commentary, such as the roles of marriage in the Othniel/Samson accounts, Ephraimites in the Ehud/Jephthah accounts, and female warriors in the Deborah/Abimelek accounts. The geographical orientations are also the same for each parallel section: Othniel/Samson are set in the south, Ehud/Jephthah deal with eastern (Transjordanian) people groups, and Deborah/Abimelek are set in the north.

(4) *Indicators to mark individual sections*: "Some method for marking the consecutive units of structure is technically necessary," including "key words," "specific signals to indicate beginnings or endings of the sections," "repeating a refrain," and "alternation."[12] The sections are clearly indicated in Judges primarily through the inclusion of formulaic opening refrains and

concluding summaries (3:7 with 3:11; 3:12 with 3:30; 4:1 with 5:31; 6:1 with 8:28–32; 10:6 with 12:7; 13:1 with 16:31). The opening and closing indicators for the Abimelek narrative, while clearly marked (8:33–35 and 9:22–24, 56–57), are different in form from the other narratives (likely for intensified rhetorical effect).

(5) *Central loading* (6:1–8:32): The "middle . . . uses some of the same key word clusters that were found in the exposition. As the ending also accords with the exposition, the mid-turn tends to be in concordance with them both."[13] The Gideon account serves as a transitional pivot for the entire book, and its themes clearly echo those of both the prologue and epilogue (see table 1).

Table 1: Correspondence between Central Pivot and Peripheral Frame

Prologue	A	Israel fights enemies (1:1–2:5)
	B	Israel faces idolatry (2:6–3:6)
Center of Ring	B	Gideon faces idolatry (6:1–32)
	A	Gideon fights enemies (6:33–7:25)
	A	Gideon fights Israel (8:1–21)
	B	Gideon forges idolatry (8:22–32)
Epilogue	B	Israel forges idolatry (17:1–18:31)
	A	Israel fights Israel (19:1–21:25)

Notice especially how both enemies and idolatry transition from the outside to the inside of Israel in the Gideon story as well as in the outer frame.

(6) *Rings within rings*: "The major ring may be internally structured by little rings. . . . A large book often contains many small rings. They may come from different sources, times, and authors."[14] Smaller rings are in fact quite prominent in Judges (e.g., see 4:1–24; 17:1–13; 19:1–30). Numerous literary scholars have identified complex chiastic devices—many of which may qualify as "rings"—in many passages of the book.[15]

(7) *Closure at two levels* (the double-prologue in 1:1–3:6 and the double-epilogue in 17:1–21:25): "By joining up with the beginning, the ending unequivocally signals completion. . . . Just arriving at the beginning by the process of inverted ordering is not enough to produce a firm closure. The final section signals its arrival at the end by using some conspicuous key words from the exposition. . . . Most importantly, there also has to be thematic correspondence."[16] The themes of Israel's military and religious failures saturate the outer framework of Judges, and many key words/phrases are readily apparent in episodes such as Judah going up first (1:1–2; 20:18), acquisition of wives (1:11–15; 21:1–25), application of the ban (1:17; 21:11; cf. 20:48), Jebusites in Jerusalem (1:21; 19:10–11), and Israel weeping (2:4–5; 20:26).

Douglas's seven characteristics of ring compositions are all demonstrably present in the book of Judges. This is not surprising given the common employment of the term "cycle" to describe the patterns evident in this period of Israel's history. But the term "cycle," or even the term "ring," may not actually go far enough in characterizing the structure of the book of Judges. On both the micro and the macro levels (i.e., regarding the smaller rings and the comprehensive ring) there is a movement from positive to negative portrayals—either from good/ambiguous to bad or from bad to worse. Thus the term "spiral" is also used appropriately to characterize the book (cf. 2:19). The beginning of the ring (prologue) is on a higher moral/political plane than the end of the ring (epilogue), just as the first triad of judges is higher than the second triad, and as the early Gideon stories are higher than the latter ones. This descending progression is even demonstrated in themes such as the changing portrayal of women in the book, ranging from honorable (Othniel's wife in chap. 1) to horrific (Benjamite wives in chap. 21).[17] The structure of the book of Judges when viewed from the side therefore reveals a spiral, whereas the structure when viewed from the top or from the bottom reveals a ring.

The movement from positive to negative presentations is also evident in the proportion of verbiage that the narrator devotes to each literary unit. Thus Younger observes: "The more moral, the less verbiage; the less moral, the greater the verbiage."[18] This insightful observation certainly characterizes the sequence of the six major parallel stories of the ring structure. The best

Table 2: Relationship between Verbiage and Morality in the Book of Judges

Literary Units			Verse Count	Word Count[a]
Framework and Pivot	Prologue	1:1–3:6	65	1,390
	Gideon	6:1–8:32	97	2,371
	Epilogue	17:1–21:25	147	3,473
Parallel Panels	Othniel	3:7–11	5	108
	Ehud	3:12–30	19	417
	Deborah/Barak	4:1–5:31	55	1,023
	Abimelek	8:33–9:57	60	1,272
	Jephthah	10:6–12:7	60	1,396
	Samson	13:1–16:31	96	2,291
"Minor" Judges	Shamgar	3:31	1	24
	Tola, Jair	10:1–5	5	87
	Ibzan, Elon, Abdon	12:8–15	8	117
Totals	Whole book	1:1–21:25	618	13,969

[a] The word-count totals were computed in Bible Works software (based on the Hebrew text, search version WTM).

and shortest account (Othniel) is eclipsed by that of Ehud, which is eclipsed by Deborah/Barak, which is eclipsed by Abimelek, which is eclipsed by Jephthah, which is finally eclipsed by the worst and longest account (Samson). But Younger's observation about the "major" judges (i.e., what I call the "parallel panels") is also borne out in the remaining sequences of the ring structure (see table 2).

As for the framework and pivot, the prologue is eclipsed by the size of the Gideon account, which is finally eclipsed by the massive epilogue. The same building sequence is even apparent for the so-called "minor" judges: Shamgar is relatively better than Tola and Jair, who are relatively better than Ibzan, Elon, and Abdon.

Theological Contribution

Israel's Failure

The downward spiral is the most extensive structural mechanism used by the narrator to convey his point. As a reader, it is difficult to miss the impression that this period was a "dark age" (cf. 1 Sam. 3:1–2), or perhaps an "intermediate period,"[19] in the history of Israel. The message is that the generations following the death of Joshua have increasingly failed to uphold the torah/covenant. This failure is illustrated in all levels of Israelite society. All the people, especially the religious and military leaders, are guilty of disobedience and apostasy. Block aptly describes this failure as "the Canaanization of Israel,"[20] which captures the idea that Judges essentially recounts a reversal of Joshua's conquest.[21]

Refrains

The narrator explicitly makes his point through the use of refrains. The first refrain—that the Israelites did "evil in the eyes of the LORD"—occurs seven times, once in the prologue (2:11) and six more times in the body of the book (3:7, 12; 4:1; 6:1; 10:6; 13:1). The so-called major judge cycles are meant to be interpreted through the lens of this refrain. The narrator is essentially telling the same story seven times,[22] even though the characters and circumstances keep changing and the stories keep growing in depth and length. Moreover, the opening formula for the Abimelek story ("When Gideon had died the Israelites relapsed and whored after the Baals" [8:33; author's translation]) is a variant form of this refrain that signals an intensification of the apostasy for the second triad of parallel stories.

The second refrain is introduced in the extended epilogue of the book. It has two related components, and it is employed in four places corresponding to the four units of the epilogue. The first and final occurrences, which form an inclusio for the epilogue, are stated in full—"In those days there was no king in Israel; each would do what was right in his own eyes" (17:6; 21:25; author's translation)—whereas the two middle occurrences are truncated so that the second component is implied by ellipsis (18:1; 19:1).[23] Again, this refrain is intended as an interpretive lens for viewing the stories of chapters 17–21.

The relationship between the two refrains of chapters 3–16 and 17–21 should not be missed. The descent from shallow to deep waters, which is the narrator's operative principle of literary arrangement, may also describe the shift from the first refrain to the second. Doing evil in the eyes of the Lord is a description of breaking covenant (i.e., disobeying God's commands; see 2:11–13, 20), and it is difficult to imagine what could be worse than that. But indeed the second refrain goes even further. Doing what is right in one's own eyes, as if there were no authority structure whatsoever, is worse than breaking covenant, because it implies that God's word and works have been left entirely out of the picture! Thus in the epilogue the reader deeply senses the *absence* of God's covenant and presence.[24] Israel is depicted here thinking and acting as though the torah does not exist, which poses the question, "Is there any difference between an Israelite and a Canaanite?"

God's Faithfulness

So far the above discussion has mainly focused on the negative message of Judges. But there is an ironic twist to this dark presentation. By emphasizing Israel's *un*faithfulness, the narrator subtly reveals *God's* faithfulness. While Israel's judges are increasingly depicted as failures, readers are ironically reminded that Yahweh is the ultimate "Judge" (11:27). Moreover, while Israel wrestles with the meaning of kingship, readers are reminded that Yahweh shall ultimately "rule" (8:23). After all, God alone is the one who graciously delivers Israel time and time again (e.g., 1:2, 4; 2:16, 18; 3:9–10, 15, 28; 4:14–15; 6:36–37; 7:7, 9, 15, 22; 10:12–14; 11:9, 32; 12:3; 15:18), not because Israel deserves it but because God chooses to preserve his covenant people.[25] Thus God is revealed in Judges as the consummate Rescuer of his people, which is among the greatest themes of Scripture (e.g., Pss. 3:8; 68:19–20; Isa. 33:22; 43:3, 11; Hosea 13:4; Matt. 1:21; Luke 2:11; 19:10; Acts 4:12).

God's Kingship

This theocentric perspective may help to explicate the meaning of the refrain "no king," which is the theme of the epilogue. Is this refrain merely referring to monarchy as the preferred polity for ancient Israel, or is it also subtly referring to theocracy (the kingship of God) as the ideal for any Israelite polity? Perhaps the reader does not need to decide between theocracy and monarchy. If the ambiguity is intentional, then the point may be that Israel needs a theocratic monarchy in which the human king helps the people to do what is *right* in God's eyes (in accordance with Deut. 17:14–20; cf. 1 Kings 15:5), rather than to do what is right in their own eyes (as illustrated in Judg. 17–21).[26]

Canonical Reflections

There are a number of important theological relationships that may be noted in the canonical juxtapositions of the books of Joshua, Judges, Ruth, and Samuel (see table 3).

Table 3: The Canonical Position of Judges

Hebrew Canon	Joshua	Judges	Samuel	
Greek Canon	Joshua	Judges	Ruth	Samuel

First, the prologue of Judges is clearly related to the book of Joshua. While Joshua emphasizes the total fulfillment of God's promises regarding the conquest and allotment of the land (see Josh. 21:43–45; 23:14–15), Judges 1:1–3:6 emphasizes Israel's partial/failed conquest of the land due to Israel's disobedience. Second, the epilogue of Judges is clearly related to the book of 1 Samuel. Both Judges 17–21 and 1 Samuel explore the relationship between theocracy and monarchy: the former serves as preface for the latter. This relationship is best appreciated in the arrangement of the Hebrew/Jewish canon, in which Samuel immediately follows Judges. Third, the book of Ruth, which is included among the Writings in the Hebrew/Jewish canon (see the introduction to Ruth), is positioned between Judges and Samuel in the Greek/Christian canon. This latter arrangement is also important because Ruth appears to qualify the negative message of Judges with the clarification that there were in fact some bright moments of faithfulness during the dark "days when the judges ruled" (Ruth 1:1). Ruth thus serves a transitional function

Judges as a Mirror for the Church?

"No book in the Old Testament offers the modern church as telling a mirror as this book. From the jealousies of the Ephraimites to the religious pragmatism of the Danites, from the paganism of Gideon to the self-centeredness of Samson, and from the unmanliness of Barak to the violence against women by the men of Gibeah, all of the marks of Canaanite degeneracy are evident in the church and its leaders today. This book is a wake-up call for a church moribund in its own selfish pursuits."[a]

[a] Block, *Judges, Ruth*, 586.

by accounting for the eventual rise of a person like David from Bethlehem (cf. Ruth 4:17, 22).[27]

Methodology

If the book of Judges is primarily about both the unfaithfulness of Israel and the faithfulness of God, then there are important methodological implications for preaching and teaching the book. First, God is the only real hero; therefore, interpretation and application must primarily be theocentric.[28] It is always appropriate to ask, "What does this story teach about God?" Second, the human characters are not role models, either for positive or negative examples. The point is never to (not) be like Samson or even to be like Othniel, whose brief record is pristine in Judges. Rather, Scripture exists to reveal God's character so that his people can know him and become like him.[29] Third and finally, the human condition has not changed. The propensities of disobedience and infidelity among God's people are, sadly, just as rampant today as they were in the days of the judges. Throughout the book, one deeply feels humanity's desperate need for a restored relationship with God—a need that can now be met directly through Jesus Christ.

Historical Setting and Composition

The period of history covered by the book of Judges spans from roughly the death of Joshua to the coronation of King Saul. While most scholars agree that the end of the judges period (or the beginning of the monarchy) was in the late eleventh century BC, there is ongoing discussion regarding the beginning of the judges period. This question is complex due to several factors.

First, there is debate concerning the date of the exodus-conquest.[30] If the exodus occurred in the middle of the fifteenth century BC, the so-called judges period would begin in the early fourteenth century. But if the exodus occurred in the mid-thirteenth century BC, the judges period would begin in the early twelfth century. The difference between these two views can be as much as two centuries, and one's interpretation depends in large part upon crux passages such as Exodus 1:11 and 1 Kings 6:1.

Second, the years of oppression, peace, and judging provided in the Masoretic Text of Judges total as many as 410 years,[31] but this span is too long even for those who hold to an early exodus date. A certain degree of overlap between the judges is therefore acknowledged by most contemporary interpreters. Indeed, the narrator of Judges appears to be more concerned with selectively presenting regional/tribal (as opposed to national) stories in a highly structured literary pattern than with presenting an exhaustive historical account in strict chronological sequence (e.g., see Judg. 10:7, 11–12).[32]

Third, numerical figures may be rounded or employed in a hyperbolic or symbolic manner, in keeping with the conventions of biblical and ancient Near Eastern literature.[33] For example, a biblical generation, which is typically construed as forty years, may account for the prominence of the number forty (and its divisions/multiples) in the book of Judges (see 3:11, 30; 4:3; 5:31; 8:28; 13:1; 15:20; 16:31; cf. 1 Sam. 4:18). Similarly, while Jephthah's three hundred years (Judg. 11:26) could be understood as a round number or as a symbolic reference to a few generations (see Gen. 15:13, 16, where a century may stand for a generation), it may also be a hyperbolic expression in the context of his politically charged speech. In any case, such numbers may offer limited help for historical reconstruction.

To compound the problem, these three factors are all interrelated. Determining the date of the exodus depends in large part on the degree of overlap between individual judges and on the interpretation of numbers as either literal or figurative. Since this is not the proper venue to try to settle this dispute, the matter must be left unresolved. For the purpose of this commentary, historical data may be considered from the whole range of possibilities—that is, from the early fourteenth century to the late eleventh century BC. In archaeological terms this period spans the Late Bronze Age II (ca. 1400–1200 BC) and Iron Age I (ca. 1200–1000 BC). At the end of the Bronze Age, Canaan was overshadowed by the mighty Egyptian Nineteenth Dynasty, but the early Iron Age was characterized by Egyptian withdrawal and a power vacuum in which many people groups (including Philistines and Israelites) were vying for survival.[34]

Even more complex than the dates for the historical context of Judges are the possible dates for the composition of the book. The composer is ultimately unknown, although Jewish tradition maintains that the author is the prophet Samuel.[35] Recent proposals for the composition date range from the late tenth century to the sixth century BC.[36] Since the book clearly displays editorial activity, it is possible that some portions originated as early as the eleventh century BC (e.g., 1:21) but that the final shaping took place in the eighth century BC or later.[37] This is indicated by the remark in 18:30 about "the time of the captivity of the land," which can refer to either the Assyrian or Babylonian exile, although the former is more likely.

Synopsis of Contents in the Book of Judges

Military Failure (1:1–2:5): Israel's failure to supplant the Canaanites and to occupy the tribal allotments is because of covenant disobedience after Joshua's death.

Religious Failure (2:6–3:6): Israel's failure to keep the covenant after Joshua's death is demonstrated through the cycle of sin, oppression, and deliverance and through God's testing of Israel by the nations.

Othniel (3:7–11): Due to Israel's apostasy, God gives them over to a distant northern oppressor and delivers them by the power of his Spirit through the foreigner Othniel.

Ehud (3:12–30): God providentially delivers Israel from Moabite oppression through the risky and tricky schemes of Ehud even though Israel has neglected God's commands.

Prose Account of Deborah and Barak (4:1–24): God is the ultimate hero who commands Israel and miraculously delivers Israel from the Canaanites while God's people are faith challenged and their participation is partial.

Poetic Account of Deborah and Barak (5:1–31): The song of Deborah and Barak reveals the kingship of God by celebrating his miraculous acts of deliverance and the blessings that are received by the individuals and tribes who participate.

Gideon's Rise (6:1–32): God affirms his presence with Gideon, commissions him to deliver Israel from the Midianite oppression, and initiates him through direct confrontation with Baal.

Gideon's Battle (6:33–7:25): God gets the glory by empowering Gideon to conscript Israel, reducing the number of troops and defeating Midian while Gideon is doubtful, controlling, fearful, and egotistical.

Gideon's Demise (8:1–32): Gideon leaves behind God's miraculous defeat of the Midianites and is consumed with selfish vendettas, aggrandizement, and the consolidation of economic and religious power in Ophrah.

Abimelek (8:33–9:57): Israel's worship of Baal-Berith and Abimelek's three-year oppression are followed by God's retribution on both Abimelek and the Shechemites for their violence against Gideon's house.

Israel's Problem (10:6–16): God responds to Israel's habitual apostasy by sending more oppression, refusing to deliver them, and rejecting their superficial repentance as a manipulative ploy.

Jephthah's Rise (10:17–11:28): Jephthah emerges as a leader in Gilead despite his sordid past, selfish ambitions, and theological ignorance, and Jephthah exclaims that God is the ultimate Judge who can bring justice in Israel's dispute with Ammon.

Jephthah's Fall (11:29–12:7): God delivers Israel from the Ammonites but passively lets Jephthah and the Israelites destroy themselves through gratuitous acts of human sacrifice and civil war.

Minor Judges (3:31; 10:1–5; 12:8–15): The minor judges reinforce the progressive patterns and themes of the book, provide thematic transitions between cycles, and bring the total number of leaders to twelve in order to indict all Israel.

Samson's Beginning (13:1–25): God graciously raises up Samson from an apathetic Danite family, and God equips him in order to initiate Israel's deliverance from the Philistines.

Samson's Marriage (14:1–20): God's plans against the Philistines are accomplished through Samson even though he is self-absorbed, marries a Philistine, and is disengaged from God.

Samson's Revenge (15:1–20): God's plans against the Philistines are accomplished in spite of Judah's opposition and Samson's vengeful and selfish behavior.

Samson's End (16:1–31): God's victory over Dagon is accomplished by graciously empowering Samson despite his foolishness with Delilah, his apathy toward God, and his vengeance against the Philistines.

Micah's Shrine (17:1–13): The story of Micah's shrine shows that Israelite worship was indistinguishable from Canaanite worship because of a disregard for God's authority and instruction.

Danite Migration (18:1–31): The story of the Danite migration shows that judgment is inevitable when religious leaders and whole tribes reject God's presence and revelation and live for their own interests.

The Levite's Concubine (19:1–30): The disturbing story of a concubine's rape and murder shows a degenerate religious leader and a Canaanized Israel who operate apart from God's authority and according to their own self-interests.

Israel versus Benjamin (20:1–48): God judges Canaanized Israel as the tribes precipitously unite under the Levite, consult God on their own terms, and apply the ban to the Benjamites because of the reported atrocities at Gibeah.

Wives for Benjamin (21:1–25): Israel's spiraling descent into Canaanization reaches its lowest point as God lets Israel partially destroy itself through hateful oaths, increased genocide, and the violent exploitation of women.

Military Failure

Big Idea

Disobedience can result in hardship and the failure to appropriate God's promises.

Key Themes

- God selects the tribe of Judah to lead the nation.
- Victory comes from the Lord.
- Israel's tribes are all unfaithful to the covenant.
- God is faithful to uphold his covenant promises.
- Obedience leads to successful occupation of the land.
- Disobedience leads to foreign oppression and loss of land.

Understanding the Text

The Text in Context

The book of Judges continues the story of the conquest, which was introduced by the book of Joshua. Whereas Joshua emphasizes God's faithfulness in giving the land to Israel, the book of Judges—especially chapter 1—emphasizes Israel's ongoing responsibility and delinquency in occupying the land. The apparent differences between the accounts of Joshua and Judges should be viewed not as contradictory but as complementary accounts that serve distinct theological purposes.[1]

The prologue to the book of Judges consists of two parts, 1:1–2:5 and 2:6–3:6. These two passages focus, respectively, on the military and religious failures of Israel and set the theological stage for the "deliverer" stories that will follow in 3:7–16:31. The general theme of chapter 1 is Israel's military fight against their external enemies. Midway through the book, this same theme will be first revisited and then reversed in the Gideon narrative (in 6:33–7:25 and 8:1–21, respectively). Then at the very end of the book, in the second part of the epilogue (19:1–21:25), the theme of chapter 1 will be mirrored so that Israel's military fight is against their *internal* enemies.

The rhetorical connections between the opening and closing sections of the book include the following: (1) designation of Judah's leadership (1:1–2; 20:18); (2) employment of the key verb "to go up" (1:1–4, 16, 22; 2:1; 20:3, 18,

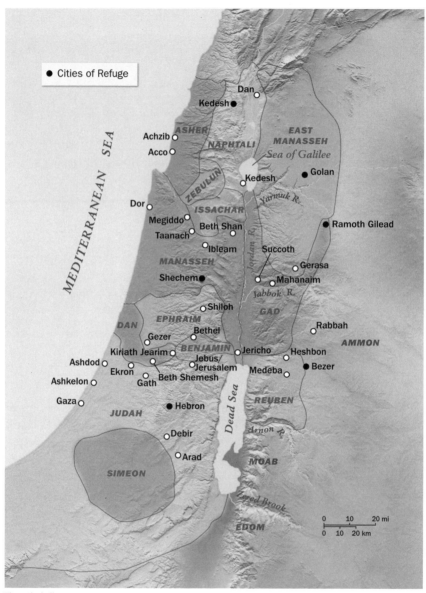

The tribal allotments

23, 26, 28, 30–31; 21:5, 8); (3) inquiring of the Lord (1:1; 18:5; 20:18, 23, 27); (4) prominence of women (1:12–15; 19:1–30; 21:1–25); (5) application of the ban (1:17; 21:11; cf. 20:48); (6) attention to all Israel (1:1–2:5; 20:1–21:25); and the mention of (7) Jerusalem/Jebus (1:7, 8, 21; 19:10–12), (8) Bethel (1:22–26; 20:18, 26, 31; 21:2, 19), (9) weeping and sacrifice (2:4–5; 20:23, 26; 21:2, 4), and (10) dispersing "each to his inheritance" (2:6; 21:24; author's translation).

Structure

A great deal of symmetry is evident in this opening passage. It is framed by the assembly of all Israel receiving a word from the Lord: first a word of commissioning (1:1–2) and finally a word of indictment (2:1–5). Between these bracketing units are two sections: one about Judah (1:3–20) and the other about the remaining Cisjordanian tribes (1:21–36),[2] although Issachar is not mentioned. These four units form an A-B-B'-A' structure, and each unit employs the key verb "to go up" (1:1–4, 16, 22; 2:1).[3]

The geographical progression for 1:3–36 moves from the southernmost tribe to what will become the northernmost tribe (from Judah/Simeon to Dan), but the section dealing only with Judah (1:3–20) moves from north to south. The general south-to-north geographical arrangement of 1:3–36 is paralleled by a good-to-bad pattern in the tribal success rate for possessing the land. Relatively speaking, Judah gains ground while Dan loses ground. Both the south-to-north and the good-to-bad patterns will be utilized again by the composer for arranging the sequence of deliverer stories in the parallel sections of the book (3:7–16:31).

Historical and Cultural Background

The numerous place names in this chapter are prominent in Bronze Age texts (see the "Additional Insights" following the unit on Judg. 2:6–3:6). Perhaps the most important document regarding the historical geography of Judges 1 is the Merneptah Stele (ca. 1209 BC), in which Pharaoh boasts: "Canaan is plundered, Ashkelon is carried off, and Gezer is captured. Yenoam is made into non-existence; Israel is wasted, its seed is not; and Hurru is become a widow because of Egypt."[4] This is the earliest extrabiblical reference to Israel in ancient Near Eastern sources, and it indicates that Israel was an ethnic group (rather than a region or city) that was present in the land at the end of the thirteenth century BC.[5] In a similar fashion, the Israelites are designated as "the *people* of YHWH/God" during this period (see Num. 11:29; 16:41 [Heb. 17:6]; Judg. 5:11, 13; 20:2; 1 Sam. 2:24; 2 Sam. 1:12; 6:21; 14:13).

Interpretive Insights

1:5 *Adoni-Bezek.* This is most likely a title meaning "Lord of Bezek," with the second element designating a place (identified with either Khirbet Salhab or Khirbet Ibzik; cf. 1 Sam. 11:8).

1:6 *cut off his thumbs and big toes.* Physical mutilation of enemies is well attested in biblical and ancient Near Eastern texts[6] and is illustrated in the iconography of Egypt and Assyria. This wartime practice was intended not merely to punish and incapacitate but especially to humiliate the enemy.[7]

1:7 *Seventy kings.* This number is often employed in royal contexts and should be understood as a figure of speech.[8]

God has paid me back for what I did to them. The words of this Canaanite ruler introduce the prominent theme of retribution. In the first half of the book, justice is often meted out by God (1:7; 2:2–3, 20–21; 5:23), but in the second half revenge often characterizes the Israelites (esp. chaps. 8; 9; 12; 15–16; 19–21).

1:8 *Jerusalem . . . on fire.* Apparently the Judahite razing of Jerusalem is short lived, and the Jebusites quickly assume control (1:21; 3:5; 19:10–12). The site would not become Israelite until David's conquest (2 Sam. 5:6–9). This pattern of initial gain with subsequent loss may also be observed for the region of Philistia (cf. Judg. 1:18–19; 3:3).

1:10 *Kiriath Arba . . . Sheshai, Ahiman and Talmai.* Sheshai and Talmai are Hurrian names, whereas Ahiman is West Semitic.[9] These are the "three sons of Anak" (1:20; cf. Num. 13:22; Josh. 15:14), who are elsewhere described as having "great size" (Num. 13:32; see the "Additional Insights" following the unit on Judg. 2:6–3:6). Arba is also a personal name. He was apparently the founding father of Hebron and is called "the greatest man among the Anakites" (Josh. 14:15) and "the forefather of Anak" (Josh. 15:13; 21:11).

1:16 *City of Palms.* This most likely designates Jericho; see the comments on Judges 3:13.

1:17 *totally destroyed.* See the sidebar "The Ban" in the unit on Judges 21:1–25.

1:18 *Judah also took Gaza, Ashkelon and Ekron.* In the Septuagint this sentence is negated ("did not capture"), most likely due to an apparent contradiction between this verse and the following verse stating that Judah was not able to dispossess the inhabitants of the plain (cf. Josh. 13:2–3). But the supposed contradiction between verses 18 and 19 can be resolved by noting the semantic distinction (between the verbs "capture" and "dispossess") and/or by positing a historical gap between the two remarks (perhaps the region was Canaanite in v. 18 and Philistine in v. 19; cf. 3:3). For further reference on the Philistines, see the sidebar "The Philistines" in the unit on Judges 15:1–20.

1:19 *chariots.* The early Israelites who were based in the hill country had little use for chariots, which were employed by the Canaanites and Philistines in the plains (cf. Josh. 17:16, 18; Judg. 4:3). The style of these chariots represented newer technology (cf. 1 Sam. 13:19–21), as they were likely plated or reinforced with iron.[10]

1:21 *to this day.* This phrase, both here and in Joshua 15:63, may indicate that this particular account was composed prior to David's conquest of Jerusalem (2 Sam. 5:6–9).

2:1 *angel of the* L<small>ORD</small>. This is apparently the divine messenger promised in Exodus 23:20–23; 33:2. See the "Additional Insights" following the unit on Judges 8:1–32.

Theological Insights

The key to understanding this passage is the speech from the angel of the Lord (2:1–3). His indictment, "Why have you done this?" (2:2), makes explicit what was only implicit in chapter 1, that Israel's military failures are actually the consequences of spiritual failures. Israel cannot blame the Lord for their situation. While the Lord asserts that he is the covenant keeper (2:1) and that Israel is the covenant breaker (2:2; cf. 2:20), he explains that the ongoing oppression and testing is his punitive response to Israel's disobedient behavior (2:3; cf. 2:21–23).

From Judah to Dan, both the level of spiritual offense and the extent of military failure are therefore expressed on a continuum from relatively best to worst. While Judah accomplishes more than any other tribe, they appear to be a reluctant leader since Judah persuades Simeon to join them on their God-given mission (1:3). Block also suggests that Judah's retributive dealings with Adoni-Bezek are very "Canaanite" in character (1:6–7).[11] The final note on Judah is the mixed report that although the Lord was "with" them, Judah did not dispossess the inhabitants of the plain (1:19)—an unacceptable outcome in light of Deuteronomy 7:2, 17–21; 20:1.

God's presence is also affirmed for the house of Joseph (1:22), although they fail to carry out the ban by showing kindness to a Canaanite family from Bethel (1:24–26; cf. Exod. 23:32; 34:12; Deut. 7:2, 16; 20:16–17). Canaanites have persisted to dwell with Manasseh (Judg. 1:27) so that "possessing, they did not in fact possess it" (1:28; author's translation). Canaanites also dwell in the midst of both Ephraim and Zebulun (1:29–30). Rather than hosting the Canaanites, both Asher and Naphtali actually have done the reverse: they live "among the Canaanite inhabitants of the land" (1:32–33; cf. 3:5). The repeated pattern of subjecting Canaanites to "forced labor" (1:28, 30, 33, 35) might sound like a relatively positive outcome if such were not explicitly forbidden in Deuteronomy 20:10–18. Finally, Dan's failures are the greatest because they have been pushed out of their inheritance altogether by the Amorites (Judg. 1:34), who are ironically honored with the only border description in the passage (1:36).[12]

Thus, chapter 1 is a most depressing account on which to begin the book. The period of the judges is characterized by occasional local victories and losses as well as foreign oppression and general political instability. Nevertheless, the angel of the Lord reminds us that God is still in complete control of Israel's identity and destiny. In fact, any military successes recorded in chapter 1 are wholly credited to God (1:2, 4, 7, 19, 22).

Teaching the Text

Since Judah meets with some success and is depicted in a relatively positive manner in 1:1–20, one might be tempted to apply this passage by upholding that tribe as a faithful model to imitate. But to do so would ignore the other explicit teachings of the text regarding Judah's compromises. After God commissions Judah and promises deliverance, Judah (the largest tribe!) enlists the help of Simeon, possibly treats Adoni-Bezek according to Canaanite terms, applies the ban explicitly to only *one* city (in Simeon's territory), and is intimidated by iron chariots (despite the affirmation of Deut. 20:1; cf. Josh. 17:18).

Clearly, the point here is not that we should be like Judah. Rather we learn that the tribe of Judah, although imperfect, is nevertheless God's choice for leadership after the death of Joshua. Judah is therefore special not because the tribe shows some obedience but because Judah is chosen by God to succeed Joshua. This is part of God's revelatory plan of divine kingship through the Davidic dynasty.[13] Eventually this will be expressed through the coming of Israel's ultimate king in the form of the Messiah. Thus Judges 1 builds on the promises to Judah from the Pentateuch (Gen. 49:8–12; Deut. 33:7; cf. Num. 10:14), and it lays the groundwork for the next phase of God's program, which is the subject of the books of Samuel (cf. 2 Sam. 2:1).

Additionally, a number of principles may be derived from this passage concerning the covenant relationship between God and his people. First, there is no legitimate substitute for obedience. Judah's compromises of their divine calling and the lack of trust in God result in a smaller inheritance (1:19). When God's people have a "mixed" response to God's commands (cf. 1:3–26), the results may also be a mixture of blessing with curse.

Second, God's people must acknowledge that just retribution concerns pagans as well as saints (i.e., the nations as well as God's people). This principle is ironically acknowledged by Adoni-Bezek (1:7), and it is reinforced as the angel of the Lord applies it to the nation of Israel (2:2–3; cf. 2:20–21). Sometimes great hardships in life may come as a direct result of spiritual failures such as foolish choices or actions.

Third, God's agendas are not derailed by the disobedience of his people. God may override the principle of retribution by graciously granting blessings despite compromises or rebellion (cf. 1:2, 4, 7, 19, 22). God is indeed the righteous judge of all people, but he also shows mercy and grace whenever and to whomever he wills (cf. Exod. 33:19; 34:6–7).

Finally, success is not always an indicator of obedience. While the house of Joseph succeeds in occupying Bethel, they do not follow God's instructions related to the ban (1:22–26; cf. 2:2; Deut. 7:2, 16; 20:16–17). Success must be defined on God's terms; or stated differently, the end should never justify the means.[14]

Illustrating the Text

God doesn't measure disobedience on a sliding scale; a small trace can bring big consequences.

Logic: Ask your listeners to consider math, and percentages in particular. Ask if they would be satisfied if they got their way 75 percent of the time. What about 98 percent? Ask if they think God is the same. What if, in 98 percent of circumstances, we say, "God, you are the wisest, and I will yield to you," but in 2 percent we say, "This, however, is an exception; this is one area where I am right and you are wrong." How will that work out for us? With God, doing things 98 percent his way is still 100 percent our way—we are modifying his standard to match our preferences. For a biblical illustration of this principle, cite James 2:10: "For whoever keeps the whole law and yet stumbles at just one point is guilty of breaking all of it."

In his graciousness, God often gives blessings in spite of our disobedience.

Parenting: Ask your listeners to consider how parents often give gifts to their children on special occasions such as birthday parties, even when the children are grumpy or otherwise not at their best. This does not mean the parents approve of all their child's behavior—it means that the parents have a gracious, loving relationship with the child that is big enough to eclipse the momentary misbehavior.

A successful end does not justify sinful means.

Sports: Rosie Ruiz Vivas is a Cuban American who appeared to win the female category for the eighty-fourth Boston Marathon in 1980 with the third-fastest time in the world of 2:31:56. Later, questions arose about her performance, as she had not been sweaty, did not appear to be in the same shape as other runners, and had not been seen by the top runners she would have had to pass to win. In the end, it was proved that Rosie had slipped into the crowd near the finish line and only run the end of the race. She was stripped of her title, and the real winner was rewarded. Despite the short-term glory of an apparently successful finish, her illicit means of winning was eventually found out and judged. A similar illustration could reference famous cyclist Lance Armstrong's illicit steroid use.

Religious Failure

Big Idea

Habitual sin and generational drift from God can result in God's discipline.

Key Themes

- Every generation must be taught to keep the covenant.
- God's people are prone to forget God's past work.
- People have a propensity toward idolatry.
- God's deliverance, presence, and compassion are undeserved.
- God is patient and long-suffering with his people.
- God may test the obedience of his people in order to teach them.

Understanding the Text

The Text in Context

The repetition of the note that Joshua died (1:1; 2:8) indicates that this story is not historically sequential to chapter 1 but is rather a concurrent or parallel perspective on the same period of time. In fact, the arrangement of stories for the whole book is based more on literary, thematic, and geographical concerns than on a strict linear sequence (see the introduction to Judges).

In the ring structure of the book of Judges (see the introduction to Judges), the double prologue is mirrored by the double epilogue, forming an A-B-B′-A′ pattern. The present passage should therefore be viewed in juxtaposition with chapters 17–18. Both 2:6–3:6 and 17:1–18:31 are about religious failure and generational drift (2:7, 10; 18:30), and they focus on the external and internal problems, respectively. Just as Israel faces idolatry in 2:6–3:6 and then forges its own idolatry in 17:1–18:31, so the midsection of the book shows Gideon following the same pattern (facing idolatry in 6:1–32 and forging idolatry in 8:22–32).

Structure

This passage is presented in four paragraphs. It opens with a summary of previous generations (2:6–10) and closes with a summary of the outcomes for the period of the judges (3:5–6). Between these summaries is an exposition of the cyclical pattern for this period (2:11–19) and the divine perspective on Israel's testing (2:20–3:4).

Historical and Cultural Background

The cyclical pattern of apostasy, oppression, and deliverance in 2:11–19 expresses not a modern but an ancient understanding of historiography, which places a high value on recurrence and endurance.[1] While numerous ancient Near Eastern texts could be cited to illustrate similar cyclical patterns in history,[2] one example can suffice from the inscriptions of the Neo-Assyrian king Esarhaddon (681–669 BC). His accounts of the destruction and restoration of Babylon reveal the following pattern: (1) human offenses (often ritual in nature), (2) divine anger/reactions (including abandonment and resulting oppression), and (3) divine change of heart (irrespective of human behavior) resulting in the election of a leader and restoration of security.[3]

Interpretive Insights

2:11 *did evil in the eyes of the* LORD. This familiar refrain is clearly defined in this passage as religious apostasy or disobedience to the covenant (2:11–13, 20).[4] It will appear six more times in Judges to introduce the stories of Othniel, Ehud, Deborah, Gideon, Jephthah, and Samson (3:7, 12; 4:1; 6:1; 10:6; 13:1). The opening statement for the Abimelek story ("When Gideon had died the Israelites relapsed and whored after the Baals" [8:33; author's translation; cf. 2:17, 19]) serves as a rhetorical variant of this refrain to signal an intensification of the apostasy for the second triad of stories (Abimelek, Jephthah, and Samson) in the body of the book.

the Baals. The plural form *be'alim* may refer to either the many localized manifestations of the single deity Baal (cf. NLT: "the images of Baal") or to rival male deities in general.[5] Although it is one of the hallmarks of the judges period (3:7; 8:33; 10:6, 10; 1 Sam. 7:4; 12:10), serving the Baals unfortunately would continue to be a problem into the sixth century BC (1 Kings 18:18; 2 Chron. 34:4; Jer. 2:23; 9:14; Hosea 2:13, 17). See the "Additional Insights" following this unit.

2:13 *Baal and the Ashtoreths.* The plural form *'ashtarot* refers either to the many local manifestations of the goddess Astarte (like "the Baals" in 2:11) or to goddesses in general who were viewed as the consorts of Baal (cf. "the Baals and the Asherahs" in 3:7).[6] Known as Ishtar in Mesopotamia, Astarte has some associations with fertility but in ancient Near Eastern sources is primarily connected with warfare.[7]

2:16 *judges.* The term "judge" (*shopet*) is often used in the Bible to designate an individual who makes legal rulings concerning disputes (e.g., Exod.

18:13–26; Deut. 1:16; 16:18; 17:9, 12; 19:17–18; 21:2; 25:1–2), but this is generally not the way it is employed in the book of Judges. While Deborah alone may function in such a judiciary capacity (Judg. 4:5), all the other "major" judges primarily offer military leadership in response to a crisis (3:10; 4:4; 12:7; 15:20; 16:31; cf. 2 Sam. 7:10–11). Therefore, some suggest that more precise translations for this term are "administrator" or "governor" and that the individual functions as an agent of Yahweh's justice or as a "deputy of Yahweh."[8] Interestingly, apart from this passage (Judg. 2:16–19), none of the characters in the book of Judges are actually identified with the noun form *shopet* except for the Lord himself in Jephthah's speech (11:27). In all other cases, the verb form is employed to describe the administrative function of the human leaders (3:10; 4:4; 10:2–3; 12:7–9, 11, 13–14; 15:20; 16:31).

3:3 *five rulers of the Philistines.* The five Philistine city-states, commonly called the Pentapolis, were Gaza, Ashdod, Ashkelon, Gath, and Ekron (cf. Josh. 13:3; 1 Sam. 6:4, 16, 18). Often translated "lord/ruler," the term *seren* is only used for Philistine leaders and most likely has an Anatolian origin (cf. Luwian *tarwanis*; Greek *tyrannos*).[9] For additional reference on the Philistines, see the sidebar "The Philistines" in the unit on Judges 15:1–20.

3:6 *marriage.* These marriages (between Israelites and the nations listed in the preceding verse) violate God's command in Deuteronomy 7:3 (cf. Exod. 34:15–16; Josh. 23:12). The downward progression in verses 5–6 moves from settling in the midst of the nations to intermarrying with them and finally to worshiping their gods (cf. Deut. 7:1–4; 17:17; 1 Kings 11:1–6). The theme of intermarriage with the nations is an important theme of the book of Judges: Othniel's marriage to Aksah is the ideal scenario (1:11–13), whereas Samson's marriage to a Philistine leads to disaster (chaps. 14–15).[10] The female partners of Gideon and Gilead (8:31; 11:1), birthing Abimelek and Jephthah respectively, may also be non-Israelites. The minor judge Ibzan marries his children to outsiders (12:9). While the marriages described in the epilogue of Judges (chaps. 19–21) are not with outsiders, Israelites take oaths against marrying each other, and they treat their own women in the way that Canaanites victimize their enemies (cf. 5:30).

Theological Insights

In the first paragraph (2:6–10), there is a movement from relatively good to bad (cf. chap. 1). While the period of Joshua and the elders was characterized by serving the Lord and experiencing God's work on behalf of Israel (cf. Josh. 24:28–31), the following generation lacks such knowledge because they neither personally experienced the exodus nor have they learned of it from parents or Levites.

The second paragraph (2:11–19) then explains the inevitable result summarized in the refrain of verse 11a. Doing "evil in the eyes of the LORD" is defined as the opposite action of the previous generations, who "served the LORD" (2:7). Instead, the Israelites have served "other gods"[11] and abandoned the Lord (2:11–13). Thus the cyclical pattern is introduced that will serve as a rubric for the stories of chapters 3–16 (cf. Neh. 9:26–28). The cycle is related in the following sequence: (1) Israel does evil by serving foreign gods (2:11–13); (2) the Lord responds by giving Israel over to foreign oppressors (2:14–15) and then by (3) graciously delivering Israel by raising up a "judge" (2:16–18), which is often God's compassionate response to Israel's "groaning" (2:18). Finally, after the judge dies, Israel does not change its stubborn ways and goes deeper into apostasy than before (2:19), and the cycle repeats itself.

The third paragraph (2:20–3:4) opens with the words of God himself, who reinforces the indictment previously made by the angel in 2:1–3. He explains that since Israel has broken the covenant, the Lord will no longer drive out the nations (2:20–21; cf. 2:2–3). Furthermore, the Lord will "test" Israel by these nations to teach them holy war (3:1–2; cf. Deut. 7:1–5)[12] and to determine whether or not Israel will obey the covenant (2:22; 3:4).

The final paragraph (3:5–6) is a brief but depressing summary of the outcome for the period of the judges. Instead of applying the ban as prescribed by God (Deut. 7; 20), the Israelites have settled in the midst of the nations (3:5; cf. 1:32–33), intermarried with them (3:6; cf. 2:2), and served/worshiped their gods (3:6; cf. 2:3; contrast with 2:7).

The downward spiral expounded in this chapter is Israel's own making. That is, Israel's experience of oppression and testing is the consequence of disobeying God's commands (2:2–3, 20–22). At the same time, the narrator clearly reveals that God is the one who has given/sold them into the hand of plunderers/enemies (2:14). This is not a contradiction of terms but rather an explanation of how covenant blessings (such as enjoying the land that God gave them) are contingent on obedience. In the same way, the Lord himself will later send his people into exile because of their disobedience (1 Kings 9:6–9; 2 Kings 17:7–23; 21:10–15; Jer. 29:4, 7, 14, 20), but the Lord will also restore them to the land because of his gracious plan (Jer. 29:10–14), which is analogous to how he graciously has "raised up judges" who would deliver Israel from its enemies (Judg. 2:16, 18).

Teaching the Text

This passage explicitly presents the fundamentals of the theology of the book of Judges. The story of this period is summarized in terms of Israel's intractable unfaithfulness to God and God's unmerited faithfulness to Israel. Judges

2:18–19 says it all: the Lord would deliver them by raising up a "judge" and by providing his presence out of compassion (v. 18), while Israel would relapse and go deeper into its stubborn apostasy (v. 19). But here we also learn that God is not only the "superhero" who always rescues his distressed people; he is also the consummate parent of Israel who disciplines his children through tough love. Such discipline consists of temporarily giving them over to oppressors (2:14–15) in order to test their faithfulness to the covenant (2:22; 3:4).

In addition to these macrothemes, we learn many lessons about the nature of trials, sin, and faithfulness. The following teachings from 2:6–3:6 are developed later as they resurface in chapters 3–21: (1) Sometimes God's people may go through hard times as a consequence of unfaithfulness to God (2:2–3, 11–15, 20–21),[13] and this principle is not just limited to Old Testament saints (cf. John 5:14; 1 Cor. 11:29–32). (2) Sometimes God may will that his people go through hard times for a period of probationary testing (Judg. 2:22; 3:1–2, 4).[14] The Lord disciplines those he loves (Deut. 8:5; Prov. 3:12; Rev. 3:19), and such experiences are "for our good, in order that we may share in his holiness" (Heb. 12:10; cf. Rom. 5:3–5; 1 Cor. 11:32; James 1:2–4; 1 Pet. 1:6–7).[15] (3) People are inclined to forget what God has done in the past (Judg. 2:7, 10; 3:7; 8:34; 18:30).[16] Remembrance is, however, essential for growing in the faith (2 Pet. 1:9, 12–15). (4) People are prone to rebel against God (Judg. 2:2, 20; 3:5) and to worship "other gods" (2:11–13, 17, 19; 3:6). This runs directly against the first commandment, which demands exclusive allegiance to Yahweh (Exod. 20:1–3; Deut. 5:6–7). While Christians today may not be tempted to worship Baal or Astarte, they may face the spiritual equivalent by expressing allegiance to creation (through materialism or selfishness) rather than to the Creator (Rom. 1:23, 25).[17] (5) The cycle of sin is a downward spiral (Judg. 2:19), and sinful compromises lead to further sinful compromises (3:5–6). It is wise to remember that this pattern of cohabitation-marriage-idolatry is the general rule while the reverse pattern of influence is the exception.[18] Believers must be very careful not to put themselves in potentially compromising situations (relationships, employment contracts, etc.) with the world. (6) Each new generation must learn how to be faithful to God (2:7–10, 12, 17, 19, 20–23; 3:1–2, 4, 6).[19] Perhaps Joshua and the elders failed to pass the baton of faith to their successors, or the following generation failed to apply what they were taught by/about their "ancestors." Either way, the consequences are disastrous for Israel. Likewise, in the church and in the home, Christian leaders carry the huge responsibility of schooling their young people in the way of Christ · (cf. Eph. 6:4; 2 Tim. 1:5–6, 13–14; Titus 2:4–7), and all Christians bear the responsibility to know and apply what is handed down to them (cf. 1 Tim. 6:20; 2 Tim. 3:14–15; Titus 1:9).

Illustrating the Text

God loves us with a tough love that includes discipline and correction.

Church Government: This might be a great time to explain in a few broad brush strokes your church's beliefs and policies regarding church discipline. If you have a document or bylaws that explain, consider handing it out. People need to know that the church is a place made safe by measured, biblical tough love.

Quote: *A Severe Mercy*, **by Mark J. Boda.** Boda says of God's discipline, "It is his justice that explains his regular discipline of sin but his grace that offers hope to a disciplined people. His justice has gracious intent, as he seeks to eliminate the sin that threatens human existence and severs relationship with him."[20]

Sin is a highly contagious and progressive disease.

Quote: *Not the Way It's Supposed to Be*, **by Cornelius Plantinga Jr.** Plantinga attributes an almost epidemiological nature to sin, saying,

> Sin is remarkably generative: sin yields more and more sin. In a standard scenario, each episode of sin gets triggered by trouble from the last. . . . Sin is a plague that spreads by contagion or even by quasi-genetic reproduction. It's a polluted river that keeps branching and rebranching into tributaries. It's a whole family of fertile and contentious parents, children, and grandchildren.[21]

Health: Give the statistics on a pandemic. For example, the first outbreak of bubonic plague (also known as the Plague of Justinian) cut human population by 25 to 50 percent wherever it broke out from AD 541 to 750. Constantinople lost an estimated ten thousand people per day. The plague broke out again from the fourteenth to eighteenth centuries, killing an estimated seventy-five million people worldwide. Point out to your listeners that by comparison to sin, this is all mere child's play. Sin infects 100 percent of humans from the moment of conception, and has a 100 percent mortality rate.[22]

One compromise usually begets many, many more.

Lyrics: Many are familiar with the old folksong about the old woman who swallowed a fly. The first verse concludes, "I don't know why she swallowed that fly—perhaps she'll die." Each verse lists another strange creature she swallows to consume the previous creature. She swallows a spider to catch the fly, a bird to catch the spider, a cat to catch the bird, a dog to catch the cat, and so on, until finally she eats a horse and "she died, of course!" The point is that often we start off with just a small compromise with sin, like accidentally swallowing a fly. This one small compromise unleashes a series of increasingly alarming events until we are consumed.

Giants | Bronze Age Cities | Baal

The prologue of Judges (1:1–3:6) makes a number of references that call for background elucidation. The first is the giants who were displaced by the tribe of Judah (see 1:10). The second is the prominence of Bronze Age cites in 1:1–36. The third concerns the identity of the Canaanite deity Baal (see 2:11–13).

Giants

Various terms for giants are employed in the Old Testament. Anakites, Emites, and Zamzummites are the names designated by individual nations (i.e., the Israelites, Moabites, and Ammonites) for the giant aboriginal inhabitants of their respective territories (Num. 13:31–33; Deut. 2:10–21).[1] Rephaites and Nephilim, on the other hand, are more general designations that are not necessarily restricted to specific territories (e.g., Gen. 6:4; 1 Chron. 20:4). While Rephaites and Nephilim were not necessarily people of gigantic proportions, a gigantic person could certainly be included among them (Num. 13:33; Deut. 2:11; 3:11). It is likely that all of these terms had pejorative meanings (e.g., Emites may designate "dreadful people"). Furthermore, these terms share a common literary function in that they designate peoples who must be destroyed or displaced. Their demise was something the Lord required or even executed himself (e.g., Deut. 2:21; 9:1–6; Amos 2:9).

Some scholars have theorized that the biblical references to giants are a form of military hyperbole or that they are embellished legends stemming from the sight of megalithic structures, but these theories fail to account for the fact that giants were living simultaneously (and interacting) with the Israelites. The Bible even preserves the personal names of giants such as Og, Goliath, and the four individuals mentioned in 1:10 (see the comments on Judg. 1:10, above). While no gigantic skeletal remains have yet been recovered from bona fide excavations, there is some evidence for the historical presence of giants in Egyptian texts. Papyrus Anastasi I describes Canaanites who were four or five cubits tall (i.e., between 7 and 8.5 feet) in the late thirteenth century BC.[2] The Execration texts also refer to a place called Iy-anq (linguistically related to the biblical Anakites) in southern Canaan (ca. 1800 BC).[3]

Bronze Age Cities

The first chapter of Judges is replete with place names, many of which are identified in Bronze Age texts. Sites like Jerusalem and Ashkelon first appear in the Egyptian Execration texts (ca. 1800 BC).[4] Akko, Megiddo, Taanach, Beth Shan (or Beth-shean), Ibleam, Gezer, and Gaza all appear in the inscriptions of Thutmose III in the fifteenth century BC.[5] Sidon, Akko, Megiddo, Taanach, Beth Shan, Gezer, Aijalon, Jerusalem, Ashkelon, and Gaza all appear in the Amarna letters from the fourteenth century BC.[6] From the thirteenth century BC, there is mention of Sidon, Akko, Megiddo, Beth Shan, and Gaza in Papyrus Anastasi I,[7] and there are also references to Sidon, Akko, and Ashkelon in Ugaritic letters.[8] The Merneptah Stele, mentioned in the unit on Judges 1:1–2:5, also references Ashkelon and Gezer at the end of the thirteenth century BC.

Baal

Baal was by far the most popular god of the Canaanites during the Late Bronze and Iron Age periods.[9] He was primarily associated with storms, fertility, and war. The name Baal is also a general term for "lord/owner" and as such may be used as a title for other male deities (cf. 9:4; see also 9:46). While Baal is well attested in Phoenician, Old Aramaic (often as Hadad), and Egyptian (often as Seth) sources, he is best known from the Ugaritic corpus of mythological and ritual texts. In these texts Baal is the son of El and Asherah, and his consorts are Anat and Astarte (and occasionally Asherah).

The worship of Baal became a problem for Israel starting with the incident at Peor (Num. 25:1–5). In the judges period Baal worship is a recurring feature of the cycles (2:11–13; 3:7; 6:25–32; 8:33; 10:6, 10; cf. 1 Sam. 7:4; 12:10) and is especially vivid when Gideon is commissioned to tear down Baal's altar at Ophrah (Judg. 6:25–32). Later on, Baal worship—especially in ninth-century Israel and seventh-century Judah—becomes one of the reasons for exile.[10]

Othniel

Big Idea

God's deliverance and empowerment of his people are undeserved and are based on his compassion and plan.

Key Themes

- God does not tolerate apostasy.
- God's deliverance is based on grace, not good works.
- Gentiles may be incorporated into the community of faith.
- God's Spirit may empower his people for a task.
- God executes his sovereign plan as he sees fit.

Understanding the Text

The Text in Context

Judges 3:7–16:31 constitutes the body of the book and features a series of seven[1] stories that illustrate the cycle of apostasy, oppression, and deliverance (see the introduction to Judges). The first three and the last three accounts share thematic parallels even though the former are relatively positive, briefer accounts and the latter are relatively negative, lengthier accounts. The fourth account (Gideon) stands alone in central position to serve as a transition between the first and second triads of stories.

The first major "cycle" is the only one featuring an individual who was previously introduced to the reader. It is evident from 1:12–15 that Othniel has been assimilated into the tribe of Judah and that his marriage within the tribe played a positive role in the conquest of Debir / Kiriath Sepher (Khirbet Rabud). These details are important background for understanding the literary placement of the Othniel cycle, which demonstrates the following thematic parallels with the Samson cycle in chapters 13–16: (1) the geography of both cycles has a southern orientation (1:11–13; 13:1–16:31); (2) marriages play a pivotal role in the outcome for both accounts—Othniel marries within his tribe, while Samson marries a Philistine outsider (1:12–15; 14:1–15:20); (3) the tribe of Judah is depicted positively in 3:9–11 (cf. 1:11–15) and negatively in 15:9–13 (see the comments on Judg. 15:11, below); (4) Othniel is a foreigner who assimilates into Israel, while Samson is an Israelite who assimilates into

Philistia (1:12–15; 3:9, 11; 14:1–3, 7, 10; 15:1, 10–11; 16:1, 4, 30; cf. 3:6); and (5) the Othniel account closes with forty years of tranquility (3:11), while the Samson account opens with forty years of oppression (13:1).[2]

Structure

The pivot for this short account is in 3:9: "Then the LORD raised up a deliverer for the Israelites; so he delivered them" (author's translation). Verses 7–8 describe the negative situation leading up to God's deliverance, while verses 10–11 describe the positive situation following God's deliverance. Each half employs the phrase "into the hands" (3:8, 10) and twice mentions the name Cushan-Rishathaim (3:8, 10). Incidentally, the name Cushan-Rishathaim even rhymes with the location Aram Naharaim.[3]

Historical and Cultural Background

The foreign king mentioned in this passage is not identified with confidence in the ancient Near Eastern sources, although scholars propose a number of theories.[4] The region Aram Naharaim (cf. Gen. 24:10; Deut. 23:4), or "Aram of the Two Rivers," refers not to the Tigris and Euphrates (like the term "Mesopotamia"; cf. ESV, NASB, NKJV) but to the region between the upper Euphrates and the Habur River in north-central Syria. Egyptian inscriptions from the Eighteenth Dynasty refer to this region as Naharin.[5] Cushan-Rishathaim is therefore the most geographically distant oppressor in the book of Judges.

Interpretive Insights

3:7 *the Baals and the Asherahs.* (For Baal, see the comments on Judg. 2:11 and the "Additional Insights" following the unit on Judg. 2:6–3:6.) The plural form *'asherot* may refer to multiple local manifestations of the one goddess Asherah, or it may refer to goddesses in general (cf. *'ashtarot* in 2:13).[6] Asherah is well known from Ugaritic epics as the consort of El and mother of the gods who is primarily associated with fertility.[7] While Asherah is here paired with Baal, Hebrew inscriptions from later periods (at Kuntillet 'Ajrud and Khirbet el-Qom) indicate that she was also occasionally viewed as Yahweh's consort.[8]

3:8 *Cushan-Rishathaim.* This name, apparently meaning "the Dark, Double-Wicked One,"[9] is likely not the actual name of this king but rather a playful pejorative that may sound something like the original name (cf. the royal names in Gen. 14:2).[10] Perhaps this designation was meant to epitomize this oppressor as the worst from the period. Furthermore, each time he is mentioned in the passage his name is duplicated so as to highlight his doubly wicked nature.

3:9 *deliverer.* Leaders such as Othniel and Ehud (see 3:15) are designated as "deliverers," but many of the leaders in chapters 3–16 are said both "to judge/govern" and "to deliver" Israel.[11] While some modern scholars prefer to call chapters 3–16 the "Book of Deliverers/Saviors" rather than the "Book of Judges,"[12] the narrator seems to make little, if any, functional distinction between his use of these words (cf. 2:16, 18; 3:9–10; 10:1–2; 13:5; 15:20; 16:31).[13]

Othniel. The name Othniel (cf. 1:13–14) means God Is My Strength,[14] and this name is appropriately positioned immediately following a clause with an ambiguous subject: "Then he delivered them" (author's translation). God did in fact deliver the Israelites, but Othniel was instrumental, as indicated by the meaning of his name.

son of Kenaz. Whether the phrase "son of Kenaz" (cf. Josh. 15:17) indicates that Othniel's father is Kenaz or that Othniel is a descendant of Kenaz is difficult to ascertain,[15] but it is clear that the ethnicity of Caleb, Othniel, and Aksah is non-Israelite and that this family has been assimilated into the tribe of Judah. The incorporation of foreigners into the covenant is an important biblical motif (cf. Rahab, Ruth, etc.) that underscores the role of faith in the

Spirit of the Lord[a]

To understand the Spirit of the Lord in the Old Testament it is first necessary to recognize that the Christian understanding of the Holy Spirit (as a distinct person of the Trinity) is due to progressive revelation and is not exactly how the Israelites would have viewed the Spirit of the Lord. In the Old Testament, and especially in the book of Judges, the Spirit of the Lord is portrayed as an extension of the presence, power, and authority of Yahweh.[b] The Spirit would come upon certain people to enable them to perform a specific task (or set of tasks) for a limited amount of time. Ministries of the Holy Spirit such as "indwelling," "baptism," or "filling," which are hallmarks of the Christian experience, are not fully revealed in the Old Testament. The judges, for example, are occasionally empowered to accomplish God's work, often despite their own inclinations (note esp. Gideon, Jephthah, and Samson). Interestingly, the presence of the Spirit seems to have no effect on the moral character of the recipient (see esp. the cases of Jephthah and Samson in 11:29–31; 13:25–14:2; 14:6–7, 19–20; 15:14, 18). Rather, the deliverers who receive the Spirit in the book of Judges demonstrate the surprising ability to conscript the armies of Israel (3:10; 6:34–35; 11:29; 13:25; cf. 1 Sam. 11:6), which was the prerogative of the Lord as Israel's commander in chief.[c] This kind of empowerment by the Spirit of the Lord was exceptional and should therefore not be viewed as a normative experience in the lives of God's people.[d] As God sees fit for the execution of his plan, he strategically sends his Spirit upon a person. When this happens, God's people immediately recognize it as the work of God.

[a] For additional references, see Averbeck, "Holy Spirit in the Hebrew Bible"; Block, "Empowered by the Spirit of God"; Hildebrandt, *Old Testament Theology of the Spirit of God*; Walton, "Ancient Near Eastern Background"; Walton and Hill, *Old Testament Today*, 187, 422.

[b] Cf. Hill and Walton, *Survey*, 244.

[c] See ibid., 245.

[d] See Block, "Empowered by the Spirit of God," 45.

relational plan of God (cf. Rom. 11:11–32). It also appears that the narrator is emphasizing the foreignness of Othniel (Judg. 1:13; 3:9, 11) in order to bring a subtle indictment on the tribe of Judah by noting that the ideal deliverer, although representing the tribe of Judah, is ironically a proselyte. There were apparently no good candidates from ethnic Judah![16]

Caleb's younger brother. While many English translations indicate that Othniel is Caleb's younger "brother," the NJPS translation more cautiously translates the term *'ah* as "kinsman." Othniel may be Caleb's nephew and would therefore represent the next generation (cf. Josh. 15:17; Judg. 1:13).[17]

3:10 *Spirit of the* Lord. See the sidebar.

3:11 *forty years.* The eight years of oppression in 3:8 appears to be a precise historical datum, whereas the forty years of peace is likely a figurative reference to a single generation (perhaps referring to the lifetime of Othniel).

Theological Insights

The Othniel account is an ideal case study for the period of the judges because all the major components of the cycle (as expounded in 2:11–19) are present, without any extended narrative distractions.[18] This account has the shortest length out of all the so-called "major" judges, and Othniel is therefore portrayed without any obvious character flaws (see the introduction to Judges). In the arrangement of the book of Judges the Othniel cycle is placed first, not only because he epitomizes the role of deliverer but also because he represents the tribe of Judah, which was chosen to "go up first" (1:1–2)[19] and to lead the nation following Joshua's death.

It is important to notice that God's deliverance of Israel—indeed, God's change of heart toward Israel—is not in response to Israel's repentance or good works. In fact, Israel shows no signs of repenting; they merely "cried out" (3:9) to the Lord because of the intense oppression. In 2:18 it is explained that God's deliverance is based only on his compassion, which is triggered by Israel's "groaning." Thus the grace of God in delivering his people from bondage is one of the most important teachings of this book. The cycle of this period is apostasy-oppression-deliverance, *not* apostasy-oppression-repentance-deliverance.[20] God's deliverance is given on the basis of who God is and what he has planned for his people (through the covenant); it is not based on who Israel is or what they have done or not done.

Teaching the Text

Two cautions must be expressed regarding the applicability of this passage to the modern context. First, as stated in the sidebar, the phenomena related to the Spirit of the Lord should not be equated with the ministries of the Holy Spirit as revealed in the New Testament. Even if the reality of the former activity is arguably attributed to the Third Person of the Trinity, the interpreter must still take progressive revelation into account and not force later theology into earlier passages of Scripture.[21]

Second, while Othniel is set forward as an ideal deliverer on literary grounds, he should not be viewed as a behavioral role model for our imitation. Othniel's story is selectively presented and arranged by the narrator to show what God was doing in response to Israel's failure at that time. It should be noted that Othniel is ideal only in a relative sense (in comparison to the other deliverers) and because so little is said about him. In fact, his foreignness may actually be intended as an indictment on the tribe of Judah (see above), and the Spirit of the Lord may come upon him because of his lack of initiative (see the sidebar). Although he may stand out positively in the book of Judges, Othniel is never depicted teaching the Israelites to obey the Lord in the manner of a judge like Samuel (see 2:17; cf. 1 Sam. 7–12; 2 Sam. 7:7 // 1 Chron. 17:6).

So what then does this passage teach? Like the other cycles in the book, this story reveals God's grace and sovereignty in delivering his people. But this story does so in an explicit and comprehensive manner, whereas the other cycles will increasingly also include numerous narrative distractions.

God's grace is displayed here in the following ways: (1) God delivers on the basis of his own character rather than according to people's worthiness (2:16, 18; 3:9). Israel, showing no signs of repentance from apostasy, has not earned the Lord's favor. Likewise, a Christian's salvation from sin is "not by works, so that no one can boast" (Eph. 2:9). (2) God is moved by the cries/groans of his people (Judg. 2:18; 3:9). As the consummate parent and covenant keeper, the Lord is "the compassionate and gracious God, slow to anger, abounding in love and faithfulness" (Exod. 34:6; cf. Num. 14:18; Neh. 9:17; Pss. 86:15; 103:8; 145:8; Joel 2:13; Jon. 4:2).

God's sovereignty is also displayed here in the following ways: (1) God's plans cannot be thwarted (2:16, 18; 3:9–10). God ensures that his plans for his people are carried out, and no obstacle—such as a disobedient tribe or a foreign ethnicity—can stand in his way. At the same time, God desires our participation in his agenda, and we should pray, "Your kingdom come, your will be done, on earth as it is in heaven" (Matt. 6:10). (2) God may use people to carry out his plan (Judg. 2:16, 18; 3:9). This is certainly the case with the proselyte Othniel, who delivers and judges Israel (3:9–10). But the meaning of Othniel's name ("God Is My Strength") is also a reminder that his noteworthy accomplishments are not his own; they are achieved by God's Spirit (cf. Zech. 4:6). Likewise, the "good works" of Christians have been "prepared in advance" by God himself (Eph. 2:10), indicating that Christians are to function as God's instruments.

Finally, God's grace and sovereignty are balanced by his justice. God does not tolerate lapses of allegiance and therefore responds with just retribution and discipline (Judg. 2:11–15, 19–23; 3:7–8; cf. Exod. 34:7; Num. 14:18).

Illustrating the Text

God often uses surprisingly unlikely people.

Film: _Simon Birch_. This 1998 movie leads off with this quote from the narrator:

> I am doomed to remember a boy with a wrecked voice, not because of his voice, or because he was the smallest person I ever knew, or even because he was the instrument of my mother's death, but because he is the reason I believe in God. What faith I have, I owe to Simon Birch, the boy I grew up with in Gravedown, Maine.[22]

This movie goes on to show how Simon believes that God has a purpose for his life, despite the many rebukes and rejections he faces due to his diminutive size, handicaps, and social class. In the end, Simon is proven a hero not just because he saves others but because he inspires others to believe in God. Ask your listeners to consider which unlikely heroes God has used in their lives to teach them about himself. Are there any unlikely heroes sent by God whom they are ignoring right now? Are they loving and believing heroically for others?

Quote: _What's So Amazing about Grace?_, by Philip Yancey. "Grace teaches us that God loves because of who God is, not because of who we are."[23]

When the Lord calls an individual, his Spirit empowers that person for the work.

Literature: _The Hiding Place_, by Corrie ten Boom. In her book, ten Boom describes an example of how God provides strength for his calling exactly when we need it. After confessing to her father that she did not have the strength to face death in pursuit of God's calling, he asked her to consider that he never gave her the ticket for the train until the moment she was about to board. "Exactly. And our wise Father in heaven knows when we're going to need things, too. Don't run out ahead of Him, Corrie. When the time comes that some of us will have to die, you will look into your heart and find the strength you need—just in time."[24] God often calls us to do difficult or impossible things. We need to step courageously into those situations, trusting that he will give us the strength through his Spirit just in time to accomplish his calling.

Ehud

Big Idea

God may arrange circumstances to fulfill his plan even if people act contrary to his will.

Key Themes

- Deliverance comes through the agency of Ehud's unique skills and deceptive scheming.
- God orders circumstances to bring about deliverance.
- Foreign oppression is the result of Israel's spiritual negligence.

Understanding the Text

The Text in Context

In the ring structure of the book of Judges the Ehud account is paralleled with the Jephthah account (10:6–12:7), and both stories share the following thematic connections: (1) an eastern geographical orientation dealing with Transjordanian oppressors (the descendants of Lot); (2) the Israelite leader brings a message to a foreign king (3:15–25; 11:12–28); and (3) an eighteen-year oppression (3:14; 10:8). These parallel passages also feature some striking contrasts: (1) both accounts may depict forms of human sacrifice: the Moabite king Eglon may be viewed as a sacrificial victim (note the allusive terminology in 3:17, 22) and the Israelite daughter of Jephthah tragically becomes a burnt offering (11:31); and (2) both accounts relate the role of Ephraimites at the fords of the Jordan—positively aiding Ehud in smiting the enemy (3:27–29) and negatively opposing Jephthah and being slaughtered by the Gileadites (12:1–6).[1]

Structure

Although the literary structure of this passage is analyzed differently by various scholars, most agree that the central unit of the pericope includes the graphic description of the assassination (3:21–22).[2] This unit is framed by the term for idols (3:19, 26; NIV: "stone images") and is further framed by the verb for smiting (3:13 [NIV: "attacked"], 29 [NIV: "struck down"]). The narrator also employs the *Leitwort* ("leading word") "hand" in a number of key phrases (3:15, 21, 28, 30; see ESV).

Historical and Cultural Background

The scene of this "perfect murder" is the second-story throne room (3:20) of a palatial structure in or near Jericho. The architectural layout of the facility may be modeled after the Syrian-style palace known as a *bit hilani*.[3] It appears that the throne room has double doors with tumbler locks that Ehud is able to secure from the outside (3:23). But such locks, which were mounted on the inside, could be opened from the outside only with a large wooden key (3:25) that had to be inserted through a hand hole.[4] Ehud then proceeds down the stairs to the portico (3:23), which is likely a pillared entryway, and makes his escape before the servants can even suspect foul play (3:24–26). Ehud goes toward Seirah (3:26), which is probably "a topographical feature with the meaning 'the woody hills.'"[5]

Interpretive Insights

3:12 *Eglon king of Moab.* The name Eglon, composed of the elements *'egel* and *-on*, means "Calfish/Calfy" or "Calf Man." Animal names were quite

Moab

According to Genesis 19:30–38 the Moabites and Ammonites were the children of Abraham's nephew Lot.[a] Their territory was on the east side of the Dead Sea between the Zered Brook and the Arnon River but often extending north into the territory allotted to Reuben. That their national deity was Chemosh is amply attested in both the Bible and Moabite inscriptions. The first Moabite king to clash with the Israelites in the biblical record is Balak, who hires Balaam to curse Israel (Num. 22–24), and the second king is Eglon, who is assassinated by the deliverer Ehud (Judg. 3:12–30). While the Israelites are clearly the tribute-paying vassals of Moab in the time of Ehud, the reverse scenario is recorded for the reigns of David and Ahab.[b] The earliest extrabiblical occurrences of the name Moab are in Egyptian inscriptions from the reign of Ramesses II (thirteenth century BC).[c] A basalt stele from about 1200 BC was also recovered from Balu'a depicting a Moabite king with hands raised before an Egyptian-style deity. The most important Moabite discovery is a monumental building inscription from the late ninth century that features more than thirty-four lines of Moabite (a dialect very similar to Hebrew) about King Mesha's dealings with the kings of Israel and Judah.[d]

[a] See Dearman, "Moab, Moabites"; Mattingly, "Moabites"; Routledge, *Moab in the Iron Age*.
[b] See 2 Sam. 8:2 // 1 Chron. 18:2; 2 Kings 3:4–5.
[c] See Kitchen, *Reliability of the Old Testament*, 195; Rainey and Notley, *Sacred Bridge*, 98.
[d] See *COS* 2.23:137–38.

common in Semitic languages (e.g., Caleb, "Dog"; Deborah, "Bee" (?); and Jael, "Ibex") and should not necessarily be understood pejoratively. Eglon's name may also be an epithet for his god or express his religious devotion.[6]

3:13 *City of Palms.* This phrase is commonly linked with the city of Jericho (cf. 1:16; Deut. 34:3; 2 Chron. 28:15), and date palms are still thriving today at this desert oasis.

3:15 *Ehud.* The name means "Where Is Majesty?"[7] and may ambiguously indicate the heroic presence of Ehud/God, which is dually expressed in 3:28: "Follow after *me*, for the LORD has given your enemies, Moab, into your hand" (author's translation).

a left-handed man. By juxtaposing the words "Benjamite" and "left-handed," the narrator is likely showing the irony of the fact that this "son of the right/south" (the meaning of "Benjamite") is actually ambidextrous! The phrase typically translated "left-handed" is rendered more precisely as "bound right hand/arm." It describes not a handicap or a predisposition from birth but rather a skill acquired by deliberately restricting use of the right hand in order to train the left hand for tactical military purposes (cf. Judg. 20:16; 1 Chron. 12:2). Thus Ehud is the only judge who is demonstrably *not* left-handed. As a trained assassin, Ehud serves as Israel's secret weapon.[8]

3:16 *double-edged sword.* This weapon is described with the term *gomed* (NIV: "cubit"), which occurs only here in the Old Testament. Instead of measurement this term may actually describe the dagger's design as a single piece; thus, it was "rigid or stiff over its entire length."[9] Although it was undoubtedly customized for the length of Ehud's thigh, the design may be analogous to the longer Naue Type II sword (pictured on both the Trojan Horse vase and the Sea People reliefs from the time of Ramesses III at Medinet Habu), which was double edged, made of one piece, and typically lacked a cross guard, which would allow the hilt to penetrate the victim (cf. 3:22).[10]

3:17 *presented the tribute.* Although the type of tribute is unidentified here, vassal payments would often consist of precious metals, agricultural produce, livestock, or some other valued commodity. While the words "presented" and "tribute" are used elsewhere as sacrificial terms, neither one requires such a nuance in the present context.[11] However, the sacrificial interpretations of this passage—viewing Eglon as an implicit "calf readied for slaughter"[12]—may be strengthened by comparing the sacrifice of Jephthah's daughter (11:29–40), which is rhetorically parallel in the ring structure.[13]

very fat. Modern English translations have, unfortunately, missed the mark on the meaning of this parenthetical statement. The term *bari'* (NIV: "fat") occurs fourteen times in the Old Testament and never refers to obesity but rather refers to health, prosperity, or attractive appearance (see esp. Ps. 73:4; Dan. 1:15). The Septuagint even renders the word as "handsome" in this passage. The narrator is thus informing us that Eglon is not an easy target but rather a "beefy" or "strapping" man, which explains why he would have little need for guards and heightens the dramatic impact of God's deliverance through Ehud (cf. the description of Moabite soldiers as vigorous [*shamen*] and valiant in 3:29). Likewise, the reference to the "fat" (*heleb*) closing over the blade (3:22) should be understood as the internal fat that protects the abdominal organs (see esp. 2 Sam. 1:22 [e.g., ESV]; Isa. 34:6–7).

3:19 *stone images near Gilgal.* The term used here for idols (*p^{e}silim*) refers to hewn images that were likely monoliths of stone or metal (cf. 17:3–4; Isa. 30:22). Gilgal, apparently meaning "Circle," has some history as a sacred place. It is where Joshua set up twelve memorial stones, circumcised the Israelites, and observed Passover (Josh. 4:19–5:12). It is also the place from which the angel of the Lord went up (Judg. 2:1; cf. Josh. 5:13–15), and it was included with Bethel and Mizpah as part of Samuel's circuit (1 Sam. 7:16). The site is later associated with apostasy by the eighth-century prophets (Hosea 4:15; 9:15; 12:11; Amos 4:4; 5:5). Here the site appears to function as one of the numerous cult spaces that should have been destroyed according to Deuteronomy 12.

3:20 *message from God.* This "secret/divine word" (cf. 3:19) is understood by Eglon as an oracle received at the Gilgal sanctuary. Such divinatory information could provide strategic intelligence appropriate for the king's ears only. Ironically, this "word/thing" (*dabar*) is revealed as Ehud's dagger!

3:21 *plunged it into the king's belly.* This verb used with the preposition means to thrust something "through," not just "plunge into" (cf. 4:21; 16:14; Isa. 22:23, 25). The term for belly (*beten*) refers to the lower abdomen, and it seems likely that this is a calculated thrust that is angled upward so as to sever the aorta and result in "almost immediate incapacitation."[14]

3:22 *his bowels discharged.* The final Hebrew clause in verse 22, absent in the Septuagint, is extremely difficult to interpret because the word *parsh^{e}don* (NIV: "bowels") occurs nowhere else in the Old Testament and its meaning is presently uncertain. While the masculine singular subject of the verb ("it went out") has been interpreted as "dung/refuse/entrails," or even as Ehud (exiting the murder scene toward the *parsh^{e}don*), it is more likely that the subject is the blade (*lahab*), which would have exited Eglon's back (cf. NLT footnote).

3:24 *relieving himself.* The Hebrew expression "to cover one's feet/legs" is clearly a euphemism for defecation whereby one's garments could provide privacy by concealing what happens in the seated position (cf. 1 Sam. 24:3). It is important to point out that this scenario is humorously *imagined* by the courtiers and is not in reality what *is* happening. There is actually no extrabiblical evidence indicating that latrines were located in/under throne rooms, and it is more likely that the scenario would involve a chamber pot.[15]

In general, the popular scatological readings of this story are overemphasized in scholarship, especially for the final clause of verse 22.

Theological Insights

The beginning and the end of the story tell readers what they need to know about the divine perspective on events (i.e., the Lord "strengthened Eglon" [3:12], "raised up . . . Ehud" [3:15], "has given . . . Moab into your hand" [3:28]; author's translations), whereas the midsection of the account relates the events from a human perspective (3:16–27). Ehud and the Israelites accomplish astounding feats through their own "hands" (3:15, 21, 30; see ESV), but the parallel reality is that God orchestrates the events (3:28). The riskiness of the scenario is emphasized in the endless list of circumstantial variables. What if the servants frisk Ehud's right leg? What if Ehud's "divine word" is uninteresting to Eglon? What if Eglon does not rise before Ehud? What if Eglon fights back or cries out for help? What if the servants see Ehud lock the doors? What if the servants do not assume Eglon is "on the pot"? The point is that, left to their own skills and schemes, the Israelites can never succeed. Only the Lord can guide events to bring about a successful outcome, and he does.

The specific spiritual offenses of Israel, which lead to the Moabite oppression (cf. 1 Sam. 12:9), are subtly indicated in the incidental details of the story. First, the existence of the Amalekites who are allied with Moab (Judg. 3:13) is problematic because Israel was explicitly commanded to annihilate them (Deut. 25:17–19; cf. Exod. 17:14–16; Num. 24:20). Second, Jericho, which is here occupied by Moab (Judg. 3:13), was completely destroyed under Joshua (Josh. 6), allotted to Benjamin (Josh. 18:21), and never to be rebuilt (Josh. 6:26). Third, there should not be any idols at Gilgal (Judg. 3:19, 26; cf. Exod. 20:4; Lev. 26:1; Deut. 4:16, 23, 25; 5:8; 7:5, 25; 12:3; 27:15) in the territory of Benjamin. An additional problem that is apparent only by its absence is that the Transjordanian tribes (Gad and especially Reuben) should have prevented the Moabite incursion. The Israelites obviously have neglected to follow through on God's commands related to the conquest.

Teaching the Text

The most important truth to acknowledge is that this story—like all of Scripture—is primarily about God and his plan. Therefore, the story is not showcasing unique human talents that God bestows on people, nor does it teach the ethics of war or regicide. Rather, the story reveals the providence of God through a series of apparent "coincidences."[16]

On the human level, the Ehud story depicts the heroic and daring actions of an ambidextrous deliverer, but on the divine level it is revealed that there is no deliverance here except for that arranged and executed by the Lord. This providential antinomy is nicely encapsulated in verses such as Psalm 127:1 ("Unless the Lord builds the house, the builders labor in vain. Unless the Lord watches over the city, the guards stand watch in vain") and Proverbs 16:9 ("In their hearts humans plan their course, but the Lord establishes their steps"). One is also struck by the way God deals with the Moabite king in this story: God "strengthened" the king for a time (Judg. 3:12 ESV) and dispatched the king when he was finished (3:28). Such actions reveal the identity of the ultimate king in this story. Indeed, the heart of the human king is "a stream of water that [God] channels" wherever he pleases (Prov. 21:1; cf. 21:31).

The deceptive or tricky schemes of Israel and Ehud are not necessarily endorsed by the divine or human composer, even if God is using these actions for his own purposes. The theme of God accomplishing his purposes through imperfect or ignorant individuals will become increasingly pronounced in the book of Judges (see esp. Samson's marriage to a Philistine, which is "from the Lord"; Judg. 14:4). It is helpful in such cases to make a theological distinction between God's will and God's plan.[17] While it may not be God's will that Ehud uses deceptive measures to assassinate Eglon, it is certainly part of God's plan for the deliverance of Israel at this time. Similarly in Genesis 50:20, the sons of Israel plan evil against Joseph, while God through the same circumstances plans for the deliverance of many people.

A secondary lesson from this story may be derived from the implicit spiritual causes of the Moabite oppression. Israel neglects God's commands regarding conduct in the promised land with respect to the Amalekites, the city of Jericho, and the practice of idolatry. God's people must always take care not only to know what God has said (through Bible study) but also to follow through and practice it if they are to experience God's blessing (cf. James 1:22–25).

Finally, the violent and gruesome details of this story may not be appropriate for all ages (esp. 3:22), but the teachings on God's providence and Israel's negligence are accessible to all.

Illustrating the Text

A perfect God can deliver his people perfectly through the imperfect actions of flawed people.

Film: Show or describe a clip from a spy comedy with a bumbling hero, like Peter Sellers in one of the *Pink Panther* films, Bill Murray in *The Man Who Knew Too Little*, or Rowan Atkinson in *Johnny English*. Illustrate how the hapless and clueless hero still gets the job done, despite completely misunderstanding or botching the assignments given to him. Point out that it is often that way with us—while we should always seek to grow in effectiveness and integrity, God is perfectly capable of using us in the meantime while we struggle and bumble our way through. In the end, our imperfection is neither an insuperable impediment nor a legitimate excuse—we can be used by God today.

Bible: Share a brief list of some of the imperfect people God has used in the Bible: Abraham lied, and Sarah laughed at God's promise; Moses stuttered and was a murderer; David was an adulterer; Jacob was a liar; Miriam was a gossip; Jeremiah and Elijah were depressed; Martha was a workaholic; Noah got drunk; and so on.

God can use even ungodly rulers to direct human affairs and prepare the way for his work.

Bible: Cyrus, king of Persia, is a perfect example of God using a pagan ruler for his purposes. Though Cyrus was a foreigner and pagan, in Isaiah 44 God calls him his anointed servant for liberating Israel from the tyranny of the Babylonians. Another great biblical example is Caiaphas, the high priest who helped condemn and crucify Jesus. Though he was wicked, he still spoke true prophecy because of his God-given office (cf. John 11:45–53). Even his role in the crucifixion was the will and work of God through him, despite his wickedness and hatred of Christ.

Current Events: Talk a little bit about the persecuted church in a country your listeners would think of as despotic or tyrannical. Describe the kind of persecution being meted out, and then compare that to the growth of Christianity in that nation. Often the persecution will correlate to increased growth of the church. For example, beginning under Chairman Mao, in communist China the number of professing Christians in China grew from 1.5 million in 1970 to 65 million by 1990. Point out that sometimes even the most ungodly rulers and their cruelty are used to direct the affairs of humans and prepare the way for God's kingdom to grow. In that sense, all earthly rulers are both equally corruptible and equally useful to God's gracious purposes.

Prose Account of Deborah and Barak

Big Idea

God's deliverance is not dependent on human initiative, but blessings may come to those who trust and obey.

Key Themes

- Female leaders have a strategic role in God's work.
- God is overtly revealed as Israel's King and Deliverer.
- God's blessings may be withheld from those who hesitate to trust and obey.

Understanding the Text

The Text in Context

The account of Deborah and Barak (chaps. 4–5) is the third major cycle that completes the first parallel panel (or triad of stories) in the body of the book. The brief note on Shamgar (3:31), which is treated along with the other "minor judges" in a separate unit in this commentary (see the unit on Judg. 3:31; 10:1–5; 12:8–15), serves a transitional function and is not presented by the narrator as a full-fledged cycle (note how 4:1 mentions only Ehud as the previous deliverer/judge).

A number of important themes emerge from comparing this account with the parallel story of Abimelek in chapter 9. The themes that are common to both passages are as follows: (1) resolution is achieved by the heroic efforts of a woman independently killing the villain by a blow to his head with an unconventional weapon (4:21; 5:26; 9:53); (2) both stories blend poetic quotations (song and fable, respectively, in 5:1–31 and 9:8–15) with the events of the prose narratives; (3) both stories have a northern geographical orientation (note especially the absence of Judah/Simeon in chaps. 4–5); and (4) both stories conspicuously omit reference to a solo human judge/deliverer so that God's role is elevated.

---

*3:31 is discussed with 10:1–5 and 12:8–15 in the unit "Minor Judges," which is after the unit on 11:29–12:7.

There are also some important contrasting themes in these parallel passages: (1) the enemy in chapters 4–5 is external/Canaanite, whereas the enemy in chapter 9 is internal/Israelite (Abimelek); (2) while both stories are about proper leadership, the former story shows Barak hesitating to take leadership when he should, and the latter story shows Abimelek taking leadership when he should not; and (3) Jael's extreme acts of altruism and communal interest are sharply contrasted with Abimelek's extreme acts of narcissism and self-interest.[1]

Structure

The story in 4:1–24 displays a chiastic structure with the "battle" account in central position (4:12–16) featuring Yahweh's miraculous deliverance (v. 15).[2] That central unit is framed by references to "tent" and "Heber the Kenite" (4:11, 17), and those units are framed by the accounts showcasing extraordinary female leaders (Deborah's prophecies in 4:4–10 and Jael's heroics in 4:18–22). Finally, the outer framework of the story features "Jabin king of Canaan," who is introduced as the oppressor (4:1–3) and is summarily subdued by God (4:23–24).

Historical and Cultural Background

Excavations at Tel Hazor in northern Israel may provide some context for the setting of Judges 4–5, which has to be after the time when Joshua burned the city (cf. Josh. 11:10–14). According to the early date of the exodus-conquest, Deborah's Hazor could be any time from Stratum XIV–1B to XI (fourteenth–eleventh centuries BC). According to the late date (see the introduction to Judges), Deborah's Hazor would be during strata XII–XI (twelfth–eleventh centuries BC).[3]

Interpretive Insights

4:1 *Again . . . did.* It is preferable to translate this idiom as "continued to do" since Israel's apostasy, except for the brief incident in 10:16, is unceasing in the book.[4] Within the ring structure sequence it may be noteworthy that this idiom is added to the refrain only in the stories that are in the second and third positions of each triad (i.e., it appears in Ehud and Deborah and in Jephthah and Samson, but not in Othniel or Abimelek, which are in first position, and not in Gideon, because 6:1 is uniquely echoing the prologue statement in 2:11).

4:2 *Sisera.* The name Sisera most likely is non-Semitic and derives linguistically from the west. Since similar names are identified in Sardinia and Crete, it is possible that Sisera's origins were with the "Sea Peoples."[5] His military station at Harosheth Haggoyim ("Farmland of the Gentiles") may designate a region in the plain east of Megiddo;[6] or alternatively, it may be located at el-Ahwat.[7]

4:3 *chariots fitted with iron.* See the comments on Judges 1:19; see also 4:13.

4:4 *Deborah.* This name may denote "(Honey) Bee," but more likely the root means "to lead/pursue."[8] The latter derivation fits the context best as Deborah is depicted leading both Barak and the Israelites (or better: God is the one leading them *through* Deborah). Lest readers overlook the feminine form of this name, the narrator goes out of his way to stress her gender in the Hebrew. Instead of designating her merely as a "prophetess" (a sufficient designation by itself),[9] she is a "prophetess-woman" (to be contrasted with the "prophet-man" in 6:8). Furthermore, she is the "wife of Lappidoth" (or perhaps "Light/Torch Woman";[10] i.e., a spiritual guide, rather than the "wife of Lappidoth"). And finally, we are told that it is "she" who is "governing [*shoptah*] Israel at that time" (author's translation). The narrator actually uses seven grammatically feminine words in a row to introduce Deborah into the story. By emphasizing her gender, the narrator may underscore her extraordinary role as an authority in a patriarchal society (cf. 5:7).

4:5 *Palm of Deborah.* Deborah's professional address is under a specific palm tree (or perhaps "scarecrow"; cf. Jer. 10:5) that is located between the sacred spaces at Ramah and Bethel (cf. Samuel's circuit in 1 Sam. 7:15–17). The Israelites come up to her for "the judgment/decision," which is probably ascertained through oracular means.[11] This "judicial" function is evidently unique in the book of Judges since she offers only religious guidance and never directly engages in battle as do the other major leaders. Although her prophetic status is exceptional, it does not preclude her functioning as a judge (see 4:4): she brings justice to Israel *through* her prophetic status.[12]

4:6 *Barak.* This name means "Lightning," but ironically Barak fails to live up to his name, as he always appears to be a step behind in following orders (4:6–9), routing the enemy (4:15; cf. 5:12), and slaying Sisera (4:22). His hometown, Kedesh in Naphtali (probably Khirbet Qedish), is near the Kenite tent settlement where Jael resides (see 4:11).

4:7 *Kishon.* This river (Wadi el-Muqatta) is the location of God's choosing, to which Sisera will gather his troops and experience panic due to a cosmic display (cf. 5:4, 21a; Ps. 83:9; see also Judg. 4:13).[13]

4:11 *Heber.* This background note on Heber the Kenite, which initially seems superfluous to readers, is foundational for verses 17–22, where Heber's wife plays a decisive role. Like the Kenizzites (see the comments on Judg. 3:11), the Kenites were ethnically foreigners.[14] They were Moses's in-laws who settled in the tribal region of Judah (1:16), but Heber separated himself

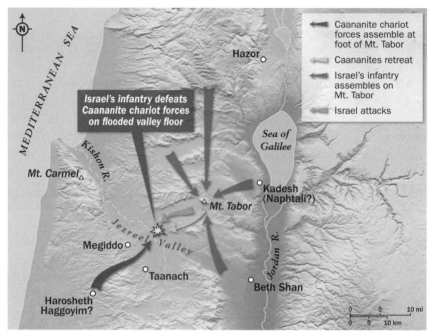

Israel defeats the Canaanite chariots in the Jezreel Valley.

from his family to this northern setting, in which he maintained some kind
of friendly (political/professional?) relationship with King Jabin (4:17). This
explains why Sisera might perceive Jael as an ally and seek temporary asylum
in her tent.

4:14 *Has not the Lord gone ahead of you?* This rhetorical question (note
the same syntax in 4:6; cf. ESV, NKJV) is equivalent to saying: "It is definitely
the case that the Lord has marched before you!" This is an emphatic affirmation about Yahweh as Israel's commander in chief. In the absence of any
single human hero in this passage, perhaps this is intended as a reminder that
theocracy is the ideal for Israel regardless of the forms of their ever-changing
political structures.

4:21–22 *picked up . . . went quietly . . . drove the peg through his temple . . .
and he died.* The rhetoric and scene in these verses echoes the assassination of
Eglon (3:21–25) and foreshadows the demise of Abimelek (9:52–55; cf. 16:14).

4:23 *God subdued Jabin.* The verb for "subdued" is most likely a pun on
the name "Canaan" (both are from the same root).

Theological Insights

The theological contribution of this story must be viewed according to its
place in the sequence of major cycles. That is, deliverance previously came

Jabin

The king named in Judges 4 should already be familiar to Bible students as the one slain by Joshua (Josh. 11:1, 10–12). The apparent naming of the same king at the same place in both Joshua 11 and Judges 4 has led some scholars to propose that the Judges account is earlier than the Joshua account or that the contradictory accounts refer to the same historical event. Neither of these solutions is satisfactory based on the available data. It is preferable to maintain that the Joshua account was historically prior to the Judges account and that they refer to two different events in the history of Hazor. Jabin was most likely a royal dynastic name at the city of Hazor (similar to "Ramesses" in Egypt or "Henry" in England).[a] The name appears as early as the eighteenth century BC in the Mari archives, where Hazor's king is Yabni-Addu (Yabni = Ibni = Jabin);[b] and more recently, the same name was discovered in part on a letter fragment from Hazor dating to the same period.[c] In the Bible, "Jabin" therefore appears to be the name of two different rulers: (1) the "king of Hazor" during Joshua's northern campaign who formed a coalition of Canaanite kings who fought the Israelites at the Waters of Merom (Josh. 11:1–5); and (2) the "king of Canaan, who reigned in Hazor" during the war of Deborah and Barak (Judg. 4:2; cf. Ps. 83:9). It is likely that the king in Judges is a direct descendant of the king killed by Joshua.

[a] See Malamat, *History of Biblical Israel*, 106; Younger, *Judges, Ruth*, 138n3.
[b] See Hess, "Non-Israelite Personal Names," 207; Malamat, *History of Biblical Israel*, 26, 106n19.
[c] See Horowitz, Oshima, and Sanders, *Cuneiform in Canaan*, 77–78, 212, 229.

by means of solo heroes who were empowered by the Spirit of the Lord (e.g., Othniel) and aided by the providential orchestration of events (e.g., Ehud). But here in the third account, there is no single human hero (there are merely three participants), and while there is certainly providential orchestration, God's deliverance is presented as a solo miraculous event credited to no character except himself (4:15; cf. 5:4–5, 11a, 20–21a).[15] Thus God's role in the first three cycles is emphasized more and more as the human characters contribute less and less.

Like the previous cycles, this story displays the pattern of apostasy-oppression-deliverance, but this time an important detail is absent—that God "raised up" a deliverer (cf. 3:9, 15). In place of such a remark, the prophetess Deborah is introduced as a de facto judge (4:4; contrast with 6:8), and then she reveals that a leader has been summoned by God but that he is reluctant to cooperate! When Deborah tells this leader about God's commissioning (4:6–7), he immediately presents his own terms (possibly doubting God's word; cf. 4:8), and Deborah reveals that Barak has therefore forfeited the "honor" because of the "course" he has taken (4:9). Barak should have been the military "hero" in this story, but alas, he is no Ehud, and he is certainly no Othniel. So, along with Barak's reluctant service, God unexpectedly employs

Judges 4:1–24

the contributions of two women (and one of them is a foreigner!). In the end, however, none of the participants can claim the victory for themselves. The divine King is clearly the commander in chief (4:6, 14), and the victory belongs to him alone (4:7, 9, 14, 15, 23).

The nature of Israel's apostasy (4:1) is unclear in chapter 4, but the song in the following chapter specifically mentions that they "chose new gods" (5:8; author's translation). Perhaps this renewed Canaanite occupation of Hazor (which was formerly put under the ban; cf. Josh. 11:10–14) implies Israel's religious negligence. Or perhaps one should pause to consider the image of the "Palm of Deborah" and the association of trees with the goddess Asherah (Judg. 4:5; cf. 6:25–30). Deborah's divinatory role as a prophetess is also very curious: her provision of oracular services for Israel (see 4:5b) may imply the absence of a functioning priesthood.[16] The narrator, however, has chosen not to dwell on such ambiguous details but to focus his attention on revealing the identity of the Deliverer and the fulfillment of prophecies.[17]

Teaching the Text

The most important thing to recognize in this passage is the hierarchy of characters.[18] God rules alone at the top with his own plan and its execution. All the other human characters are on the same terrestrial level (regardless of social standing; cf. 5:10), far below the Lord. Each of them participates in some small way—Deborah with commissioning and prophesying, Barak with pursuing the enemy army, and Jael with dispatching Sisera—but none actually causes the outcome. This principle is always true in life. God's people each have unique positions to play in God's game plan, and the goal is not to win as individuals but to give glory to God. The apostle Paul likewise explains: "I planted the seed, Apollos watered it, but God has been making it grow. So neither the one who plants nor the one who waters is anything, but only God, who makes things grow" (1 Cor. 3:6–7). God, of course, does not "need" our participation, but he desires to meet our deepest needs through our participation.

Our participation in God's program, however, requires faith. Barak's faith is certainly present (cf. Heb. 11:32), but it seems feeble (see Judg. 4:8). Apparently, God's command and promise are not sufficient grounds to proceed, and Barak needs more assurances for whatever reason (this foreshadows Gideon's spiritual deficiencies in 6:33–7:25). So he makes a "deal" with Deborah, and contrary to expectation (4:9),[19] she agrees to accompany him. After his own terms are met, Barak agrees to obey God. The tragedy of this scenario is that God apparently has blessings ("honor"; 4:9) in store for Barak but distributes them elsewhere (to Jael) because Barak seemingly lacks faith. So also, the extent to which Christians can enjoy God's unlimited gifts may be related to their measure of trust. On requesting wisdom, James explains: "When you ask, you must believe and not doubt, because the one who doubts is like a wave of the sea, blown and tossed by the wind. That person should not expect to receive anything from the Lord. Such a person is double-minded and unstable in all they do" (James 1:6–8).

Jael, on the other hand, displays no inhibitions. She is providentially presented with an opportunity, and she decisively acts. She seemingly has much to lose and little to gain by killing Jabin's general. Her marginalized social status (by ethnicity and gender) and her husband's friendly relationship with Jabin, as well as the prospect of reward for protecting this fugitive, are all strong deterrents, yet she opts—for whatever reason—to risk everything by grasping the mallet.[20] Thus, in contrast to Barak (see 4:9), Jael is honored as the "most blessed of women" (5:24; cf. Luke 1:42, 48). Now, before one presumes that the point is to "be like Jael and not like Barak," it must be noted that Jael's faith in God is never explicitly mentioned in the text. She is blessed and Barak is bereft to the extent that each is receptive to God's agenda. The point is that God's work and word must come first in our lives. We must "seek first his kingdom and his righteousness, and all these things will be given" to us (Matt. 6:33; cf. Luke 14:26).

Illustrating the Text

The one who hesitates loses.

Quote: You are probably familiar with the popular saying, "He who hesitates is lost." This popular quote is an adaptation from James Addison's play *Cato*. The original quote is "The woman who deliberates is lost." Interestingly enough, the rewrite is necessary in this passage, where Barak (the man) hesitates in his lack of faith and trust in God. Jael and Deborah (both women) are more decisive and spend no time in deliberation when opportunity arises to be part of God's story. The point is about not women or men but rather hesitation. Male or female, will we respond in faith and boldness when God calls or waste time in deliberation and miss out on the honor and reward God offers?

We are called by God to obey without delay, excuse, or challenge.

Christian Book: *Shepherding a Child's Heart*, by Tedd Tripp. In this parenting classic, Tripp explains that "submission to authority means that [children] obey without delay, excuse, or challenge."[21] It is easy to get fuzzy in our thinking about obedience, especially in a culture that prizes independent thought and discourages people from being mindless robots that are taken

Judges 4:1–24

in by false authorities. However, Tripp's book does a great job in explaining that our obedience here on earth and in families is a great training ground for the obedience God desires. We are to respond to him immediately without back talk, excuses, or procrastination. Ultimately, this is the example we see in Jesus.

Poetic Account
of Deborah and Barak

Big Idea

God's people should function as one family and celebrate God's sovereign works in their community.

Key Themes

- God may freely employ miraculous events to deliver his people from oppression.
- God's kingship must be recognized by every class of people.
- God may lavish blessings on his people when they participate in God's battles.
- Blessings may be withheld from God's people who are disengaged.
- Curses are placed on covenant breakers and enemies of God.

Understanding the Text

The Text in Context

The song of Deborah and Barak is part of the third major cycle (chaps. 4–5) that completes the first parallel panel (or triad of stories) in the body of the book of Judges. The thematic connections between the accounts of Deborah/Barak and Abimelek (chap. 9) are listed for the previous pericope (see "The Text in Context" in the unit on Judg. 4:1–24). Like the literary function of Jotham's fable in the narrative that follows about Abimelek, the song of Deborah/Barak (chap. 5) complements the previous narrative account (chap. 4). That the narrator intends for the song to be integrated with the juxtaposed narrative is indicated by (1) the phrase "on that day" (4:23; 5:1) and (2) the final formulaic remark that "the land was tranquil forty years" (5:31b NJPS). The song is therefore "embedded or character's text";[1] or as Younger explains, the poetic and prose versions are like two different sides of the same coin.[2] The poetic version is more overtly theological—or even celestial—in perspective than the prose account, which describes the terrestrial roles of the human players. While Jotham's fable (9:7–20) is about a person in a wrong relationship with the divine King, the song of Deborah/Barak depicts people in a right relationship with the divine King (relatively speaking).

Structure

The poetic units of this song may be identified from smallest to largest as cola, verses, strophes, stanzas, and larger sections that may be called acts.[3] The most important units for holistic exposition are the acts and stanzas.

Act 1	Stanza 1 (5:2–5)
	Stanza 2 (5:6–8)
Act 2	Stanza 3 (5:9–13)
Act 3	Stanza 4 (5:14–18)
Act 4	Stanza 5 (5:19–23)
Act 5	Stanza 6 (5:24–27)
	Stanza 7 (5:28–31a)

Act 3 is the central section of the poem. Furthermore there is a progressive shift in subject matter from the general to the specific[4]—that is, from the whole nation in acts 1–2 (5:2–13) to the ten northern tribes in act 3 (5:14–18) to a city in act 4 (5:19–23) to individual women in act 5 (5:24–31a).

Historical and Cultural Background

One of the ways to determine the historical setting of a biblical passage is by onomastic analysis (i.e., the study of personal names). Hess has performed such analysis on the names in this poem and determines that names like Deborah, Barak, Abinoam, Shamgar, Jael, Heber, and Sisera are characteristic of the late second millennium (i.e., pre-1000 BC), rather than the first millennium BC.[5] Thus it is not surprising that many philologists and historians suggest that this poem is among the earliest sources in the Bible and that it originates in the Iron Age I period (1200–1000 BC).[6]

The genre of this poem may be described as a "victory song" or "triumph hymn" that honors a military leader (either divine or human). Another lengthy example from the Bible is the Song of the Sea/Miriam in Exodus 15:1–21, while shorter examples are found in Judges 16:23–24 and 1 Samuel 18:6–7 (cf. Judg. 11:34). This genre is also well attested in Egyptian and Mesopotamian sources (see, e.g., the poetic triumph hymn of Ramesses II and the epic of Tukulti-Ninurta I, both from the thirteenth century BC).[7] Additionally, the recording of battle accounts with complementary versions in both prose and poetry is documented in the inscriptions of Thutmose III, Ramesses II, Merneptah, Tukulti-Ninurta I, Tiglath-Pileser I, and Shamaneser III.[8]

Interpretive Insights

5:2 *When the princes in Israel take the lead.* Right at the beginning, translators are confronted with one of the many exegetical challenges of this poem. The NRSV, NJPS, and NJB are most likely correct by interpreting $p^e ra'ot$ as "locks/hair" ("when locks are long in Israel"; NRSV) rather than "leaders" (for the latter, cf. NLT, NKJV, NASB, ESV, HCSB). The practice of soldiers leaving their hair unshorn during wartime may also be expressed in Ugaritic and may inform the portrayal of Samson as a long-haired Nazirite.[9]

5:4 *went out from Seir.* Seir/Edom in this context is poetically parallel with Sinai (see 5:5), but this need not indicate that Sinai is located in Edom. Rather, Edom was a station through which Yahweh passed on his journey to the promised land.[10]

5:7 *mother.* On analogy with the title "father" (used for Levites, prophets, and diviners in the Bible; see the comments on Judg. 17:10), the title "mother" seems to designate Deborah as an expert adviser on matters in the cultic domain.

5:8 *God chose new leaders.* Only the NIV and NET supply the word "leaders" and take *'elohim* as the subject of the verb in this ambiguous clause. The other English translations and LXX take *'elohim* as the object of the verb (e.g., "new gods were chosen"; ESV), an interpretation which makes the best sense in the context of the book (see Judg. 10:14, referring to "the gods you have chosen"; cf. Deut. 32:15–18; 1 Sam. 12:9).

forty thousand. This is also the number of Israelites who crossed over the Jordan with Joshua (Josh. 4:13). In such military contexts, it may be preferable to interpret high, rounded numbers hyperbolically or to translate the term *'elep* as "contingent/company," which would consist of far fewer than a thousand men.[11]

5:14 *Amalek.* This cryptic reference to Amalek is probably related to the remark about Abdon's burial place "in Ephraim, in the hill country of the Amalekites" (12:15). While a relationship with the Amalekites would normally be grounds for reproach (cf. Deut. 25:19), the poem ironically commends Ephraim for their participation in battle.

5:19 *At Taanach, by the waters of Megiddo.* This location may be the poetic synonym for the prose term Harosheth Haggoyim, if the latter refers to the plain east of Megiddo.[12]

5:20 *stars fought.* This may refer to negative celestial omens that caused panic for the Canaanites. Similar astronomical phenomena are described in Joshua 10:12–14 and Habakkuk 3:11 (regarding the sun and moon) and in battle accounts from Egypt and Mesopotamia.[13] It is also possible, in light of Ugaritic parallels, that the ancients viewed the stars as a source of rain (cf. 5:21a).[14]

5:23 *Meroz.* The otherwise unknown site of Meroz seems to designate a town of foreigners who were in treaty relationship with Israel yet failed to uphold the stipulation of supporting Israel in battle and therefore incurred God's curse. The inhabitants of Meroz are an example of God's "enemies," rather than his "friends" (i.e., covenant partners), who are mentioned in 5:31a. For the angel of the Lord, see the "Additional Insights" following the unit on Judges 8:1–32.

5:25 *she gave him milk.* Similar to the function of Ehud's "secret/divine word" (3:19), Jael's hospitable provision of milk (or a milk product like curds/yogurt) disarmed Sisera for the murder. The sedative qualities of milk are widely recognized and were ingeniously exploited by Jael (cf. 4:19).

5:26 *crushed his head.* The ignominious manner of Sisera's death, which parallels that of Abimelek (9:53), may also be appreciated in light of the common Egyptian depictions of Pharaoh smashing the head of his enemy.[15] This victorious image of Jael standing over her vanquished foe (4:21; 5:26–27) is to be contrasted with the anxious image of Sisera's mother in verses 28–30.

5:28 *window.* The motif of a woman peering through her window is commonly associated with opulence, power, and security (cf. 2 Sam. 6:16; 2 Kings 9:30–32). But ironically, the image is here invoked to show the imminent reversal of fortunes for Sisera's mother.[16]

5:30 *a woman or two for each man.* The term for "womb," translated here as "woman," is likely a macho pejorative designation for women who are viewed as plunder (cf. English "broad/wench"). This remark—surprisingly from a woman—implies that Canaanite military victories involved the routine raping of conquered women. For the theme of women in the book of Judges, see the "Additional Insights" following this unit.

Theological Insights

Both the prose and poetic versions of this account reveal the kingship of Yahweh. In chapter 4 Yahweh issues the marching orders to Barak and assures deliverance (4:6–7), and then he goes out before Barak and his army to rout the enemy (4:14–15). In chapter 5 kings and potentates are invoked (5:3; cf. 5:19) to recognize Yahweh's royal victory for his people. Yahweh is also revealed here as the true storm deity (5:4; cf. 5:21a) in place of Baal.[17]

One of the unique contributions of the poem is its revelation of exactly how God's miraculous deliverance was accomplished. The angel of the Lord was present and most likely played a significant role (5:23).[18] God is in sovereign control of cosmic forces like earthquakes, rain storms, celestial omens, and flooding (5:4–5, 20–21a), and these served as his weapons of choice in the battle so that Sisera's chariots were disabled in the muddy plains and his men were forced to flee on foot and face the sword (4:15). Thus, the poem provides an exposition primarily from a divine perspective on the meaning of the verb *hmm* (4:15; best rendered "threw into a panic"; cf. NRSV, NJPS, NLT),[19] which is used only in the prose account. It is noteworthy that this literary pattern of featuring a poetic version after a prosaic account of God's *hmm* warfare is also evident in Exodus (14:24; 15:1–21) and in Joshua (10:10, 12–13).

The second major contribution of the song is the background information it provides about the extent of tribal involvement. While the involvement of Naphtali and Zebulun was already recounted in chapter 4, the poem adds Ephraim, Benjamin, Makir (= Manasseh; cf. Gen. 50:23; Num. 32:39–40; 1 Chron. 7:14–15), and Issachar to the list of participants. But the poem chides four tribes (Reuben, Gilead [= Gad; cf. Josh. 13:24–28], Dan, and Asher) for their failure to participate in God's battle. Thus all ten of the northern tribes are accounted for while the southern tribes (Judah and Simeon) go without mention. The six participating tribes were apparently all from the central highlands (and were probably economically independent agriculturalists), while the four nonparticipating tribes were perhaps "tied down" by economic dependence on outsiders in the eastern pastoral regions (Reuben and Gilead) and in the western coastal regions (Dan and Asher).[20] The omission of Judah (and Simeon) in the song may indicate that they also were delinquent in some way (cf. 1:1–20; 3:9–11; 15:9–13; 20:18); or perhaps it is implied that the foreigner Jael is the only faithful representative of Judah participating in these events (cf. 1:16; 4:11).

The poem also identifies Israel's apostasy as choosing new gods (5:8a), which resulted in a time of foreign oppression when Israel lacked the weapons needed for self-defense (5:8b; cf. 1 Sam. 13:19–22). This likely coincided with restrictions on Israelite travel and trade (5:6). Such difficult circumstances were probably characteristic of Jabin's twenty-year oppression and factored into Israel's cry to the Lord for help (4:3). Only the "righteous acts of the Lord" could turn this tide and make it possible for Israel to "march down to the gates" (5:11b; author's translation).

Teaching the Text

There are two applications that must be emphasized based on the song of Deborah and Barak. The first one concerns commemoration. Imbedded poetry such as this piece serves the function of slowing down the reader so that one can pause to acknowledge and appreciate the significance of what has taken place. In this sense, the song certainly "interrupts" the flow of the narrative. It is an occasion for meditation, for praise, for worship, even for introspection. This song may certainly be used to serve such liturgical functions in the church today. But it also serves as a reminder that any miraculous work of God that is experienced in life should be formally commemorated (e.g., see Josh. 4; 1 Sam. 7:10–12; 2 Sam. 22; Ps. 18). We celebrate personal accomplishments like promotions and educational milestones. We celebrate births, marriages, and building projects. Should we not also celebrate God's life-changing victories in our own lives and in the lives of others? We should be constantly looking for evidence of God's miraculous works in our lives. When they are identified, those special events should be marked as occasions for corporate praise and worship in the community of believers.[21]

The second application concerns participation. While the southern tribes receive no comment, four northern tribes are confronted (though notably not cursed) for standing on the sidelines while their brothers went out to fight God's war (see 5:15b–17). Evidently, these four tribes were too invested or distracted with other relationships and commitments. What a shame that in the moment of truth they took the path of comfort and ease at the expense of their covenant community. While Barak was reluctant in responding to the martial summons (see 4:6–9), these four tribes failed to show up altogether. There was also the city of Meroz, whose people probably defaulted on a treaty obligation to assist Israel and thus placed themselves under a curse (5:23). The main point here is that the collective community of God's people (the people of Yahweh [5:11, 13]; those who love him [5:31a]) is meant to function as a family unit. Thus, "if one part suffers, every part suffers with it; if one part is honored, every part rejoices with it" (1 Cor. 12:26; cf. Rom. 12:15).[22] Christians are not called to stay on the sidelines while their brothers and sisters face spiritual battles or experience God's victories. Rather, all God's people are called to be willing participants in God's program (Judg. 5:2, 9; cf. Ps. 110:3).

Illustrating the Text

God is able to arrange natural circumstances for the benefit of his people.

Parenting: Talk about the way parents often augment their children's early experiences in sport or adventure. Moms and dads run behind bicycles, boost kids to the first branch, catch to buffer big leaps, and let children ride on their backs in the water. Even in board games, parents suspend overcomplicated rules or partner up with younger players to make the odds more even. Invite your listeners to consider that, in the same way, our Father in heaven is actively beside us in our walk of faith, supporting us, boosting our efforts, pulling us back from temptation, catching our fall after extreme risks and mistakes, and partnering with us to level the playing field. Sometimes he even suspends the rules he made for nature, space, and time in order to facilitate our success when we obey. Just like an earthly parent, he does this to see us grow under an umbrella of protection as we engage ever-increasing challenges and trials. It is a natural thing for him to bend the rules and arrange natural circumstances for the benefit of his people.

God wants us to stop and celebrate his blessings as they unfold.

Human Experience: Ask your listeners to think about local monuments with which they are familiar. Your locality may have special parks, statuary, attractions, or points of interest that are part of the psychological landscape for your listeners. (Consider sharing images of these landmarks to enhance your listeners' experience of the illustration.) Ask them to consider what or whom each one commemorates. Explain that stopping to commemorate (literally "remember together") important events is a part of the human experience. Invite them to think about the fact that they even do this at home by planting trees, making height marks on the wall to remember children's growth patterns, and so on. In the same way, we ought to "remember together" the way God has worked in the past and revealed his faithfulness.

Applying the Text: Invite your listeners to create a "God Sightings" scrapbook or journal in their home. Any time God does something amazing, answers prayers, heals, sets free, or otherwise delivers someone in your home, they should record the event and keep it in the family journal. Suggest that they take it out once a year, perhaps at Thanksgiving or on New Year's Day, to recount God's mighty works for them over the course of the year. Perhaps your congregation could have an annual service of commemoration at which attenders are allowed to share God sightings the congregation has experienced throughout the year. This could also be done electronically via a blog, social media page, or other means of group communication. The regular rituals of baptism and communion are also perfect opportunities to corporately commemorate God's works.

Those who bond together and participate in the battle gain a stake in the spoils.

Sports: Talk about a sports competition in which the players all share a trophy after winning. A great example is the Stanley Cup, the annually awarded prize for the National Hockey League's Championship series. The giant silver cup is engraved with the names of every player on the winning team, and each player gets a chance to keep the cup at his home for a time during the following year. The "player's day with the cup" is overseen by a member of the Hockey Hall of Fame. The tradition became the subject of an ESPN marketing campaign that showed players using the cup: one player (Ken Daneyko) is depicted eating cereal out of it, another (Derian Hatcher) used it as a cooler, and another (Brett Hull) locked himself out of his car with the cup inside. Players have been shown using the cup to baptize their children, feed their dogs (Clark Gillies), and serve their kids chocolate milk (Dustin Brown). The point is that all members of the team play a part in winning the cup, and all share a stake in the fun and spoils.

Women in the Book of Judges

Women are featured more prominently in Judges than in any other book of the Bible.[1] Women tend to play more positive roles toward the beginning of the book and increasingly negative roles toward the end. With the exception of Delilah, the women in the latter half of the book remain nameless. Their roles can be summarized under the headings of wives, leaders, mothers, and victims.

First, the prologue opens with the one and only positive picture of matrimony: Aksah is the wife of the ideal deliverer Othniel (1:11–15). The prologue closes by describing spiritual apostasy in terms of Israelites marrying non-Israelite "daughters" (3:6). This theme of marriage with outsiders appears to be illustrated in the body of Judges by the references to Gideon's concubine (8:31), Gilead's prostitute (11:1), and Ibzan's arrangements for his children (12:9). The theme is then overtly illustrated in Samson's illicit relationships with women: a wife, a prostitute, and Delilah (chaps. 14–16). The epilogue features a thematic reversal of the positive prologue (esp. 1:11–15) with its depressing stories about the estranged concubine (19:1–2), vows against marrying Benjamites (21:1, 7, 18), and the forcing of many women to marry Benjamites (21:12–14, 20–23).

Second, a few women in Judges are heroically depicted in leadership roles. Deborah uniquely leads Israel in her "judicial" function as a prophetess (4:4–5; 5:7). Jael and a "certain woman" (9:53 ESV) each singlehandedly slay ruthless villains (4:17–22; 5:24–27; 9:53).

Third, the biological mothers in the book are mostly portrayed negatively. Sisera's mother expresses a depraved fixation on plunder (5:30). Abimelek's mother is Gideon's Canaanite concubine (8:31). Jephthah's mother is a prostitute (11:1). While Samson's nameless mother is honored by the messenger of the Lord (13:2–23), she appears to be apathetic to God's instructions (13:4, 7, 14, 24), and her progeny brings her only dishonor (e.g., 14:2–3). Micah's mother invests her money in idolatry (17:3–4).

Finally, the most dark and disturbing depictions of women in Judges concern victimization. The first reference is to the Canaanite pillaging of conquered women through rape (5:30). The second instance is the sacrifice of Jephthah's only daughter (11:30–40). Next is the Philistine burning of Samson's wife (15:6). Then the epilogue features a cluster of horrific accounts, including the rape and dismemberment of the Levite's concubine (19:16–30), the slaughter of Benjamite women (implied in 20:48), the slaughter of married women from Jabesh Gilead (21:10–11), and the seizure of virgins from both Jabesh Gilead and Shiloh (21:12–23). Such stories are concentrated in the epilogue of Judges and are especially symptomatic of Israel's Canaanization and rejection of God.

Gideon's Rise

Big Idea

God's presence is a resource for his people, and God deserves exclusive worship.

Key Themes

- God indicts Israel for polytheistic practices.
- God sends his messenger to commission Gideon.
- God affirms his presence with Gideon.
- God commands Gideon to challenge Baal and to assert the exclusive worship of Yahweh.
- Baal is impotent.

Understanding the Text

The Text in Context

The Gideon cycle (chaps. 6–8) is the fourth story in the sequence of seven stories that compose the body of Judges. But the story is set apart from the other six because it is positioned alone in the center and serves as a pivot for the entire book. As is characteristic of ring compositions, the middle section echoes the themes and rhetoric of both the prologue and epilogue (see "Literary Structure" in the introduction to Judges and table 1 there).

The Gideon story may also be divided into four units (6:1–32; 6:33–7:25; 8:1–21; 8:22–32): the themes of the first and second units are revisited in reverse/chiastic order in the third and fourth units. Furthermore, the first and second units complement the two-part prologue of Judges, while the third and fourth units complement the two-part epilogue of Judges, also in reverse/chiastic order.

The battles and idolatry that are recounted in the prologue and in the first half (i.e., the first and second units) of the Gideon story are portrayed as external/foreign problems, whereas the idolatry and battles in the second half of the Gideon story and in the epilogue are portrayed as internal/domestic problems. This shift reflects the downward spiritual spiral that was previously described as Israel's Canaanization.

The present pericope, recounting Gideon's rise, is the first unit of the Gideon narrative. Some rhetorical connections with the prologue (primarily chap. 2) may be noted as follows: (1) a review of the exodus traditions (2:1, 12; 6:8–9, 13); (2) the indictment that Israel has disobeyed God's voice (2:2; 6:10); (3) the problem of idolatry—especially Baal worship (2:3, 11–13, 17, 19; 3:6; 6:10, 25–32); (4) the appearance of the angel of the Lord (2:1–4; 6:11–22); (5) emphasis on God's presence (2:18; 6:12, 16); (6) recollection of God's works on Israel's behalf (2:7, 10; 6:13); (7) the tearing down of altars (2:2; 6:28–32); and (8) the people's rejection of God's leader (2:17; 6:29–30).

Historical and Cultural Background

The Baal altar and the Asherah described in 6:25–26 exemplify the persistence of polytheism in ancient Israel. Although this high place belongs to Joash, it apparently serves the whole community of Ophrah (cf. 6:27–32). Similar open-air cult sites from Iron Age I are identified in the territory of Manasseh—namely, the altar on Mount Ebal and the "Bull site" (featuring a bronze bull figurine and a possible standing stone or altar) located east of Dothan.[1] Closely associated with the altar of Baal in this passage was "the Asherah." This was a wooden cult object (see 6:25–26), perhaps in the form of a pole or tree, which probably symbolized the fertility of the goddess. Charred remains of a possible Asherah pole have been identified beside a standing stone in a later (tenth century BC) context at Israelite Lachish.[2]

Interpretive Insights

6:1 *Midianites.* The history of Midian in the biblical text extends from the friendly descendants of Abraham (Gen. 25:2, 4) with whom Moses dwelled (Exod. 2:15–16) to enemies who opposed Israel in the Balaam incidents (Num. 22; 25; 31) and oppressed Israel in the time of Gideon (Judg. 6–8).

6:7–10 Verses 7–10 of the Masoretic text (and the ancient versions) are absent from one of the fragmentary scrolls of Judges that were recovered from the Dead Sea / Qumran.[3] However, these verses are marked as a self-contained paragraph in the Masoretic text and may have been inadvertently omitted or even intentionally moved or skipped for various reasons by a scribe at Qumran.[4]

6:8 *prophet.* Like the introduction of Deborah in 4:4, this prophet enters the narrative immediately following the Israelites' cry to the Lord for help (6:7; cf. 4:3). But in contrast to Deborah, who is presented as a de facto leader, this prophet is clearly sent by the Lord. Furthermore, the narrator employs a similar redundant phrase to highlight the individual's gender: "prophet-man" (contrast with "prophetess-woman" in 4:4).

6:11 *angel of the* LORD. For the identity of the angel of the Lord, see the "Additional Insights" following the unit on Judges 8:1–32 and the comments on Judges 13:2–3. In the present context, the title "angel/messenger of the LORD" is synonymous with the title "angel/messenger of God" (6:20; cf. 13:6, 9). Furthermore, a number of factors indicate that the angel of the Lord may be equated with the prophet-man of 6:8–10. First, a prophet can also be called a messenger of the Lord (see Hag. 1:13). Second, the prophet-man of 6:8–10 reinforces the same basic message as that of the first angel of the Lord in 2:1–3. Third, the fact that the prophet-man has been "sent" by the Lord while the angel merely "came" (without any introductory formula) implies that the prophet is the same as the angel.

Ophrah. This place name apparently denotes "dusty place," and in the present literary context it may connote economic or spiritual desolation.[5] It was located in the territory of Manasseh, possibly at Khirbet 'Awfar, just southwest of Shechem.[6]

Gideon. For the meaning of this name, see the comments on 6:32, below.

6:15 *weakest . . . least.* Gideon's response does not indicate that he has a low economic status in society (he actually commands a large number of servants; cf. 6:27). Rather, he is most likely referring to his limited authority (perhaps in contrast to that of his older brothers) to summon his family and tribe to battle. This is why the Lord responds with the promise that Gideon will in fact defeat Midian as "one man" (6:16 NASB, ESV, NKJV)—that is, "despite Gideon's lack of official authority the Israelites would fight in concert, unified behind his leadership."[7] This nuance is lost in a number of English translations that apply the phrase "one man" to the Midianites (e.g., NIV, NLT, NRSV, NJPS, HCSB).

One Bull or Two?

In 6:25–26 the Lord instructs Gideon (probably through a dream) to offer a specific bull as a burnt offering on the new altar that is to be built according to proper procedure (i.e., according to God's specifications in Exod. 20:24–26). While some scholars take 6:25 as referring to two distinct bulls (cf. ESV, NASB, NJPS, HCSB), the following verse (which instructs Gideon to offer a single bull and lacks any further mention of another bull) strongly indicates that there was only one bull to begin with (cf. NIV, NRSV, NLT, NKJV). Thus the bull belonging to Gideon's father is further identified (through parallelism and explicative conjunction) as "the *sheni* bull seven years old." The meaning of the term *sheni* is still, however, a matter of debate. The term could mean "second(ary)" (i.e., distinguished from the firstborn) or, by modifying the first vowel (thus *shani*), it could mean "aged," "full grown," "shining," or "red."[a]

[a] For helpful discussion, see Bluedorn, *Yahweh versus Baalism*, 90–97.

6:24 *Gideon built an altar to the Lord there.* While some scholars suggest that there are two altars to Yahweh mentioned in this passage,[8] it is preferable to take this verse as a summary statement about the one altar to Yahweh built by Gideon in Ophrah after the angel has appeared to him. That is, the story about the supplanting of Baal's altar in verses 25–32 is a detailed elaboration on the origins of the altar, which is here named "The Lord Is Peace" and which still stands in Ophrah at the time of this story's composition. The practice of naming altars is also attested for Abraham (Gen. 22:14) and Moses (Exod. 17:15).

6:32 *Jerub-Baal.* This name, which ambiguously means "Let Baal Contend" or "Baal Will Contend," is employed by the narrator to characterize Gideon both positively (as one who challenges Baal) and negatively (as one associated with apostasy). It is possible that Jerub-Baal is his original birth name (given by his Baal-worshiping father) and that it takes on additional significance when he contends with Baal. Likewise it is possible that "Gideon" is an official (throne?) name taken as a result of the events in chapters 6–7 (see esp. 7:1; 8:35). The name Gideon probably denotes "hacker/cutter" (from *gd'*), and appropriately in this story Gideon lives up to his name by cutting down his father's altar and Asherah (Deut. 7:5; 12:3; cf. Judg. 6:25, 28).[9]

Theological Insights

Two attributes of God are especially revealed in this passage: God's presence and God's exclusivity. The very first statement of the messenger to Gideon is that "the Lord is with you" (6:12). Gideon immediately retorts—in words anticipated by the Lord in Deuteronomy 31:17—that God's *absence* is indicated by the current political crisis (Judg. 6:13). Then, in order to make God's presence known through the messenger, the narrator relates that the Lord himself turns (*pnh*) to Gideon and commissions him to deliver Israel (6:14). Gideon therefore shifts his form of address from "sir" to "Lord" (6:13, 15 ESV) and humbly responds in the manner of Moses (cf. Exod. 3:11). Then, in the language of both Moses's and Joshua's commissioning (cf. Exod. 3:12; Deut. 31:23; Josh. 1:5; 3:7), the Lord promises, "I will be with you," or better, "*'Ehyeh* is with you" (Judg. 6:16). God's very presence is the basis on which Gideon will defeat Midian (cf. 2:18). Finally, in order to reinforce God's presence with Gideon, the narrator documents that God continues speaking to Gideon (6:23, 25; see also 7:2–11) even *after* the messenger has "disappeared" (6:21).

Now that God's presence is assured for Gideon, the Lord reveals Gideon's first task. He is to tear down his father's Baal altar, cut up the Asherah that is beside it, construct an altar to the Lord, and sacrifice his father's bull on the new altar (6:25–26). The existence of this idolatrous high place in an Israelite town and the furious reaction of the "people of the town" (6:28–30) concretely illustrate the type of apostasy described by the prophet in 6:10 (fearing "the gods of the Amorites"). Gideon's bold actions enforce not only God's instructions concerning Canaanite cult paraphernalia (Exod. 34:13; Deut. 7:5; 12:2–3; 16:21) but also the first commandment, requiring the exclusive worship of Yahweh (Exod. 20:3; Deut. 5:7). Under Deuteronomic law the men of the city are actually guilty of a capital crime (see Deut. 13), but they ignorantly view the situation in reverse. While the men of the city want to avenge Baal's case themselves (Judg. 6:30), the patriarch Joash places the burden of vengeance directly on Baal since he is the putative deity (6:31). The fact that Baal never comes to his own defense during Gideon's life suggests that he is no god at all (or that he is a weak god and therefore unworthy of worship).[10] In contrast to Baal, the Lord is known to frequently defend himself when a desecration occurs.[11]

Teaching the Text

This passage certainly introduces Gideon as God's designated deliverer, but it does not put Gideon on a pedestal as a role model to follow. While Gideon is hiding from the Midianites (6:11), the messenger appears and ironically dubs him a "warrior of means" (6:12; author's translation). But the passage makes it clear that his future accomplishments will be achieved not by his own strength but rather because God is "with" him (6:12, 16; cf. 2:18). Additionally, he expresses a skewed understanding of history and theology (6:13; cf. Deut. 31:17). His request for a sign (6:17; cf. Exod. 3:12) foreshadows his lack of trust and need for assurances, which will be addressed in the next pericope (see 6:36–40; 7:9–11). And his speedy obedience is actually motivated by his fear of people (6:27).[12] Once again, instead of analyzing Gideon's character qualities in this account, it is prudent to focus on the revelation of God.

Any lesson or sermon on this passage would do well to emphasize the presence and exclusivity of God. As for presence, it is important to understand that God gives Gideon the necessary spiritual resources to fulfill his calling (cf. 6:12, 16). The task of delivering Israel from oppression is an impossible task for Gideon unless God himself accompanies him. But God's presence with Gideon was also something special for that time and place; so it does not necessarily follow that Christians today should expect to have Gideon's exact experience. Under the new covenant, God actually has made his presence more accessible to all of his people because they function as his temple and are indwelled by the Holy Spirit (see Eph. 2:22).[13] Believers today are therefore fully equipped to do whatever God commissions them to do (cf. 2 Pet. 1:3).

Second, God demands exclusive worship. The replacement of the Baal altar and the Asherah with an altar to Yahweh (6:25–26) shows that the Lord works alone and that there are no other gods in his presence (Exod. 20:3; Deut. 5:7).[14] Furthermore, Baal's failure to defend himself (cf. Judg. 6:31–32) reveals either that he is not a god to begin with or that he cannot compete with the Lord (or the person empowered by the Lord). All of this is a lesson to both Gideon and Israel that Yahweh (and not Baal!) is worthy of worship and that proper worship is exclusive in nature. God does not distribute his power or share his authority with anyone else. In the same way Jesus Christ, who is of one substance with the Father, has authority over all things "in heaven and on earth and under the earth" (Phil. 2:10; cf. Col. 1:16–17, 20), and he therefore has supremacy in everything (Col. 1:18).

Illustrating the Text

Power flows from presence; God's nearness is the underwriting behind deliverance.

Object Lesson: Find a powerful magnet (usually a neodymium or "rare earth" magnet is the most powerful) and some objects that are big enough to be seen and to respond to magnetism (e.g., steel washers or nails). Show your listeners how the objects react to the magnet based on proximity. The closer the magnet gets to the objects, the more they will react by shifting their orientation to the magnet's poles and eventually sticking to it. Show them also how once an object adheres to the magnet, it also becomes magnetic and can pass on the power to another object. Just like the magnet affects the objects, so God affects us. As he draws near to us, his power and influence begin to call our hearts into alignment with his Spirit. Once we are adhering to him, he often uses us to draw others to himself.

Human Experience: Ask your listeners to consider the various ways we address problems. Point out that there are some situations we can address remotely (via virtual technology, letter writing, voice calls, persons sent as our proxy, etc.), while others must be addressed in person. The situations we address remotely tend to be matters of material concern that do not require our personal presence. The ones we show up for in person tend to be matters of the heart that deserve our full focus, authority, and physicality to be properly solved. In the same way, God comes in power for his children. When we are in distress, we get him—he brings power with him, but his presence is also a solution in and of itself.

Proper worship is always exclusive; God demands to be the sole focus of our attention.

Object Lesson: Bring a variety of everyday objects to display. Ask your listeners to vote by cheering or raising hands about which are appropriate to share and which are not. You should have some that are appropriate to lend, like a golf club, hedge trimmers, DVD, good book, and so on. Other objects should be more ambiguous, like the keys to your car, a favorite sweater, or a hot water bottle—these should produce a mixed response. Then, bring out a series of objects that are entirely inappropriate to share: for example, a toothbrush, an irreplaceable family heirloom, or contact lenses. Finally, bring out a final item: an envelope that appears to have a letter in it. Tell your listeners that it contains an extremely private love letter between a husband and wife, in which the deepest secrets and dreams of one's soul are poured out to the other; ask if it would be appropriate to share it out loud from the pulpit. The last series of items ought to clearly elicit a "not for sharing" response. Explain that this is OK—some things just are not for sharing. Assert that the exclusivity and privacy we naturally sense when thinking of these objects is the way God feels about our love and worship of him. These attentions are precious and intimate; he is unwilling to share them with idols of any kind.

Human Experience: Some types of attention are meant to be exclusive. Consider what behaviors or actions are only suitable between spouses and should not be shared with others. (E.g., what kind of attention is appropriate for a husband to give another woman—a compliment, flirtation, a personal gift, a kiss?)

Gideon's Battle

Big Idea

God's glory and kingship must trump our doubts, fears, and desires to control or take credit.

Key Themes

- The Spirit of the Lord empowers Gideon.
- Gideon is fearful and needs assurances from God.
- Gideon attempts to control his situation by manipulating God.
- The Lord patiently and graciously accommodates Gideon's faults in order to encourage him.
- The Lord wants the glory for delivering Israel.
- Gideon wants some glory for himself.
- The Lord miraculously defeats the Midianites.

Understanding the Text

The Text in Context

This pericope is the second unit of the centrally positioned Gideon story, and it has thematic connections with the first part of the prologue. That is, (1) both 1:1–2:5 and 6:33–7:25 recount Israel's confrontation with external military threats; (2) both emphasize that victory comes from the Lord (1:2, 4, 7, 19, 22; 6:36–37; 7:2, 7, 9, 14–15, 22; cf. 6:16); and (3) both feature the employment of war oracles (1:1–2; 6:36–7:15; see also the epilogue [20:18, 23, 27–28]).[1] This unit is also juxtaposed to 8:1–21, which continues the military focus of chapter 7 but shifts to an internal orientation. Thus, in the ring structure of the book of Judges, this pericope serves as the final account for the first half of the book.

Historical and Cultural Background

The declaration "For the Lord and for Gideon" in 7:18 is strikingly similar to a number of dedicatory inscriptions that feature a divine name followed by a royal name: (1) "For Baal and for Padi," on a Philistine store jar from Tel Miqne-Ekron (604 BC); (2) "For Astarte, for Pygmalion," on a Phoenician gold medallion from Carthage (ca. 800 BC); and (3) "to revere god and king" in Neo-Assyrian inscriptions from the eighth century BC (cf. Exod. 22:28; 2 Sam. 15:21; 1 Kings 21:13; Prov. 24:21).[2]

Interpretive Insights

6:34 *the Spirit of the* LORD *came on Gideon.* The verb here (*lbsh* in Qal) probably means not "to clothe" but "to put on" or "to possess."[3] Thus the Spirit of Yahweh is not enveloping Gideon but is rather wearing or donning Gideon.[4] The rallying of the tribes (6:35) is thus made possible by the initiative of the Spirit, perhaps because Gideon is incapable of doing so by himself (see the sidebar "Spirit of the Lord" in the unit on Judg. 3:7–11). The Spirit's action here appears to be in fulfillment of God's promise to provide his presence for Gideon (cf. 6:16).

6:37 *I will place a wool fleece.* Provoked oracles by means of a fleece are unattested outside of this passage. Since Gideon apparently does not have access to the regular divinatory devices (such as lots, Urim and Thummim, ephod, or teraphim), he here improvises by employing a common item as an ad hoc medium for binary manipulation.[5] Later on, Gideon will construct and install an ephod as a more permanent device to accomplish similar functions (8:27; see the sidebar "Ephod" in the unit on Judg. 8:1–32). The verb translated here as "placing" (*ytsg* in Hiphil) seems to have a technical cultic use as it is also applied in this story to the lappers (7:5) and the ephod (8:27), and it is applied elsewhere to Jacob's rods (Gen. 30:38) and the ark of the covenant (1 Sam. 5:2; 2 Sam. 6:17 // 1 Chron. 16:1).

dew. Yahweh's control of the dew may be significant following the desecration of Baal's altar in 6:25–32. Rain and dew were thought to be the domain of the storm deity Baal, and Yahweh here demonstrates his sovereignty over these phenomena.[6]

6:39 *test.* Gideon's first procedure (6:37) is based on the usual patterns of nature, while his second (primary) procedure is based on unusual patterns.[7] Gideon describes his inquiry as a test (*nsh* in Piel), which must be understood in the context of Old Testament theology.[8] God is the one who tests his people in order to improve them,[9] and this is especially true in the period of the judges (2:22; 3:1, 4). Israel is not to test God, and doing so may incur severe judgment.[10] That God indulges Gideon's presumptuous tests of validation is a striking display of his grace. While repeated forms of confirmation are typically posed by ancient Near Eastern diviners,[11] Gideon should not assume that Yahweh operates by the same protocol.

7:2 *too many.* After Gideon's double testing of God, God initiates a two-part process of sifting the people. Just as Gideon has presented God with the terms and means of his test, so also God now presents Gideon with the

The Jezreel Valley

The geographical setting of Gideon's surprise attack is the Jezreel Valley (6:33; 7:1). Jezreel is a town located on the eastern end of the valley. This fertile region extends from the Jordan Valley (near Beth Shan) to the Akko plain (on the Mediterranean), passing northwest between Mount Gilboa and Moreh Hill and between the Carmel Range and the lower Galilee (see the map in the unit on Judg. 4:1–24). The strategic location and topographical features of the Jezreel Valley have made it a common battle site throughout history (e.g., Judg. 4–5). Gideon's army is located at the spring of Harod ("trembling"), which is at the northern base of Mount Gilboa (traditionally identified with 'Ain Jalud; cf. 1 Sam. 29:1), and the Midianite camp is located to the north at the Hill of Moreh ("teacher")—probably at Endor, which is at the northeastern base of Moreh (see Ps. 83:10).[a]

[a] Rainey and Notley, *Sacred Bridge*, 139.

terms and means of his own refinement process (*tsrp*; 7:4; NIV: "thin out"), apparently through direct speech. The first step is to remove the fearful (7:3), and the second is to remove the kneelers (7:4–8). Yahweh does this in order to make the source of the victory unmistakable for Gideon and Israel (7:2, 7, 9, 22; cf. Deut. 8:17–18).

7:3 *Anyone who trembles with fear.* The act of sending home the fearful (*yare'*) is in keeping with the battle instructions given in Deuteronomy 20:8. This event, or possibly a recurring tradition at this location, probably accounts for the name of the spring (Harod, "trembling"; 7:1).

7:15 *the dream and its interpretation.* After God reaffirms his promise to bring deliverance (7:7, 9), Gideon is still afraid (7:10; cf. 6:27). So God sends him to eavesdrop in the enemy camp to hear yet another confirmation through a foreign dream omen (7:10–14). The symbolic dream, which applies negatively to the Midianites and positively to the Israelites, is surprisingly more convincing to Gideon (7:15) than the direct statements of Yahweh in 6:16; 7:2, 7, 9. The word for "interpretation" (*sheber*) in this context is from a root meaning "to break" and is comparable to modern English idioms such as "breaking news" or "cracking codes."

7:18 *For the LORD and for Gideon.* For the striking similarity of this declaration to a number of dedicatory inscriptions from the ancient Near East, see "Historical and Cultural Background" above. That Gideon himself would demand use of this formula indicates at least his desire to take some credit for the victory and at most indicates his royal aspirations. A comparison of Gideon's statement with that made by David when he faces Goliath (1 Sam. 17:47; cf. 2 Chron. 20:15) may indicate that Gideon has a skewed view of theocracy.[12]

Judges 6:33–7:25

Theological Insights

God is revealed in this passage as the victorious commander of the armies of Israel. God's promise of his presence with Gideon (6:16) is fulfilled as his Spirit has "donned" Gideon (6:34–35), making it possible for him to summon the northern tribes (minus Issachar, as in chap. 1). God also makes it very clear to Gideon and to Israel that God must receive all the glory for this deliverance (7:2; contrast with 8:22). So he drastically reduces the size of Gideon's army by purging the fearful and the kneelers and leaving only three hundred warriors (7:3–8). Then God employs a negative dream omen to create panic in the camp of Midian (7:13–14). Finally, as Gideon's army surrounds the Midianite camp wielding only their torch-jars and trumpets, "the LORD set every man's sword against his comrade and against all the camp" (7:22; author's translation). This victory is an unmistakable, solo act of God, not unlike the miraculous defeat of Sisera's army.[13]

Although he is God's choice, Gideon is here portrayed as a "mixed bag" in his relationship to God. Like Barak in Judges 4, Gideon is also reluctant to obey God, and he requires some assurance. But Gideon's need for assurance exceeds Barak's in both number and intensity, and Gideon is further characterized by fear and a selfish desire for glory.[14] God's promises to Gideon that he will deliver Israel (6:14, 16, 36) are apparently insufficient. So Gideon demands that God confirm his intentions through a series of oracular experiments or "tests" (6:36–40), so that he can "know" that God will bring deliverance (6:37). Then God indulges him, notwithstanding his command to "not put the LORD your God to the test" (Deut. 6:16; cf. 1 Cor. 10:9). But Gideon apparently does not uphold his end of the bargain since, after this, it is noted that fear—which is also rampant in the ranks of Israel (Judg. 7:3)—continues to persist with Gideon (7:10; cf. 6:11, 27). So God instructs him to go down into the camp of Midian with his squire in order to hear a dream account and its interpretation, which again confirms victory for Gideon (7:9–14). Encouraged by this additional revelation, Gideon is finally able to rally his army (7:15) and propose the nighttime strategy (7:16–18). But in the excitement of the moment, Gideon gets overly zealous for glory and commands the troops to shout, "For the LORD and for Gideon" (7:18, 20), which smacks of royal prerogatives.

What is most surprising in this account is not Gideon's feeble faith (which one grows accustomed to seeing in the book of Judges) but God's patience with Gideon and his inclination to meet Gideon in his place of weakness. God does not need to cooperate with Gideon's manipulative schemes, yet he does so repeatedly, and he unexpectedly gives Gideon an additional confirmation through the dream omen. God's actions toward Gideon in this story are totally unnecessary, and they poignantly illustrate his grace in action.

Teaching the Text

This passage neither condones nor instructs anyone to "lay out a fleece" for spiritual guidance. Just because God answers Gideon (i.e., indulges his weaknesses) through this means does not indicate that God will do so again or that God is pleased by such methods.[15] Sadly, such approaches to decision making have become far too common in popular Christian practice today. Gideon audaciously acknowledges that he is questioning God's intentions and spoken word (6:36–37), and he even describes his actions as a "test" (6:39), which is self-incriminating according to the teachings of the torah (see Deut. 6:16).[16] Gideon's method is motivated by doubt, and after he receives no fewer than three confirmations from God (Judg. 6:17–21, 36–40), it is evident that he still needs additional corroboration (7:10–14; cf. Luke 16:31). Gideon is clearly *not an example* of faithfulness (even though he has some faith); and even if he did demonstrate strong faith, he should still not be employed as a role model for modern believers (on Hebrews 11 and hermeneutics, see the "Additional Insights" following the unit on Judg. 8:1–32).

The purpose of this story (and all biblical stories) is to reveal God's attributes in action.[17] Here, God's kingship is revealed as he receives all the glory for defeating the enemy without much assistance from Gideon or Israel. It is important when teaching this story to focus on the miraculous elements rather than on the military tactics or strategies of Gideon and his three hundred men.[18] God loves to do big things for the benefit of his people—especially things that they are incapable of doing themselves. The proper role of God's people is to let God be King and to give him the glory due to him. We fail to give him glory if we test him by ignoring his spoken word or questioning his intentions (cf. 6:36–37, 39). We fail to give him glory when we boast about our own abilities and powers (cf. 7:2, 18; 8:22; Deut. 8:17–18; Zech. 4:6; 2 Cor. 12:9–10). We fail to give him glory when we back God into a corner with a manipulative "fleece" that forces God to respond to our own terms in our own time (cf. Judg. 6:36–40).[19]

This passage also powerfully reveals that God is patient, long-suffering, and gracious toward Israel and especially toward Gideon. As Gideon's flaws become more apparent in this story, God's patience and grace come into sharper relief (cf. Rom. 5:20–21). But instead of acknowledging God's grace and changing his actions, Gideon appears to take advantage of God through manipulative methods and selfish aspirations. This is a most dangerous way to relate to the divine King! God's gracious indulgence of Gideon's bad methods does not justify Gideon's approach. The apostle Paul makes a similar point about responding to God's grace: "What shall we say, then? Shall we go on sinning so that grace may increase? By no means! We are those who have died to sin; how can we live in it any longer?" (Rom. 6:1–2).

Finally, something can also be learned about decision making from this passage. Gideon seeks God's confirmation about something God has already clearly revealed to him (6:36–37). This is an example of testing God, because it supplants his authority with one's own. A modern example of this is seeking God's will about dating or marrying an unbeliever: God has revealed clear instructions (see 1 Cor. 7:39; 2 Cor. 6:14–18), yet many people are tempted to rebel by rationalization and following their own desires. Making life decisions can certainly be difficult, but ignoring or disregarding God's Word in the process only makes it more so. The most important resource at our disposal *after* consulting God's revelation in Scripture is the guidance of the Holy Spirit through prayer and Christian counsel.[20]

Illustrating the Text

While God may make concessions to help us through doubts, it is better to trust and obey the first time.

Hymn: "Trust and Obey," by John Sammis. Singing or discussing this classic hymn is a great way to evoke the heart of this premise.

Quote: *Experiencing God*, by Henry Blackaby. Blackaby writes, "God's commands are designed to guide you to life's very best. You will not obey Him if you do not believe Him and trust Him. You cannot believe Him if you do not love Him. You cannot love Him unless you know Him." [21] Invite your listeners to think about times when they may have missed out on life's very best because they were unwilling to trust and obey or because they did not yet deeply love or know God.

God specializes in backing underdogs—they accentuate his role and give him glory.

Film: Showing a clip or describing a scene from a sports-themed underdog movie would help evoke this truth in your listeners. Consider movies like *The Bad News Bears, Hoosiers, Rudy, Seabiscuit,* or *Remember the Titans.* Or use this classic line from *Rocky,* the movie about a prizefighter whose whole life was a million-to-one shot:

> I was nobody. But that don't matter either, you know? 'Cause I was thinkin', it really don't matter if I lose this fight. It really don't matter if this guy opens my head, either. 'Cause all I wanna do is go the distance. Nobody's ever gone the distance with Creed, and if I can go that distance, you see, and that bell rings and I'm still standin', I'm gonna know for the first time in my life, see, that I weren't just another bum from the neighborhood.[22]

Sometimes just committing to go the distance by relying on God's power is all it takes to see God's glorious deliverance.

Do not seek new answers to issues God has definitively addressed in his Word.

Humor: There is an old joke about a man who had fallen off of a cliff and was dangling by a cluster of roots. He cried out, "God, if you're really up there, save me!" God replied audibly, "I will save you if you have faith—let go of the branch and fall the rest of the way. It will all be OK." The man thought for a moment and replied, "Is there anybody *else* up there I can talk to?" The reality is that God has given us a path of salvation and insights that are reliable in his Word. Sometimes when we cry out for help, we do not like his answers, and we say something very similar in our hearts. We consult all sorts of other sources, or even look for false teachers to twist what the Bible clearly teaches into something we find more palatable. In the end, this is all self-deception. If God has already spoken, we do best to put our energy into implementation, not negotiation.

Gideon's Demise

Big Idea
God's kingship must be acknowledged in actions as well as words.

Key Themes
- Gideon is unnecessarily vengeful and acts like a ruthless tyrant.
- Gideon's military and economic authority is acknowledged by Israel.
- Gideon's actions do not match his pious words.
- Gideon assumes dynastic and priestly control of Israel from Ophrah.
- Gideon leads the Israelites into religious apostasy.

Understanding the Text

The Text in Context

Chapter 8 contains the third and fourth units (that is, the second half) of the Gideon story. While the first half of the Gideon story (as well as the first half of the book, chaps. 1–7) emphasizes God's power and presence, God's absence is the predominant theme of the second half of the Gideon story (and of the second half of the book, chaps. 8–21).[1] The second half of the book also has an internal/domestic orientation, whereas the first half of the book has an external/foreign orientation.[2] While Gideon is portrayed as extremely fearful and reluctant in chapters 6–7, he is extremely confident and ruthless in chapter 8.

There are also some internal parallels within the chiastic structure of the Gideon story. The first and fourth units focus on religious matters in Gideon's hometown of Ophrah (the place name is mentioned in the Gideon story only at 6:11, 24; 8:27, 32). The second and third units focus on the battle with the Midianites: note how the Midianites are described as "fallen" (*noplim*; 7:12 [NIV: "had settled"]; 8:10; cf. 20:46) and the stories each conclude with the dispatch of a pair of leaders (Oreb and Zeeb; Zebah and Zalmunna).[3]

Since the Gideon story is the core of the ring structure for the book, its units also echo the themes and rhetoric of the prologue and epilogue (see "Literary Structure" in the introduction to Judges and table 1 there). The third unit of the Gideon story (8:1–21) anticipates the themes of the second part of the epilogue (chaps. 19–21) by recounting stories of vengeful retribution and the slaughter of Israelites.[4] The fourth and final unit of the Gideon story (8:22–32) anticipates the first part of the epilogue (chaps. 17–18) by its focus on aberrant religious practices and the construction of an ephod (the ephod is only mentioned in the book of Judges at 8:27; 17:5; 18:14–20).

Historical and Cultural Background

The Transjordanian locations mentioned in 8:4–17 may be identified as follows (from northwest to southeast): Sukkoth is at Tell Deir 'Alla; Penuel (= Peniel) is at Tell edh-Dhahab esh-Sharqi; "the route of the nomads" (8:11) apparently refers to the caravan route leading to the site of Karkor, which is probably located in the Wadi Sirhan in the northern Hejaz.[5]

Interpretive Insights

8:6 *hands.* The hands of slain foes (cf. 8:15) were often removed and counted by the victors after battles in the ancient Near Eastern world. This practice is attested in Bronze Age archaeology, texts, and reliefs from Egypt.[6]

8:14–16 Gideon's tactics in this passage are reminiscent of those used for taking the city of Bethel in the first part of the prologue (1:23–26). In both instances representatives from the tribes of Joseph interrogate a man of the city in order to obtain strategic intelligence. The difference, however, is that Bethel was a Canaanite city while Sukkoth appears to be Israelite at this time, and the Lord was "with" the house of Joseph (1:22) while an overt reference to God's presence with Gideon is lacking.

8:23 *The LORD will rule over you.* While this statement appears prima facie to be on the right track, Gideon's actions in the immediate context indicate otherwise. That is, Gideon's conception of God's rule appears to be that which is mediated to the people by means of the ephod (see the sidebar).[7]

8:24 *gold earrings.* Since this precise phrase occurs elsewhere only in the golden calf episode (Exod. 32:2–3; cf. Judg. 8:26), it is likely that the term is intended as an intertextual allusion to apostasy. The association of rings with cultic paraphernalia (also attested in Gen. 35:4) likely reflects aspects of the worshiper's relationship to deity.[8]

8:26 *rings . . . ornaments . . . pendants . . . chains.* Jewelry pieces with shapes of rings, crescents, and drips have been excavated from numerous sites (e.g., Tell el-'Ajjul and Tel Beth Shemesh).[9] Camels with neckbands are actually depicted among the items of tribute presented to Shalmaneser III on the Assyrian Black Obelisk from the ninth century BC.[10]

8:27 *prostituted.* The verb *znh* paints an extremely graphic depiction of Israel's covenant unfaithfulness to her divine husband.[11] The NIV and NLT

Ephod

Based on the descriptions in the Pentateuch (Exod. 25:7; 28:4–35; 29:5; 35:9, 27; 39:1–26; Lev. 8:7), the ephod was a sacred vestment that was worn and employed by the high priest.[a] It was associated with the Urim and Thummim and the procurement of oracular information (Exod. 28:15, 29–30; Lev. 8:7–8). In the historical books the ephod is employed by various priests, Levites, and rulers of Israel (Judg. 8:27; 17:5; 18:14–20; 1 Sam. 2:18, 28; 14:3; 21:9; 22:18; 23:6–12; 30:7–8; 2 Sam. 6:14; 1 Chron. 15:27). In the context of the book of Judges the ephod is clearly an illicit device since "all Israel whored after it" (8:27 ESV), and it is paired with teraphim (Judg. 17–18;

cf. Hosea 3:4; NIV: "household gods"), which also serve divinatory functions (on teraphim, see the sidebar "Teraphim" in the unit on Judg. 17:1–13). It is unclear in Judges whether or not the ephod was made to be worn. If it was to be worn, would it be for the human practitioners (Gideon or the Levite), for the teraphim, or for (an image of) Yahweh himself? It is possible that the problem with the ephod in Judges is that it demonstrates syncretistic assumptions about how Yahweh mediates his will and presence. That is, the incidents concerning Gideon and Micah's shrine may illustrate ignorance of (or disregard for) the second commandment (Exod. 20:4–6; Deut. 5:8–10).

[a] For additional references, see Bray, *Sacred Dan*, 112–18; Cryer, *Divination in Ancient Israel*, 277–81; Meyers, "Ephod," *ABD* 2:550; Oppenheim, "Golden Garments of the Gods"; cf. *COS* 2.135:367.

may mislead readers by translating this phrase "prostituted themselves by worshiping it." Here all Israel is unfaithful not because of worshiping other gods directly but because of the syncretism of presuming that Yahweh can be manipulated (through the ephod) in the same way as other gods. The ephod is thus not itself an object of worship; it is rather a means of apostasy (see the sidebar). The composer of Judges previously warned his audience (in the second part of the prologue; 2:17) that spiritual prostitution was coming. In 8:33—which introduces the Abimelek story—it is clear that such activity becomes the new normal for the second half of the book.

snare. As previously announced by the angel of the Lord (see 2:3), Israel here becomes entrapped in apostasy by means of the ephod. The metaphorical use of this fowling term (*moqesh*) is elsewhere employed to describe Israel's entrapment by the nations (Exod. 34:12; Josh. 23:13), their gods (Exod. 23:33; Deut. 7:16; Judg. 2:3), and their idols (Ps. 106:36). Significantly, the snare in this passage is not external/foreign but Israel's own creation.[12]

8:28 *the land had peace.* This refrain, identifying a generation or two of tranquility, is employed only in the first half of the book of Judges (cf. 3:11, 30; 5:31). After the Gideon account, there is no more rest for the land, and the leaders are said to rule/judge only for a short number of years—always less than a generation.[13]

8:30 *seventy sons.* The royal figure of "seventy" sons for Gideon may foreshadow the mention of the same number of donkeys for the (grand)sons of Abdon (12:14). In order to father this many children, Gideon would need a harem of at least fourteen wives.[14]

8:31 *concubine, who lived in Shechem.* It is likely that this remark serves as the first example of intermarriage with Canaanites as described at the end of the second part of the prologue (3:6).

Theological Insights

The Gideon "cycle" (of Israelite apostasy, Midianite oppression, and deliverance through Gideon) was technically concluded at the end of chapter 7.[15] But instead of ending on a positive note, the Gideon story continues as chapter 8 takes the reader down a new path and the emphasis shifts more directly toward the destructive roles of Israel's human leaders. Increasingly these leaders will be driven by impulsiveness and self-interest,[16] and God's presence in the accounts will grow more ambiguous.[17] Tribal tensions also continue to increase.[18] Chapter 8 recounts Gideon's moral/spiritual demise because it shows him to be a self-absorbed leader who fails to properly apprehend divine kingship. The previous themes of Gideon's doubt and fear are totally absent in this chapter, and the previous themes of his arrogance and desire to control God (see 6:36–40; 7:18) are now totally dominant.

Chapter 8 opens with Gideon placating the contentious Ephraimites (8:1–3). Gideon then needlessly pursues the defeated kings and their armies into the Transjordan, and on the way he threatens to punish ruthlessly the Israelites who cautiously refuse to assist him (8:4–9). His threat to the men of Sukkoth (8:7) indicates how he confuses the Lord's victory with his own accomplishments. Then, upon his successful return from battle with the enemy kings in his custody (8:10–13), Gideon follows through on his vengeful threats. When he reaches Sukkoth, he claims that they previously "taunted" him (8:15)—which just highlights Gideon's narcissistic perspective—and he "teaches" them a lesson through torture (8:16). Then Gideon proceeds to Penuel (Peniel), where he destroys the tower (as he said) and also gets carried away by impulsively slaughtering the men of the city (8:17). After this, Zebah and Zalmunna are forced to acknowledge Gideon's royal status (8:18), and Gideon reveals that he is predisposed to be more merciful to the enemy kings than to his fellow Israelites (8:19; cf. v. 17). Gideon finally dispatches the pair of kings, and he takes the royal spoil for himself (8:21, 26).

These events form the basis for Israel's perception that Gideon (rather than God!) has delivered them and that Gideon and his dynasty should rule over them (8:22). Gideon responds with an ironic reminder that the Lord is technically king (8:23), but this statement likely serves as a humble acceptance speech rather than as a rejection of their offer.[19] After all, Gideon is already functioning in a royal capacity (note his actions in 8:1–21), and his actions following this speech are mainly royal prerogatives. He issues his first decree—that the Israelites turn over their gold spoil (totaling about 43 lb. / 19 kg)[20] for the purpose of manufacturing and installing an ephod at Ophrah (8:24–27), where Gideon has already constructed an altar to Yahweh (cf. 6:24, 26, 28). The narrative goes on to say that he "went and dwelled in his house/palace" (8:29; author's translation), had "many wives" (8:30), and had seventy biological sons (8:30), one of whom he named "My father is king" (= Abimelek; 8:31). Furthermore, Gideon's "kingship" displays obvious tensions with the teachings of Deuteronomy, such as appointing the one God chooses (Deut. 17:15; cf. Judg. 8:22), not taking many wives (Deut. 17:17a; cf. Judg. 8:30), not accumulating excessive wealth (Deut. 17:17b; cf. Judg. 8:21, 24–26), and not considering himself to be better than his brothers (Deut. 17:20; cf. Judg. 8:7–9, 15–17).

Teaching the Text

While this account may explain how Gideon becomes established as an official leader in Israel, the narrator is more concerned about expressing what is wrong with this picture. Rather than revealing "a man of moderation and a model of every virtue" (as suggested by Josephus),[21] chapter 8 reveals a leader and a nation who know little or nothing about proper kingship. For the first time in the book of Judges, one of the deliverers appears to "cross over" (note the use of the verb 'br in 8:4)[22] from the role of judge to that of king. But the view of "ruling" (mshl; 8:22–23) that is expressed by Gideon and Israel in this passage falls short of theocratic principles.

The proper application of this passage should derive from Gideon's statement that "I myself will not rule over you, nor shall my son rule over you; the LORD shall rule over you" (8:23; author's translation). The surprising and ironic nature of this statement is made evident by Gideon's royal attitudes and actions (expressed both before and after the statement) and by the fact that his son Abimelek will certainly "rule" over them (see 9:2; cf. 9:6, 22). In other words, this statement shows Gideon's hypocrisy. He may say the right words (for the record, so to speak) while he does all the wrong actions. So here we have what appears to be a solid theological statement ("the LORD shall rule over you") but a failure to understand and apply its meaning.

Gideon fails to apply the kingship of God in a number of significant ways. First, Gideon takes personal credit for God's work of deliverance (8:7, 22; cf. 7:2, 18). Notice especially how he fails to correct the men of Israel when they assert, "because you have saved us from the hand of Midian" (8:22). Second,

Gideon abuses his newfound power by lording it over the Israelites through unreasonable demands, impulsive acts of retribution, and even opportunistic extortion (8:7–9, 14–17, 19, 24–27). Third, Gideon thinks too highly of himself (8:7, 9, 15–17, 31). This point is driven home in the closing remark that Gideon has made his son's name (i.e., "designated him")[23] Abimelek, meaning "My Father Is King" (8:31). Fourth, Gideon takes more money than he should for himself. This detail is twice noted by the composer, who distinguishes between the people's booty and that of Gideon (8:21, 26). Fifth, Gideon serves as God's mediator for the people. By installing an ephod in Ophrah (8:27), Gideon can control or manipulate God's revelation and presence for the Israelites. Even as a king, Gideon has no right to commandeer the priestly domain to serve his own political purposes. Finally, Gideon leads others into sin. After manufacturing and installing the ephod in Ophrah, "all Israel whored after it" and it became a "snare" for Gideon and his house/dynasty (8:27 ESV).

These six examples show that Gideon's affirmation of God's kingship (8:23) is hypocritical. Contemporary applications of the kingship of God in the Christian life may also take their cue from Gideon's mistakes. Thus, stated positively, God's people should (1) "do it all for the glory of God" (1 Cor. 10:31);[24] (2) "serve one another" (Gal. 5:13);[25] (3) "humble yourselves" (James 4:10);[26] (4) "be generous and willing to share" (1 Tim. 6:18; cf. Matt. 23:25; Heb. 13:5); (5) "be a holy priesthood" (1 Pet. 2:5; cf. 1 Pet. 2:9) with Jesus as our "one mediator" (1 Tim. 2:5);[27] and (6) "spur one another on toward love and good deeds" (Heb. 10:24–25). Such lessons from the story of Gideon are merely illustrative of what it looks like to live properly under God's authority. Many additional applications and scenarios could be imagined. Of course, one should ever look to Jesus, who modeled the perfect example of a theocratic life.

Illustrating the Text

There is a big difference between knowing the godly thing to do and actually doing it.

Quote: Benjamin Franklin once said, "Well done is better than well said." An unknown author said, "After all is said and done, a lot more will have been said than done."

Bible: The apostle Paul lays this tension out clearly in Romans 7:7–24. So did James in James 2:14–26.

Drama: This would be a great topic to explore via drama or video. Set up a series of vignettes in which an alleged believer passes by people in various states of distress or vulnerability who are possibly looking for help or advice. While encountering each, the believer should give an obviously biblical answer, like James presents in James 2:16, but then do nothing. A hungry person could be given a good quote about Jesus being the bread of life as the speaker gnaws on a sandwich and then walks away without sharing. A hurting person could be told that the best solution to a problem is prayer; as the hurting person seems open to receiving prayer, the speaker could walk away and—instead of praying—say, "Well, good luck with that!" A person observing an injustice should say, "Wow—somebody should do something about that." And then walk away. The idea is to painfully illustrate the heartbreaking difference between knowing the right thing to do and actually doing it.

Broken deliverers must be careful not to become hypocrites in the aftermath of victory.

Quote: *The Challenge of the Disciplined Life*, by Richard J. Foster. It is easy for broken deliverers to forget where they began and allow victory to go to their heads. In speaking about the corrupting influence power can have, Foster says, "Power can destroy or create. The power that destroys demands ascendency; it demands total control. It destroys relationship; it destroys trust; it destroys dialogue; it destroys integrity." He also says, "The power that creates gives life and joy and peace. It is freedom and not bondage, life and not death, transformation and not coercion. The power that creates restores relationship and gives the gift of wholeness to all. The power that creates is spiritual power, the power that proceeds from God."[28]

Comics: *Pogo*, by Walt Kelly. In his classic comic strip, Kelly's main character coins a famous twist on an older saying. (Oliver Hazard Perry, after winning the battle of Lake Erie in the War of 1812, said, "We have met the enemy, and he is ours.") Pogo says, "We have met the enemy, and he is us." This twist is a playful way of saying that no matter how many external enemies we may vanquish, we still have to face off against our own wicked hearts; usually, the heart is the hardest enemy to outwit. If we don't, we find that after defeating ungodly foes, we ourselves become ensnared in ungodliness as Gideon did in the end.

Angel of the Lord | Hebrews 11 and Hermeneutics

Angel of the Lord

The phrase "angel/messenger of Yahweh" occurs more times in Judges than in any other biblical book, but these occurrences are limited to only four passages: 2:1–4; 5:23; 6:11–22; 13:3–23.[1] While some scholars have identified the appearances of the angel of the Lord as theophanies or Christophanies in which God (or the Second Person of the Trinity) himself is revealed, there are a number of problems with such a view. First, the Christophany view forces New Testament theology onto earlier Old Testament texts, which violates the concept of progressive revelation and makes exegesis secondary to theology. Second, the Christophany view dilutes the uniqueness of the incarnation event and undercuts the teaching of Hebrews 1, which reveals Christ's superiority over angels (cf. 1 Pet. 3:22). Third, both views ignore what is now widely known from ancient Near Eastern practices that envoys, who were sent by kings or deities, functioned as authoritative mouthpieces for their superiors. Like a prophet, who occasionally shares the same title (*mal'ak*; see Hag. 1:13; cf. 2 Chron. 36:15–16; Isa. 42:19; 44:26; Mal. 1:1; 3:1), the messenger would often speak the words of his sender in the first person, and the recipients would respond to it as though they were dealing directly with the sender. Thus it is preferable to understand the angel of the Lord not as an ontological equivalent to God himself (e.g., note how the Lord is distinguished from the angel in Judg. 6:21–23 and 13:16) but rather as a function that is filled by a human or angelic intermediary who is sent by God to speak and act on his behalf.

Hebrews 11 and Hermeneutics

Gideon is notably mentioned in Hebrews 11:32, and so are Barak, Jephthah, Samson, and other prominent Old Testament figures.[2] The composer of Hebrews seems to set up these men as role models of faith for Christian inspiration. That these men each exhibited some measure of faith is not at all problematic for interpreting the book of Judges. But to argue on the basis of Hebrews 11 that the book of Judges therefore provides behavioral role models for Christians to imitate would be to put aside more objective hermeneutical methods and impose a more subjective reading on the text of Judges that ignores authorial intentions. One must concede that the lead human characters of the book of Judges increasingly show signs of apostasy or "Canaanization," and that is precisely the theological agenda expressed in the book. It is also important to affirm that Hebrews 11 has its own authoritative message in the context of that book and that the ultimate focus, even there, is on the example of Jesus, who is "the author and perfecter of our faith" (Heb. 12:2 NASB). But the subjective hermeneutic employed by the inspired composer of Hebrews 11 should not be replicated by Christians today as they exegete Old Testament texts because Christians are simply not inspired in the same sense as biblical composers. Walton aptly explains: "God's use of allegory to inspire Paul [in 1 Cor. 10:6, 11] or His use of role model by inference to inspire the composer of Hebrews does not suggest we should use those methods any more than the star of the magi suggests we should practice astrology."[3]

Abimelek

Big Idea

God may orchestrate disastrous consequences when his people reject his rule and become like those who surround them.

Key Themes

- Israel is disloyal to Yahweh by worshiping Canaanite gods.
- Israel is disloyal to Gideon by slaughtering his heirs.
- Israel is internally oppressed by Abimelek's tyranny.
- Abimelek is like his father Gideon, but much worse.
- God brings justice for Israel without sending an oppressor or raising up a deliverer.

Understanding the Text

The Text in Context

The lengthy Abimelek story should be viewed not as merely a sequel to the Gideon story but as the first account in the second parallel panel (or triad of stories) of the body of the book. In the ring structure this story is rhetorically parallel with the account of Deborah and Barak (chaps. 4–5). The themes common to these parallel accounts are as follows: (1) both stories have a northern geographical orientation (note that Shechem is on the border of Ephraim/Manasseh); (2) resolution is achieved by the heroic efforts of a woman independently killing the villain by a blow to his head with an unconventional weapon (4:21; 5:26; 9:53); (3) both stories conspicuously omit reference to a human judge/deliverer so that God's role is elevated; and (4) both stories integrate poetic quotations (song and fable, respectively, in 5:1–31 and 9:8–15) with the events of the prose narratives. Like the literary function of Jotham's fable in the narrative that follows about Abimelek, the song of Deborah/Barak (chap. 5) complements the previous narrative account (chap. 4). In addition to these common themes, there are a number of contrasting themes in these parallel passages (see "The Text in Context" in the unit on Judg. 4:1–24).

Historical and Cultural Background

The precise temple building that is the center of events in Judges 9 was identified at Tell Balatah in 1927 by the German archaeologist Ernst Sellin.[1] It is described by Stager as "the premier religious center in the highlands of Canaan."[2] The temple of "El/Baal-Berith" (9:4, 46) should be equated with the "tower of Shechem" (9:46–47, 49). This kind of temple, known as a *migdal* or fortress temple, is also attested at sites such as Megiddo (Temple 2048), Pella (Jordan), and Tel Haror (Area K). Temple 1 at Shechem is particularly large (70 x 86 ft.) with wide stone foundations (17 ft. thick) that supported a multistoried superstructure (cf. 9:46, 49) and two large towers flanking the entrance on the east. This structure was apparently in use from Middle Bronze II until Iron Age I. It had an altar (cf. Gen. 12:7; 33:20), a large standing stone (designated "Massebah 1"; cf. Josh. 24:26–27; Judg. 9:6), and a sacred tree (cf. Gen. 12:6; 35:4; Josh. 24:26; Judg. 9:6, 37) in its forecourt. The destruction of this temple by Abimelek is likely dated to about 1100 BC (Shechem, Stratum XI).

Interpretive Insights

8:33 *Baal-Berith*. Clearly distinguished from Yahweh (cf. 8:27), minimally this new god is supplementing Yahweh; maximally it is displacing Yahweh. Since the deity at Shechem is called both Baal-Berith (8:33; 9:4) and El-Berith (9:46), it seems likely that "El" is the proper name and "Baal" is the epithet.[3] A full identification for this deity is thus "El, Baal-Berith" (i.e., "El, Lord of Covenant"). The name El-Berith (cf. 9:46) may elsewhere occur in a Hurrian hymn from the late second millennium.[4] The reference to Berith ("covenant/ treaty") is especially disturbing because Yahweh's covenant that was renewed at Shechem (see Josh. 24:1–28; cf. Gen. 12:6–7; Deut. 27–28; Josh. 8:30–35) is now eclipsed by some other kind of covenant associated with El, head of the Canaanite pantheon.[5] El is most likely represented by figurines from the Late Bronze Age such as those excavated at Shechem (Field VII) and Megiddo (Temple 2048) and another that was reportedly from the area of Shechem.[6] While Shechem was previously de-Canaanized and became "the holy place of the LORD" (Josh. 24:26; cf. Gen. 33:20), it is here re-Canaanized as the domain of El in the following period (about a century after Joshua's time).

9:4 *reckless scoundrels*. Abimelek hires "empty men" (cf. 11:3; 2 Chron. 13:7), who are also described as "reckless." Mobley suggests that these individuals may have "lacked sturdy kinship attachments" or lacked "a portion of the family estate," but that they "compensated by forming pseudofamilies

Abimelek's Geography

The Abimelek story is rich with geographical names.[a] While Shechem (8:31; 9:1; etc.) is certainly identified with Tell Balatah, near modern Nablus, the other sites in the story are more obscure. As previously noted (see the comments on Judg. 6:11), Ophrah (9:5) may be identified with Khirbet 'Awfar southwest of Shechem in the territory of Manasseh. Beth Millo (9:6, 20) may designate both a place and a group of people (cf. the English use of a term like "the White House" for the building and/or its occupants) within the city of Shechem, such as the priestly class who reside in quarters on the temple platform. Beer, the place to which Jotham flees (9:21), is probably identical with Beeraim in the territory of Manasseh.[b] The NIV's "central hill" (9:37) renders a phrase that could refer either to the "center/navel of the land" (cf. Ezek. 38:12)[c] or to "an elevated plateau without external fortifications."[d] Abimelek's residence, Arumah (9:41), is identified with Khirbet el-'Urmah, southeast of Shechem. Mount Zalmon (9:48) may designate any local hill, including Ebal, which is not otherwise mentioned in this passage, and Gerizim, which serves as Jotham's podium (9:7). Finally, the location of Thebez (9:50) is unknown, although some have identified it with Tirzah (Tell el-Farah North), northeast of Shechem.[e]

[a] See Rainey and Notley, *Sacred Bridge*, 139–40.
[b] See Samaria Ostracon 1 in Ahituv, *Echoes from the Past*, 261–63.
[c] See Walton, *Ancient Near Eastern Thought*, 174–75.
[d] Block, *Judges, Ruth*, 329; Block, "Judges," 2:173.
[e] See Malamat, "Period of the Judges," 3:150, 320n61.

under the patronage of warlords, trading their services for portions of martial harvests and brigandage."[7]

9:5 *one stone.* This probably does not refer to the slaughtering location (as does 7:25, "at the rock of Oreb," which uses different terminology) but refers to an unconventional weapon employed by Abimelek's men. "By a single stone" (cf. 9:18) may indicate that a mace was used as the instrument of slaughter.

seventy brothers. Establishing kingship through the slaughter of seventy princes (cf. 9:18, 24, 56) is a motif that also appears in the Jehu story (2 Kings 10:6–7) and in the Panamuwa inscription (ca. 730 BC).[8]

9:8–15 *trees.* Jotham's perspective, communicated parabolically through a fable,[9] is in line with the narrator's (= God's) perspective (see 9:57). Although they are relatively rare in the Bible (cf. 2 Kings 14:9–10), fables also appear in Aramaic, Akkadian, and Sumerian texts.[10] Olives, figs, and grapes are staple products that may represent "domestic prosperity and successful foreign relationships—both the result of a competent king's rule."[11] While the domestic thorn tree is equated with Abimelek, the foreign cedars of Lebanon are equated with the elites of Shechem (see 9:15, 20).[12]

9:23 *God stirred up animosity.* In this story God brings deliverance for Israel not by his Spirit coming upon a judge (cf. 3:10) but by sending a "spirit of disaster" between Abimelek and the Shechemites (see 9:56–57). This phrase refers to the spirit as an agent of God's judgment.[13]

9:26 *Gaal.* Although it means "dung beetle"[14] and may sound pejorative to the modern ear, the name Gaal connoted prestige because the dung beetle was widely known as the sacred scarab beetle associated with the morning sun in Egyptian mythology.

9:28 *Hamor, Shechem's father.* Gaal advances a compelling argument to Shechem's aristocracy that is based on his superior ancestry (in contrast, Abimelek is half-Israelite; 8:31; 9:1–3), claiming kinship with the founding fathers of the city (see Gen. 33:18–34:31; Josh. 24:32). It is possible that the name Hamor (meaning "Donkey") was given at birth since animal, even equid, names were common in the ancient Near East.[15] Another possibility is that Hamor is an honorific title acquired later that alludes to the practice of treaty/covenant ratification by means of slaughtering donkeys.[16] The ceremonial dispatch and subsequent burial of donkeys is well attested in Near Eastern archaeology, and a decapitated donkey skeleton was even excavated from a Late Bronze Age pit at Shechem.[17]

9:45 *salt.* Abimelek not only captures and razes the city and kills the people in it; he continues to make his point by sowing the city with salt. Salt can render a land infertile and desolate.[18] Whether it is a literal act, a ritual, or a figure of speech, the salting of conquered land was practiced by a number of victorious kings and is mentioned in Old Aramaic curses.[19]

9:46–49 *stronghold.* In the present context this rare term (cf. 1 Sam. 13:6) is used to describe an architectural feature of the temple and may be translated as "corridors" or "ambulatory." Based on the dimensions and features of the Shechem temple foundations, the analogous 'Ain Dara temple in Syria, and the description of side chambers in Solomon's temple (1 Kings 6–7), it is probable that there were multistoried hallways that wrapped around three sides of this temple. Such a feature could accommodate the large number of people described in verse 49, who probably died by asphyxiation.[20]

9:53 *upper millstone.* In order to survive and stop the oppressor, a single nameless woman hurls the means of her livelihood from the roof. An "upper millstone" is a small handheld stone, known as the rider, that was used to grind grain on the large lower stone, known as the saddle quern. Typically made from basalt, an upper millstone weighed between four and nine pounds.[21]

Theological Insights

Pretty much everything is wrong with the picture painted in this story. The patterns and problems introduced by Gideon in chapter 8 are repeated and intensified in chapter 9. Abimelek is just like his father in all the worst possible ways. Not only are their speech and actions strikingly similar (7:17; 9:48), but they both victimize innocent people based on personal vendettas (8:7–9, 13–17; 9:5, 43–52). Both assume kingship despite the rule of Yahweh (8:22–32; 9:1–6, 15–20, 22), and both lead Israel into spiritual prostitution (8:27, 33). Worst of all, when Abimelek repeats the sins of his father, he does so with amplified intensity. All of this shows that the behavior of Israel and its leaders looks increasingly like that of the Canaanites.[22] It is therefore very difficult to distinguish ethically between the insiders and the outsiders. In the first half of the book of Judges, many outsiders surprisingly act like insiders (e.g., 1:7, 12–15; 3:9–10, 31; 4:17–22; 5:24–27); in the second half—epitomized by Abimelek—the insiders appear more and more like outsiders.

Furthermore, the three components of the cyclical rubric (apostasy, oppression, and deliverance) are all present in this story, but the details of each component are totally out of whack.[23] First, Israel's apostasy (8:33–35) has intensively devolved from merely doing "evil in the eyes of the LORD" to now prostituting after the Baals and setting up "the lord of [another!] covenant" as their own god. Second, the oppressor (9:1–22) is not sent by Yahweh but is instead homegrown. Although he is the son of Gideon, Abimelek functions more like an "anti-judge"[24] who slaughters fellow Israelites. Third, deliverance is accomplished by God (9:23–57), but not by raising up a judge in the usual sense. God himself rescues Israel from itself by sending a spirit of disaster (9:23) and meting out exactly what each party deserves (9:15–20, 24, 56–57). Abimelek's elimination "has the effect of surgical amputation. In the removal of this cancer . . . the nation has been saved."[25] Since God acts alone here as the ultimate Judge and sovereign King (cf. 8:23; 11:27), he is presented as the sole hero in this narrative. Israel's/Abimelek's disloyalty is contrasted with God's loyalty (8:33–35), and Israel's/Abimelek's treachery is contrasted with God's integrity (8:35; 9:5, 15–20, 23–24, 56–57).

Teaching the Text

Appropriate applications of this passage should be based on the theological emphases of the narrator. First, one should carefully expound the matter of kingship. While the narrator certainly endorses Jotham's critical speech about monarchy (9:57), this story does not categorically condemn all forms of monarchy. Rather, it condemns a "certain kind of kingship" that supplants theocracy,[26] because Israel's kings are instructed elsewhere to uphold God's authority (see Deut. 17:14–20).

Second, one should emphasize that God is the righteous Ruler who providentially orchestrates history (9:20, 23–24, 56–57). In this story God himself functions as the true Judge, King, and Deliverer of Israel, despite the fact that a human judge is missing from the account and Abimelek is crowned as Israel's king (9:6, 22). This theocratic principle is to be normative for God's people whether they live during a polity of judges, monarchy, democracy, or even anarchy. Just as the anti-judge Abimelek eventually gets what he deserves (9:56), so evildoers will inevitably get what they deserve.[27] During times of oppression, tyranny, and injustice, God's people are reminded to always trust in the ultimate Judge who brings justice (cf. 11:27). God's retribution is always righteous, never lacking integrity or truth (see 9:15–16, 19). Sometimes God sends a spirit of disaster (9:23) to expedite a just outcome. At other times God lets evil persist until the final judgment (Rev. 20:11–15). But in all cases, justice is God's prerogative, and his wise orchestration of the cosmos is always operative.

Third, one should emphasize that without God's help human beings tend to stray from God and destroy themselves. In the book of Judges this tendency is revealed in the plummeting pattern of Israel's Canaanization. In this story Israel exchanges their covenant with Yahweh for a covenant with El (8:33; 9:46). Israel exchanges theocracy for mere monarchy (8:22–9:22). Israel exchanges communal solidarity for self-interests and power-grabbing (8:33–9:57). Block aptly observes that "this chapter reads like a page out of a Canaanite history notebook."[28] All of this is evidence that Israel's greatest nemesis is not external but internal, and God's response to this is complex. On the one hand, God lets Israel reap the disastrous consequences of their own actions (9:5). On the other hand, God intentionally rescues Israel by inciting strife (9:23) and destroying both Shechem and Abimelek (9:45–57). The point is that God's people put themselves in grave danger when they become functionally like the world around them. It is therefore crucial to follow Paul's instruction in Romans 12:2: "Don't copy the behavior and customs of this world, but let God transform you into a new person by changing the way you think" (NLT).

Fourth, it is also helpful to highlight the generational pattern of sin that is revealed in this story. Abimelek follows in the footsteps of both his Canaanite mother (cf. 11:1) and his Israelite—though Canaanized—father. Gideon's seeds of syncretism and selfishness in chapter 8 have germinated, grown, blossomed, and reproduced in the tragedies of chapter 9. In this vein, Plantinga notes that "sin is both fatal and fertile" and that "sin tends both to kill and to reproduce. Indeed, like cancer, sin kills *because* it reproduces."[29] This deadly cycle can be broken only by yielding to God, and the family unit is one of the primary fronts where believers can fight against the progress of generational sin (for further discussion on maintaining the family, see "Teaching the Text" in the unit on Judg. 11:29–12:7).

Illustrating the Text

God's people put themselves in grave danger when they become like the world around them.

Science: There is a classic science experiment in which a cold-blooded creature (usually a frog) is placed in a beaker of water. The beaker is then slowly heated over a Bunsen burner, and the frog sits there calmly as the temperature steadily rises. Eventually, he will have been calmly cooked without a bit of protest. This is because his cold-blooded nature enables him to adjust to a changing environment by tolerating changes in his internal temperature. As long as the change happens steadily, he is cooked before he even knows it. Christians can face the same problem; if we are adapting to the surrounding culture and are functionally like the world around us, eventually we will be calmly cooked and not even know it.

Bible: 2 Corinthians 6:14–18. Paul addresses the calling to be holy and separate. He says (indirectly quoting Isa. 52:11), "Come out from them and be separate, says the Lord. Touch no unclean thing, and I will receive you." God is holy and set apart—he asks us to be the same in reverence for him.

Apart from God's intervention, humans tend to spiral toward self-destruction.

Human Experience: It is a common experience in life that the spaces in which we live easily devolve into a mess. The dishes in the kitchen pile up and spill out of the sink onto the surrounding counters. Stacks of papers on a desk become disheveled heaps falling onto the floor. Laundry goes from clean and neatly folded to dirty and in a heap. (A series of pictures could help visualize the advancing mess.) There is a steady creep of chaos. It can seem as though stuff is alive and taking over our rooms. The point is that our lives tend toward chaos, entropy, and destruction unless energy is expended by a benevolent outside force, namely, God.

Patterns of false worship in one generation sow seeds of tragedy for the next.

Health: Explain to your listeners about Fetal Alcohol Syndrome, the name ascribed to a constellation of mental and physical defects in children exposed to high levels of maternal alcohol consumption during pregnancy. Alcohol crosses the placenta, affecting development and even causing distinctive facial distortions. Neurons and brain structures are damaged, which can produce psychological or behavioral problems. These can include poor memory, attention deficits, impulsive behavior, poor cause-effect reasoning, predispositions to mental health problems, and drug addiction. In other words, false worship of alcohol in one generation can sow seeds of tragedy for the next in literal, biological ways. Generational sin is vicious and ugly.

Power tends to corrupt leaders.

Quote: Lord Acton. This late nineteenth-century baron said, "Power tends to corrupt, and absolute power corrupts absolutely"; "Great men are almost always bad men"; "The danger is not that a particular class is unfit to govern. Every class is unfit to govern."[30]

Israel's Problem

Big Idea

God may get exasperated and withhold deliverance when his people are addicted to sin or manipulate him.

Key Themes

- God does not tolerate manipulation.
- God becomes exasperated with Israel.
- Israel's addictive track record reveals their true loyalties.
- Israel's confession and repentance are insincere.
- Israel's worldview is polytheistic.

Understanding the Text

The Text in Context

The Jephthah story (10:6–12:7) constitutes the fifth major "cycle" in the body of the book of Judges. In the ring structure it is paralleled with the Ehud account (3:12–30). Some of the thematic connections between the Ehud account and the present pericope include the eastern geographical orientation (dealing with Transjordanian oppressors) and the eighteen-year oppression (3:14; 10:8).

Structure

The Jephthah story is composed of five episodes that are each defined by a confrontational dialogue: (1) Israel and the Lord (10:6–16); (2) elders and Jephthah (10:17–11:11); (3) Jephthah and the king (11:12–28); (4) Jephthah and his daughter (11:29–40); (5) Jephthah and the Ephraimites (12:1–7).[1] All five episodes reveal the themes of self-interest and/or manipulative measures.[2] The first episode is the focus of the present unit ("Israel's Problem"), the second and third episodes are the focus of a second unit ("Jephthah's Rise"), and the fourth and fifth episodes are the focus of a third unit ("Jephthah's Fall").

---

*10:1–5 is discussed with 3:31 and 12:8–15 in the unit "Minor Judges," which is after the unit on 11:29–12:7.

Interpretive Insights

10:6 *Again . . . did.* As in 3:12; 4:1; and 13:1, it is best to translate this idiom as "continued to do" (see the comments on Judg. 4:1). Israel's apostasy is not intermittent but habitual.

the gods. This comprehensive litany of seven deities (two by name and five by national domain) is the only list of its kind in the Bible, and it seems to echo the description of apostasy in 2:11–13 (cf. 3:7). For "Baals" (also in 10:10), see the comments on Judges 2:11 and the "Additional Insights" following the unit on Judges 2:6–3:6. For Ashtaroth (NIV: "Ashtoreths"), see the comments on Judges 2:13. The problem here is that Israel seems to have a polytheistic worldview in which "other gods" (10:13) are served alongside Yahweh. While the Israelites apparently still believe that Yahweh has the power to deliver them (10:15), they view him as one god among many (cf. 6:10, 25–26; contra Exod. 20:3; Deut. 5:7; 6:14; 7:4, 16; 8:19; 11:16, 28). Israel's worship of seven foreign gods (and oppression by seven foreign peoples; Judg. 10:10–12) is a disturbing reversal of God's instructions in Deuteronomy 7:1–2 regarding the protocol for the seven nations in the promised land (cf. Josh. 3:10; 24:11).

10:7 *the Philistines and the Ammonites.* On the Ammonites, see the sidebar in this unit; on the Philistines, see the sidebar "The Philistines" in the unit on Judges 15:1–20. While the Jephthah story focuses on the Ammonite

Ammon[a]

The Ammonites, or Bene-Ammon, were descended from Lot, according to Genesis 19:30–38. Their territory was settled prior to Israel's arrival in the mid- to late second millennium (Gen. 19:38; Num. 21:24; Deut. 2:19–21), but they continued to exist well into the Persian period in the mid-first millennium (Neh. 2:10, 19; etc.). Centered at Rabbah (i.e., Rabbath-Ammon; modern Amman) on the King's Highway, their territory was in the Transjordan, east of the allotment of Gad and south of (or within the circle of) the Jabbok River. In the book of Judges, the Ammonites are the allies of Moab during Eglon's oppression (3:13) and are the oppressors of Israel in the Jephthah story (10:6–12:7). While the identity of the king in 11:12–28 is uncertain, many Ammonite royal names are attested in epigraphic and biblical sources (e.g., Nahash, Hanun, Shanip, Padoel, Amminadab, Hissalel, Baalis). Milkom (NIV: "Molek") was apparently their national deity and is named both in Ammonite inscriptions and in the Bible (1 Kings 11:5, 33; 2 Kings 23:13). The Ammonite language is related to Hebrew and Phoenician and is best represented by inscriptions from the Amman Citadel (ninth century BC), Tell Siran (late seventh century BC), Tell Hesban (early sixth century BC), and the Amman Theatre (late sixth century BC).

[a] See Block, "*Bny 'mwn*"; COS 2.24–26:139–40; 2.71:201; 3.84–85:202–3; MacDonald and Younker, *Ancient Ammon*; Mattingly, "Who Were Israel's Transjordanian Neighbors?"; Younker, "Ammon, Ammonites."

oppression, the next major story (the Samson cycle in chaps. 13–16) will focus on the Philistine oppression. This verse may indicate that these two oppressions overlapped historically.[3] Thus it is possible that God's reluctance to deliver Israel in this passage (10:13–14) anticipates the Samson cycle (see esp. 13:5).[4]

10:8 *shattered and crushed.* The action of the oppressors in this verse is described with two verbs that sound very similar in Hebrew (*r'ts* and *rtsts*). The alliteration is beautifully captured by the Septuagint and a number of English translations (NJPS: "battered and shattered"; cf. CEB, MSG). The second verb (*rtsts*) may be employed here to recall the covenant curse in Deuteronomy 28:33 (ESV), "you shall be only oppressed and *crushed* continually" (cf. Judg. 9:53).

10:10 *We have sinned.* While Israel cries out a number of times (3:9, 15; 4:3; 6:6–7; 10:12; cf. Neh. 9:27–28), this is the first and only confession of sin that Israel makes in the book of Judges (cf. 1 Sam. 12:10). Unfortunately, this confession is hollow, as indicated by the Lord's rebuff in verses 13–14.

10:11–12 *the Egyptians, the Amorites, the Ammonites, the Philistines, the Sidonians, the Amalekites and the Maonites.* There are seven parties listed as Israel's past oppressors. The total of seven is most likely used to show comprehensiveness (cf. Deut. 7:1; Judg. 10:6; Amos 1:3–2:5). Since some of the oppressors mentioned in verses 11–12 have no corresponding stories in the book of Judges (e.g., the Amorites and Sidonians; cf. 1:34–36; 3:3), one may deduce that the narrator's agenda is not merely to preserve a history of the period but to instruct his audience by strategically selecting and arranging the stories.[5] Interestingly, at this point in the narrative, precisely seven judges have been named (including the "minors").[6]

10:14 *Let them save you.* The Lord's sarcastic retort here indicates that he is sick and tired of Israel's addiction to apostasy (cf. 2:19–21). Similar divine responses to Israel's disloyalty and insincerity appear in Isaiah 57:13; Jeremiah 2:28; 14:1–15:9; Ezekiel 20:3, 31, 39; and Amos 4:4–5. Yahweh's reaction here is understandable in light of the depressing developments of Judges 8–9, where it is shown that "the people would never stay faithful no matter how conclusive Yahweh's victory."[7] Yahweh's reaction is also similar to that of Jephthah in 11:7.[8]

10:16 *he could bear Israel's misery no longer.* The interpretation reflected in the NIV is like most of the modern English translations. However, the narrator employs the idiom "his soul was short," most likely to indicate that God was exasperated with Israel's effort (cf. Num. 21:4; Judg. 16:16; Job 21:4; Zech. 11:8).[9] This first and only instance of Israel's repentance in the book may look commendable on the surface but is deemed a manipulative affront to the God who can see through the veneer into their hearts. It is important to note that this remark is made by the narrator to describe God's impatient feelings toward Israel, not a change of his tactics as defined in verses 13–14 (the gracious change will not come until after Jephthah's lengthy speech invoking Yahweh as the Judge).

Theological Insights

For the first time in the book, Israel confesses sin and seems to repent (10:10, 15–16). Also for the first time in the book, God refuses to deliver Israel (10:13) and tells them to do what comes naturally to them: "Go and cry out to the gods you have chosen. Let them save you!" (10:14). Elsewhere in the book, Israel cries out for deliverance without any signs of repentance, and out of his mercy and compassion God raises up a deliverer (cf. 2:18; 3:9, 15; 4:6–7; 6:14; 10:12). Here Israel cries out for deliverance *with* a show of repentance, and God withdraws out of frustration and anger (10:16). What is going on?

God is not impressed by the outward religious gestures that may convince other people. God can see into the heart and can discern motives and loyalties (see 2 Chron. 16:9; Pss. 17:3; 139:23–24; Jer. 11:20; 17:9–10; Acts 15:8). In this passage, Israel's heart is far from God, even though their actions look momentarily pious. Israel's problem is that they are loyal to any and every god who will give them what they want (Judg. 10:15). Thus Israel has "chosen" and "served" other gods when it has seemed beneficial to do so (see 10:6, 10, 13, 14), and in the same way, Israel has "served" the Lord when it has seemed like the best option (see 10:16). But God sees this for what it is—a disloyal display and a manipulative measure—and he is fed up (10:16).

The dialogue between Israel and Yahweh (10:10–15)—which is also a first in the book—serves an important function at the beginning of the Jephthah cycle because it explains the rationale for God's absence (or passivity) in the events that will follow. Both Jephthah's rise to power (10:17–11:28) and the atrocities of human sacrifice and tribal genocide (11:29–12:7) will be related without overt references to divine involvement. It is evident that the cyclical rubric presented in 2:11–19 and illustrated in the first half of the book (3:7–7:25) is no longer intact—the deliverance component dissolves in the second half of the book.[10] While Jephthah is a deliverer who is not ostensibly raised up by God, Samson is raised up by God but does not exactly bring deliverance (see 13:5; 15:20).

Teaching the Text

First, God's response to Israel, described in 10:16, should not be interpreted in the traditional sense (see the modern English translations) as an expression of divine pity or compassion provoked by Israel's desperate need. Certainly, God is compassionate and merciful (see Deut. 32:36; Judg. 2:18), but here God is impatient, insulted, and incensed. God temporarily abandons his people in this incident because he is exasperated. This is similar to the way a parent might put a child in time-out for demanding to have something she wants or for presumptuously enjoying a privilege whenever he wants to.

Second, the God who gets exasperated with his people should be very familiar to readers of the Gospels. Jesus frequently displays grief and righteous anger toward hypocrites and hardened people (see Mark 3:5; 10:14). Jesus even has moments of rage (Mark 11:15–17; Luke 19:45–46; John 2:13–17) and expresses his exasperation (Matt. 17:17; 21:18–19; 23:37; Mark 8:12; 9:19; 11:12–14; Rev. 3:16; cf. Judg. 10:13–14, 16), sometimes with surprising sarcasm (Matt. 16:8–11; 23:25–28; Mark 8:17–21; cf. Judg. 10:14). Today, the people of God should consider whether their view of Yahweh/Jesus is correct—whether God is merely meek and mild or is also mean and wild.[11]

Third, Israel's condition in this passage is self-centered, manipulative, and addictive. These characteristics would be exasperating to anyone (how much more so to God!). Dealing with a loved one who has a destructive addiction sometimes calls for extreme measures of intervention—or possibly temporary abandonment. These measures are painful to all parties involved, but they have corrective intent. The same is true with God's refusal to deliver Israel (10:13). God is grieved by their addiction to idolatry, so he responds with tough love. Christians today should ponder whether or not they exasperate God, or perhaps how they may be exasperating God right now in their lives. For Ephesians 4:30, *The Message* states, "Don't grieve God. Don't break his heart. His Holy Spirit, moving and breathing in you, is the most intimate part of your life, making you fit for himself. Don't take such a gift for granted."

Plantinga demonstrates how "addiction is a dramatic portrait of some main dynamics of sin, a stage show of warped longings, split wills, encumbered liberties, and perverse attacks on one's own well-being."[12] Addiction may be described as a cycle of delusion, obsession, and ritual behavior.[13] These behaviors often lead to feelings of despair, and despair is often relieved by indulging again in the obsession.[14] But this cycle must be broken, and it can be broken only at the place where it begins—surrender. The road to recovery begins when sinners admit that they need help and trust in God, who alone offers forgiveness and healing through Christ. Recovering sinners should understand that this is a protracted and multifaceted process—sometimes involving professional therapists—whereby one unlearns old habits, makes amends with others, takes personal inventory, and shares lessons with others who are on the same road.

Illustrating the Text

God is not to be manipulated.

Quote: *Jesus Mean and Wild*, by Mark Galli.

> Perhaps the greatest danger—and the most tempting idol—is to imagine that God is the servant of our desires, who meets all our needs and is there for us in crises in exactly the way we need him to be there for us. But this idol is built on a false base, as if our desires are the measure of what is best for us, as if our "needs" are really our deepest needs, as if the only and best way to resolve a crisis is to do so in the way we think it should be resolved—as if we were all-wise, all-knowing, and all-loving.[15]

The God we really need is not the safe, tame creation of our own imaginations.

Children's Book: *The Lion, the Witch and the Wardrobe,* by C. S. Lewis. In this first book in the Chronicles of Narnia series, Mr. Beaver describes what it will be like for human children to meet the Christ figure in the book—a lion named Aslan. Lucy admits she will feel uncomfortable meeting a lion in person. Mr. Beaver explains that this is only natural—Aslan is a fierce and mighty king, a powerful lion. Lucy then asks if Aslan is safe. Mr. Beaver responds, "Safe? . . . Who said anything about safe? 'Course he isn't safe. But he's good. He's the King, I tell you."[16]

There is a big difference between mere worldly sorrow and true repentance.

Human Experience: Talk about the way children mature in their ability to experience grief over their sin. When they are very young, most children experience only regret about being caught in wrongdoing, displeasure at being disciplined, or possibly rejection in relationship to disciplinarians. As they progress in age, some even develop techniques to conceal wrong acts and insulate themselves from the unpleasantness of guilt. They are mostly experiencing worldly sorrow, or regret for the consequences their sin brings on themselves. As they mature in the Lord, however, they begin to be able to think outside themselves more and to appreciate the intrinsic evil in sinful actions. They may actually even start to intuitively see the need to repent, make amends, and reconcile with God and others they have wronged. The earlier pattern is worldly sorrow—the latter is true repentance. Ask your listeners to consider the last time an adult person apologized to them—was it based on worldly sorrow or true repentance?

Jephthah's Rise

Big Idea

God is the Judge who brings ultimate justice even in times when it feels like God is absent.

Key Themes

- God appears to be withdrawn from the events.
- Jephthah's rise is due to human initiatives.
- Jephthah comes from a flawed family.
- Jephthah and the Gileadites are acting manipulatively and selfishly.
- Jephthah is theologically ignorant and confused.
- God is ultimately the Judge who brings justice.

Understanding the Text

The Text in Context

The account of Jephthah's rise is part of the fifth major "cycle" in the body of the book of Judges. In the ring structure this pericope is paralleled with the Ehud account (3:12–30). Both stories are set in an eastern geopolitical context and emphasize a message to a Transjordanian king (3:15–25; 11:12–28).

Historical and Cultural Background

The geographical references in the Jephthah story are numerous.[1] Jephthah hails from a town named Tob (11:3, 5), which is identified with et-Tayibeh, southeast of Edrei/Der'a, in the territory of east Manasseh. The place name Tob is literarily anticipated in the Israelites' plea that the Lord does what is "best" (*tob*) in 10:15. Mizpah/Mizpeh, Israel's military base in Gilead (10:17; 11:11, 29) and Jephthah's new home (11:34), is not to be equated with Benjamite Mizpah (see 20:1, 3; 21:1, 5, 8). Although its exact location is unknown, this Mizpah is located in Transjordan (11:29; cf. Gen. 31:48–49; Josh. 13:26), probably on the western edge of the Ammonite territory "in the vicinity of Jebel Jel'ad and Khirbet Jel'ad."[2] In 11:33 three uncertain Ammonite sites are mentioned: Aroer is located "near" Rabbah/Amman (Josh. 13:25); Minnith is probably equivalent to Eusebius's Maanith (perhaps Umm el-Basatin); and

Abel Keramim is probably equivalent to Eusebius's Abila (perhaps Sahab). Finally, Zaphon (12:1) can be identified with either Tell Mezar or Tell es-Saidiyeh in the Jordan Valley (cf. Josh. 13:27).

Interpretive Insights

11:1 *Jephthah*. The name means "He (Will) Open(s)." Although it probably referred to God opening the womb when the name was given at birth,[3] the narrator likely employs the name here as a pun for the man who frequently opens his mouth in speech (note the many examples of Jephthah's "OMS: open mouth syndrome"[4] in 11:7, 9, 11, 12, 15–27, 30, 35–36, 38; 12:2–3).[5]

mighty warrior. This term, *gibbor hayil*, is also used of Gideon (Judg. 6:12) and Boaz (Ruth 2:1 [NIV: "man of standing"]) and generally refers to a man of means.[6] In this context, the term must be qualified by the fact that a gang of "empty men" (NIV: "scoundrels"; 11:3; see the comments on Judg. 9:4) were gathered to him and "went out with him" (11:3 ESV, NASB). That is, Jephthah has a reputation as the feared local warlord. Rainey comments: "Sociologically, it can be said that Jephthah and his militia had become like the Late Bronze Age *'apîru* men,"[7] who were generally regarded as renegades. The pattern of rejection, exile, association with renegades, and return is also observed in the autobiography of King Idrimi (ca. 1500 BC).[8]

11:2 *son of another woman*. In addition to surrounding himself with "empty men" (11:3), Jephthah has an illegitimate pedigree that is ominously similar to that of Abimelek (see 8:31; 9:1–3, 5). The breakdown of the family is a major motif in the second half of the book that starts with Gideon and Abimelek and progressively escalates in the stories of Jephthah, Samson, Micah, and, finally, in the story of the Levite and its aftermath.[9]

11:11 *head and commander*. The sequence and negotiations in this passage indicate that the term for "commander/chief" (*qatsin*) is lower in rank than "head" (*ro'sh*), and that "head" is still less than "king" (*melek*) because the "head" is subject to the rulers/elders of Gilead.[10] Interestingly, the term for "judge" (*shopet*) is not employed here at all, indicating that the narrator probably has bestowed that status only in hindsight (see 2:16–19; 12:7). Also, it is theologically noteworthy that "the people," not the Lord, "made him head and commander over them."

before the Lord. Here Jephthah opens his mouth to speak "all his words" at what appears to be a swearing-in ceremony, like the modern oath of office at a presidential inauguration with a hand placed on a holy book. Like Israel's notorious actions in 10:10, 15–16, this ceremony appears to be "a glib and calculated effort to manipulate Yahweh."[11] Furthermore, Mizpah is not a legitimate worship place for Yahweh (see Deut. 12:5–7, 10–14; but cf. Gen. 31:48–49).

11:24 *your god Chemosh.* There are a number of problems in Jephthah's statement. First, Chemosh is known from inscriptions and the Bible to be the national god of the Moabites rather than the Ammonites (see Num. 21:29; 1 Kings 11:7, 33; 2 Kings 23:13; Jer. 48:7, 13, 46).[12] Thus, Jephthah is either ignorantly making a diplomatic faux pas or, more likely, he is intentionally muddling the Ammonite theology in order to provoke his opponent.[13] Second, and more important, Jephthah demonstrates his ignorance of the torah when he avers that the Ammonites received their land from their god (on the contrary, they received it from Yahweh; see Deut. 2:19; cf. Deut. 32:8–9; Amos 9:7) and when he infers that Yahweh has a limited/localized domain that is functionally parallel to that of the Ammonite deity.[14] This inference exemplifies thinking that is both polytheistic (cf. 10:6, 10, 13–14) and syncretistic, which on the narrative level may prepare readers to understand why Jephthah will later associate Yahweh with human sacrifice (see 11:30–31). This verse offers one of those cases where interpreters must carefully "distinguish between the presumably reliable narrator of a biblical book and an unreliable speaker whose words are reported within that book."[15]

11:26 *three hundred years.* This period of Israelite occupation, if understood rigidly, can be used to bolster the argument for the early date of the exodus event in the mid-fifteenth century BC. However, this round number may also be taken figuratively or hyperbolically (see the introduction to Judges).[16] Interestingly, the ninth-century BC Mesha Stele also acknowledges that "the men of Gad lived in the land of Ataroth from ancient times."[17]

11:27 *Judge.* The statement that Yahweh is the Judge who will bring justice (NIV: "decide") is striking for at least two reasons: (1) it is from the mouth of Jephthah, who otherwise expresses questionable or unorthodox theology (see 11:11, 24, 30, 35); and (2) it is the only time in the book when Yahweh is called the Judge. In fact, the noun form *shopet* (traditionally translated "judge") occurs only here and in 2:16–19. Perhaps the narrator intends to remind his audience about theocracy at this precise point because Jephthah apparently has emerged through human initiatives. The reminder that Yahweh is Judge is therefore rhetorically similar to the ironic reminder (in the mouth of Gideon) that "the LORD will rule over you" (8:23). While these quotations are essential for understanding the narrator's theological agenda, they are not necessarily indicative of the speakers' spirituality. As Younger points out, "Jephthah is a pragmatic Yahwist."[18]

Theological Insights

First, it is important to identify what is wrong in this story. It begins on a sobering note: "The Ammonites were called to arms and camped in Gilead" (10:17). This encroachment follows right on the heels of Israel's superficial "repentance" and cry for help and God's exasperation with Israel (10:10–16). Then, instead of God raising up a deliverer as in the previous cycles (2:16, 18; 3:9, 15; 4:6–7; 6:14; 10:12), the rulers/elders of Gilead begin to devise their own plans (10:18). They start seeking a military "head" without consulting God (contrast 1:1–2) and thereby "usurp Yahweh's role"[19] of appointing an agent of deliverance.

Jephthah is then parenthetically introduced as a powerful but marginalized troublemaker from a messed-up family (11:1–3)—qualities that are reminiscent of Israel's domestic oppressor, Abimelek (8:31; 9:1–5). This does not bode well for Israel. When military engagement ensues, the Gileadites desperately seek Jephthah's help—probably as a last resort (11:4–5). The negotiations with Jephthah reveal both the manipulative measures and self-interests of both parties (11:6–11).[20] While the elders and Jephthah give lip service to God (11:9–10), "God is relegated to the role of silent witness to a purely human contract"[21] that takes place at an illegitimate cult space (11:11).

Second, it is essential to identify God's role in this story. While God's absence in the human developments of 10:17–11:11 is palpable, Jephthah's speech to the Ammonite king serves as an ironic reminder that God is in the business of leading, protecting, and delivering his covenant people (11:15–27; cf. Num. 20–24; Deut. 2–3). Most important, Yahweh is identified—for the first and only time in the book of Judges—as the ultimate Judge who will administer justice between Israel and their enemies (11:27). Unfortunately, Jephthah's affirmation of Yahweh as Judge is qualified by his syncretistic view that Yahweh's jurisdiction is merely national/regional rather than universal/ cosmic (see 11:24). Nevertheless, Jephthah's invocation of Yahweh as Judge seems to be the primary factor that explains God's change in tactics toward Israel in the following pericope (from refusing deliverance in 10:13 to giving some deliverance in 11:32).

Teaching the Text

Since God is seemingly absent from the human developments in this passage, one might be tempted to make the human characters the focus of a lesson or sermon. Indeed, many interpreters, like Josephus, attempt to elevate the leadership qualities of Jephthah.[22] But instead of working hard to find something commendable in Jephthah's status as a "mighty warrior" (11:1), and instead of highlighting traces of Jephthah's feeble faith expressed in his religious talk (11:9, 11, 21, 23–24, 27; 12:3; cf. Heb. 11:32), it is far better to apprehend the theocentric issues that are broached by the narrator in this passage.

The first issue is the absence of God. The present pericope shows the human characters attempting to rectify their problem through their own machinations.

God's involvement in this process is passive or ambiguous at best and must be understood in relation to God's response in the previous account (see 10:13–16). Galli, in a chapter called "Forsaken by Grace," makes some helpful remarks about divine absence. He suggests that God's withdrawal "is good news, first, because it signals that he desires a genuine, mutual relationship."[23] Since God is omnipresent (e.g., Ps. 139:7–12), he is never *actually* absent. The *sense* of absence is "something God has to manufacture, an experience he has to take special pains to create."[24] Second, divine absence is also good news because "it is one of the ways God topples our idols."[25] It is essentially the tough love expressed by a parent toward a rebellious child or by a spouse toward an unfaithful/addicted partner. The sense of forsakenness can therefore serve as a "rude awakening"[26] that can impel one to abandon false gods and return to the true God (cf. 2:19–21).

The second issue is the justice of God. While Israel's judges are increasingly depicted as failures, readers are appropriately reminded that Yahweh is the ultimate Judge who can bring equilibrium to the world (11:27). This is one of the many ways the book refers to the kingship of God (see also 8:23; 17:6; 18:1; 19:1; 21:25). The theme of God as Judge is found throughout the biblical corpus.[27] In this story it is God's status as Judge that makes all the difference for Israel (cf. Judg. 11:32). God is "the true arbiter of Israel's destiny, not the nations who threaten them or the human judges who arise to rescue them."[28] Justice is not something that God's people are able to fully achieve or maintain by themselves. Rather, justice is God's business, and God accomplishes it in his time either with or without the participation of his people. However, by following the example of Jesus, Christians may entrust themselves "to him who judges justly" (1 Pet. 2:23).

Additionally, there are important issues that arise in this passage that will be addressed further in the next pericope (11:29–12:7). These include (1) the importance of theological accuracy in the lives of God's people (see 11:24), (2) the strategic role of the family in God's program (see 11:1–3), and (3) the importance of controlling the tongue (see 11:7, 9, 11, 12, 15–27).

Illustrating the Text

Sometimes God's way of making us hungry for his presence is to give us a taste of his absence.

Popular Saying: You probably have heard the saying "Absence makes the heart grow fonder." It is usually meant to describe the effect of travel or distance on human romances. However, it is also true in a deeper theological sense—when we experience God's apparent absence or obscurity in a crisis and/or have to wait on him for prolonged periods, we begin to focus on him more, reach out for him more, and long for him more deeply. Perhaps a brief tour of some psalms of lament would be a good illustration of the biblical background behind this phenomenon. For an example, try Psalm 22.

Sometimes a bad example can help you understand the real thing better.

Human Experience: Talk about the way in which many people discover a lot about whom they want to marry by simply inverting the traits they have experienced in others they have dated. In other words, sometimes we learn about what kind of a person we *do not* want to marry before we are able to articulate the kind of person we *do* want to marry. In the same way, putting up with increasingly awful human judges helps Israel to learn about the perfect Judge they truly desire.

Philosophy: Plato talked about the idea of "forms" in philosophy. He posited the idea that everything we can see and experience is an imperfect manifestation of a more perfect ideal that exists in an invisible, foundational reality. For example, the inherent nature of all chairs lies in the fact that they imperfectly mirror a perfect and invisible chair in the realm of forms. By the same token, a thing's failure to satisfy or function properly can be explained by its imperfect representation of its true form. In other words, when a chair fails, it is because it does not faithfully represent the full "chairness" of the ultimate and invisible chair. In the afterlife, it was supposed, we might encounter the forms in person and finally see the perfected versions of the things we have known here. While this is not expressly Christian philosophy, there is a sense in which it expresses a dimension of the relationship we have with God: he is the full manifestation of a just Judge—when an earthly judge falls short, we lean into the juxtaposition and are able to intuit more about what a perfect God must be like.

Jephthah's Fall

Big Idea
God may passively let his people destroy themselves when they persist in selfish obsessions.

Key Themes
- Jephthah attempts to manipulate God.
- Jephthah's theology is syncretistic.
- Jephthah's words are unnecessary and self-serving.
- God uses Jephthah and delivers Israel from the Ammonites.
- God appears to be passive in Israel's domestic tragedies.
- The Israelites are destroying themselves.

Understanding the Text

The Text in Context

The account of Jephthah's fall closes the fifth "cycle" in the body of the book of Judges. In the ring structure this pericope is paralleled with the Ehud account (3:12–30), and both stories share an eastern geographical orientation dealing with Transjordanian oppressors (the descendants of Lot). Additionally, these parallel passages offer some striking contrasts: (1) both accounts relate the role of Ephraimites at the fords of the Jordan—positively aiding Ehud in smiting the enemy (3:27–29) and negatively opposing Jephthah and being slaughtered by the Gileadites (12:1–6), and (2) both accounts may depict forms of human sacrifice: the Moabite king Eglon may be viewed as a sacrificial victim (note the allusive terminology in 3:17, 22), and the Israelite daughter of Jephthah tragically becomes a burnt offering (11:31). These contrasts are examples of the spiraling pattern of decline that moves from synergy to civil war or from conquest to Canaanization in the narrator's literary agenda.

Interpretive Insights

11:29 *Spirit of the* Lord. See the sidebar "Spirit of the Lord" in the unit on Judges 3:7–11. Here the Spirit of the Lord appears to empower Jephthah to rally the army for battle (cf. 6:34–35), and Jephthah may thus be regarded as a legitimate judge of Israel (12:7). The Spirit does not, however, sanctify his character or enhance his moral judgment, for he proceeds to make a foolish vow.

11:31 *whatever comes out.* Jephthah's terminology could also be rendered "whoever." Maybe he is expecting a servant or a wife to exit the door and meet him, or perhaps he is not thinking at all (except about victory). It is also possible that he is intentionally vague in order to leave the choice up to God.[1] While his word choice is broad enough to include both humans and animals, the latter would generally not be expected to "meet" him, and the only animals that *might* act this way (dogs, donkeys, etc.) were unclean for Israelite sacrifice (cf. Lev. 11:2–7, 26–27; Deut. 14:4–8). Regardless of what Jephthah intends by his statement, his vow lingers in the narrative without a divine response. God's silence suggests his scorn.

burnt offering. The term translated "burnt offering" (*'olah*) is never used metaphorically and always entails slaughter and incineration. Thus Jephthah's vow clearly allows for the possibility of human sacrifice.[2] This is an example of syncretism in which Yahwistic worship is blended with the local worship practices in Transjordan. Jephthah's wartime vow is very similar to the one made by Israel in Numbers 21:1–3, except that in the latter Israel properly proposes to apply the ban on the Canaanites and God responds positively, whereas here Jephthah improperly proposes human sacrifice and God responds negatively by silence.[3] For further discussion on human sacrifice, see the sidebar in this unit.

11:32 *the LORD gave them into his hands.* This deliverance was anticipated by the statement that Yahweh is the Judge who will bring justice (11:27). What has happened here is God's work, not Jephthah's (cf. 1 Sam. 12:11). Although Jephthah and his daughter (see Judg. 11:36) may wrongly assume that Yahweh has honored the vow by giving deliverance, the narrator and the implied readers know better than this. By deemphasizing the actual battle (a mere two verses) and emphasizing the vow and its application (nine verses), the narrator shifts attention to what is wrong with the picture—Jephthah's unnecessary negotiations with God, which effectively demonstrate his Canaanization.

11:34 *only child.* It is striking that Jephthah has only one child, a nameless daughter, of whom he will be bereft. It is even more striking to read this verse in light of the preceding and following accounts of "minor judges" who are blessed with scores of sons (see 10:4; 12:9, 14; cf. 8:30–31).[4]

11:35 *I cannot break.* The mouth-opener here blames his daughter ("You have brought me down") for his own stupidity. It is bad enough that he makes this illicit vow, but it is even worse that he follows through with it (see 11:39). He is totally ignorant of God's provisions in the torah. While breaking a vow is indeed a sin (Num. 30:2; Deut. 23:21–23), monetary redemption is also allowed as damage control (Lev. 27:1–8; cf. 1 Sam. 14:24–46).[5] Ironically,

Jephthah shamefully keeps his vow, while Yahweh graciously retracts (at least partially) his own resolution concerning deliverance (Judg. 10:13; 11:32).[6]

12:4 *fought against Ephraim*. The theme of civil war characterizes the second half of the book of Judges, as it is a major focus in chapters 8–9; 12; 20–21. In all of these dark accounts, God lets the Israelites destroy themselves as they see fit (cf. 21:25).

12:6 *Shibboleth*. This word simply means "ear of grain" or "torrent (of water)." More important, the incident reveals what is indicated in the local inscriptions (e.g., Ammonite, Deir ʿAlla)—that there were dialectical differences between the tribes of Cisjordan and those living in Transjordan. Apparently, the same phoneme was pronounced by the Ephraimite westerners with an *s*- sound and by the Gileadite easterners with a *sh*- sound.[7] Dialectical diversity is also noted in 18:3.

Theological Insights

Jephthah's tenure as a judge concludes without any period of rest for the land (12:7). The cycle begins with God refusing (temporarily) to deliver Israel (10:13–14) and then taking a passive role in the developments of the narrative (starting in 10:17). God's passivity is perpetual in the domestic sphere of the cycle, while his active deliverance of Israel (11:32) is surprisingly granted in the foreign sphere. God responds as Israel's ultimate Judge, and he brings justice as only he can do (cf. 11:27). But God's gracious deliverance is not the primary focus of the present pericope. God's victory is supplanted by the literary interruption of Jephthah's vow (11:30–31) and its aftermath.[8] Since divine empowerment and deliverance are given, Jephthah can be properly regarded as one of God's agents of justice (12:7). However, Jephthah also unnecessarily obstructs the process and simultaneously serves as an "agent of atrocity"[9] in Israel.

The story of Jephthah's fall can be viewed as relating one step forward (God's deliverance from the Ammonites, though not from the Philistines) and two steps back. If Jephthah is one part deliverer of Israel, he is also two parts destroyer of Israel. Both steps backward in this pericope are induced by unnecessary words that reflect and lead to increased Canaanization for Israel.

The first step backward is Jephthah's rash vow. This is a manipulative attempt to control God and ensure that he will act in accordance with Jephthah's wishes. God has already expressed his exasperation about Israel's attempts at divine manipulation (10:13–16), but Jephthah does not seem to know any better. Jephthah apparently does not really believe his own argument that he made to the Ammonite king—that God would deliver Israel (11:21–27). His vow is therefore totally unnecessary and self-serving. Also, by proposing human sacrifice, Jephthah is demonstrating a syncretistic theology in which

Human Sacrifice

Jephthah's horrific sacrifice of his daughter does not happen in a historical-cultural vacuum.[a] The practice of human sacrifice is, sadly, quite common in Scripture. While it is strongly forbidden in the Pentateuch (Lev. 18:21; 20:1–5; Deut. 12:31; 18:10; cf. Gen. 22:2, 12–13), the Israelites nevertheless partake in various forms of the practice from the settlement period to the exile.[b] This abomination is associated with Canaanite religion (Deut. 12:31; 18:9–14; cf. 2 Kings 17:31; Isa. 66:3) and is modeled by the Moabite king Mesha in 2 Kings 3:27 (cf. Amos 2:1). The votive offering of a child appears to be an extreme and desperate wartime measure in the cases of Jephthah and Mesha, and perhaps also in Egyptian reliefs of besieged cities in the thirteenth century BC (e.g., the depiction of Merneptah's siege of Ashkelon). Evidence for human sacrifice may also be represented at archaeological sites throughout the Mediterranean world and in Phoenician-Punic and classical texts. It is arguably the case that all forms of human sacrifice in the ancient Near East were motivated by self-interests (preserving life, appeasing deity, demonstrating loyalty, etc.) at the cost of victimizing others. Perhaps this is why the practice is so repulsive to God and why it is antithetical to the human sacrifice of Jesus Christ, who selflessly victimized himself in order to preserve and save the lives of others. Ironically, human sacrifice motivated by selflessness is the greatest expression of love and life.[c] Thus, human sacrifice can be at once a most disturbing and inspiring theme of the Scriptures.

[a] See Finsterbusch, Lange, and Römheld, *Human Sacrifice in Jewish and Christian Tradition*; Hennessy, "Thirteenth Century B.C. Temple"; Hess, *Israelite Religions*, 101–2, 132, 136, 224–25, 293, 326–27; Kaufman, "Phoenician Inscription of the Incirli Trilingual"; King and Stager, *Life in Biblical Israel*, 48, 359–62; M. S. Smith, *Early History of God*, 6, 171–81, 201–2; P. Smith, "Infants Sacrificed?"; Stavrakopoulou, *King Manasseh and Child Sacrifice*; Tatlock, "Place of Human Sacrifice in the Israelite Cult."
[b] Judg. 11:30–40; 1 Kings 16:34 (cf. Josh. 6:26); 2 Kings 16:3; 17:17; 21:6; 23:10; 2 Chron. 28:3; 33:6; Ps. 106:37–38; Isa. 57:5; Jer. 7:31; 19:5–6; 32:35; Ezek. 16:20–21, 36; 20:26, 31; 23:37–39; Hosea 13:2; Mic. 6:7.
[c] See Matt. 10:38–39; 16:24–25; Mark 8:34–35; Luke 9:23–24; John 15:13; Rom. 12:1; Eph. 5:2, 25; Phil. 2:1–18; 2 Tim. 4:6; cf. Isa. 53.

the worship of Transjordanian deities is conflated with the worship of Yahweh. This kind of worldview was previously expressed in 11:24, and it contradicts God's command about human sacrifice in Deuteronomy 12:31. Essentially, Jephthah places higher importance on his vow/sacrifice than on God's instructions or on obedience (cf. 1 Sam. 15:22; Prov. 15:8; Isa. 1:11–17; Mic. 6:6–8).[10]

The second step backward is in 12:1–6. Again Jephthah's open mouth—his rash and unnecessary words (12:2–3)—leads to disaster. Just as Jephthah single-handedly slaughters his own daughter and blames her for it (11:35), so he leads the Gileadites to slaughter a breathtaking number of Ephraimites and blames them for it (12:2–4). Jephthah was himself a victim of domestic violence (11:2, 7), and here he perpetrates even greater violence on his own extended family. Jephthah leads Israel into self-destruction through senseless civil war, and God lets the Israelites do this to themselves.

Teaching the Text

Due to the extremely disturbing descriptions of violence, this passage is not appropriate for younger audiences. It is now notoriously known as a "text of terror,"[11] and it is therefore important to respond to the question of why God did not intervene in these instances of human sacrifice and tribal genocide.[12] First, it must be affirmed that God is indeed passive in this account. God's exasperation with Israel is expressed at the beginning, where he gives over the Israelites to their own depraved devices (10:13–16; cf. Rom. 1:24). The Israelites' aberrant actions are their own, and God is not culpable for them. Second, it is important to clearly condemn Jephthah's actions. In the literary context, the Jephthah cycle must be viewed as the penultimate example of apostasy in the descending spiral of Judges 3–16 (see the introduction to Judges). Thus the narrator does not need to proffer his obvious disapproval; his censure is already implied by the strategic placement of the story.[13]

Once these issues are sufficiently addressed, then one can focus on other implications that emerge from the emphases of the narrator. The first implication is about *minding theology*. Jephthah demonstrates ignorance of (or disregard for) the torah when he wrongly assumes that Ammon received its land from its own god, that Yahweh is localized, and that Yahweh is pleased by human sacrifice (11:24, 31). His syncretistic assumptions, which are especially offensive to God (see Deut. 12:31), also have tragic consequences on others (Judg. 11:35–40). Christians must take note that accurate knowledge of God through Scripture is essential for life and growth (see Deut. 8:3; 30:15–16, 19–20; Ps. 1:2–3; Prov. 8:35; 9:11; Matt. 4:4; 1 Tim. 4:8, 16), that ignorance can lead to death and disaster (Deut. 30:15, 17–19; Ps. 1:6; Prov. 8:36; 9:18; Hosea 4:1–6; Rom. 1:18–32), and that perseverance in theology "will save both yourself and your hearers" (1 Tim. 4:16; cf. 1 Tim. 6:20; 2 Tim. 1:13–14; 3:14–15; Titus 1:9).[14]

The second implication from this passage is about *manipulating God*. Jephthah's vow is an attempt to bribe God so that victory—and perhaps Jephthah's own legitimacy as head—is assured (11:30–31). Divine manipulation was also the issue in 10:10–16, where the Israelites tried to cow God into delivering them, and God refused to be bought (10:13–14, 16; cf. Deut. 10:17). Thus it is important to clarify that God grants victory in this passage not in response to Jephthah's vow but because he is gracious and just (Judg. 2:18; 11:27). So also, Christians should never presume that God must meet their needs, nor should they expect God to comply with their selfish agendas. Even in prayer, a Christian may be tempted to "strong arm" God into answering in a certain manner or time frame. This is manipulation, and it exasperates God. Instead, Christians are called to focus on God's will rather than their own (see Matt. 6:7–10; 26:39, 42; Luke 22:42; James 4:3, 15).

The third implication from this passage is about *managing the mouth.* "open mouth syndrome" is a prominent theme in the Jephthah account (see the comments on Judg. 11:1). Whenever he opens his mouth in negotiations, diplomacy, God-talk, or lament, Jephthah's self-interests are revealed (cf. Matt. 12:34; 15:18; Luke 6:45). His words may also be manipulative (Judg. 11:7, 9, 11, 30–31), confused (11:24, 31), ignorant (11:24, 31, 35), judgmental (11:35), and possibly dishonest (12:2–3). Most of these words—including the term "Shibboleth" (12:6)—are unnecessary and lead to disaster and destruction for those around Jephthah. This story offers a sobering reminder about the power of words (cf. Prov. 18:21; James 1:19, 26; 2:12; 3:1–12) and the necessity of managing input (i.e., minding theology) so that output and outcomes are pleasing to God (Matt. 6:19–23; Luke 11:34–36; James 1:21; 3:11–12).

The fourth implication is about *maintaining the family.* Jephthah comes from a broken and abusive home (11:1–3, 7), and in turn he abuses—actually slaughters!—members of his own family (11:30–39; 12:4–6). This is an alarming demonstration of how hurt people hurt people.[15] But it does not have to be this way. The family is designed by God to be a vehicle of life and growth, and it is the place where God's teachings are studied, modeled, and taught (see Exod. 20:12; Deut. 4:9; 5:16; 6:2, 7–9, 20–25; Josh. 4:6, 21; 24:14–15; 2 Tim. 1:5–6; 3:15; contrast Judg. 2:6–3:6). While destructive behavior in the family (such as abuse, violence, addiction, abortion, and infidelity) can replicate exponentially over generations, it is essential to break the cycle of sin by receiving forgiveness through the cross and by making Christ and his word central to family life.

Illustrating the Text

God is willing to give us over to the school of self-inflicted consequences.

Parenting: A father once saw his toddler daughter sneaking a fistful of extremely spicy cinnamon mints he had forbidden to her. He called out, "Don't eat those—they're yucky!" She quickly stuffed them into her mouth and then stared defiantly at him as she began to suck on them. The father sat down calmly and waited for her reaction. As her eyes began to water and her cheeks began to sweat, he gently said, "How are those tasting? Do you see why I said not to eat them?" The tearful child spit them out and came over for a hug. The father did not need to enforce a secondary punishment—there had already been a self-inflicted consequence that taught the lesson amply.

The Bible describing a behavior and the Bible endorsing that behavior are two separate things.

Church Fathers: Augustine, *Questions on Judges*. Commenting on Jephthah's vow, Augustine writes,

> The Scriptures never approve or disapprove of the act explicitly but let the matter stand, to be evaluated and contemplated after consulting the righteousness and law of God. Therefore, the Scriptures of God do not offer any comment in either the vow or its fulfillment, so that our mind might be put to work to pass judgment on this matter and so that we might now say that such a vow displeased God and led to the punishment that his only daughter, of all people, ran out to meet her father.[16]

Church Fathers: John Chrysostom, *Homilies concerning the Statues*. In a homily, Chrysostom considered God's attitude toward Jephthah's vow:

> And I know, indeed, that many of the unbelievers impugn us of cruelty and inhumanity on account of this sacrifice; but I should say that the concession in the case of this sacrifice was a striking example of providence and clemency; and that it was in care for our race that he did not prevent that sacrifice. . . . By suffering this vow to be actually fulfilled, he put a stop to all such cases in the future.[17]

Hurt people hurt people—until the cycle is broken.

Literature: *Les Misérables*, by Victor Hugo. The story of Jean Valjean in this novel is one of the most compelling pictures of the concept of breaking the cycle of hurting others. Having been imprisoned twenty years for stealing bread to feed his family, Valjean is stigmatized as a former convict. He is shown kindness by a local bishop, who houses and feeds him overnight. Valjean steals his silverware and flees. When Valjean is caught and brought back, the bishop says he gave him the silver willingly. The authorities leave, and the bishop tells Valjean that he has given the silver to ransom his soul—he must use it to become an honest man. This act of grace changes Valjean forever. The scene is a great picture of how hurt people play out a pattern of hurting others, but grace can break the cycle.

Quote: Martin Luther King Jr. In his message of love and nonviolence, Dr. King provides an example of breaking the cycle of hurt: "Darkness cannot drive out darkness; only light can do that. Hate cannot drive out hate; only love can do that."[18]

Minor Judges

Big Idea

Canaanization may be a corporate trend that is expressed through self-promotion or worldly alliances.

Key Themes

- The leaders act like kings by asserting status, building dynasties, and making alliances.
- God's leadership is increasingly ignored by human leaders.
- The leaders arrange marriages with outsiders (probably Canaanites).
- The leaders represent all Israel, both in number and in their actions.
- The Canaanization of Israel intensifies as the leaders are multiplied.

Understanding the Text

The Text in Context

The accounts of the six minor judges punctuate Judges 3–16 at strategic points. The Shamgar note relates to the previous accounts (Othniel and Ehud) because all three bring deliverance for Israel (3:9, 15, 31). Shamgar also relates to the following account (Deborah) due to the sociohistorical parallels with the time of Jael (see 5:6). And like the Ehud and Deborah accounts, Shamgar features the use of makeshift weapons (3:31; cf. 3:16; 4:21; 5:26). The second note of minor judges (Tola and Jair) relates to the preceding Gideon and Abimelek material because of the emphasis on royal prerogatives, such as having many sons to ensure dynastic succession (10:4; cf. 8:30–31). The identification of Jair as a Gileadite (10:3) relates to the following Jephthah account that shares the same geographical setting.[1] The third note of minor judges (Ibzan, Elon, Abdon) relates to the preceding accounts by revisiting the royal theme of many sons (12:9, 14; cf. 8:30–31; 10:4),[2] and more important, it anticipates the Samson account by introducing the theme of foreign marriages (12:9; cf. 14:1–3).

In the ring structure of the book, the first minor judge is placed among the first triad of stories (3:7–5:31), which share a relatively positive portrayal of Israel's leaders. The second and third lists of minor judges are positioned among the second triad of stories (8:33–16:31), which share a relatively negative portrayal of Israel's leaders (see the introduction to Judges). In fact, the three minor judge passages show a moral/spiritual progression from the ambiguous Shamgar (3:31) to the royal aspirations of Jair (10:4) to the foreign alliances of Ibzan (12:9) and the intensified royal aspirations of Abdon (12:14). This progression is also evident in the relative proportions of the three passages: 3:31 is the shortest (24 words in Hebrew), with one leader; 10:1–5 is larger (87 words), with two leaders; and 12:8–15 is the largest (117 words), with three leaders.[3] Additionally, the geographical pattern evident in the parallel panels of the ring (Othniel/Samson, Ehud/Jephthah, Deborah/Abimelek) is also apparent in the trifold sequence of minor judges: 3:31 has a southern orientation (dealing with the Philistine threat), 10:1–5 has a Transjordanian orientation (at least for Jair the Gileadite), and 12:8–15 has a northern orientation.

Interpretive Insights

3:31 *Shamgar.* This name is probably non-Israelite and may derive from the Hurrian language.[4] While the foreigner Othniel was associated with the tribe of Judah (1:13; 3:9), no tribal or territorial identification is recorded for Shamgar. Shamgar's foreign status may also be indicated by his pairing with the Kenite Jael (5:6). Since the first deliverers of the major and minor sequences (Othniel and Shamgar, respectively) are apparently foreigners, the composer may be indicating that there is a "dearth of native leadership in Israel."[5]

son of Anath. This title may identify Shamgar as a member of a special warrior class and/or as a disciple of the goddess Anath (cf. 5:6).[6] The phrase is also attested on inscribed bronze arrowheads from the early Iron Age (including one from southern Palestine).[7] Anath is the adolescent sister of Baal who is closely associated with warfare and hunting in Ugaritic texts.[8] While it is a little disturbing that the only divine name mentioned in the Shamgar account is Anath, Shamgar is nevertheless noted as an agent of deliverance for Israel. Perhaps Shamgar functions as a foreign mercenary (for Israel or Egypt), or perhaps he delivers Israel unknowingly while fighting his own battles (cf. Samson).

oxgoad. The term used for goad/prod (*malmad*) only occurs here; the Septuagint has "plowshare" (*arotropous*). It was most likely made of hard wood with a metal tip.[9] Unconventional weapons are noted frequently in Judges, probably to emphasize that God's victories are not dependent on state-of-the-art weaponry or technology (cf. Josh. 6; 1 Sam. 13:19–14:23; 17:45–47; etc.).[10] Apparently, Shamgar's defeat of the Philistines is only temporary (cf. Judg. 10:11; 13–16), since they continue to threaten Israel until the time of David (cf. 2 Sam. 8:1; 1 Chron. 18:1).

10:1–2 *Shamir.* Tola is likely buried in the family tomb in a region that is later attributed to Shemer and purchased by Omri to become Samaria, the capital of the northern kingdom (cf. 1 Kings 16:24).[11]

Donkey Riders

In an epic Hittite text known as the Tale of Zalpa, a queen is said to have borne thirty sons and thirty daughters, and the sons are said to be driving donkeys.[a] It is noteworthy that the donkeys in this text are closely associated with royalty. The story bears striking resemblance to the descriptions of Jair, Ibzan, and Abdon, where the motif of "thirty sons" (and thirty donkeys) also occurs (10:4; 12:9, 14). It is possible that this motif is a kind of "type-scene"[b] that signifies prestige, power, wealth, or kingship in the ancient Near Eastern world. Such an approach is preferable to positing that the biblical account is borrowed from the Hittite version.

The donkey is often associated with royalty in the Bible (cf. Gen. 49:10–11; 1 Sam. 25:20, 23, 42; 2 Sam. 16:1–2; 19:26; Zech. 9:9) or with people of high social standing (cf. Num. 22:21–34; Judg. 5:10; 1 Sam. 9–10; 1 Kings 13:13–29). In Ugaritic epic texts, the donkey is also employed by riders of high status, including deities and noblemen.[c] Finally, donkeys are frequently interred with elite human graves in Bronze Age burials all over the Near East and Egypt.[d]

  [a] See COS 1.71:181; Hoffner, *Hittite Myths*, 81–82; cf. Beem, "Minor Judges," 155–56; Tsevat, "Two Old Testament Stories," 322–26.
  [b] See Alter, *Art of Biblical Narrative*, 47–62, 181–82, 188.
  [c] E.g., see COS 1.86:258–59; 1.103:352.
  [d] See Way, "Assessing Sacred Asses," 210–13, 219–25.

10:4 *donkeys.* The term used for "donkey" (*'ayir*) in 10:4 and 12:14 is not a "foal," "colt," or young animal (as translated by LXX, NKJV, etc.) but is rather a male equid, most likely a jackass.[12] The remark about Jair's thirty sons/donkeys/cities characterizes his family as wealthy and powerful,[13] and the rhetorical impact might be analogous to noting that a modern person drives a Mercedes-Benz. Moreover, the term *'ayir* in this verse sounds similar to both the name of the judge (*Ya'ir*) and the common term for "city" (*'ir*). The NJPS translation cleverly preserves part of this Hebrew wordplay in English: "He had thirty sons, who rode on thirty *burros* and owned thirty *boroughs*."[14]

12:8–10 *Bethlehem.* This is probably the northern Bethlehem (cf. Josh. 19:15), not the one located in Judah (cf. Judg. 17:7–9; 19:1–2, 18; Ruth 1:1–2).

12:13 *Abdon.* The name, which is based on the common root meaning "serve," is also attested on an unprovenanced arrowhead from Iron Age I.[15]

12:14 *seventy.* Just as Abdon's numerous progeny and donkeys are indicative of royal behavior, the number seventy may carry the same connotation. The number seventy frequently occurs as a figure of speech in royal contexts in both the Bible and ancient Near Eastern texts (see the comments on Judg. 1:7). Therefore, it may be more than coincidental that the total number for the years of administration by the minor judges (i.e., 23 + 22 + 7 + 10 + 8) comes to exactly seventy.[16]

12:15 *hill country of the Amalekites.* While this enigmatic location is unidentified (cf. 5:14), it should be noted that the memory of the Amalekites should have been blotted out by this time (see Deut. 25:19). Concluding the passage in this manner echoes the mention of Amorites in 1:36 and foreshadows the mention of Canaan in 21:12. It causes the reader to ask, "Whose land is this?"[17]

Theological Insights

Since these passages are so strategically arranged in the book (see "The Text in Context," above), it is evident that the term "minor" (apparently coined by Albrecht Alt)[18] can be a misnomer. These accounts are "minor" only in the sense that they are shorter than the other stories and they lack cyclical features. However, their selective thematic emphases (especially on kingdom building and foreign alliances) reveal that they are included with authorial purpose. The minor judges therefore have major importance for theology.

The cycle that was expounded in 2:11–19 and illustrated so well in 3:7–30 is barely recognizable in the brief Shamgar account. Apostasy is not explicitly described (although Shamgar's likely foreign ethnicity and religion may indirectly indict Israel), and Philistine oppression as well as God's role in deliverance may only be implied (cf. 10:11). Deliverance is also mentioned in connection with Tola, but the oppressor's identity is unstated (10:1). All of the minor judges after Shamgar are said to govern (*shapat*) Israel, but exactly how they brought justice is unclear. What is clear is that the rubric of 2:11–19 is progressively breaking down and that God's involvement in the leader's tenure is either ambiguous or absent.[19] None of these individuals is explicitly raised up by God (each simply "arose"; 10:1, 3 ESV, NASB, NJPS)[20] or empowered by his presence, and the land never enjoys any rest. One might go as far as to say that as God's sovereign role decreases in these narrations, the role of the human leader increases as each one pursues his own agenda. This trajectory of increasing human kingship at the expense of God's kingship comes to maturity (or degeneracy) in chapters 17–21, where there is no king in Israel and each does what is right in his own eyes (17:6; 21:25).

Another important issue that deserves consideration is the likelihood that the composer selected these six minor accounts in order to bring the total number of deliverers/judges in the book to twelve. The number twelve is arrived at by excluding Abimelek from the roster, since he has illegitimately "ruled" (*srr*; 9:22) and actually functions as an oppressor of Israel. The literary quota of twelve is likely intended as an indictment against all Israel so that no tribe is exempted from the trend of covenant rebellion (or "Canaanization") that characterizes the period (cf. 19:29; 20:6). Apostasy is a corporate offense, and every Israelite holds a stake in the responsibility.

Teaching the Text

The application of these passages to God's people today can be treated under the following categories: kingdom building, alliances with the world, and corporate responsibility.

First, kingdom building can be good or bad, depending on who is ruling. Jair, Ibzan, and Abdon all appear to act as leaders who promote their own reputation by strutting on donkeys and building a dynasty (10:4; 12:9, 14). It may not be a stretch to say that they are all enthroned at the top of their own social ladders. When their initiatives are viewed in light of the crucial statements about the Lord as both Ruler and Judge (8:23; 11:27), it is revealed that these minor judges are competing with God's authority. Today, Christians must also come to grips with the deep-reaching implications of Christ's position as "head" of the church: "so that in everything he might have the supremacy" (Col. 1:18).[21] Perhaps the most basic principle of the Christian life—and the one that is hardest to grasp—is that he is God and we are not.[22] We are to take our marching orders from the King of kings (Rev. 17:14; 19:16),[23] and our modus operandi must be to deny ourselves (Matt. 16:24; Mark 8:34; Luke 9:23).

Second, alliances with the world are often a bad idea because they can divide (or displace) our allegiance to God. Intermarriage with the Canaanites was forbidden because it inevitably would lead to idolatry (Exod. 34:15–16; Deut. 7:3–4; Judg. 3:6; cf. Josh. 23:12). Yet the minor judge Ibzan apparently makes such arrangements for all sixty of his children (Judg. 12:9). He brings thirty foreign wives into his own family (presumably with their own infectious religious allegiances), and he gives his thirty Israelite daughters to idolatrous Canaanite families. As the following "major judge" story will show (i.e., Samson; see esp. 14:1–3), Ibzan will not be the only leader who engages in this kind of Canaanization. Christians likewise are instructed to marry only "within the fold"—that is, within the community of believers (cf. 1 Cor. 7:39; 2 Cor. 6:14–18). Failing to do so may lead to divided loyalty or to compromised faith. An alliance with the world can come in many forms. It can be any relationship or input that steers one away from God. James warns that "friendship with the world means enmity against God" (James 4:4).

Third, corporate responsibility is generally not a comfortable idea in modern Western cultures.[24] It may not seem "fair," from an individualistic perspective, that all twelve tribes of Israel (loosely corresponding to the number of leaders in chaps. 3–16) are collectively held responsible for breaking covenant, especially when some tribes have done better or worse than others. But this communal concept is emphasized throughout Scripture and is not taught just in the Old Testament. As the one body of Christ, the church is also responsible for maintaining corporate holiness. The church is indwelled by the Holy Spirit, and believers function as a community of priests to keep their space free of all impurities.[25] My sin is therefore my sisters' and brothers' concern, and their sin is my concern.

Illustrating the Text

Kingdom building is only good if the builder is God and the kingdom is his.

Bible: Psalm 127. A short exposition of Psalm 127:1–3 could be used as a devotional complement to this point.

Contrasting Concept: Sketch out a recent example of unhealthy kingdom building in the human sphere, such as Nazi Germany or some other fascist state with which your listeners are familiar. The idea is to show how building a kingdom and wielding absolute power are only good things if the one building has proper motives, is incorruptible, and is inherently benevolent. The problem is that history confirms what the Bible says—no human can sustain those qualities because of sin. The only way such kingdom building works is when God is the one at the helm.

Poetry: "Invictus," by W. E. Henley. Henley writes, "I am the master of my fate, I am the captain of my soul,"[26] but only God holds this position.

We must not be unequally yoked in alliances with the world.

Visual: Shoot video of two dogs, vastly different in size and temperaments, bound together on a short leash. Look for a shih tzu lashed to a Labrador retriever, or a Newfoundland lashed to a pug. Film the interaction, and bring it as an illustration of what two different kinds of dogs will endure if unequally yoked. Consider following the first video up with a video of sled dogs from the Iditarod race in Alaska. The comparison ought to show the stark difference between being evenly and unevenly yoked.

Faith is a team sport—we struggle, fall, rise, and win together.

Sports: Compare and contrast for your listeners a few different sports. Talk about some that are individual endeavors, like singles tennis, and others that are team endeavors, like American football or soccer. Explain that Christianity has a lot more in common with the team sports. No matter how individualistic the culture's mind-set is, the church is meant to function interdependently. We share corporate responsibility and ownership of our successes, failures, and goals.

Applying the Text: Invite your listeners to prayerfully consider if there are any corporate sins in their home, church, nation, or region for which God is calling them to repent. Sometimes we are so individualized that we do not take time to notice and hate systemic injustices in which we inherently participate by silence, passivity, or indifference. Perhaps there are some that you could suggest that would fit the context of your congregation and could be used by God to speak prophetically into their lives.

Samson's Beginning

Big Idea
God may initiate a plan of deliverance for his people because he is gracious, not because they deserve it.

Key Themes
- Israel's apostasy continues, and foreign oppression intensifies.
- The angel of the Lord announces the birth and identity of a quasi deliverer.
- Manoah's wife fails to remember and practice what God has said.
- Manoah is reluctant to trust his wife's report and tries to assume control of the situation.
- God blesses and empowers Samson.

Understanding the Text

The Text in Context

The Samson story is the seventh and final account in the body of the book of Judges. The first story (Othniel) is the shortest, and it is a positive portrayal of conquest that is connected to the tribe of Judah. This final story is the longest, and it is a negative portrayal of conquest that is connected to the tribe of Dan (13:2, 25; 16:31), which never occupies its allotment and instead conquers a city far to the north (see chapter 18). The literary movement from Judah to Dan forms both a geographical pattern (south to north) and a moral/spiritual pattern (best to worst) that is also precisely expressed in the prologue (1:1–36). Just as the Amorites possessed the Danite allotment in 1:34, so the Philistines possess the same region in chapters 13–16.[1]

In the ring structure, the long Samson account is rhetorically parallel with the short Othniel account. The most important parallels between chapter 13 and Othniel are the following: (1) both accounts have a southern geographical orientation (1:11–13; 13:1–16:31; i.e., Samson's story is set in the south even though his tribe is associated with the extreme north); and (2) the Othniel account closes with forty years of tranquility, while the Samson account opens with forty years of oppression (3:11; 13:1).[2]

Structure

Chapter 13 is a self-contained literary unit that both begins and ends with references to Zorah and the tribe of Dan (13:2, 25). This chapter shares a number of rhetorical connections with chapter 16 (see "The Text in Context" in the unit on Judg. 16:1–31), and the whole story from chapter 13 to chapter 16 exhibits a chiastic structure of its own, in which 13 is parallel with 16, and 14 is parallel with 15 (i.e., A-B-B′-A′).[3]

Historical and Cultural Background

The geographical setting of the Samson story is in the region where the territories of Dan, Judah, and Philistia converge. The border between Philistia and Israel was in a buffer zone of foothills known as the Shephelah (1:9). In the northern Shephelah, the Valley of Sorek (16:4) runs from the southeastern hill country toward the northwestern coastal plains. The towns of Zorah and Eshtaol (13:2, 25; 16:31; 18:2, 8, 11) were in Danite territory just north of the Sorek Valley. The town of Beth Shemesh (curiously not mentioned in Judges) was in Judahite territory just south of the Sorek Valley. Timnah (14:1, 2, 5) was in the lower Philistine territory just south of the Sorek Valley. Ashkelon (1:18; 14:19) and Gaza (1:18; 6:4; 16:1, 21) were located on the coast much farther south in Philistine territory. The more obscure sites of Etam (15:8, 11) and Lehi (15:9, 14, 19) were located in Judah.

Interpretive Insights

13:1 *Again . . . did.* On the patterns of variation for the refrain statements, see the comments on Judges 4:1.

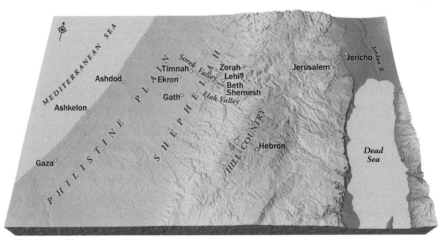

The places of Samson's exploits

13:2–3 *childless, unable to give birth.* Although Manoah's wife is unable to have children, God graciously decides to open her womb (13:2–5, 7, 24). The type-scene of a miraculous male birth is attested for the matriarchs of Genesis, for Hannah, and also for Elizabeth and Mary.[4] The inclusion of Samson's mother in this list may raise readers' expectations temporarily and then deeply disappoint readers in the ensuing story.[5] For an evaluation of Samson as a type of Christ, see the sidebar "Samson as Type?" in the unit on Judges 16:1–31.

angel of the LORD. On the identity of the angel/messenger of the Lord, see the comments on Judges 6:11 and the "Additional Insights" following the unit on Judges 8:1–32. Manoah and his wife initially perceive the angel as a prophet in 13:6–8 (i.e., a "man of God"; cf. Deut. 33:1; 1 Sam. 2:27; 9:6–10; 1 Kings 12:22), and they upgrade their perception only after he has "ascended" in 13:19–20. Importantly, the angel distinguishes himself from the Lord by refusing to accept a burnt offering (13:16)—a similar ontological distinction is also evident in 6:21–23.

13:5 *take the lead.* This key verb (*hll* in Hiphil), often translated as "begin," is employed at both the beginning and the end of the Samson account in order to chart Samson's destiny with reference to the Philistines, the Spirit, his strength/weakness, and his hair. The first occurrence of the verb is in the mouth of the angel, who identifies Samson as a quasi deliverer (13:5; cf. 10:13–14), while the three other occurrences are all employed by the narrator at strategic points in the story (13:25; 16:19, 22). The angel's announcement implies that Samson will commence God's deliverance, that others may contribute to this mission (e.g., Shamgar, Samuel, Saul), and that the process may be completed only by King David (2 Sam. 7:1, 9–11; 8:1; 1 Chron. 17:8–10; 18:1).[6] Interestingly, Manoah's wife omits this information in her testimony and instead mentions Samson's death (Judg. 13:7). She therefore "speaks better than she knows," and her substitution is "anticipatory of the climax" (see 16:16, 30).[7]

13:19 *Manoah.* While Samson's mother remains anonymous, his father bears a name that offers an ironic literary effect for readers. The name Manoah is based on a Hebrew root denoting "rest."[8] However, Israel receives no rest at this point in the book (cf. 3:11, 30; 5:31; 8:28; 18:7, 27), and Manoah himself is presented as a "restless and insecure individual."[9]

13:24 *Samson.* This name, meaning "Sunny" or "Sun-Man," is highly unusual given the miraculous manner of his birth. Instead of choosing a name that overtly acknowledges Israel's God (e.g., Samuel; see 1 Sam. 1:20), the nameless mother ambiguously names her child after the sun, which could implicitly refer to Yahweh or to some other god.[10] It may be more than coincidental that the town of Beth Shemesh (or "Temple of Shemesh") is located near Samson's hometown.[11]

13:25 *Spirit of the* LORD. Samson is the fourth and final deliverer to be empowered by the Spirit in the book of Judges (see the sidebar "Spirit of the Lord" in the unit on Judg. 3:7–11). This instance is unique in stating that the Spirit "began to move/impel him in the encampment of Dan" (author's translation). The three other instances of the Spirit that follow in the Samson account are all alike ("rushed upon"; 14:6, 19; 15:14 ESV). It is implied in this verse that, starting here, the Spirit's empowerment is continuous and constant until the end, when the Lord temporarily departs from Samson (16:20).[12]

Mahaneh Dan. The name Mahaneh ("Camp of") Dan occurs only in the book of Judges (cf. 18:12). It is apparently located west of Kiriath Jearim (Tell Deir el-'Azhar) and between Zorah and Eshtaol. It is the place where six hundred Danite warriors camp during their migration before they come to the house of Micah in the Ephraimite hill country (18:11–13). The name most likely designates a temporary Danite enclave located in the Judahite hill country, since the Danites never assume control of their God-given allotment due to overwhelming pressures first from the Amorites (1:34–36) and then from the Philistines (13:1, 5; 14:4; 15:11, 20) during the period before Israel's united monarchy.[13] Historically speaking, the Samson story most likely postdates the migration story of chapter 18.

Theological Insights

Samson's beginning looks very promising, but be advised that the narrator is setting up readers for a fall. In this chapter, Samson's birth, identity, and destiny are announced by the angel of the Lord, who appears two times and then ascends in a flame. Samson's birth is miraculous, he is a "Nazirite of God" (13:7; cf. 13:5; 16:17), and he is blessed and empowered by the Lord (13:24–25). What could go wrong? Starting in the first verse of the very next chapter, it will be revealed that Israel's last hope is in "a 'judge/deliverer' who chases women instead of enemies and who avenges personal grievances instead of delivering his nation from the oppression."[14]

A closer reading of chapter 13 also reveals subtle hints that the opening scene for Samson is far from perfect. First, "forty years" constitutes the longest period of oppression in the entire book, which may be proportional to the amount of apostasy in Israel (13:1). Second, the double mention of barrenness (13:2–3) may be interpreted as a curse for breaking covenant (Deut. 7:13–14; 28:18). Third, the triple mention of dietary prohibitions implies that the Israelites are ignorant or apathetic about the torah (Judg. 13:4, 7, 14). Fourth, Manoah's wife fails to report to Manoah the most important news of all—that this child will begin to deliver Israel from the Philistines (13:5; cf. 13:7). Fifth, Manoah displays distrust toward his wife, the angel, and God (13:8, 17, 22). Sixth, Manoah tries to assume control of the situation by

Nazirite of God

Numbers 6 explains that a man or woman can voluntarily take "a special vow, a vow of dedication to the LORD as a Nazirite" (Num. 6:2). This entails a temporary abstinence from three things: (1) consuming grape-related products (Num. 6:3–4), (2) cutting one's hair (Num. 6:5; cf. Judg. 5:2 NRSV), and (3) contact with corpses (Num. 6:6–12). The first two items are explicitly mentioned by the angel in Judges 13 (13:4–5), while the third item is not mentioned at all.

The first item is applied to the mother (13:4, 7, 14), while the second item is applied only to Samson (13:5; cf. 16:17), and the Nazirite status here is neither voluntary nor temporary for Samson (13:5, 7; 16:17; cf. 1 Sam. 1:11, 22, 28; Luke 1:15). In the following chapters, Samson has contact with innumerable corpses (14:6–9, 19; 15:8, 15–16), partakes in feasting that probably involves grape products (14:10; cf. Amos 2:12), and has his hair shorn (16:16–22).

taking his wife's place and asking for the angel's name (13:11, 12, 17). And finally, Manoah's wife chooses the unorthodox name Samson (13:24), which may have pagan connotations.

These are the indicators that much is wrong with the picture of Israel in this chapter, but the most important message relates to what God is doing for his people. First and foremost, God is taking the initiative to start the process of deliverance even though Israel never cries out for his help (13:1–5). God helps them because they need it, not because they want it or deserve it. This is grace. God also graciously answers Manoah's prayer, even though his request is unnecessary and incredulous (13:8–9). By opening a barren womb (13:2–3, 24), blessing the child (13:24), and moving him with his Spirit (13:25), the Lord is essentially growing Samson "from scratch"[15] and giving him every possible advantage. While Samson eventually squanders God's blessing and power (see chaps. 14–16), God still accomplishes his own purposes for Israel and the nations (see 14:4).

Teaching the Text

Like the other pericopae in the book of Judges, this chapter must be taught in light of the broader literary context. If the chapter is taken in isolation, one might be inclined to emphasize the dynamics of good/bad parenting, the makings of a "hero," or the typological connections to Christ. However, none of these themes would be a concern of the composer of Judges. Instead, applications should derive from the emphases that are consistent with the preceding and following contexts, where God's involvement is paramount and human involvement is increasingly deficient.

Therefore, the role of God in this chapter must be emphasized. First, God is the Deliverer. Davis aptly remarks: "We must not allow our focus on the savior

God raises up to eclipse the God who saves."[16] God's plan of deliverance in this account (13:5) is totally unsolicited, and it is initiated here only because of who God is. Rather than employing a leader who is already available to some extent, like in the previous stories (chaps. 3–12), God now creates a customized new agent for his own purposes. It is essential "that we see this, lest we think Yahweh's salvation is always an ad hoc, Band-Aid affair, a piece of divine crisis management instead of a plan that Yahweh has had in view far in advance."[17] This Deliverer is, of course, the same God who chose Christ "before the creation of the world" and revealed him "in these last times" for our sake (1 Pet. 1:20).

Second, God is gracious. In addition to God revealing his rescue strategy to Manoah's wife (13:5), God also meets Manoah in his place of unbelief by answering his prayers (13:8–9). This pattern will be repeated in the following chapters as God will later answer Samson's self-centered requests for both life (15:18–19) and death (16:28–30). God's grace is further revealed in blessing (13:24) and empowering (13:25) Samson regardless of his level of commitment to God. Indeed, without God's gracious actions toward Samson and his parents, there would be no story here worth telling!

A by-product of focusing on God's character and actions in Judges is the contrast that it provides in relation to the human players. God's heroic acts in chapter 13 come without much cooperation from Israel, the parents, or Samson. Apathy (general disregard for God's instructions) is a spiritual disease that is rampant in Israel. It is exemplified by Samson's mother (13:4, 7, 14, 24), and in the following chapters it will become evident that Samson quickly follows suit (regarding his Nazirite status, philandering with Philistines, etc.). Block observes: "No other deliverer in the Book of Judges matches his potential. . . . Despite all these advantages and this special attention, Samson accomplishes less on behalf of his people than any of his predecessors."[18] What a sad scenario! The hero of chapters 13–16 is clearly not Samson, who squanders God's gifts. Rather, the hero is introduced in chapter 13 as the Gracious One who plans deliverance for his covenant people (13:5).

Illustrating the Text

God starts out from the beginning with a plan to save—he isn't making it all up as he goes along.

Bible: Revelation 13:8. This passage clearly states that Jesus is "the Lamb who was slain from the creation of the world." Explain to your listeners that this is a great assurance to us—God did not invent salvation as an afterthought or a backup plan—he intended it from the moment he created, and Jesus's identity has been as a willing, suffering servant from before the words "let there be light" were ever uttered.

Television: *MacGyver.* Many people will be familiar with the classic TV series *MacGyver* (1985–92). The hero, MacGyver, is renowned for his ability to improvise munitions, solutions, and traps and to escape plots using only the most rudimentary tools and supplies. Given a Swiss army knife, a pack of gum, and a paper clip, MacGyver is likely capable of blowing up an enemy fortress. Point out that, while God is also able to use rudimentary tools and resources (flawed people like us), he is not an improviser like MacGyver. God had a plan from the beginning and never has to "MacGyver" his way out of anything. He is sovereign and in control.

Apathy actively antagonizes God.

Human Experience: Ask listeners to admit to themselves how many times they have been provoked to anger by another's apathy. When one family member cleans passionately while another carelessly plays video games or takes a nap, apathy can actively antagonize. It is similar with God. He is passionately seeking and saving the lost and fighting for holiness and reconciliation. When we claim to be his but cannot be bothered to care about such things, it is an affront to him.

We may be sidekicks, villains, or extras in God's story; he is the only real hero.

Human Metaphors: Ask your listeners to imagine their lives as a television series or movie. Would it be an adventure? A love story? A mystery? A documentary? Now ask them to consider these questions: Whom would they cast for various roles? Which actor would they cast as the villain? Who would play their part? Would they have a sidekick? A love interest? Now ask them to consider this: in the real story of their lives, there is one casting decision that has already been irrevocably made—the hero is God. Point out that everyone naturally imagines that they are the hero in their own story. The Bible teaches that this role is already taken. Open parts include sidekick (adopted son or daughter in Christ), villain (captive to the devil's schemes and trapped in wickedness), or extra (timidly trying to stay off the radar but inevitably getting drawn into the crossfire and being used by the enemy). God is already the author, producer, and protagonist. Which part will your listeners play?

Samson's Marriage

Big Idea

God can accomplish his plans even through people who are self-absorbed, disobedient, and disengaged from God.

Key Themes

- God employs Samson's selfish antics for God's own purposes.
- Samson follows his senses instead of God.
- Samson's lifestyle contradicts his identity and calling.
- Samson's extraordinary gifts are God given.

Understanding the Text

The Text in Context

In the ring structure of the book of Judges, the story about Samson's marriage to the Timnite should be viewed as a stark contrast to Othniel's marriage to Aksah (1:12–15). While Othniel marries a faithful insider, Samson marries a Philistine outsider. It is also ironic that Othniel is a foreigner who assimilates into Israel (Judah), while Samson is an Israelite (Danite) who assimilates into Philistia.[1] Samson's actions here show total disregard for the teachings of Moses and Joshua concerning marriage to outsiders (Exod. 34:15–16; Deut. 7:3; Josh. 23:12).

Chapter 14 contains a single story about Samson's wedding and its aftermath, but verses 4–9 are an intentional literary interruption. Note how verse 4 begins with a Hebrew disjunctive marker, "Now/However" (see HCSB, NASB), and verse 10 continues the story line from verse 3. This interruption reveals to the audience both God's agenda and Samson's weaknesses. It is a parenthetical paragraph that provides crucial information that must inform one's interpretation of the marriage story and the stories that follow in chapters 15–16.

Historical and Cultural Background

Samson's altercation with the lion (14:5–9) can be compared to the feats of the Sumerian king Gilgamesh and the Greek hero Heracles, both of whom were said to defeat lions with their bare hands (cf. 14:6). Biblical analogies may be identified in the exploits of King David (1 Sam. 17:34–37) or of his mighty men (2 Sam. 23:20 // 1 Chron. 11:22). Lions were a common symbol for royalty in the biblical world.[2] Kings throughout the ancient Near East and Egypt hunted lions with spear, bow, or sword to demonstrate their prowess in battle and their sovereignty as "Master of the Beasts."[3] This image is similar to the portrait of the "Wild Man" Samson, who is also able to capture and harness three hundred foxes (15:4).[4] In the Samson story and in other biblical narratives, the now-extinct Asiatic lion (*Panthera leo persica*) is depicted as an agent of Yahweh.[5] The lion is associated with the tribes of both Dan and Judah,[6] and skeletal remains are identified at a few places, including Jaffa, Tel Miqne-Ekron, and the sacred precinct of Tel Dan.[7] There is also now a seal from Beth Shemesh (eleventh century BC) picturing a man handling a lion.

Interpretive Insights

14:1 *Timnah.* The Philistine town of Timnah is identified with Tel Batash, Stratum V (Iron IB; late twelfth and mainly eleventh centuries BC).[8] It was located in the Sorek Valley about four and a half miles to the west of Israelite Zorah.

Philistine woman. The Hebrew phrase used here ("of the daughters of the Philistines") recalls the earlier statement about the inhabitants of Canaan, from the second part of the prologue, that the Israelites "took their daughters in marriage and gave their own daughters to their sons, and served their gods" (3:6). The theme of marriage with outsiders, which is illustrated only in the second half of the body of the book (i.e., the narrative from Gideon to Samson; 8:31; 11:1; 12:9; 14:1–3, 10–11), demonstrates Israel's spiritual decline and increasing loss of distinctiveness.

14:3 *She's the right one for me.* Samson is a man who repeatedly sees something that is potentially gratifying and impulsively seizes it (14:1, 2, 8–9; 16:1). Since the Timnite woman is right in his eyes (cf. 14:7), he demands to marry her. The problem with his perspective is that it is not what is right "in the eyes of the LORD" (cf. 2:11; 13:1). Samson's selfish orientation, as described in this phrase, also serves a transitional function in the book of Judges, since the epilogue (chaps. 17–21) illustrates how each does what is right in his own eyes (cf. 17:6; 18:1; 19:1; 21:25).

14:5 *young lion.* The phrase used for the animal here designates a subadult (2–3.5 years old), nomadic lion that is (possibly ousted) from a pride.[9] This can help to explain its location in the vineyards and its aggressive ("roaring") behavior. Thus Samson's foe is not just any lion; it is "perhaps the most dangerous instance of the world's dominant land predator that one could possibly encounter."[10]

14:8 *carcass.* Samson's contact with a corpse in verses 6–9 is ritually problematic but not irreparable. Numbers 6:9–12 prescribes the necessary steps for restoration. The problem, then, is not that Samson defends himself (in the power of the Spirit) against the attacking lion. Rather, the problem is that he keeps it a secret and does not bother to follow God's instructions (Judg. 14:6). What is worse is that his actions spiral downward as he later has "turned aside to look at the lion's carcass" (14:8) and extracted some unclean honey for himself and then passes the impurity to his parents (14:9). These actions show a total disregard for his Nazirite status (see 13:4, 7, 14).

bees . . . honey. Wild honey from bees is also mentioned in 1 Samuel 14:24–30. Traditionally, historians have assumed that the honey in the phrase "land of milk and honey"[11] referred to fruits such as dates and figs, but recent research has shown that bee honey was also cultivated in the land and should not be excluded. Excavations at the Israelite site of Tel Rehov have revealed the existence of an elaborate bee-keeping industry dating to slightly later than the time of the judges.[12]

14:10 *held a feast.* Although it is not explicitly stated in this verse, it seems likely that Samson's wedding "feast" (*mishteh*) entails the consumption of some form of alcohol. If so, then Samson is once again disregarding his Nazirite status (Num. 6:3–4; Judg. 13:4, 7, 14). The so-called beer jug (or strainer-spout jug) is in fact a common artifact discovered at Philistine sites,[13] and virtually all wedding ceremonies in the biblical world (like today) would have included the consumption of alcohol (cf. John 2:1–11). For additional explanation of marriage customs, see "Historical and Cultural Background" in the unit on Judges 15:1–20.

14:12–18 *riddle.* From Samson's standpoint, it appears that this verbal game is analogous to "Heads, I win; tails, you lose." The exchange thus provokes the first of six "occasions" for retaliation against the Philistines (cf. 14:4). While "riddle" is not the best translation of the term *hidah*, the analysis of lexicography[14] and the Aegean cultural background of this scene favor the understanding that Samson's "(enigmatic) saying" is topped by his opponents and that Samson is demonstrating his adeptness at the Philistines' own game.[15]

14:19 *Ashkelon.* This was one of the five capital cities of Philistia (cf. 3:3). It was located on the Mediterranean coast, about twenty-three miles southwest of Timnah. It is unclear why Samson travels so far since other Philistine cities (especially Ekron) were much closer. The Iron Age I period is represented at Ashkelon in Strata XVII–XIV (1175–950 BC).[16]

Theological Insights

Verses 4–9 offer essential theological insights about both God's agenda and Samson's weaknesses. Most important, verse 4 reveals that God is the one who is really orchestrating the events in the story. The narrator explains that the parents "did not know that" Samson's demand "was from the Lord" and that God was "seeking an occasion/opportunity against the Philistines" (14:4; author's translation). This theological statement is undoubtedly the most important one for interpreting chapters 14–16. In 14:5–9 it is evident that God is pulling the strings, so to speak, not only by the Spirit empowering Samson (14:6) but also in the highly unusual incidents of the lion's attack (14:5) and the bees inhabiting the carcass (14:8). Clearly, these unusual developments are providentially prompted by God.[17]

But 14:4–9 also reveals the basic problems with Samson's character, which will resurface again and again. Basically, Samson is foolish and selfish. He is driven by his senses (note the many references to his sight in 14:1, 2, 3, 7, 8 [see ESV]; cf. 16:1, 28). He also shows disregard for God in his handling of a corpse (contra his Nazirite status; cf. Num. 6:6–12) and disregard for others by offering unclean honey to his parents (Judg. 14:9). Similar disrespect toward his parents (contra the fifth commandment; see Exod. 20:12; Deut. 5:16; Eph. 6:1–3; Col. 3:20) was already revealed in 14:2–3, where he commands his parents with imperative verbal forms ("get her"; contrast with 15:1).

Fooling Around in Philistia

It is ironic that the "wise" wordsmith in Judges 14 is actually characterized as a fool. This conclusion is evident when Samson's actions are evaluated against the teachings of the book of Proverbs.[a] A fool is one who brings sorrow, grief, bitterness, and ruin to one's parents (Prov. 10:1; 17:21, 25; 19:13), which is aptly illustrated in the exchange between Manoah and Samson (Judg. 14:2–3). A fool also displays disregard for parents (Prov. 15:20), which is evident in both Samson's commands and his sharing of uncleanness (Judg. 14:2, 3, 9). The wedding celebration and verbal contest even show how "a fool finds pleasure in wicked schemes" (Prov. 10:23; cf. Judg. 14:10–14), "a companion of fools suffers harm" (Prov. 13:20; cf. Judg. 14:11), and "the lips of fools bring them strife" (Prov. 18:6; cf. Judg. 14:14–18). Samson's isolation, selfishness, contentiousness, and poor judgment are addressed in Proverbs 18:1, and his penchant for foreign women epitomizes foolishness (Prov. 2:16–19; 5:3–6, 20; 7:5–27; 22:14; 23:27–28; cf. Judg. 14–16) and leads to his demise (Prov. 2:19; 7:23; 16:25; Eccles. 7:26; cf. Judg. 16:16, 30–31). Samson also naively fails to see the consequences of his behavior (Prov. 1:32; 22:3; 27:12; cf. Judg. 16:20), and he foolishly tries to get even (Prov. 24:29; cf. Judg. 15:3–11). But the most important teaching in the Samson story is the theological perspective that is succinctly summarized in Proverbs 16:9: "In their hearts humans plan their course, but the Lord establishes their steps" (see also Prov. 19:21; cf. Judg. 14:4).

[a] See Brettler, Book of Judges, 50–54; Chisholm, "What's Wrong with This Picture?," 178–79; Younger, Judges, Ruth, 301n38, 310.

The primary story of chapter 14 should be understood as Occasion 1 (à la 14:4). It is essentially the beginning of the beginning (cf. 13:5, "he shall *begin* to save Israel"; ESV).[18] Although Samson's marriage to the Timnite goes squarely against God's will,[19] it is part of God's plan for commencing Israel's deliverance from Philistine oppression (see 13:5; 14:4). Samson initiates this "occasion" (or divine appointment) by propounding his enigmatic saying, which leads to a back-and-forth pattern of retaliation that begins in 14:15–19 and escalates in 14:20–15:17.

Teaching the Text

Samson's case of selfishness and willful disengagement from God is the worst example of judgeship in the whole book. Nevertheless, God still accomplishes his own agenda through his agent Samson. The point is that deliverance is God's business, and he gets it done regardless of how cooperative his agents are. Although Samson may foolishly plan his own way, it is the Lord who directs his steps (see Prov. 16:9).

Samson is indeed an agent of God's deliverance (and is thus a judge; cf. 13:5; 15:20; 16:31) even though he is often passively unaware and unworthy of this function. Instead of being used by God unwittingly, it is far better to be actively engaged in God's work. Ideally, God's people should not only know their calling and identity, they should also live in accordance with them (see 1 Cor. 6:20; 7:23). This is precisely what James talks about when he writes,

> Anyone who listens to the word but does not do what it says is like someone who looks at his face in a mirror and, after looking at himself, goes away and immediately forgets what he looks like. But whoever looks intently into the perfect law that gives freedom, and continues in it—not forgetting what they have heard, but doing it—they will be blessed in what they do. (James 1:23–25)

In this story Samson does appear as one who "goes away and immediately forgets what he looks like" (James 1:24). This is evident in his slavish obedience to his sensual instincts, his determination to marry an "uncircumcised" Philistine, and his apathy toward contracting and spreading ritual impurity. All of these actions reveal his selfish lifestyle, which contradicts his divine calling and God-given identity. This kind of spiritual apathy is a matter of life and death for God's people (cf. Prov. 16:25). Again, James explains that "faith without deeds is dead" (James 2:26; cf. Matt. 7:21–23).

Samson would have done well to look "intently into the perfect law" and to do it (James 1:25) rather than be enslaved by his carnal senses. Contemporary culture may also encourage people to trust their feelings and to follow their "hearts" (i.e., "If it feels good, do it"), but that is pagan wisdom and not

God's wisdom. Instead of following one's heart, it is far better to *lead* one's heart (Prov. 23:19). Since feelings and emotions can often mislead a person, they must be subordinated to God through the human will that is informed by Scripture.[20]

Another point emphasized in this passage is that the secret of Samson's extraordinary feats is not in himself. It is not his long hair, Nazirite status, muscular physique (which is never described in the text!), military prowess, or clever sayings that make him effective. The narrator makes it absolutely clear that—when God deems it necessary—the Spirit of the Lord rushes upon him[21] to deal a blow against the Philistines. Since God may graciously empower his agents to accomplish his purposes, his agents cannot claim any credit for themselves.[22] Thanks must always go to God since "every good and perfect gift is from above" (James 1:17). The secret of Samson's strength (and the Christian's strength) is always the Spirit of God.

Illustrating the Text

Being used by God does not equal being right with God; it is best when both go together.

Human Experience: Invite your listeners to think about jobs they have worked. In many cases, they have had to work over, under, or alongside people they found repugnant. In the end, they may have been able to accomplish something with or through such people. However, that is very different from establishing rapport with them, liking them, or inviting them into the inner circles of one's life. In other words, we have all learned to work with people with whom we would never want to be friends. If we allow our relationship with God to function this way, it is possible that we may become very useful to him or even be used by him mightily; however, what will matter in the end is whether or not we had been reconciled to him by Christ's blood, or whether we have been only a useful enemy to him. Matthew 25:31–46 is a biblical point of reference for this concept. It clearly teaches that there will be some who were used mightily *by* God but never experienced reconciliation *to* God through a saving faith in Jesus Christ.

It is dangerous to follow your heart unless it is being shaped by Scripture.

Quote: E. E. Cummings. Modern literature and entertainment are full of the notion that if only we trust our hearts, all will come out right. Author Cummings is frequently quoted as saying, "Trust your heart if the seas catch fire, live by love though the stars walk backward." The problem, biblically, is that sin makes the human heart deceitful and unreliable. Cummings does not seem to take into consideration the fact that, unless the heart is being reformed and shaped by the Spirit of God through exposure to holy Scripture, it is not inherently reliable or prone toward God. It would be powerful to cite Jeremiah 17:9, followed by Ezekiel 11:19 (and/or Ezek. 36:26). Ask listeners to consider if their hearts are being reformed by God and, therefore, becoming increasingly reliable, or whether they are still highly carnal and deceitful through isolation from God and his Word.

Film: *Fireproof.* In this 2008 movie, Caleb Holt (played by Kirk Cameron) is struggling with whether his heart is really in his efforts to save his marriage. His friend Michael counsels, "Don't just follow your heart, man, because your heart can be deceived. But you gotta lead your heart."

Exceptional strength comes from the Spirit of God, not the flesh.

Science: There are documented incidents in which frail mothers are suddenly able to lift cars off pinned children after a crash. A scientific explanation for this cites the sudden burst of endorphins that can flood a person's body under extreme duress and alarm. In other words, we carry chemicals on board that theoretically can grant momentary superhuman powers far beyond our normal physical abilities. However, these phenomenal results are not reproducible in a laboratory—at least not to that extreme. It takes a moment of real crisis (and probably divine intervention). Isn't it possible that the Spirit of the God who designed us is also able to rush upon a person in such a way as to bring strength and endurance far beyond the norm? The Bible lists other examples besides Samson (e.g., Elijah running in front of Ahab's chariot all the way to Jezreel in 1 Kings 18:46). Point out that the Bible never even mentions Samson being of abnormal physical size or strength—that is merely assumed by modern readers. The only explanation given is the Spirit of God. Challenge your listeners to trust the Spirit of God as the source of exceptional strength.

Samson's Revenge

Big Idea
God can accomplish his plans in spite of opposition or vengeful and selfish behavior.

Key Themes
- God employs Samson's vengeful antics for God's own purposes.
- Samson's actions and attitudes are identical to those of the Philistines.
- The tribe of Judah is against God's deliverer and for Philistine oppression.
- Samson's extraordinary gifts are God given.
- God graciously grants Samson's demands.

Understanding the Text

The Text in Context

In the ring structure of the book, chapter 15 presents some contrasts with the Othniel material. First, Othniel could be described as a foreigner who is more Judahite than the tribe of Judah (1:12–15; 3:9, 11), whereas Samson could be described as an Israelite who is more Philistine than the Philistines (15:1, 10–11; cf. 14:1–3, 7, 10, 14; 16:1, 4, 30). Second, the tribe of Judah plays a very surprising role in 15:9–13 as it capitulates to the enemy and rejects God's deliverer. In contrast, the parallel account of Othniel depicts the same tribe ideally as conquering the enemy (1:11–15; 3:9–11). The generally positive portrayal of Judah in the early chapters of the book (with some possible subtle indictments; see 1:3, 6–7, 13, 19; 3:9, 11) has thus shifted to a decidedly negative portrayal in the later chapters (with the explicit indictment of 15:9–13). Judah's actions here show total disregard for the instructions concerning warfare in Deuteronomy 7:2, 5, 16–26; 20:1, 16–18.

In the structure of the Samson story itself, which exhibits an A-B-B'-A' pattern corresponding to the biblical chapter divisions, chapter 15 is parallel with chapter 14. Rhetorically and thematically, these two chapters share many similarities: (1) both begin with Samson speaking to a disagreeable father about a wife (14:1–3; 15:1–3); (2) both show Samson's mastery over wild animals (14:5–9; 15:4–6); (3) both mention the Philistine *hegemony* over Israel (*moshlim*; 14:4; 15:11); and (4) both show the Spirit rushing upon Samson immediately after an aggressor comes roaring/shouting *to meet him* (*liqra'to*; 14:5–6; 15:14).[1]

Historical and Cultural Background

It is helpful to keep in mind that the marriage customs described in 14:10–15:2 may be somewhat unique because the setting is Philistine rather than Israelite. This cultural distance is indicated by the narrator's remark that "Samson held a feast, *as was customary for young men*" (14:10). Indeed, Greek marriage customs provide a rich background for understanding how Samson's "wife" could be given to his best man (see 14:15, 20; 15:2). Yadin explains that "the marriage was never completed, since instead of proceeding to the unveiling, procession and consummation, Samson flew into a rage over the Philistines' perfidy and stormed back to his parents' home, leaving behind a woman who could be married to another."[2] In 15:1, when Samson returns with goat in hand (the cultural equivalent to a bouquet of roses!), he wishes "to complete the wedding ceremony by taking his intended bride to the bridal chamber (*thalamos*; literally 'chamber' or 'room') and consummating the marriage."[3]

Interpretive Insights

15:4 *three hundred foxes.* The species designated as *shu'al* is probably a fox (*Vulpes palaestinus*), rather than a jackal,[4] and it is elsewhere associated with desolation (cf. Song 2:15; Lam. 5:18; Ezek. 13:4). Since the text does not explain how Samson gathers and handles these wild animals, one can only deduce that it is by the Spirit of the Lord (cf. 13:25).[5]

15:5 *He burned.* The torching of the grain fields and olive orchards of the Philistines would be totally devastating to the economy, especially as it takes place during the summer dry season (see 15:1). Samson's vindictive actions express the opposite of what is taught in Exodus 22:6 and bring suffering to many innocent commoners. But it is also possible that Samson's (or even God's) agenda is to humiliate the Philistine deity Dagon, who is probably the god of grain (cf. 16:24).[6]

15:7 *I won't stop until I get my revenge.* Samson's statements in this story (cf. 15:3, 11) and at the end of his life (16:28) show that he is consumed with revenge. Yet the Lord uses this vice for his own providential purposes (cf. 14:4).

15:11 *the Philistines are rulers over us.* In their speech to Samson, it is revealed that the tribe of Judah is content with the political status quo (compare the opposite sentiment portrayed in 1:1–20). Moreover, they seek to maintain the oppressive situation by handing their (Danite-Israelite) deliverer over to the enemy (15:12–13). This is a selfish act of tribal preservation that runs

The Philistines[a]

Perhaps the most infamous of Israel's oppressors during the settlement period, the Philistines are prominently featured in the books of Joshua, Judges, and Samuel. In the book of Judges, Shamgar (3:31), Samson (13–16), and the tribe of Judah (1:18–19; 15:9–13) all have confrontations with the Philistines. The Philistines are also grouped among Israel's enemies in 3:3; 10:6, 7, 11. Their tenure in the land of Israel extends from the early twelfth century to the late seventh century BC. Their geographical base is the southern coastal plains, especially the "Pentapolis" cities of Gaza, Ashdod, Ashkelon, Gath, and Ekron (cf. Josh. 13:3; Judg. 3:3; 1 Sam. 6:4, 16, 18). Excavations at these sites (and others, such as Qasile and Timnah) have revealed many distinctive cultural features, such as raised hearths, pork consumption, incised bovine scapulae, bathtubs, and painted pottery decorated with fish, birds, and geometric patterns. The earliest pottery manufactured at Philistine sites (called Mycenaean IIIC:1b or "monochrome") bears close resemblance to Aegean styles. Most archaeologists today believe that the Philistines arrived in Canaan-Israel around 1175 BC. Their arrival was part of a wider phenomenon known as the Sea Peoples movement. This took place mostly during the time of Ramesses III and is documented in Egyptian texts and iconography (especially the Medinet Habu reliefs).

[a] See Ben-Shlomo, *Philistine Iconography*; Ehrlich, "Philistines"; Hitchcock and Maeir, "Yo-ho, Yo-ho, A *Seren's* Life for Me!"; Killebrew, *Biblical Peoples and Ethnicity*, 197–245; Oren, *Sea Peoples and Their World*; Stager, "Biblical Philistines"; Yasur-Landau, *Philistines and Aegean Migration*.

contrary to God's command that Judah should provide leadership for the nation of Israel (see 1:1–2; 20:18). It is therefore disappointing that the three thousand men of Judah do not step up and fight against the mere thousand men of Philistia (15:15–16).[7]

did to them what they did to me. Since Samson's childish statement reflects the same terminology and sentiments as that of the Philistines (see 15:10), this serves as another example of Samson's acculturation into Philistia.

15:15 *fresh jawbone of a donkey.* The incident at Jawbone Hill (= "Ramath Lehi"; 15:17) is reminiscent of Shamgar, who smote six hundred Philistines with an oxgoad (3:31), and it can be compared to other occasions where unconventional weapons are employed in the book of Judges (cf. 3:16; 4:21; 5:26; 9:53). That Samson's weapon is "fresh" may indicate that it is strong and not yet brittle. However, this weapon is also unclean because it is both part of a corpse and part of an animal that is ritually unclean (implied in Lev. 11:2–7; Deut. 14:4–8). Thus it appears that Samson is once again disregarding his Nazirite status (see Num. 6:6–12).

15:16 *I have made donkeys of them.* The NIV translation effectively communicates an implication of Samson's wordplay—he essentially declares that the Philistines are now his beasts of burden (a situation that will be ironically reversed in 16:21). The wordplay here is based on the different meanings of the Hebrew root *ḥmr*—"ass/donkey" and "heap."[8] This is accurately captured by the NJPS translation, which brilliantly preserves the original alliteration: "With the jaw of an ass, Mass upon mass!" The "ass-mass" is therefore a reference to the heap of Philistine corpses.

15:18 *this great victory.* In the wake of Samson's amazing feat, it is essential to understand that this victory is ultimately God's accomplishment. God is the Rescuer par excellence in the book of Judges,[9] and he can bring deliverance even through unworthy vessels. The self-centered manner in which Samson speaks to God in this prayer (and also in 16:28) reveals much about his spiritual deficiencies. Yet God still graciously works through him and grants his requests (15:19).

15:19 *God opened up the hollow place in Lehi.* Similar to God's provisions of water in the wilderness (Exod. 17:1–7; Num. 20:2–13), this incident is an undeserved gift of divine grace. In fact, this miracle of water eclipses the previous miracle of battle so that God emerges as the ultimate hero in the narrative.[10]

15:20 *Samson led Israel.* Samson's tenure as judge only lasts half of a generation (cf. 16:31). In fact, all the judgeships following Gideon are less than a generation (10:2, 3; 12:7, 9, 11, 14), and they all lack a notice about tranquility. This summary remark about Samson is also the only one that is qualified with "in the days of the Philistines," because the foreign oppression remains ongoing (cf. 13:1, 5; 14:4; 15:11). This raises some question about how Samson can legitimately be counted as a judge. While Samson neither effects total deliverance nor consciously acts on behalf of the tribes of Israel, he is certainly still acting as Yahweh's agent to bring some measure of justice (see the comments on Judg. 2:16).

Theological Insights

Chapter 15 continues the theological theme introduced in the previous chapter—that God was seeking an occasion against the Philistines (14:4). If Samson's enigmatic saying at the wedding provided the first occasion against the Philistines (see 14:19), then chapter 15 presents three more "occasions." First, the marriage of the Timnite to the best man leads to the destruction of Philistia's crops (14:20–15:5). Second, the brutal execution of the Timnite and her father leads to a "great blow" (15:8 ESV), presumably at Timnah. Third, the Philistine pressure on Judah leads to Samson's Spirit-empowered slaughter of a whole contingent of Philistines (15:9–17).

In each of these occasions, God is accomplishing his own plan, while the human players are completely self-absorbed. Samson's self-interests are revealed in his appetite for ever-increasing levels of retaliation (15:1–17). His vengeful attitude is actually identical to that of the Philistines (notice how Samson speaks the same way as the Philistines in 15:10–11). His boast in 15:16 demonstrates his arrogance. His selfishness is also revealed in the way that he manipulatively speaks to God: "You yourself have given by the hand of your servant . . . , and must I now die" (15:18; author's translation). Another player in this account that is disturbingly self-absorbed is the tribe of Judah, who appear to be content with the political status quo (15:11; cf. 1:18–19) and who cooperate with Philistia by handing over God's agent of deliverance (15:12–13; cf. 13:5).

Teaching the Text

This passage primarily reveals God and secondarily reveals the selfish condition of humanity. It is therefore not appropriate to emphasize Samson's courage or his prayer life as behavioral models for believers today. Also, Samson's cruel treatment of animals in 15:4–5 is a topic that may not be appropriate for younger children.

When teaching this passage, it is essential to stress two things about God. First, God may use unworthy human agents to accomplish his plans. Even though Samson's actions are often incongruent with God's will (as revealed elsewhere in Scripture), God is nevertheless directing the course of history to bring about his own ends (see 14:4). Since God is the first and the last (Isa. 41:4; 44:6; 48:12; Rev. 1:8, 17; 2:8; 21:6; 22:13) and humans make their own choices, God's ends should not be used to justify the human means. That is, people are still responsible for their own decisions and the consequences.

Second, God may give grace to unworthy human agents whenever and however he sees fit. Certainly God's empowerment of Samson by his Spirit (15:14) is a gift that Samson has not earned. But this grace theme is even more pronounced in God's timely answer to Samson's prayer. The prayer in 15:18 is more like a demand based on manipulation ("you yourself"), hubris ("by the hand of your servant"), and fear of death ("must I now die"). Nevertheless, God meets him in the "fox hole," so to speak, and graciously grants him water to preserve his life (15:19). God's response is unnecessary and undeserved from a human standpoint, but it is part of God's plan for Samson, for Israel, and for the Philistines.

A secondary theme in this chapter—which flows from the primary one—is the selfish human condition. Selfishness dominates Samson's verbal expressions of justice, strength, and prayer. For Samson, "justice" is met by escalating acts of revenge (15:3, 7, 11) rather than by appealing to the divine Judge. Samson's God-given power becomes the occasion for an arrogant boast (15:16) rather than for humility or thankfulness. Samson's desperate prayer (15:18) also reveals his narcissistic perspective. Such selfish preoccupations come naturally to people of all places and times. Believers, however, must be disciplined through the work of Christ and the power of the Spirit to give vengeance to God (Matt. 5:38–40, 44; Rom. 12:14, 17, 19; 1 Thess. 5:15; Heb. 10:30),[11] to give glory and thanksgiving to God (Ps. 118:1; 1 Cor. 15:57; 2 Cor. 2:14; 1 Thess. 5:18), and to converse with God continually in prayer (Matt. 6:9–13; Rom. 12:12; Eph. 6:18; 1 Thess. 5:17).[12]

Illustrating the Text

God's good ends do not excuse wicked human means.

Human Experience: If we abuse the idea of God's sovereignty, we could make any action seem godly. Play this out with your listeners briefly. Ask them if God will use a person being robbed to sanctify and deepen that person by the refining of his or her faith through struggle. Does that good end, then, make robbery morally acceptable? Of course not. Has God ever brought redemption and healing to a marriage after adultery, such that it ends up stronger than before? Of course. Does that then sanction adultery as a means of marriage building? Ridiculous! The fact that God makes good endings to horrible stories does not mean horrible stories ought to be proliferated. Therefore, in every human story (including Samson's and ours) there are two lessons to be learned: (1) the goodness, grace, and amazing sovereignty of God, and (2) the utter holiness of God and our constant calling to progress toward his standard by repentance and learning from our mistakes. This is true, even when he has used our mistake to bring deliverance.

God shows grace to whom he wishes, when he wishes.

Object Lesson: Bring something wonderful and desirable. (Food items are probably your best bet. If it has a wonderful smell, so much the better.) Reflect on what an elementary school teacher would likely say about the situation: "Did you bring enough to share with the rest of the class?" Then simply say, "No. I didn't. I only brought enough to share with one person. This gift is only for *one* of you. Now how does that make you feel?" The reactions will be mixed. Some will focus on hurt, others on hope (i.e., "maybe it's me . . ."). Ask them to think it over with you: Who brought the treat? Whose is it to give? Why do we feel entitled to be the one to receive it? The answer is that you brought it and may give it to whomever you like. The entitlement many will feel is a preexisting condition that has nothing to do with the treat or you. It is human nature to compare and want what others have. It is God's right, however, to distribute his gifts and grace however he sees fit without giving an account to us. Give the treat to a random person in the room (a visitor might be a nice extra touch). Explain that grace is *undeserved* favor. God gives it to whomever he pleases whenever he pleases.

We spoil God's favor when we use it to boast and bully; the cure is intentional selflessness.

Quote: **Saint Francis of Assisi.** An often-quoted prayer of selflessness is attributed to Saint Francis: "O Divine Master, grant that I may not so much seek to be consoled, as to console; to be understood, as to understand; to be loved, as to love. For it is in giving that we receive. It is in pardoning that we are pardoned, and it is in dying that we are born to Eternal Life."

Self-gratification drives much advertising today.

Advertising: Modern advertising is often meant to feed selfish desires. In 2011 restaurant chains Carl's Jr. and Hardee's developed an edgy media campaign around the slogan "That's just the way it is." One ad asserted, "We believe that life is short. So if it feels good, do it, and if it tastes good, eat it."[13]

Samson's End

Big Idea

God may graciously empower his people to accomplish his purposes even if they are foolish, apathetic, or vengeful.

Key Themes

- God answers and empowers Samson for God's own purposes.
- God is victorious over the Philistine god Dagon.
- God's power and presence are gifts, not givens.
- Samson is lustful and foolish in his dealings with Philistine women.
- Samson is apathetic about his Nazirite status.
- Samson is driven by selfishness and revenge.

Understanding the Text

The Text in Context

In the ring structure of the book of Judges, the Samson story is parallel with the Othniel story (1:11–15; 3:7–11). Othniel and Samson are similar in terms of their southern geographical settings, but they are dissimilar in terms of cultural settings. While Othniel is a foreigner who makes his home in Israel, Samson is an Israelite who makes his home in Philistia (16:1, 4, 30; cf. 14:1–3, 7, 10, 14; 15:1, 10–11).

In the structure of the Samson story itself, which exhibits an A-B-B′-A′ pattern, chapter 16 is parallel with chapter 13. Thematically, chapter 13 recounts Samson's beginning in Israel (13:2, 25), while chapter 16 recounts his end in Philistia (16:21–30). Rhetorically, these chapters share a number of parallels: (1) both mention the important theme of the razor not coming upon his head because he is a Nazirite of God from the womb (13:5; 16:17); (2) both employ the key verb *ḥll*, "to begin" (13:5, 25; 16:19, 22); (3) both refer to the source of Samson's strength—the Spirit begins to impel him in 13:25, and the Lord departs from and returns to him in 16:20, 28; and (4) both close with Samson located "between Zorah and Eshtaol" (13:25; 16:31).[1]

Chapter 16 contains the final episodes for the body of the book of Judges (3:7–16:31). The body mostly illustrates the three-part cycle of apostasy, foreign oppression, and deliverance (cf. 2:11–19), but here in the Samson story it appears that the cyclical pattern is finally exhausted.[2] The final element of the cycle (divine deliverance) is not fully realized; Samson is only the beginning of this process (13:5). But the Samson story also introduces some new motifs that serve to transition the reader into the epilogue (chaps. 17–21). These are (1) the theme of doing right in one's eyes (14:3, 7; 17:6; etc.); (2) the figure of eleven hundred shekels (16:5; 17:2); and (3) the theme of God's absence (16:20; cf. 2:18; 19:1–30).

Historical and Cultural Background

Dagon's temple in Gaza was apparently a large complex that incorporated two pillars that structurally supported an upper level where a large crowd could gather (cf. 16:25–26). This type of temple architecture, with "two central pillars," is not common in the Levant, but it is attested in the Aegean world (thirteenth–twelfth centuries BC) and in Philistine temples that are excavated at Tell Qasile (eleventh–tenth centuries BC) and Tell es-Safi/Gath (tenth century BC).[3]

Interpretive Insights

16:1 *Gaza*. Judges 16 both begins and ends at the Philistine city of Gaza (vv. 1–3, 21–30). The ancient site, identified as Tell Harube / Tell 'Azza, lies beneath the modern Palestinian city of Gaza.[4] It is strategically situated in southern Palestine near the Egyptian border and is approximately three miles from the Mediterranean Sea.

16:3 *Hebron*. Hebron (Tell er-Rumeideh) was located deep in the Judahite hill country, about forty miles east of Gaza. This distance seems excessive if Samson's only objective is to humiliate the Philistines. It is also possible that Samson is "embarrassing weak-kneed Judah for turning him over to the Philistines" (cf. 15:9–13).[5]

16:4–18 As the only woman named in the Samson account, Delilah plays a prominent role in the narrative both as the trap for Israel's last/worst judge and as a parallel to Aksah, who served the opposite function for the first/ideal judge (cf. 1:11–15). While the text does not identify her ethnicity, one may infer that Delilah is Philistine (or at least non-Israelite) based on her geographical location and her political affiliations.[6] The etymology of her (foreign?) name is uncertain, but because it sounds like the Hebrew word for "night" (*laylah*; cf. 16:2–3) it is possible that the narrator exploits the name Delilah as a pun contrasting day (the Sun-man, Samson) with night (Delilah).

16:4 *Valley of Sorek*. While the exact location of Delilah's home is unknown, she appears to be in Philistine territory (cf. 16:5, 18). The Sorek Valley (Wadi es-Sarar) is Samson's primary passageway from Dan to Philistia. The term "Sorek" denotes "choice (grape) vine," and the valley includes the area of Timnah's "vineyards" (14:5). This familiar location may be associated with the motif of Samson's propensity to flirt with forbidden things (cf. Num. 6:3–4; Judg. 13:14).

16:5 *eleven hundred shekels.* Eleven hundred shekels of silver is a generous reward (equal to about 27.5 lb. / 12.6 kg), and when the figure is multiplied times five (the number of the Philistine lords), the amount is overwhelmingly large (139.4 lb. / 63.2 kg), possibly "equivalent to 550 years' wages."[7] This is an offer that Delilah cannot refuse (see 16:18).

16:19 *she called for someone.* The identity and role of this "someone" are obscure. While he could be Delilah's servant, a barber, or a Philistine warrior, it seems more likely that he is Samson, as suggested by Jack Sasson. That is, Delilah calls to the man (i.e., Samson) to ensure that he is really asleep before she wields the razor.[8]

shave off the seven braids of his hair. The Israelites and Canaanites were generally known to be hairy people, whereas the Philistines were apparently clean shaven. The shaving of Samson may therefore be a symbolic act whereby Israelite identity is removed and Philistine identity is imposed.[9] At the same time, the act of shaving marks a ritual transition from holy to common status (cf. Num. 6:5; Judg. 16:17).[10] That Samson would so easily capitulate to Delilah and thereby risk losing his sign of ethnic and sacred identity tragically reveals his moral delinquency.

16:20 *the LORD had left him.* The source of Samson's strength has always been God: "his strength left him" (16:19) only because the Lord has left him. This means that Samson's hair is not magical (although the Philistines probably perceive it as such; cf. 16:5), and it suggests that Samson is not an unusually large or muscular man (if he were, then the Philistines would not wonder what made him so strong; cf. 16:5).[11] Thus Samson's foolish error is not that he has disclosed the secret of his strength per se. Instead, he foolishly presumes (or perhaps gambles with the hypothesis) that he is invincible because God's power always seems to be present regardless of his apathetic behavior. He probably thinks that shaving will have no consequence since he frequently compromises his Nazirite status (see the sidebar "Nazirite of God" in the unit on Judg. 13:1–25). While he fully expects to break free from the Philistines as he did previous times, God seems to view his presumption as a test that has crossed a line.

16:21 *eyes . . . shackles . . . grinding.* The Philistines' treatment of Samson as a prisoner of war is typical of ancient Near Eastern practices.[12] Grinding grain was often the work of slaves, women, and animals.[13] Prisoners were often humiliated through physical mutilation (cf. 1:6–7) and, in some cases, blindness.[14] From a literary standpoint, there is some poetic justice in Samson's blindness, since his eyes are frequently fixed on forbidden objects (cf. 14:1–3, 7–9; 16:1).

16:22 *the hair on his head began to grow again.* By this statement, the narrator indicates that the tables are about to turn. The remark means not that Samson magically regains access to power but that he is transitioning back to his holy Nazirite status and to his function as a divinely empowered judge-deliverer.

16:23 *Dagon.* The grain deity Dagon, also spelled Dagan, had numerous temples in Philistine cities like Gaza, Ashdod, and possibly Beth Shan (cf. 1 Sam. 5:1–2; 31:10; 1 Chron. 10:10), but the Philistines also worshiped other deities, according to biblical and epigraphic sources.[15] In this context it is appropriate to focus on Dagon because Samson specifically has burned the grain fields (15:4–5) and thereby "laid waste" Dagon's domain (16:24).

16:25 *to entertain us.* The words used here to characterize Samson's actions call for some explanation. The Philistines summon Samson "so that he may entertain for" them (16:25a; author's translation), and Samson apparently delivers when he acts "obscenely before them" (16:25b; author's translation). Then the crowd is said to be "looking at the spectacle of Samson" (16:27b; author's translation)—that is, Samson is the object of public ridicule/mockery. Since the form of the verb in verse 25b (*tshq* in Piel) is used euphemistically elsewhere in the Old Testament (cf. Gen. 19:14; 21:9; 26:8; 39:14, 17; Exod. 32:6), it seems likely that, when the Philistines bring out Samson for their own amusement, Samson responds with obscene gestures or with behavior that would normally be considered distasteful. Since a euphemism is intended to conceal,[16] it is difficult to pinpoint a specific gesture or behavior. However, that the nature of Samson's action is insulting, offensive, or obscene to the Philistines is implied by the term used in verse 25b.

16:29 *pillars.* On the construction of the temple, see "Historical and Cultural Background" above.

Theological Insights

Chapter 16 is composed of two stories (vv. 1–3 and vv. 4–31) that must be interpreted in light of the narrator's statement in 14:4. These two stories therefore constitute "occasions" five and six wherein God's plans are accomplished against the Philistines. Samson is apparently unaware of his divine function while he initiates contacts with the Philistines. His visit with the prostitute results in the humiliation and exposure of Gaza by Samson displacing the doors of the city (16:1–3). His love for Delilah (16:4) leads to the compromise of his God-given status (16:17), the temporary loss of divine power (16:19–20), and the loss of his eyes and freedom (16:21). But in God's plan, Samson's shenanigans result in a perfectly orchestrated scenario in which three thousand Philistines are slain, along with Samson, in the temple of Dagon (16:30). Thus God's deliverance of Israel from the Philistines is certainly begun through Samson (see 13:5).

It is also important to observe that God is the one who supplies Samson's strength. Samson's long hair is not at all magical like Rapunzel. Samson temporarily becomes weak because God is exasperated with him (see 16:19–20). Samson does not lose his power because of Delilah's wiles or some kind of magical manipulation, although this is likely how the Philistines view it (see 16:5). His loss of strength is essentially the withdrawal of God's Spirit/presence, which is a reversal of the pattern described in 2:18 (the Lord was "with the judge").[17] This motif of God's absence brings closure to the series of cycles and sets the stage for the epilogue.

In the end Samson utters a desperate prayer for strength (16:28) that is motivated by a selfish desire for revenge rather than remorse, and God acquiesces because it is part of his providential plan for Samson, Israel, and Philistia. God graciously grants Samson's requests for both life (15:18) and death (16:30). Perhaps Samson's desire to die "with the Philistines" (16:30) connotes that Samson is still more comfortable in Philistia than in Israel. From a literary perspective, it seems fitting that Samson dies among the people with whom he lives.[18]

Teaching the Text

Lessons and sermons on this story should be based on the emphases of the narrator rather than on the meager faith of Samson (Heb. 11:32) or the alleged analogies to Christ (see the sidebar). Likewise, it is inappropriate to focus on Samson's strength, prowess, or courage. When teaching this story it must always be emphasized that God is the main actor and the only real hero. All of the Samson stories in chapters 13–16 are framed by God's agenda (13:5; 14:4) and God's empowerment (13:25; 14:6, 19; 15:14). Thus, God's brief withdrawal from Samson (16:20–22) and the entrance of Dagon into the story (16:23–24) set up readers for the climax of God's return to Samson and the reversal of Philistine fortunes (16:28–30).

All of Samson's vices seem to come together in this account. He is lustful (16:1, 4), apathetic (16:17), and foolish (16:20), and right up to the very end he is selfish (16:28) and vengeful (16:28). Amazingly, God uses all these flaws to accomplish his own purposes. However, God's employment of Samson does not count as an endorsement of his lifestyle, nor does it absolve Samson from the terrible consequences of his poor choices (see 16:20–21, 30).

Like his self-centered prayer at Lehi (15:18), Samson's final prayer is one in which he speaks to/at God rather than with God (16:28). Exum notes that "no dialogue ever takes place between Yhwh and Samson."[19] What is most ironic about this prayer is that Samson pleads for personal vengeance, which is probably contrary to God's will for him,[20] and that God grants the request apparently because it coincides with God's plan to begin to bring retribution against the Philistines (13:5; 14:4).[21] Therefore, Samson is said to have judged Israel (15:20; 16:31) because he has served—perhaps inadvertently—as an agent of God's justice (see Heb. 11:33).

As the body of the book of Judges (3:7–16:31) draws to a close, it is evident that Israel's apathy and apostasy continue to increase, the human agents of deliverance are increasingly selfish and ignorant, and God's presence and blessings are increasingly withheld from his people. It is also difficult at this point to distinguish between the practices of Israel and their neighbors. The spiral of spirituality continues to twist downward, and the cyclical pattern of 2:11–19 is broken down. While the central core

Samson as Type?

Is Samson a saint or a sinner? Is he like Christ or like the antichrist? According to one ancient Christian commentary, Samson "signified" and "prefigured" Christ,[a] but according to one modern Christian commentary, "Samson and Christ are polar opposites in attitude and action."[b] Is it possible that both perspectives may be correct for different reasons? Although the New Testament never explicitly states that Samson is a type of Christ, there are certainly many striking similarities to consider in hindsight—especially the details of their miraculous births and sacrificial deaths. The differences, however, are no less striking. Samson's selfish, arrogant, and vengeful character traits are totally antithetical to the loving, humble, and forgiving character traits of Christ. Indeed, this is the nature of a type. Typology may imply both positive and negative compari-sons (cf. Rom. 5:12–21).[c] The important principle for hermeneutics is that a type is only authoritative if it derives from an inspired biblical text.[d] Therefore, from the vantage point of New Testament theology (along with sensitivity to early Christian traditions), one might tentatively infer that Jesus is both a type and antitype of Samson. But from the vantage point of the Old Testament book of Judges, one must stress primarily the faithfulness of Yahweh and secondarily the failures of Samson and Israel. That is, the human composer of Judges did not have christological typology in mind and did not intend for his readers to analyze the story in that manner. Therefore, when teaching or preaching from Judges, one must stand firmly on the inspired text by deriving lessons that are authoritatively based on the composer's communicative intention.

[a] Caesarius of Arles (sixth century AD); see Franke, *Joshua, Judges, Ruth, 1–2 Samuel*, 163.
[b] Younger, *Judges, Ruth*, 328.
[c] See Ashmon, "Sampson and Christ, Type and Antitype."
[d] See Walton, "Inspired Subjectivity," where he writes, "There may be value in types, symbols, role models, and fulfillments, but, being subjective methods, they do not carry the authority of God's Word unless they become incorporated in the inspired message of a biblical author" (57). See also Walton, Bailey, and Williford, "Bible-Based Curricula."

of the book ends here, the extended epilogue will provide an even darker denouement.

Illustrating the Text

God's power is great enough to use evil for good.

Sports: Judo is a Japanese form of wrestling that uses an opponent's own momentum, weight, aggression, and strength against him or her. In this longtime Olympic sport, practitioners spend time honing their ability to read their opponent and cause sudden shifts in balance or direction that will enable them to throw and pin their opponent. God does the same thing with evil. He is able to foreknow all of the enemy's plots and schemes and senses the moment at which Satan will overplay his hand. At those moments, God specializes in shifting the momentum and direction of history and human hearts to topple and cast out his opponent.

Bible: Psalm 2. This psalm is a great picture of human conspirators plotting against God and his anointed, only to be met by God's laughter over their defeat. Even when all the nations plot evil against God and his Messiah, he is able to bring victory and good out of the situation. This can also be illustrated in the Joseph saga from Genesis 50:20.

Samson is a carnal believer; God's power unfolds through him but never dwells in him.

Children's Book: A softer example of this might be the character Eeyore from A. A. Milne's classic children's books about Winnie the Pooh. Eeyore is very morose and deadpan, no matter what goes on around him. Good things happen around him, through him, and to him, but he always manages to put a cloud over it with a depressing statement of self-pity or pessimism that blunts the edge of the blessing. Be sure to concede that this is a very light-hearted illustration of a very deadly disorder. Samson shows us that if we are too caught up in the things of the flesh (either through excessive lust and materialism or through excessive fear and pessimism) we can be at ground zero of amazing blessing and still miss it all.

If God's people aren't holy, they will become a cautionary tale instead of a city on a hill.

Popular Sayings: You have probably heard it said, "Lead, follow, or get out of the way." You may also have heard it said, "If you are not part of the solution, you are part of the problem." When it comes to holiness, both are true statements. We can only try to lead by intrinsic holiness (a task at which we will ultimately fail, since only God is intrinsically holy) or follow in borrowed holiness (a good and workable plan, thanks to Christ). Similarly, if God's people are not part of the solution (reflecting God's holiness through the cross and sanctification), then we are part of the problem (a cautionary tale that demands severe discipline in order that God's honor and glory may be preserved). The only part that is not possible is to "get out of the way." God *will* reveal his holiness for his glory's sake. All humans will either be with him or be lost.

Micah's Shrine

Big Idea

When God's people disregard God's authority and instruction, they may become indistinguishable from those around them.

Key Themes

- The worship of Yahweh is syncretistic.
- The Levite is both ignorant and wayward.
- There needs to be a centralized place of worship.
- Yahweh is unique and must be worshiped on his own terms.

Understanding the Text

The Text in Context

This story is the beginning of the end for the book of Judges. The cyclical stories are now exhausted, and the extended literary conclusion (chaps. 17–21) begins here. The story of Micah's shrine is the first of two accounts portraying illegitimate cult places—the shrines of Micah (17:1–13) and the Danites (18:1–31). The corruption of the Levitical system, which is introduced in this chapter, is a theme that continues into chapters 18–19 and has repercussions in chapters 20–21.

In the ring structure of the book of Judges (see the introduction to Judges) chapters 17–18 display thematic parallels with the second part of the prologue (2:6–3:6). The theme of both sections relates to religious failures, but here the problem is internal (i.e., syncretism within the Israelite tribes), whereas in the prologue the religious challenges are more external. This story also relates to the last episode in the Gideon account (esp. 8:22–32), where Gideon forges idolatry by setting up an ephod (cf. 17:5; 18:14, 17, 18, 20).

Structure

One of the features of ring compositions is that they are often composed of smaller rings; that is, they may feature "rings inside a ring."[1] Chapter 17 offers an excellent example of this chiastic phenomenon, in which 17:6 serves as the literary pivot and stands alone as the interpretive lens for 17:1–13.

A Misunderstanding of Yahweh's blessing (17:1–2)
   B Illicit contents of "Micah's house" (17:3–4)
      C Priest inducted by Micah (17:5)
         D "In those days . . . " (17:6)
      C' Priest inducted by Micah (17:7–12a)
   B' Illicit contents of "Micah's house" (17:12b–c)
A' Misunderstanding of Yahweh's blessing (17:13)

Historical and Cultural Background

The geographical setting for this account is "the hill country of Ephraim" (17:1, 8; cf. 18:2, 13). While this region is also home to Deborah and Tola (4:5; 10:1) as well as the Levite who has a concubine (19:1, 18), it is most importantly the location of the house of God at Shiloh (18:31). One might therefore ask why there is a need for Micah's shrine in such close proximity to God's sanctuary. In fact, multiple cult spaces were known to have existed simultaneously at this time in ancient Israel,[2] but such practices are proscribed in Deuteronomy 12:1–14.

Monetary figures are mentioned repeatedly in this passage (17:2–4, 10). The eleven hundred shekels of silver that Micah steals and returns to his mother is quite a large sum (equal to about 27.5 lb. / 12.6 kg) and was likely the woman's dowry.[3] This sum is consecrated to the Lord, and the first two hundred shekels (5 lb. / 2.3 kg) are made into (or applied to) a cult image. The remainder of the silver is presumably used to manufacture or acquire additional cult items (ephod and teraphim) and to sustain the operating expenses of the shrine, including the salaries of the personnel—ten shekels (0.25 lb. / 0.1 kg) in the case of the Levite.

Interpretive Insights

17:1 *Micah.* This name is related to the names Mica, Micaiah, Michael, and Micayahu. The meaning of all these names pertains to the incomparability of Israel's God ("Who Is Like Yahweh/God?"). It is disturbingly ironic in this story that a man whose name denotes the uniqueness of Yahweh is portrayed as a thief and as one who establishes an idolatrous cult shrine. That is, Micah's religion, though focused on Yahweh, is indistinguishable from that of the Canaanites.

17:2 *eleven hundred shekels.* This number may be a rhetorical link to the preceding chapter, where Delilah is paid the same amount from each of the Philistine rulers (16:5). If so, the reader/hearer of Judges may deduce not that Delilah is the same person as Micah's mother but that Micah's evil even surpasses that of Delilah.[4]

Curses and Blessings

Curses and blessings are frequently attested in Hebrew inscriptions (e.g., Kuntillet 'Ajrud, Nimrud ivories, Khirbet el-Qom, Khirbet Beit Lei, Silwan tombs, Ketef Hinnom amulets, Arad ostraca, Lachish ostraca, etc.). They typically invoke the divine name and call upon deity to act for good or ill. A blessing often expresses a wish for the good things in life (land, longevity, progeny, protection, etc.), while a curse expresses a wish for the lack of such things. In 17:2 the fear generated by the mother's curse is likely Micah's motivation for returning the silver. After Micah's confession, his mother immediately counters her own curse with a blessing on her son.[a] Later, after Micah acquires the Levite, he ignorantly expects God's blessing to follow (17:13). Whether Micah will indeed receive blessing or curse is resolved in the following story (Judg. 18).

[a] See Faraone, Garnand, and López-Ruiz, "Micah's Mother (Judg. 17:1–4)."

17:3 *an image overlaid with silver.* Although the making of images is strictly forbidden in the Pentateuch,[5] the practice is nonetheless frequently attested in ancient Israel.[6] The terminology used in this passage to designate the image is actually a hendiadys (two words joined to express one idea; cf. NIV, NRSV, HCSB), which is used to describe the method of production. That is, the image is called a *pesel* because it is initially carved or sculptured (either from wood or stone), but it is further identified as a *massekah* because the *pesel* is then overlaid with molten metal (in this case, silver). A similar manufacturing process is illustrated by a small bronze bull from Canaanite Ashkelon that is overlaid with silver.[7]

17:5 *an ephod and some household gods.* Both of these were divinatory devices and were not objects of worship per se. That they were used for obtaining divine guidance is implicit in 18:5–6 and explicit in 1 Samuel 15:23; Ezekiel 21:21; and Zechariah 10:2. Divination of this sort was forbidden in ancient Israel (see Deut. 18:10, 14). On the ephod, see 8:27 and the sidebar "Ephod" in the unit on Judges 8:1–32.

17:6 *Israel had no king; everyone did as they saw fit.* This verse is the interpretive key for the conclusion of the book of Judges (chaps. 17–21). At first glance this refrain appears to be about the lack of a monarchal form of government, but kingship need not be defined merely in political terms. For Israel, kingship was about the rule of Yahweh regardless of the specific form of polity. Yahweh was to be Israel's king even during the rule of the judges. The phrase "do what is right in one's own eyes" should be understood with reference to Deuteronomy 12:1–14—and especially verse 8: "You are not to do as we do here today, each doing whatever is right in his own eyes" (author's translation). Instead, Israel was instructed to destroy the Canaanite worship places, to seek out the one place that Yahweh chooses, and to refrain from employing renegade shrines to Yahweh (like the one created by Micah!). What is depicted in the present story is Micah, his mother, and the Levite all doing what seems "right in their own eyes" instead of seeking out what is "right in the eyes of the Lord."[8] Note especially how the Levite has not found a place and is willing to go wherever his job leads him (17:8–9), regardless of God's instructions.

17:7 *A young Levite from Bethlehem . . . living within the clan of Judah.* That the Levite is a "young man" (*na'ar*) may indicate that he falls short of the prescribed age for priests (cf. Num. 4:3, 30; 8:24), or simply that he is unmarried.[9] It is surprising that his hometown is Bethlehem since that city is not listed among those ascribed to the Levites (Num. 35:1–8; Josh. 21). The phrase used here for sojourning may be an allusion to the allowance in Deuteronomy 18:6, which might imply that this Levite both comes from and goes to the wrong place.

17:10 *father and priest.* This word pair, which is repeated only in 18:19, seems to include all that is involved in the cultic domain—authority as well as expertise. The title "father" is also used for Elijah and Elisha (2 Kings 2:12; 6:21; 13:14) and may designate one who serves an advisory role by obtaining answers through divination (cf. Gen. 45:8; Isa. 22:21). This advisory function may be compared to Deborah's title, "mother" (5:7). It is ironic (or perhaps nonsensical) that a "young man" or a "son" would serve as a "father" to Micah (cf. 17:11).

Teraphim

Often translated "household gods/idols," the term *t^erapim* occurs in only eight passages of the Old Testament (Gen. 31; Judg. 17–18; 1 Sam. 15; 19; 2 Kings 23; Ezek. 21; Hosea 3; Zech. 10) and may be used as a singular or as a plural.[a] The etymology is uncertain since the term does not clearly occur in any of the cognate languages. The use of *t^erapim* is condemned in 1 Samuel 15:23; 2 Kings 23:24; and Zechariah 10:2, but they seem to be mentioned without any moral assessment in Genesis 31 and 1 Samuel 19. The physical form of teraphim appears to be anthropomorphic and variable in size (see Gen. 31; 1 Sam. 19). Although teraphim may be classified as *'elohim* (Gen. 31:30, 32; cf. Judg. 18:24), it is more appropriate to regard them not as divine images but as pertaining to the divine realm. That teraphim function as divinatory devices is clear from most of the biblical examples. While it is possible that the form of divination is necromancy in the context of an ancestor cult, it is impossible to prove such a theory with the present set of limited data. The idea of a connection with the ancestor cult may also be problematic because Micah's teraphim are perceived as useful to the marauding Danites (18:14–17), who obviously have different ancestors.

^a For further discussion, see Bray, *Sacred Dan*, 118–23; Cox and Ackerman, "Micah's Teraphim"; Giorgetti, "Nature of the Biblical Teraphim"; Lewis, "Teraphim," *DDD*, 844–50; van der Toorn, "Nature of the Biblical Teraphim."

Theological Insights

Based on 17:6, the purpose of this story is twofold. First, it is about kingship—"In those days Israel had no king." The story of Micah's shrine effectively depicts the lack of proper authority. It shows what worship looks like when *God's* kingship is not acknowledged. The problem is therefore defined as a spiritual issue (not a political one), and the solution must be defined in the same way.[10] Judges 17–21 is calling not for mere monarchy but for an authority structure that functions as a theocracy. Theocracy is maintained when God's authority is acknowledged and his instructions are followed—by the people as well as the religious and political leaders. This theocratic ideal is what later distinguishes David from Saul (1 Sam. 8–31) and leads David to centralize worship in Jerusalem (2 Sam. 6–7). It is the standard by which every king of Judah is evaluated.[11]

Second, this passage depicts religious syncretism (i.e., the assimilation of pagan religious practices). Here it is evident that "doing what is right in one's own eyes" is not so much about worshiping other gods but about worshiping God in the wrong way. Yahweh is the only deity present in this story,[12] and that is precisely the problem. The form of Yahweh worship that is depicted here looks no different from Canaanite forms of worship (note similarities to the syncretistic golden calf incidents in Exod. 32 and 1 Kings 12). Here is both aberrant provincial worship (instead of the centralization required by Deut. 12:1–14) and the breaking of numerous commandments from the Decalogue (e.g., the first, second, third, fifth, and eighth). God is worshiped here in the wrong ways and at the wrong places. God's uniqueness ("Who is like Yahweh?"), which is revealed in his instructions, must be the basis for his worship. The distinct identity and incomparable character of Yahweh is a prominent theme throughout the Old Testament.[13]

Teaching the Text

There is often a tendency, when teaching the Bible, to identify what appears to the reader as good in a story and to hold it up as a model for imitation. But such an approach often ignores the literary and theological cues that are provided in the text. Perhaps one could commend Micah's "confession" (17:2) or his mother's "consecration" (17:3), but to do so would create difficulties in the context and would run squarely against the theme statement of 17:6. There is nothing commendable here to apply, and that is partly the point. This story shows what happens when God's authority is ignored and when people and leaders do things their own way.

The mother, Micah, and the Levite all demonstrate ignorance and disregard for God's authority. Micah fails to make restitution and sacrifice for his theft (as required by Lev. 6:1–7). Micah and the Levite appear to be motivated by materialistic gain (Judg. 17:2, 10; 18:19–20). All three characters make and/or utilize illicit cult objects, and they act as though God's sanctuary at Shiloh does not exist. Worst of all, they do this with confidence—note especially how Micah is assured that God will bless him for his endeavors (17:13). The problem here is worshiping God without adherence to his revelation. It is God's revelation (or instructions) that sets him apart and makes him unique, and theocracy cannot be practiced without adhering to God's instructions.

In teaching this story it is most important to emphasize that God is unique and that his people should reflect that uniqueness in their lives. By knowing and practicing God's instructions, God's people will be set apart and will honor God's authority. The problem is that God's people may be ignorant of God's revelation and may therefore do what is "right in their own eyes" by integrating illicit things into their lives. The temptation is to live (or to worship) according to one's own terms rather than God's terms (cf. Prov. 16:2).

Of course, the use of modern forms of divination (like horoscopes and psychics) is an example of supplanting (or even supplementing) God's authority with illicit means of supernatural guidance. These practices should have no place among God's people. Other, perhaps more subtle, types of syncretism might include "muddy" thinking about the proper course of action in decision making. There is a temptation to give our primary attention to popular opinion polls instead of seeking the guidance of the Holy Spirit through Scripture and prayer.

Such syncretistic thinking runs directly against the first commandment—that God does not share his authority.[14] Acknowledging God's authority by constantly assimilating his revelation is the most effective antidote to syncretism for God's people. This is made possible by searching the Scriptures and looking to Jesus, who provides the perfect model of a unique, theocratic life.

A related lesson from this story may be derived from Micah's misplaced confidence. He expects God to bless him because he has hired a Levite (17:13). But Deuteronomy 27–28 clearly teaches that blessings are contingent on obedience to the covenant, while disobedience results in curses. The following account shows that Micah's expectations are both unfulfilled and ill-founded (18:24). Micah deserves a curse because he does things his own way. He seeks a blessing without even consulting God.

God's people should never presume that God will bless their syncretistic mess. Disobedience has inevitable consequences, and believers should not presume that their forgiven position in Christ makes them exempt from the consequences of sinful choices in this life.

Illustrating the Text

We cannot claim to be God's people and then completely ignore all of God's standards.

Military: When a soldier is caught doing something unseemly, it is often cause for strict discipline. This is even more pronounced when that behavior occurs while on duty or in uniform. There is a phrase for this that we often hear used in military movies and stories: "You are a disgrace to the uniform!" The notion is that the uniform conveys a certain dignity and honor that bespeak a long-standing tradition and ethic. When someone wearing the uniform breaks such codes, it is a hypocrisy that brings great disgrace. Something very similar occurs with those who impersonate an officer by wearing a uniform that gives the illusion of a rank they have not been granted. It is the same with God's people—if we are caught impersonating a believer or disgracing our uniform (the garment of Christ's own righteousness put on over our iniquity) by completely ignoring God's standards, harsh discipline is in order.

Once we know God's word, rolling the dice for a different answer is sinful.

Popular Culture: Discuss an example of a seemingly innocent form of sooth-saying in your culture. (Obviously, you should avoid any objects of occult worship or idolatry.) For example, you might bring in a Magic 8-Ball toy or a fortune cookie. Talk about how you can keep shaking the ball or opening another cookie if you do not like the answer you get. God is not that way! We cannot just keep rolling the dice with him, hoping that he will alter the truths he has clearly revealed in his Word. (You could order and distribute a batch of custom fortune cookies that all have the same scriptural message inside. Invite your listeners to open and compare answers before making the point above.)

Personal Stories: Share about a time in your childhood when you used a play-ful means of testing God's will. It might be pulling petals from a flower and saying, "He loves me, he loves me not . . ." to dream about love; saying "Eenie, meenie, minee, moe . . ." to pick an order on the swing set; or shooting bas-kets and saying, "If I get this one, I'll ask her to the dance." Often in those scenarios, when we do not get the result we desire, we say, "OK—best two out of three" and then try again. This is what we do with God all too often. We treat him as a cosmic vending machine, and when we put in our quarter and do not get the prize we wanted, we just keep adding quarters, hoping God will give us a better answer. But life is not child's play. If God has given us a clear answer, we ought not to keep rolling the dice.

Danite Migration

Big Idea

Judgment is inevitable when people reject God's presence and revelation and live for their own interests.

Key Themes

- Idolatry seems normal and right.
- God's orders are overridden by Dan's plans.
- God's favor is wrongly presumed.
- God's words are ignored or misappropriated.
- Levites follow rather than lead.
- God judges apostasy with exile.
- Worship must be centralized.

Understanding the Text

The Text in Context

This story is the second of two accounts portraying illegitimate cult places—the family shrine of Micah (17:1–13) and the tribal shrine of the Danites (18:1–31). Together chapters 17 and 18 compose the first part of the epilogue, and they relate how the root of Israel's apostasy is its religious leaders—the Levites. The whole epilogue (chaps. 17–21) shows God's involvement in Israel's activities as marginal at best. It appears that "Yhwh abandons Israel to its own devices."[1]

In the ring structure of the book of Judges, chapters 17–18 display thematic parallels with the second part of the prologue (2:6–3:6). Both of these passages are about religious failure (2:6–3:6 focuses on foreign religious idols, and chaps. 17–18 focus on domestic religious idols), and they emphasize the pattern of generational drift away from Yahweh (2:7, 10; 18:30). Chapters 17–18 also relate to the last episode in the Gideon narrative (8:22–32) as the Israelites forge idolatry by setting up an ephod (cf. 8:27; 17:5; 18:14–20).[2]

Historical and Cultural Background

The reference in 18:30 identifying the Levite as "son of Gershom, the son of Moses," indicates that these events likely have an early date in the period

Tel Dan

The Canaanite city of Laish, or Leshem (cf. Josh. 19:47), was renamed as Dan by the Danites (Josh. 19:47; Judg. 18:29). Thanks to the discovery of a bilingual inscription mentioning the "God who is in Dan," this biblical city is now certainly identified with Tell el-Qadi, located in Upper Galilee by the northern borders of modern Israel. The Tel Dan excavation is one of the longest ongoing archaeological projects in Israel, beginning in 1966 under the direction of Avraham Biran and presently continuing under the direction of David Ilan of the Nelson Glueck School of Biblical Archaeology at Hebrew Union College–Jewish Institute of Religion. The fiery destruction of Laish, mentioned in Judges 18:27, is likely corroborated by the "thin layer of burnt material and ash" that is associated with Stratum VII.[a] According to the excavator, Stratum VII probably represents the final urbanized inhabitants of Canaanite Laish, and the following level (Stratum VI) represents a new population having a distinct seminomadic material culture.[b] If this interpretation is correct, then the Danite migration and the conquest and settlement of Laish, described in Judges 18, took place at the beginning of the twelfth century BC, marking the transition from the Late Bronze to the Iron Age (ca. 1200 BC).

[a] Biran, *Biblical Dan*, 126.
[b] See ibid., 126–34.

of conquest and settlement. The setting may be identical with that of 1:34, where the Amorites are oppressing the Danites. These events also apparently precede those of the song of Deborah/Barak (which locates the Danites in the north; see 5:17) and the exploits of Samson (which is set during the Philistine oppression of Israel). These observations indicate that the Judges narrative is organized by themes and rhetoric rather than by strict historical sequence.

The reference in 18:30 to "the captivity of the land" probably refers to the Assyrian subjugation of the northern kingdom, which happened in the late eighth century BC.[3] This detail provides some clues about the composition date(s) for the book of Judges (see the introduction to Judges).

The place names in this passage are mostly familiar from previous accounts. For Zorah, Eshtaol, and Mahaneh Dan, see the unit on Judges 13:1–25. For the hill country of Ephraim, see the unit on Judges 17:1–13. Kiriath Jearim (18:12) is probably located at Tell Deir el-'Azhar in modern Abu Ghosh.[4] Laish (18:7, 14, 27, 29), meaning "Lion," is mentioned in numerous Bronze Age texts from Egypt and Syria, before it became Dan (see the sidebar).[5] Sidon is the well-known Phoenician port city (cf. 1:31; 3:3; 10:6, 12; 18:7, 28). Beth Rehob is an unidentified site north of Tel Dan (cf. Num. 13:21; Judg. 18:28; 2 Sam. 10:6). Shiloh (18:31; 21:12, 19–21), located halfway between Bethel and Shechem, is identified with Khirbet Seilun and was probably destroyed by the Philistines in the mid-eleventh century BC.[6]

Interpretive Insights

18:2 *to spy out the land.* Sending out spies for reconnaissance is a familiar motif from earlier conquest accounts (cf. Num. 13; Deut. 1; Josh. 2), but here the spies forsake their allotment to explore a region that is not theirs (Laish was included in Naphtali's allotment; cf. Josh. 19:32–39). Therefore, it may be helpful to view this story, along with chapter 1, as an "anti-conquest"[7] account. While chapter 1 recounts Israelites not conquering what they should, chapter 18 recounts Israelites conquering what they should not.

18:3 *recognized the voice.* Apparently the Levite from Bethlehem (17:7–9) speaks a southern Hebrew dialect that is immediately recognizable to the Danites. Israel's dialectical diversity is also noted in 12:6.

18:6 *Go in peace.* Probably by employing his divinatory devices (ephod and teraphim), the Levite gives a highly ambiguous answer to the spies. The NIV's "Your journey has the LORD's approval" is far too positive. A better translation is "Your journey is in front of the LORD" (cf. Prov. 5:21).[8] Not surprisingly, the Danites presumptuously take this as a favorable oracle (Judg. 18:10).

18:7 *at peace and secure.* This description may capture the confidence of the population "in what they assumed to be impregnable defenses. Living behind their great earthen ramparts the Canaanites must have believed that no enemy would be able to scale these and conquer Laish."[9] In addition to the security provided by the massive Bronze Age fortifications, Laish is also "very good" (18:9) and "lacks nothing" (18:10) since it is built on the most productive fresh water spring in the Near East and is situated on a main crossroads (Gen. 49:17). These factors may have fueled a complacent attitude, making Laish an easy target for the conquering Danites. The "carefree character of the city of Laish" may even be illustrated by a clay plaque depicting a dancer with his lute from the end of the Late Bronze Age (Stratum VII).[10] Ironically, Canaanites are here described as "quiet" or "at peace/rest," while the Israelites are the oppressors or "rest-disturbers" (a reversal of 3:11, 30; 5:31; 8:28).[11]

18:12 *Mahaneh Dan.* It is revealing to note the contrast between this reference to the camp of Dan and the previous one in 13:25. The Spirit of the Lord actively began to move Samson there, but in the present story the Spirit is conspicuously absent.[12]

18:14–20 For the cultic implements listed here, see the comments on Judges 17:3 and 17:5. For the ephod, see also 8:27 and the sidebar "Ephod" in the unit on Judges 8:1–32.

18:19 *father and priest.* See the comments on Judges 17:10.

18:28 *rebuilt the city.* The first urban building phase documented at Israelite Tel Dan is represented in Stratum V, which was extensively destroyed in the mid-eleventh century BC.[13]

18:30 *set up for themselves the idol.* Only future excavations in Area T can reveal the remains of the earliest Israelite shrine at Tel Dan. The first Danite high place was undoubtedly located below the exposed "sacred precinct" that dates to the tenth century BC (Jeroboam I).[14]

Jonathan son of Gershom. As with the use of Micah's name in chapter 17, this name—meaning "Yahweh Has Given"—is ironic. The Danites and this Levite have rejected the promised allotment that "Yahweh has given" to them (see Josh. 19:40–46). For Gershom, see Exodus 2:21–22, which employs some similar terms and phrases that are echoed here and in Judges 17:7–11.[15]

son of Moses. The reading "Moses" is supported by the Septuagint and is preferred over "Manasseh" because the former is shorter and the more theologically difficult reading.[16]

18:31 *house of God.* Shiloh was the first home of the tabernacle (see Josh. 18:1, 8, 10; 19:51; Judg. 21:19; 1 Sam. 1:3, 9, 24; 3:21; Ps. 78:60) and the first location where the Lord made his name dwell (Jer. 7:12; cf. Deut. 12:5, 11, 21). The excavations at Khirbet Seilun show "a high degree of probability that the Iron I sanctuary [Stratum V] was located on or near the summit,"[17] but severe erosion is evident in some areas of exposed bedrock.[18]

Theological Insights

The disturbing themes of disregarding God's authority and practicing syncretistic religion, which are illustrated in the previous story of Micah's shrine (17:1–13), continue into the present account. What previously characterizes a small extended family now applies to a large urban tribe. When it is read in the light of the Pentateuch and Joshua, the story of the Danite migration looks like the world upside down. The Danites reject God's gift (specified in Josh. 19:40–46) because of alleged insurmountable obstacles (Judg. 1:34; but cf. Deut. 7:1–2, 16–24), and they ruthlessly conquer a place that looks better. Indeed, such actions are a rejection of God's kingship and an attempt to do what seems right in a tribe's eyes.

Every Israelite in this passage is set in his own aberrant ways. Acting independently of the nation, the Danites are "seeking a place of their own" (18:1). In an anti-conquest operation, the five spies seek God's favor for "our journey" (18:5), and then they wrongly presume that God grants it (18:10). The Danites seem to know intuitively that stealing cult objects by force is "what to do" (18:14). The opportunistic Levite is "very pleased" (i.e., his *heart* is glad; 18:20) with his pagan promotion to something "better" (18:19). Then the thief Micah becomes irate about the theft of *his* gods that *he* made (18:24). And finally, the Danites set up "for themselves" the idol at their new high place where Moses's (not Aaron's!) descendants serve as priests (18:30).

The narrator provides a few necessary clues about God's relationship to the events in this story. First, the reference to "no king" (18:1) means that Israel is acting on its own apart from the rule of Yahweh (since kingship in Israel always includes the idea of theocracy). Second, the reference to "the captivity of the land" (18:30) is a reminder that God will eventually judge his people for their syncretistic, idolatrous cult practices (cf. 2 Kings 15:29; 17:7–23). Third, the reference to "the house of God" in Shiloh (Judg. 18:31) indicates that there is rampant apathy about the central place of God's presence (see Deut. 12:5–14).

Teaching the Text

Lesson plans and sermons based on this passage must be aligned with the theological trajectories that are set by the narrator. In this case, the narrator provides clear ideas at both the beginning and end of the passage. First, there is the refrain about "no king" in verse 1 and its implied second part about self-governance (cf. 17:6; 21:25). Second, there are two remarks in 18:30 that can serve as warnings for God's people today: (1) the identification of Jonathan as Moses's near descendant shows the potential power of sin; and (2) the mention of exile shows the inevitability of God's judgment. These issues are treated in order.

God's kingship. If people view God as their king, then they must view themselves as divine servants (cf. Exod. 23:25; Lev. 25:55; Matt. 6:10, 33; Rom. 6:22; 1 Cor. 7:22–23; 1 Pet. 2:16). Servants follow the king's interests, not their own. They follow the king's plans, not their own. Servants know and obey the king's law; they are not free to do as they see fit. Servants fear the words of the king; they do not misconstrue or misapply his words (cf. Judg. 18:6, 10). Servants do not presume that they have the king's favor when they are noncompliant to his law (cf. 18:5, 10). If God's authority is ignored, one may think the grass looks greener on the other side or that might makes right (like the Danites), one may become intoxicated with achieving success or reputation (like the Levite), or one may manufacture costly gods for oneself (like Micah). On the other hand, if God's authority is embraced, one can patiently trust God and experience true joy and contentment even in the midst of difficult circumstances (Prov. 16:32; Phil. 4:11–12; James 1:2).

Sin's potential. If the self is served first and God's authority is eschewed, then sin will spread quickly, even in the most respected families. Just as Micah's domestic shrine grows into a tribal cult, apostasy may start with an individual and spread to a larger group, such as a church, denomination, or even a whole society. Perhaps only two generations after Moses, Jonathan succumbs to sin's lure by pursuing a career over his calling (17:7–13; 18:19–20) and managing shrines that undermine Shiloh (17:10–12; 18:19–20, 27, 30–31). Sadly, Jonathan's "heart" (see 18:20 in ESV, KJV, NASB) becomes completely desensitized to God's will and presence, and it is led away by selfish desires (cf. Ps. 119:36). This is an example of the "psychology of idolatry," in which wrong somehow seems right.[19] Since this kind of slide into apostasy can happen so rapidly and aggressively (cf. Judg. 2:7, 10; 8:33–34), it is imperative that God's people are proactive in planning for the future and investing in the health of the next generation of Christ-followers by teaching and modeling God's word.

God's judgment. The remark about the captivity in 18:30 should serve as a wake-up call to God's people in all periods and places. Rebellion against God's authority may be sustained for a while, even with apparent success. However, God's judgment is inescapable. Disastrous consequences may or may not come during one's lifetime (18:30), but ultimate justice will certainly come after death (Heb. 9:27; Rev. 20:11–15). Providentially, the tribe of Dan (which actually means "Judge") serves as an agent of God's swift judgment on Micah (Judg. 18:17–26; cf. Gen. 49:16).[20] Meanwhile, the Danites despise God's presence at Shiloh (Judg. 18:31), moving their locus of worship to a distant place, and God passively allows them to pursue their own desires for an extended amount of time. This passivity is a compelling demonstration of God's patience (cf. 2 Pet. 3:9). Then, more than four centuries later, God responds by exiling Israel to foreign lands (Judg. 18:30), removing them even farther from his presence in Jerusalem. In the final judgment, God may also give people the desires of their hearts and send them away from himself forever. One way or another, apostasy leads to exile.

Illustrating the Text

There's only enough room for one King in this kingdom.

Popular Culture: Everyone is familiar with old Westerns in which shooters declare to one another, "This town ain't big enough for the both of us." The idea is that the two personalities and value systems represented in the showdown are incompatible and that the only resolution is for one or the other to be defeated decisively and "get out of Dodge." It is the same with the kingdom of God—there is room for only one ruler, and any high thing that exalts itself above the knowledge of God must be torn down decisively. This is true, even when it is the pride and willfulness of God's own people. (One option for illustrating the point would be to have a monologue drama in which a man or woman comes in dressed as an old Western gunfighter and attempts to have it out with God. He or she could yell at the ceiling and raise complaints against God in the struggle for control over a life decision or a desire and say things like, "There's not room in this decision for the both of us" or "C'mon—draw! What are you—yellow?!" At the end, you might have the Lord speak back: "You're right. There isn't room on the throne of your life for both of us. There is one King in this kingdom. Surrender.")

Although idolatry may make perfect sense at the time, it can breed insanity.
Quote: *Knowledge of the Holy,* by A. W. Tozer. "The idolater simply imagines things about God and acts as if they were true."[21] The capacity for us to become practical idolaters is immense. We end up worshiping a convenient but counterfeit god who arises from our own predilections and passions but who bears no resemblance to the Lord. Invite your listeners to consider how, in the end, that path leads to an inbred cycle of worship where we worship a god who comes from what we already are and leads us deeper into what we already are: poisoned by the insanity of sin.

God's silence often means he is offering a window for repentance before judgment.
Bible: 2 Peter 3:9. "The Lord is not slow in keeping his promise, as some understand slowness. Instead he is patient with you, not wanting anyone to perish, but everyone to come to repentance."

The Levite's Concubine

Big Idea

Chaos may ensue when people operate apart from God's authority and according to their own self-interests.

Key Themes

- Israelite autonomy eclipses God's kingship.
- Israelites are ironically acting like pagan Canaanites.
- Levites are corrupt, and they invert the torah.
- Murderous acts characterize Israelite life in both the village and the sanctuary.
- Women are exploited and sacrificed by depraved men.

Understanding the Text

The Text in Context

As the second part of the epilogue, chapters 19–21 compose the final movement of the Judges narrative. If the early chapters represent the moral apex of the book, then chapters 19–21 represent the nadir.[1] Judges begins with emphasis on God's presence, sovereignty, and covenant, but it ends with emphasis on God's absence (see 17:6; 18:1; 19:1; 21:25).

In the ring structure of the book of Judges (see the introduction to Judges), chapters 19–21 have thematic parallels with the first part of the prologue (1:1–2:5). These bookends form an inclusio for the whole narrative. The present pericope (chap. 19) shares a number of significant features with chapter 1:[2] (1) Both mention corporal dismemberment—one is a partial and just act against a Canaanite combatant; the other is a total and unjust act against an Israelite woman (1:6–7; 19:29; cf. 7:25). (2) Both mention Jerusalem—one shows an initial conquest; the other shows foreign control (1:7–8; 19:10–12). (3) Both mention married couples—one has names and exemplifies faithfulness; the other is anonymous and embodies apostasy (1:11–15; 19:1–30; cf. 3:9). (4) Both mention a woman transported by a donkey—one dismounts with her own voice heard; the other is only passively mounted with deafening silence (1:14–15; 19:28). (5) Both mention the failures of the tribe of

Benjamin—one by cohabitating with Jebusites, the other by gang rape in Gibeah (1:21; 19:22–26).

Structure

This chapter may contain another example of a "ring within a ring" (see the introduction to Judges). Based on the analyses of Fokkelman and Younger, this passage can be divided thematically into nine units that are arranged chiastically:[3]

A verses 1–2
  B verses 3–4
    C verses 5–7
      D verses 8–10a
        E verses 10b–14 (v. 12 as the pivot point)
      D' verses 15–22a
    C' verses 22b–26
  B' verses 27–28
A' verses 29–30

This structure is revealing because the pivotal text (v. 12) is the Levite's remark about the supposed distinction between the Israelites of Gibeah and the foreigners of Jerusalem. This remark proves to be ironic as the Israelite characters show their true Canaanite colors in the scandalous events at Gibeah. Also, the fact that Jerusalem remains Jebusite and unconquered underscores Israel's basic failures in this period before the time of David (cf. Deut. 12:5–14; 2 Sam. 5:6–9).

Historical and Cultural Background

This chapter begins in Judah, then moves to Benjamin, and ends in Ephraim. The well-known Judahite sites of Bethlehem (17:7–9; 19:1–2, 18) and Jerusalem/Jebus (1:7, 8, 21; 19:10–12) are located in the modern cities bearing the same names. In Jerusalem, meager remains from this period (Iron Age I) are represented in the City of David, Stratum 15.[4] The Benjamite sites of Gibeah (see also chap. 20 and the sidebar "Gibeah" in the unit on Judg. 20:1–48) and Ramah (4:5; 19:13) are located at Tell el-Fûl and er-Râm, respectively.[5] Ephraimite Shiloh (18:31; 21:12, 19, 21; see the comments on Judg. 18:31) is not explicitly named in this chapter but appears to be the Levite's residence (cf. 19:1, 18, 28–29).

Interpretive Insights

19:1 *Levite.* While Levites are conspicuously absent in chapters 1–16, they are notoriously present in chapters 17–20. Indeed, this nameless Levite may be the most despicable individual of the entire book, even more so than the opportunistic Jonathan from chapters 17–18![6] This Levite is apparently a man of status with multiple wives, a servant, and a number of pack asses. But he is also callously self-absorbed and is involved in raping, murdering, and dismembering his reclaimed concubine (19:25–29; 20:4–5).

concubine. Concubines were legal spouses but ranked lower than full-status wives. They typically did not bring dowries and could be divorced with relative ease. Their primary purpose was to provide sexual partnership and/or to produce offspring for the husband (cf. 8:31).[7]

19:2 *unfaithful.* Although the verb *znh,* traditionally rendered "to play the harlot" (cf. NASB, NKJV), seems to indicate that the concubine was "unfaithful" (ESV, HCSB, NIV), it is more likely that the term is employed metaphorically for walking out on her husband since "Israelite law did not allow for divorce by the wife."[8] This is probably why the versions of the Septuagint render this as "became angry with him" (cf. NET, NLT, NRSV) or "deserted him" (cf. NJPS).[9] Therefore, it seems likely that the Levite—not the concubine—is the one who has provoked the estrangement through some unstated offense, and that is why he "went to her to persuade her to return" (19:3).

19:18 *house of the LORD.* The Hebrew text states emphatically that the Levite is on his way to "the house of the LORD" (cf. ESV, HCSB, NIV, NJPS, NKJV), presumably at Shiloh,[10] but the Septuagint reads "my home/house" (cf. NASB, NET, NLT, NRSV). The Greek tradition might be preferred if one seeks harmonization with 19:29 ("his house/home") and/or if one posits an early scribal practice of abbreviating the divine name.[11] However, in the immediate context, the Levite may emphasize his special status and mission in order to procure some hospitable lodging for the night. Furthermore, there may be little, if any, distinction between his home and his place of employment in the hill country of Ephraim. It seems likely that the butchery of the human victim in "his house" (19:29 ESV, NASB) is actually performed in the Levitical quarters of the sanctuary.

19:22 *wicked men.* The nocturnal urbanites from Gibeah are characterized in the text as "sons of Belial" (KJV; cf. 20:13). The best translation of this phrase is "worthless fellows" (ESV, NASB).[12] They are "men without honor. The moral sense of the idiom is reflected by the kinds of people so characterized: murderers, rapists, false witnesses, corrupt priests, drunks, boors, ungrateful and selfish folk, rebels, and those who do not know Yahweh."[13]

19:25 *the man took his concubine and sent her outside to them.* The ambiguity here regarding which man seizes the concubine is for dramatic suspense. That the Levite master shoves his spouse out the door is confirmed by the heartless portrayal of the Levite only a few hours later when morning dawns (19:26–28).

19:28 *no answer.* Although the Greek version unnecessarily adds "for she was dead,"[14] the Hebrew text leaves her vital status ambiguous. If she was already dead on the doorstep, the Levite is at least an accessory to murder (see 19:25). If she was still alive when he "stepped out to continue on his way" (19:27), then she died either on the donkey's back or on the chopping block. Regardless of the timing, homicide has happened (note the narrator's remark in 20:4), and the sixth commandment has been violated.[15]

19:29 *sent them into all the areas of Israel.* The practice of sending a dismembered body as a dramatic call to assembly is attested in only one other biblical passage (1 Sam. 11:7) and in one letter from the Mari royal archives (eighteenth century BC).[16]

Theological Insights

This passage is about both God's absence and Israel's Canaanization.[17] Or, as Trible states, "What is not accounts for what is."[18] These two related issues form the double-sided coin that is described in the literary refrain. First, there is "no king" (19:1). Israel certainly lacks a God-fearing monarch who can help the people to uphold the torah. But more important, Israel lacks a basic understanding of their identity under the rule of the divine King. God's authority is not acknowledged in this story, and God does not intercede. Indeed, it appears that "God gave them over to a depraved mind" (Rom. 1:28; cf. Judg. 10:13–16).

Second, each person therefore lives by his own rules (see 17:6; 21:25; cf. 19:24), and disorder dominates the scene. Marriages are messed up (19:1–9).

Intertextuality[a]

Intertextuality is the name given to the phenomenon of one biblical passage alluding to another. It can create a sense of literary déjà vu. Also called innerbiblical interpretation, echo narrative technique, and polyacoustic reading, some describe it as the vertical axis of a text, such that a given text both influences later texts and is influenced by earlier texts. In Judges 19, the allusions point both forward and backward to different literary settings. Looking forward, 19:29–20:1 may relate to Saul's sending of dismembered oxen parts to all the Israelites (1 Sam. 11:7). Looking backward, 19:29a may recall the binding of Isaac (esp. Gen. 22:6, 10), and the scene of 19:15–26 is unmistakably reminiscent of Lot's debacle at Sodom (Gen. 19:1–22). The latter allusion is likely intended to cast Benjamite Gibeah as a new Sodom that is even worse than the first.

[a] See Block, "Echo Narrative Technique"; Fishbane, *Biblical Interpretation in Ancient Israel*; Hallo, "Ancient Near Eastern Texts," xxvi; Schnittjer, "Narrative Multiverse"; Tracy, "Why the Levite Lied."

Levites are disrespected and dishonored (19:15, 18, 22–24; contra Deut. 12:19; 14:27, 29; 26:12–13). Levites use their privileges for personal agendas (19:18, 25–29). Women are expendable, exploited, and exterminated (19:24–29). Israelites act worse than Canaanites (cf. 19:12) as they enjoy themselves (19:6, 9, 22; cf. 18:20), do what is good in their eyes (19:24), and excel in acts of homosexuality (19:22; proscribed in Lev. 18:22; 20:13),[19] violence (19:22–26), rape (19:25; proscribed in Deut. 22:23–29), adultery (19:25; proscribed in Exod. 20:14; Deut. 5:18; 22:22–29),[20] and murder (19:24–29; 20:4–5; proscribed in Exod. 20:13; Deut. 5:17). Ironically in the book of Judges, rape was previously associated with Canaanite practices (see Judg. 5:30), but here it is perpetrated by Israelites. It is no wonder that the eighth-century prophet Hosea views the infamous Gibeah events as the epitome of Israel's corruption (see Hosea 9:9; 10:9).

Teaching the Text

The R-rated story of the Levite's concubine is one of the most troubling of the so-called "texts of terror"[21] in the Bible. The shock and awe is even acknowledged by the Israelites when they exclaim: "Such a thing has never been seen or done, not since the day the Israelites came up out of Egypt" (19:30). This part of the book of Judges is intended to be the crescendo of Canaanization. Therefore, it is essential when teaching this text not to soften or sanitize it but to let the story do its work on its own terms.

This story is meant to disturb, to jar God's people, by showing them a world without God. Today the story should be used as an example to talk about the chaos that may result when people act instinctually and apart from God. The scene of Judges 19 is the place to which sin's trajectory leads. It is dark, cold, painful, and terrifying. It resembles hell itself: a place defined by divine absence and self-presence.[22] While this story is not developmentally appropriate for children, it can be very effective for awakening adults and sharpening their sensitivity toward sin.

Judges shows us that the cycle of sin is a habit that gets progressively worse. Habitual sin is not static. It spirals downward to exploitation, anonymity, abandonment, and death (cf. Prov. 16:25). One might be tempted to appeal to the Levite's implicit wealth, power, privileged status, or even his gender[23] as reasons for his repulsive behavior, but these are not necessarily problems. The problem for the Levite, the old man, and the wicked urbanites is that they all do what is right in their own eyes, as though they are kings and Yahweh is not (19:1). Their gods are themselves, along with hospitality, honor, and carousing, such that they confuse bad with good (see 19:6, 9, 22, 24).[24] They do what they want to do, and God lets them and leaves them.

But this story may do more than teach about human depravity. It may subtly call God's people to action. A secondary lesson that can be taught from this story is the need for rescue/deliverance. The book of Judges has presented God as the gracious Rescuer of his vulnerable people (e.g., 2:18; 6:36–37; 7:7; 10:12–14; 15:18; cf. 2 Tim. 3:11; 4:17–18; 2 Pet. 2:7–9), and his people can sometimes also function in a similar capacity (e.g., Judg. 2:16; 3:9, 15, 31; 10:1; 13:5). Since Judges 19 displays the polar opposite of rescue (on both the human and divine levels), one might suggest that the story makes an implicit call to restore this ideal way of life. God's people should be characterized by selfless acts of rescue since they are beneficiaries of the same (see Eph. 5:1–2; cf. Prov. 24:11; James 5:19–20; Jude 23).[25]

In contrast to Judges 19, the stories of Hannah and Ruth (which immediately follow in the Hebrew and Greek canons, respectively) offer positive models of rescue/deliverance on both human and divine levels.[26] Also in contrast to Judges 19, Jesus offers the perfect model of selfless rescue (e.g., Luke 19:10; Titus 3:4–6), and this applies especially to the context of marriage (Eph. 5:22–33).

Illustrating the Text

When the church looks more like the world than the world does, severe discipline is imminent.

Bible: 1 Corinthians 5. Take your listeners through a brief read and sketch of 1 Corinthians 5:1–6 to give a good scriptural example of the way loving church discipline is needed in response to extreme, willful sin. If you like, you can mention a more contemporary example, but be sure your words are edifying and appropriate.

Sin takes you further than you wanted to go and costs more than you wanted to spend.

Testimony: Tap into the resource of recovered addicts in your congregation or circle of friends. Many churches are connected with a twelve-step group or have constituents who have been delivered from addictive patterns with substances and relationships. Invite such a person—or group of persons—to share (to an appropriate level) about the ways in which sin does, indeed, take a person further than he or she wanted to go and cost that person more than he or she intended to pay.

Object Lesson: Take some time to talk about fishing. Consider bringing in a variety of lures, hand-tied flies, and baits, or possibly have someone in your congregation who fishes come up and help with this part. Explain to your listeners that the bait is meant to imitate a good food source that the fish is created to desire. However, the hook is hidden inside the bait so that, after it is set and implanted in the fish's jaw, the angler can take the fish much farther than it wanted to go and impose a cost much greater than the fish intended to pay. It may even lose its life, depending on whether or not the angler is practicing catch-and-release. In the same way, sin is designed to mimic a good thing God created us to want, but once we take hold of it, Satan sets the hidden hook deeply and drags us deeper than we intended. Only God can cut the line and set us free.

Wicked men use their strength to exploit and dominate; godly men use it to rescue and protect.

Quote: Ed Morsey. "As men increasingly wander from God, they increasingly dishonor women."[27]

Human Experience: Invite your listeners to think about godly men who have been important and edifying presences in their lives. (Admit that some will have to think hard to come up with one, depending on their experience, and say it is OK if they cannot.) Tell them to think back about how those men used their God-given strength. Did they tear down, terrorize, bully, and degrade with it? Did they build up idols and tear down people? The answer will be no, of course. The godly men in their memories will be those who used their strength to tear down idols and build up people. Judges 19 is full of awful male role models. However, many men we know have been good examples who have made us safe and secure through love, protection, shepherding, and caring discipline.

"It's my life" and "It's good to be king" are characteristics of Canaanization.

Lyrics: In the Bon Jovi rock anthem "It's My Life" (2000), singer Jon Bon Jovi extols the virtues of doing things one's own way and talks about the need for independence and self-determination. A similar example is found in Tom Petty's song "It's Good to Be King" (1994).

Israel versus Benjamin

Big Idea

When God's people become like the world around them, God may bring justice by delivering his people from themselves.

Key Themes

- Israel unites under the leadership of the lying Levite.
- Israel's corporate Canaanization is galvanized.
- Canaanized Israel is put under the ban.
- God judges Israel by helping them to destroy themselves.
- Israel consults God only after decisive actions.
- The ark of the covenant is abused, and sacred space is confused.

Understanding the Text

The Text in Context

Chapter 20 is embedded in the second part of the epilogue of the book (chaps. 19–21), and its focus is on Israel's civil war. Whereas the first chapter of Judges stressed Israel's foreign wars and the ban against Canaanites, chapters 19–21 stress Israel's ban against itself. In chapter 1 God fought on Israel's behalf, but here God fights against Israel because they are thoroughly Canaanized. Interestingly, this large-scale slaughter of Israelites was already foreshadowed in the centrally positioned Gideon narrative (see "Literary Structure" in the introduction to Judges and table 1 there), where Gideon slaughters Israelites on a smaller scale (8:1–21).[1]

The specific rhetorical connections between chapters 1–2 and 20 include the following: (1) emphasis on Judah's leadership (1:1–2; 20:18), (2) employment of the key verb "to go up" (1:1–4, 16, 22; 2:1; 20:3, 18, 23, 26, 28, 30–31; cf. 21:5, 8), (3) inquiring of the Lord (1:1; 20:18, 23, 27; cf. 18:5), (4) application of the ban (1:17; 20:48; cf. 21:11), (5) emphasis on all Israel (1:1–2:5; 20:1–21:25), and the mention of (6) Bethel (1:22–26; 20:18, 26, 31; cf. 21:2, 19) and (7) weeping and sacrifice (2:4–5; 20:23, 26; cf. 21:2, 4).

Gibeah

Although the Hebrew term just means "hill," Gibeah is also the name of a site in central Benjamin (Josh. 18:28; Judg. 19:12–20:43).[a] It is most likely identified with Tell el-Fûl (Arabic for "mound of beans"), which is located about three miles north of Jerusalem in the modern West Bank. Excavations by W. F. Albright (1920s–30s) and P. W. Lapp (1960s) have revealed meager remains from Iron Age I–II. The first two periods of occupation (Iron IA and Iron IC) at Tell el-Fûl are interpreted in relation to the events in Judges and 1 Samuel, respectively. According to the biblical record the city was torched by the Israelites (Judg. 20:40, 48; ca. 1150 BC) and later became the capital of Saul (1 Sam. 10:26; 11:4; 13:15; 14:16; 15:34; 22:6; 23:19; Isa. 10:29; ca. 1025 BC). The atrocities of Gibeah related in Judges 19–20 are also recalled by the prophet Hosea in the eighth century BC (Hosea 9:9; 10:9; cf. 5:8).

[a] Arnold, *Gibeah*; Lapp, "Ful, Tell el-"; Rainey and Notley, *Sacred Bridge*, 142–43; Schniedewind, "Search for Gibeah."

Historical and Cultural Background

A variety of significant places are introduced in chapter 20. The merism "from Dan to Beersheba" (20:1) occurs here for the first time in the Bible and refers to the entire land of Israel (cf., e.g., 1 Sam. 3:20). Dan is the northern site discussed in chapter 18, and Beersheba is located about 160 miles to the south at Tell es-Seba'. The name Gilead (20:1) refers to the Israelite territory east of the Jordan (cf. 10:3–5, 8, 17–18; 11:1–11, 29, 40; 12:4–7). Mizpah is a cult center on the border of Benjamite and Ephraimite territories (20:1, 3; 21:1, 5, 8; cf. Josh. 18:26; 1 Sam. 7:16). Located at Tell en-Naṣbeh, this Mizpah is not to be equated with Jephthah's home in Gilead (cf. 11:34). Bethel is another cult center located on the border of Benjamite and Ephraimite territories (20:18, 26, 31; 21:2, 19; cf. Josh. 18:13, 22; Judg. 1:22–23; 4:5). If it is identified with Beitîn,[2] Bethel is about three and a half miles northeast of Mizpah. For the location and archaeology of Gibeah, see the sidebar. The sites Baal Tamar (20:33) and Gidom (20:45) are presently unidentified. The rock of Rimmon (20:45–47; 21:13; cf. 1 Sam. 14:2), or "pomegranate rock," can be identified with the el-Jai'a cave northeast of Gibeah (near Geba). The shape and features of this cave resemble a split pomegranate, and it is large enough to accommodate six hundred warriors.[3]

Interpretive Insights

20:1 *came together as one.* This convocation of (almost) all Israel is a first in the book of Judges. Ironically, the dismembered body of the concubine is the occasion for this gathering of the unified body of Israel, which is about to dismember itself (see 21:6). The phrase used here to describe Israel's unity ("as one man"; 20:1, 8, 11) is previously employed in 6:16 (cf. 1 Sam. 11:7), but here there is no judge (divine or human) at the helm, only the depraved Levite.

20:2 *four hundred thousand men.* This very large number (cf. 20:17) most likely refers to four hundred contingents of soldiers (see the comments on Judg. 5:8). It is the largest Israelite army ever assembled in Judges, and Israel's "determination and thoroughness" in this battle surpasses "anything seen in Israel's wars against the Canaanites elsewhere in Judges."[4] This is an inverted conquest scenario in which Israel stands in the place of Canaan and is therefore justly conquered by God.

20:5 *intending to kill me.* As the sole witness, the Levite dishonestly misleads Israel. He adds the fact that the men of Gibeah meant to murder him, and he omits the fact that he hand-delivered his concubine to the rabid rapists. In the Hebrew text, the Levite's self-centered perspective is emphasized: "they rose up against *me* and surrounded the house against *me* at night. *Me*, they intended to kill, but *my* concubine they raped, and she died" (author's translation).[5]

20:16 *left-handed . . . sling.* On ambidextrous Benjamites, see the comments on Judges 3:15. The sling is a lethal military weapon with long-range precision.[6] Sling stones have been recovered from numerous excavations in Israel, and slingers are depicted on Assyrian battle reliefs.

20:18 *Who of us is to go up first . . . ?* In contrast to 1:1, this question wrongly presumes that the Israelites should go up against their own people.[7] In contrast to 1:2, God offers them no assurance of victory. Also, Bethel appears to eclipse Shiloh as the primary shrine (cf. 18:31; 21:19), perhaps because it is logistically closer to Gibeah.

20:23 *Shall we go up again . . . ?* After Judah suffers massive casualties on day one, the tribes inquire again—this time with tears—for God's approval. But since they have already taken up battle positions for round two (see 20:22), it is evident that their inquiry is insincere and that they are obstinately pressing on against their "fellow Israelites."

20:26 *They fasted.* Since the outcome of round two is essentially the same as round one, the Israelites now resort to extreme measures (including weeping, fasting, offerings, the ark, and the Aaronic priest) to procure God's blessing. Although the rituals include burnt and fellowship offerings, Stone notes that the sin offering is "conspicuously lacking."[8]

20:27 *In those days the ark.* The phrase "in those days" (also in 20:28 [see ESV]) occurs elsewhere only in the well-known refrain (17:6; 18:1; 19:1; 21:25). This connection suggests that the priestly activity here involving the ark is the parade example of what "no king" is all about (see also 1 Sam. 3:1). This singular mention of the ark in Judges indicates that it is homeless, displaced from the sanctuary at Shiloh. Comparable to the battle context in 1 Samuel 4, here the Israelites may view the ark as a magical relic of last resort rather than as part of Yahweh's throne.[9]

20:28 *Phinehas.* Similar to the mention of Jonathan in 18:30, the reference to Phinehas as Aaron's grandson indicates that the setting of this story is during the first generation of the conquest. Phinehas is probably very old at this point (cf. Num. 25:6–11; 31:6; Josh. 22:13–34; 24:33; Ps. 106:30–31).

20:48 *including the animals and everything else.* The application of the ban (*herem*), including the total slaughter of Benjamite women, is implicit in this verse. For further reference on the ban, see the sidebar "The Ban" in the unit on Judges 21:1–25.

Theological Insights

God is now back in the story, but he is not Israel's friend. Instead of bringing justice through delivering Israel, God here brings justice through partially destroying Israel. In chapters 1–7 God raises up deliverers/judges, routs Israel's enemies, and releases his Spirit. In chapters 8–16 God continues to deliver Israel, albeit with intermittent exasperation and silence. In chapters 17–19 God is mostly passive and seemingly withdrawn. But here in chapters 20–21 God returns to mete out justice against Israel. Since Israel is thoroughly Canaanized, God is now Israel's enemy. As Israel's ultimate Judge, God here delivers Israel from itself. The key statement in this chapter is the narrator's remark: "The LORD defeated Benjamin before Israel" (20:35; cf. 21:15). Therefore, God gives the Israelites the victory that they want, but ironically, the defeated enemy is also Israelite. Israel wins its battle against the Benjamites only because Israel loses the war against the Canaanites.

On the surface, this story seems to present some amazing achievements: the Levite succeeds in uniting all but one of the tribes, the Israelites are seeking God, and the ban (*herem*) is finally applied. These developments may appear superficially commendable, but in their literary context they are totally wrong. The scenario in this chapter is that of a world upside down. In the tradition of the anti-judge Abimelek, the Levite appoints himself as Israel's leader (19:29–20:7; cf. chap. 9). He then selfishly misleads Israel to avenge a crime for which he is at least an accomplice (20:4–7; cf. 19:25–30). The determined people ignore God's revealed procedures for investigating capital crimes (20:8–13; cf. Num. 35:30; Deut. 13:12–18; 19:15–21) and for application of the ban (20:13, 48; cf. Deut. 7; 13:12–18; 20). They also ask God all the wrong oracular questions (20:18, 23, 27–28). Finally, they are confused about sacred space (20:1–3, 18, 26; cf. 18:31; 21:1–8, 19; see also Deut. 12), and they abuse the ark of the covenant (20:27). Nothing here is the way it is supposed to be. Indeed, everyone does as they see fit (17:6; 21:25).

Teaching the Text

This story does reveal God as Israel's enemy, but one must deal carefully with this challenging subject. It would be a profound mistake to blame God for Israel's loss or to characterize God's behavior as morally problematic.[10] Rather, God's actions in this story must be understood in light of both the declining spiral pattern in the book of Judges and the realization of the covenant curses in Deuteronomy 27–28.

The most important emphasis in this story relates to the fact that God is the ideal Judge who brings justice to his world. Justice must be defined on God's terms, not human terms (cf. Gen. 18:25; Judg. 11:27; 1 Pet. 2:23). God judges those who reject his authority and live for themselves. Such people are God's enemies, and their destruction is sure (see Judg. 5:31; cf. Ps. 145:20; Heb. 10:26–27).

Corporate Israel is God's enemy in this story because Israel is morally indistinguishable from Canaan. God therefore stands against Israel and partially destroys them (or at least helps them to do so) as a necessary act of judgment. While this story can be viewed against the backdrop of biblical accounts of divine judgment against pagan groups (e.g., Gen. 6–9; 19), it is more helpful to compare it with accounts of divine judgment against Israelite groups (e.g., Exod. 32; Num. 11; 16–17; 25; Josh. 7; 2 Sam. 24).[11] These are instances when God metes out justice in order to preserve the integrity of his covenant people (cf. 1 Cor. 11:29–32; Acts 5:1–11).

The problem in this story is that Israel's will and God's will are not aligned, although they do intersect. Both God and Israel want justice in this story, but Israel's understanding of justice is distorted and misguided (19:22–20:13), whereas God's justice is perfect. In this instance, God lets Israel execute justice as they see fit (20:28, 35), but Israel's actions providentially fulfill God's judgment against the whole nation (21:3, 15). The point is that God sometimes gives people what they want as a disciplinary measure (cf. 1 Sam. 8–16).

A secondary emphasis in this story relates to the human predicament. Since Israel's Canaanization is expressed here in terms of committing terrible atrocities in God's name, it is important to remind God's people that they are capable of the same kinds of sins. In fact, the "church" already has a record for acts of genocide in eras like the Crusades or the Holocaust, and acts of abuse and violence are just as widespread in the church today as they are in society.[12] It is a sobering reality that the church seems to have an unlimited capacity for sin. Thankfully, however, the church is not hopelessly destined for such corruption, because God's "divine power has given us everything we need for a godly life" (2 Pet. 1:3–4).

Israel's Canaanization is also expressed in the way that they relate to God. The Israelites prematurely decide on a course of action, and they act on it without considering what God has already said. Then they seek God's input only when it is already too late (20:8–28; cf. 21:3). Every Christian struggles with this problem to some extent. It is called selfishness or manipulation. Too often our prayers are about "my will" rather than "thy will" (Matt. 6:10, 33; 26:39, 42; Luke 22:42), and we desire God to approve, affirm, or somehow baptize our ideas and plans. We should never assume that God will bless us just because we have done all the steps that we think are right (cf. Judg. 20:26–27; see also 17:13; Ps. 51:16–19; Hosea 6:6). Instead of asking God the wrong questions and hearing only what we want to hear from God, the proper path for decision making comes through apprehending Scripture and praying without ceasing.[13]

Illustrating the Text

God giving you what you want isn't as good as you learning to want what God gives.

Lyrics: **"Unanswered Prayers," by Garth Brooks.** In this song, the speaker explains how sometimes God's best gifts are unanswered prayers. This thought occurs after the speaker has run into an old flame while with his wife and kids and has realized that, had God answered his many juvenile prayers for the former relationship's success, he would have missed out on something far better that he had not yet imagined. The same is true for all of us in many types of situations.

Unimaginable rebellion is within the church and within each of us.

Classic Radio: There was a series of 1930s pulp novels about a hero called *The Shadow* that eventually became a radio show. The show spots always began with the tagline "What evil lurks in the hearts of men? The Shadow knows." The Shadow was one of the first dark heroes, a force for good who fought amid the unseen and seedy elements of society. He knew about evil, and knew that it was not just hiding out there somewhere—it was in the hearts of men and women just like you and me. Unfortunately, many believers like to imagine that the evil is out there somewhere hiding in someone else's heart—someone monstrous. What we fail to recognize is that the same sin that makes another man or woman monstrous is in us too. The question is not whether it *can* make monsters of us all but rather whether it *will*. If the Spirit of Christ dwells in us, it will not; if we go it alone in our own strength, it very well may.

Justice must be defined on God's terms, not human terms.

Quote: *Opening the Bible*, by Thomas Merton. "It is of the very nature of the Bible to affront, perplex and astonish the human mind. Hence the reader who opens the Bible must be prepared for disorientation, confusion, incomprehension, perhaps outrage."[14]

Quote: *The Attributes of God,* by A. W. Pink. "Our readiness or our reluctancy to meditate upon the wrath of God becomes a sure test of our heart's true attitude toward Him."[15]

Wives for Benjamin

Big Idea

God may express his judgment by letting his people suffer the consequences of their own selfish decisions.

Key Themes

- Israelites make foolish oaths.
- Israelites illicitly apply the ban to a delinquent Israelite town.
- Israelites steal virgins for the surviving Benjamite soldiers.
- God withholds his pity and lets Israel harm itself.
- Israel's morals hit rock bottom as self-rule replaces God's rule.
- God graciously preserves the nation of Israel.

Understanding the Text

The Text in Context

This final chapter of Judges concludes the second part of the epilogue (19:1–21:25), which, in the ring structure of the book, is parallel with the first part of the prologue (1:1–2:5). The most salient themes that are common to both 1:1–2:5 and to 21:1–25 are (1) both passages show Israel at war—one is against outsiders (1:1–36; cf. 6:33–7:25) and the other is against insiders (21:8–12; cf. 8:1–21); (2) both passages show the application of the ban—one is torah compliant (1:17) and the other is torah corrupted (21:10–11; cf. 20:48); (3) both passages emphasize wives and marriage—one is idyllic (1:11–15), and the other is horrific (21:1–25; cf. 19:1–30).[1] Additionally, both passages emphasize the key verb "to go up" (1:1–4, 16, 22; 2:1; 21:5, 8; cf. 20:3, 18, 23, 26, 28, 30–31) and the involvement of all Israel (1:1–2:5; 20:1–21:25). They also both mention Bethel (1:22–26; 21:2, 19; cf. 20:18, 26, 31), along with weeping and sacrifice (2:4–5; 21:2, 4; cf. 20:23, 26).

Structure

Chapter 21 divides into three paragraphs (vv. 1–7, 8–15, and 16–24) before the book concludes with the final refrain in verse 25. Webb has insightfully pointed out that these three paragraphs are thematically connected to chapters 19–20 and that the whole unit is chiastic.[2]

A Violent abuse of concubine (19:1–30)
  B Slaughter of Israelites (20:1–48)
    C Problematic oaths (21:1–7)
  B′ Slaughter of Israelites (21:8–15)
A′ Violent abuse of virgins (21:16–24)[3]

The cluster of themes in this literary unit is reminiscent of the Jephthah story (11:29–12:7), which takes place at a different Mizpah and involves a problematic vow, the violent sacrifice of a dancing virgin daughter, and the gratuitous slaughter of Israelites.

Interpretive Insights

21:1 *oath*. The oaths in this passage are made at Mizpah in the national assembly that takes place before the battle against the Benjamites (see 20:1–2). Both the oath about marriage (21:1, 7, 18, 22) and the "solemn oath" about solidarity (21:5) are rash oaths. While oaths are legally binding (Num. 30:2), the torah also makes provisions for thoughtless oaths (see Lev. 5:4–6; cf. Matt. 5:33–37). Unfortunately the Israelites are totally ignorant of these provisions and engage in a "comical tragedy of legalism" whereby they subvert the spirit of the law and tenaciously enforce the letter of the law.[4]

21:8 *Jabesh Gilead*. This site is most likely located at Tell el-Maqlub in Jordan.[5] Since this Israelite city does not participate in the Mizpah assembly (20:1), the marriage oath/curse does not apply to them. Thus the Israelites decide to procure wives from this city and at the same time enforce the solemn oath of solidarity via a selective application of the ban. This is "a case of using one oath in order to circumvent another: legally justifiable, but morally dubious to say the least."[6] The new kinship bonds forged between Benjamin and Jabesh Gilead are important historical background for the later Saul narratives (1 Sam. 11:1–11; 31:11–13; 2 Sam. 2:4–5; 21:12; 1 Chron. 10:11–12).

21:10 *twelve thousand*. This large number, also in Numbers 31:5, most likely refers to twelve contingents (see the comments on Judg. 5:8).

21:11 *Kill every male and every woman*. See the sidebar.

21:12 *Shiloh in Canaan*. This curious remark may be a subtle rhetorical reminder that even though Israelites live in the land, the Canaanites and their influence are still ever present (cf. 1:36; 12:15). One may justifiably ask, did the Israelites not already "take possession of the land" (2:6; cf. Deut. 32:49; Josh. 18:1; 21:43)? This reference to Canaan brings the entire narrative full circle as the Canaanization theme from the prologue is recapitulated.[7]

The Ban[a]

Herem is the Hebrew word for the "ban" or "utter destruction." It entails the annihilation of everything, including livestock and noncombatants such as women and children. Although practiced by many of Israel's neighbors, the ban in ancient Israel is framed by a unique theology (see esp. Deut. 7 and 20). The basis for the ban is at least threefold: God's justice, God's holiness, and God's promises. That is, the ban brings God's righteous judgment on groups of guilty people (Gen. 15:16; Deut. 9:4–5), protects Israel from cultic contamination (Deut. 18:9–14), and fulfills God's covenant promises about the land (Gen. 15:18–21). In short, the ban is God's prerogative, not Israel's. As Israel's commander-in-chief, Yahweh decides if and when it is applied. Also, the application of the ban to the inhabitants of Canaan should be viewed as a unique event that is related to covenant promises about the land. Though it is necessary for the conquest of Canaan, it is not normative for universal application (Deut. 20:10–15). The ban is mentioned in only two strategic places in the book of Judges. In the opening chapter Judah and Simeon apply it properly to a Canaanite city (1:17), and in the final chapter collective Israel applies it improperly to an Israelite city (21:11). In the first case the ban is arguably commanded by God and may be deemed as an act of justice. In the second case the ban is commanded by Israel and may be deemed as an act of genocide that is symptomatic of having "no [divine] king" (21:25).

[a] See Younger, *Judges, Ruth*, 28–30, 69, 76–77, 81. For a survey of the literature and issues, see Barrios, "*Ḥērem* and Israel's Sacred Space and Status"; Copan, *Is God a Moral Monster?*, 158–97; Copan and Flannagan, *Did God Really Command Genocide?*; Cowles et al., *Show Them No Mercy*; Trimm, "Recent Research on Warfare"; Younger, "Some Recent Discussion on the *Ḥērem*."

21:15 *the* LORD *had made a gap.* By giving Israel victory against the Benjamites (20:28, 35) the Lord creates a "breach" (ESV, NASB, NJPS, NRSV) in the tribes of Israel. As an act of judgment against Canaanized Israel, God allows them to slaughter each other, although he does not command total annihilation (see 20:48). Instead of God relenting because of their groaning (see 2:18), his stern approach to Israel here is ironically contrasted with Israel's pity toward the Benjamites (see also 21:6). However, Israel's grief about the tragic outcome should not be confused with repentance. The Israelites actually blame God for the breach (21:3, 6, 16–17) rather than take personal responsibility.[8]

21:16 *elders of the assembly.* These leaders are more national than tribal in this context, and they make for a pathetic literary comparison to the elders who serve the Lord in 2:7. They are morally no different from the Levite and the old host in chapter 19. This is yet another example of the pattern of moral declivity in the overarching narrative.[9]

21:19 *festival of the* LORD. It is striking that a festival of Yahweh is mentioned only incidentally in the elders' speech. Apparently, the festival is not well known to the Israelites, or at least to the Benjamites, since the elders provide such detailed information about the location of Shiloh. Disturbingly, the location for "the house of God" (18:31) becomes the second scene for the violent acquisition of hundreds of young women. Instead of worshiping Yahweh at this festival, Israel does what is right in their own eyes.

21:21 *young women of Shiloh.* These "daughters of Shiloh" are most likely a professional class of dancers who regularly performed in religious ceremonies.[10]

21:22 *You will not be guilty of breaking your oath.* The elders exploit a perceived loophole in the law by abducting the daughters and thereby absolving the fathers and brothers from the curse (see 21:18). This "legally justifiable, but morally reprehensible"[11] argument is apparently effective, as the narrator reports no ensuing conflict with the victims' families.

21:24 *each to his own inheritance.* This same phrase occurs at the beginning of the book, where the Israelites go out "to take possession of the land" after Joshua dismisses them (2:6; cf. Josh. 24:28). Ironically, here is an apparent reversal of the conquest as the Israelites nonchalantly go home possessing their new wives but not possessing the promised land.

Theological Insights

Judges does not have a happy ending. Israel's present problem is the threat of Benjamite extinction due to genocide and rash oaths, and Israel's own solution is more genocide and the seizure of virgins for Benjamin. A godly solution, however, would look dramatically different. It would involve taking responsibility for actions and repenting from sin, rather than asking "how this awful thing happened" (20:3; cf. 21:6, 16–17). The narrator actually explains—no fewer than four times!—why this has happened: "In those days Israel had no king; everyone did as they saw fit" (21:25; cf. 17:6; 18:1; 19:1). Essentially, God is not recognized as King anymore in Israel. Israel reigns over itself, and God is on the outside. That is why the narrator also explains that "the LORD had made a gap in the tribes of Israel" (21:15). The Lord is acting as Israel's enemy (cf. 20:35). The Lord no longer has compassion/pity as he did in the cycles (see 2:18; 21:15). Israel's comprehensive Canaanization is expressed in legal casuistry as they apply the ban on their own terms (20:48; 21:10–11; contrast Deut. 7; 20), kidnap girls as needed (21:20–23; see Exod. 21:16; Deut. 24:7), and regard young women as rightful objects of spoil—no different from the depraved perspective of Sisera's mother (see 5:30).[12] Such repulsive attitudes and behavior characterize Israel in this dark age. And sadly, life goes on as usual as the Israelites "went home" apparently content with the outcome (21:23–24; cf. 9:55).

First, it is important to clarify that God does not cause the pain or chaos in this account. Rather, people do. God created people to make their own choices, and this account shows the consequences and results of selfish choices.

Second, the book of Judges concludes here with Israel's tribal identity threatened yet retained. This ultimately and ironically reveals God's grace because he providentially preserves his covenant people. Davis rightly remarks: "The Book of Judges ends with a miracle. . . . Yahweh's grace is far more tenacious than his people's depravity."[13]

Teaching the Text

More violence and victimization leave an audience breathless as the previous texts of terror coalesce in this final crescendo of Canaanization. In just the last three chapters, what started as a private family problem escalates to the public sphere as an urban gang rape and homicide, which leads to a national civil war, which turns into tribal genocide, which spawns more genocide and more violence against hundreds of women, and there the story ends.[14] Apostasy is unabated.

When teaching this depressing account, it is essential to let the text speak on its own terms rather than to impose some other—even if biblical—message upon it. The narrator demands that we read this story through the lens of his refrain, which is his final, resounding word (21:25). This means that he gives us a real-life depiction of the "Land of Do-As-You-Please," or perhaps the "Land of Topsy-Turvy."[15] The conquest looks illusory, Israelites look like Canaanites, and God looks distant. This is because God's authority is rejected.

In light of the clear literary refrains (17:6; 18:1; 19:1; 21:25) and in light of the declining pattern in the overall design of the book, it is imperative to remind audiences that Israel's actions here are indeed aberrant. God is not indifferent about genocide, rape, and abusive treatment of women.[16] God is also repulsed by torah twisting, blame shifting, loophole seeking, and foolish swearing. That is why God as the ultimate Judge often brings justice by allowing people to reap what they sow. That is also why God here makes a "gap in the tribes of Israel" (21:15).

The R-rated nature of the book of Judges is not because God is R rated; it is because people are R rated. Left to themselves, humans wander from God. They eschew God's teaching because they think they know better than he does. Then they grow numb toward sin and eventually self-destruct because of selfish choices. This cycle is not just the problem with ancient Israelites; it is the problem with twenty-first-century Christians and non-Christians alike.

The only way to break this cycle is to adhere to God's Word and turn from sin (contrast the attitude in 21:3, 6, 16–17). This is doing "what is right in the eyes of the LORD" (Deut. 12:25, 28; 21:9) instead of doing what is right in one's own eyes. When self-interests are surrendered and God's authority is acknowledged, the spiral pattern ceases and true living begins. Thus, the apostle John writes, "everyone who does *what is right* has been born of him" (1 John 2:29). Doing what is right in God's eyes comes by abiding in Christ as a regenerated child of God (see 1 John 2:28–3:10). Because of the cross, children of God do not "continue to sin, because God's seed remains in them; they cannot go on sinning, because they have been born of God" (1 John 3:9). Through faith in Jesus, the cycle of Canaanization ceases (1 John 5:4–5).

Illustrating the Text

The Bible is about real people drowning in real sin apart from a real God; only then do we fully appreciate the good news of the cross.

Popular Saying: Many will be familiar with the statment "I've got good news and bad news—which do you want first?" The most usual answer is, "bad news first, please." We say this because we like something good to cleanse the palate after disappointing or discouraging news. In the case of the gospel, God gives us the bad news first in order to facilitate repentance that leads to a proper absorption of the good news. Put another way, we tend to overlook the profundity of the gospel unless we first feel an acute pain and grief over the bad news of our sin and desperate state. Otherwise, we tend to preach the gospel as mere "life enhancement" and end up finding it only constricting and annoying. When God begins the story with bad news and conviction, the soil of our hearts is ready to accept the seed of the gospel gladly and bear good fruit.

Judges is rated R because people do R-rated things, not because God does.

Contrasting Concept: In movies and television, the ratings a show receives are a direct reflection of the imagination of the writers and producers against the backdrop of the intended audience's sensibilities. In the Bible, however, the gruesomeness in some passages is *not* a reflection of the author. To the contrary, it is a reflection of the actors' imagination and sin against the backdrop of the author's sensibilities about what is right and wrong. The Bible documents what happened and who did it and shows God's rating on each choice depicted in each scene. The narrative is meant to reveal the perfect divine story hiding behind the scenes of the gruesome human ones. In that sense, the Bible is honest and moral, even when its pages describe people and events that were not.

Stop doing what is right in your own eyes, and do what is right in the eyes of the Lord.

Applying the Text: This passage is a great time for a call to repentance. Invite your listeners to consider where in their lives they are playing judge and to turn from the trap of doing only what is right in their own eyes. Offer a means for them to commit to do things according to God's standard instead and to recommit their lives to that purpose. For example, offer listeners a chance to write down their sins and see them destroyed. Paper slips nailed to a cross, burned in a fire pot, shredded in a shredder, and so on, all have the effect of helping worshipers release sin and turn back to God.

How a society treats women reveals much about its health.

Society: There are many metrics and indicators by which a society can be judged. One that proves fruitful is the treatment of women. As biblical scholar Daniel Block says, "The manner in which men treat women today serves as a barometer of the spiritual climate of a nation, society, church, or family."[17] In Judges, the "escalating violence parallels the escalating deterioration of the status of women."[18] This link has also been supported by recent research, which has shown that the status of women can be linked to the level of violence and volatility in a society.[19]

Introduction to Ruth

The book of Ruth presents the inspiring journey of God's people from tragedy to triumph.[1] The story is a mirror opposite of Israel's depressing journey from triumph to tragedy that is presented in the book of Judges. While Judges is about breaking covenant and leaving torah, Ruth is about keeping covenant and living torah. While Judges emphasizes Canaanization and curse, Ruth emphasizes sanctification and blessing. While Judges documents acts of self-interest, Ruth documents acts of self-sacrifice. While Judges finally depicts the lack of kingship, Ruth finally depicts the line of kingship.

Indeed, the story of Ruth teaches powerfully by means of luminous contrasts with the dark period of the judges. This understanding of the book of Ruth may come naturally for Christians, who read Ruth as a sequel to Judges (see "Canonical Reflections," below), but it is also an emphasis that emerges from the opening chapter of the story itself. The very first verse sets the historical time frame ("In the days when the judges ruled") and braces the audience for bad news. Famine, flight, and a spate of deaths leave Naomi bereft and bitter. But then the light begins to shine brightly as God providentially provides fertility, people show kindness to one another, and God rewards his people with present and future blessings.

It is important and necessary that the book of Ruth offers an exception to the dark picture painted in the book of Judges. Given the general trend of Israel's faithlessness, one might justifiably wonder how a righteous king like David could emerge. The book of Ruth effectively answers this question by placing a spotlight on a faithful family in Bethlehem of Judah that will turn out to be David's genealogical and spiritual kin. Ruth's story confirms that

God providentially has preserved faithful families and that David emerges from such righteous stock despite the shadowy conditions of premonarchic Israel.[2]

Literary Features

The poetic qualities of biblical prose are now widely appreciated in biblical scholarship, and the composer of Ruth can be described as "one of the most brilliant masters of formal technique among biblical writers."[3] The composer's artistic sophistication is expressed through numerous wordplays (see the sidebar for examples of plays on names), creative representation of dialect and register,[4] concise economy of verbiage,[5] and a high proportion of dialogue (instead of narration) that propels the plotline. Accounting for more than half the story,[6] the conversations in Ruth make "every scene intimate" and represent "the highest ratio of dialogue to narrative in any of the biblical books."[7]

Names in the Book of Ruth[a]

Hebrew names were usually rich in meaning, and speakers of Semitic languages would intuitively understand this. The primary meaning of a name may be given by the parents at birth, but secondary permutations could arise as situations developed over time. For an Israelite storyteller, names were polyvalent and offered opportunities for creative wordplay—sometimes even by tweaking the vocalization—as the context allowed (e.g., Judg. 3:8, 10; 6:31–32), but this does not imply that the names were invented out of whole cloth for literary or ideological purposes.

The short story of Ruth is packed with names, and wordplays are "densely deployed"[b] throughout the narrative. For this reason, many scholars over the centuries have suggested that the names can play literary roles in the story.[c] It is ironic, for example, that there is famine in the "food house" (i.e., Bethlehem; 1:1; cf. 1:6), that "My God Is King" (i.e., Elimelek; 1:2) would live in the days when there is "no king" (cf. Judg. 17:6; 18:1; 19:1; 21:25), and that the "sweet" Naomi may be called "bitter" (1:20). It is also fitting that "sick" Mahlon and "weak" Kilion die (1:5), that Orpah ("back of the neck/head") turns away from Naomi (1:14–15), that Ruth (possibly related to "dew" or "irrigation") becomes a source of fertility (see 4:10–17), and that Boaz is a man of "strength" ('oz), just as the latter half of his name indicates (Bo'az; cf. 2:1).[d] The narrator appropriately applies anonymity to the kinsman who fails to "maintain the *name* of the dead" (4:5; cf. 4:1). And finally, resolution is achieved as the miracle child Obed ("servant" or "guardian") serves Naomi and becomes the grandfather of the "beloved" King David (4:17).

[a] For general reference on the literary use of names, see Cooley, "Etymology, Assyriology, Philology and the Hebrew Bible." On names in the book of Ruth, see Eskenazi and Frymer-Kensky, *Ruth*, lvii–lviii, 4–7, 24, 25, 28, 71, 92; Frymer-Kensky, *Reading the Women of the Bible*, 253–54; Garsiel, *Biblical Names*, 29, 250–53, 259–61, 282; Sasson, "Ruth."

[b] Sasson, "Ruth," 321.

[c] Against the assertion of Manor, "Ruth," 2:246.

[d] Note that an additional term for strength (*hayil*) is applied to Boaz in 2:1; 4:11b.

The narrative is also beautifully arranged in chiastic form. Although some may refer to this form as a "ring,"[8] it is more precise to describe the structure as a simple chiasm, especially since Ruth lacks explicit interconnections between the outer frame and the central core (a feature that is essential in longer ring compositions).[9] Ruth's structure unfolds in a six-part parallel pattern that lacks a clear central pivot (thus, A-B-C-C′-B′-A′):

A   Past family history (1:1–5)
   B   Naomi returns with Ruth (1:6–22)
      C   Ruth and Boaz in the fields (2:1–23)
      C′   Ruth and Boaz at the threshing floor (3:1–18)
   B′   Boaz redeems the land and marries Ruth (4:1–17)
A′   Future family history (4:18–22)

This analysis essentially represents the foundational work of Stephen Bertman in 1965, although many scholars have attempted to fine-tune some details since then.[10] The A // A′ sections (1:1–5; 4:18–22) function as an inclusive envelope for the story that provides the historical and genealogical context both before the story (stressing death) and after the story (stressing birth). The B // B′ sections (1:6–22; 4:1–17) share the narrator's remarks about God's provision (1:6; 4:13), and they also feature three-way dialogues (1:8–18; 4:1–12) and the speeches of the women to Naomi (1:19; 4:14–15, 17). The C // C′ sections (2:1–23; 3:1–18) employ the term *hayil* to describe the noble character of Boaz and Ruth, respectively (2:1 and 3:11),[11] and these sections also feature "series episodes"[12] so that the sequence of events in chapter 2 is repeated in chapter 3, as follows: Ruth/Naomi initiating plans (2:1–3; 3:1–5), Boaz favoring Ruth (2:4–17; 3:6–15), and Ruth deliberating with Naomi (2:18–23; 3:16–18).[13]

For the purposes of this commentary, the book of Ruth is divided into four teaching units (pericopae) that correspond to the modern chapter divisions in the English Bible.[14] The first pericope combines literary units A and B (Ruth 1:1–22). The second pericope corresponds to literary unit C (2:1–23). The third pericope corresponds to literary unit C′ (3:1–18). The final pericope combines literary units B′ and A′ (4:1–22).

Theological Contribution

Godly Character

The story of Ruth reveals God as one who cares for the needy, expects his people to care for the needs of others, and blesses those who reflect his character by doing so. God is concerned for foreigners, orphans, and widows,[15] and he provides for their needs—sometimes directly, as in 1:6;

4:13, and at other times indirectly through the actions of his caring people toward each other.[16] God also rewards people who act in caring ways as he does (see Ps. 18:25), and he often does so by means of prayers expressed for the benefit of others (e.g., Ruth 1:8–9; 2:12, 19–20; 3:10; 4:11–12). Because God's revealed character is established in Scripture as the basis for his people's character (see Lev. 11:44–45; 19:2; 20:26; cf. 1 Pet. 1:15–16), the human character qualities exhibited in biblical narrative must be viewed in light of God's (communicable) attributes. People can act redemptively and graciously because God graciously redeems his people (e.g., Exod. 6:6; 15:13; 20:2; Lev. 11:45; Deut. 5:6). People can act in love and loyalty toward one another because God acts in those ways toward them (see Deut. 10:18–19; cf. 1 John 3:16; 4:7–12).

Covenant Themes

The story of Ruth, which has been called "a microcosm of Genesis,"[17] engages various components of God's covenant program. In the final movement of the narrative, *land* is redeemed (4:3, 9), a *descendant* is born (4:12–13), and *blessings* are realized (4:14–22)—three themes that are basic to the Abrahamic covenant (see Gen. 12:1–3, 7; etc.). Through "intertextual play,"[18] Ruth's past history is portrayed as an echo of Abraham's (see 2:11; cf. Gen. 12:1), and her future history is likened to Rachel, Leah, and Tamar (4:11–12). The genealogy at the very end (4:18–22), employing the same terminology as Genesis ("these are the generations" ['elleh tol'dot]; ESV, NASB), also situates Ruth's story in covenant history as "an important faith link between Abraham and David" (cf. Matt. 1:1–6, 17).[19]

Over the years, scholars have debated whether the primary purpose of the book is to give instruction on kindness (*hesed*), providence, redemption, and gentile inclusion or to make an apology for King David.[20] But the truth is that all these themes are important to the book of Ruth, and they are all tied to God's covenant program. Through the covenant, God reveals his loyalty (*hesed*), works out his redemptive plan despite obstacles (providence), includes the nations (especially faithful foreigners),[21] and elects his leaders (such as David). Ultimately the trajectory of the story culminates in the person of Jesus Christ, who, as the ultimate revelation of God (cf. Matt. 1:1, 5, 16–17; Luke 24:27; Rom. 10:4), embodies the theology of the book of Ruth.

Canonical Reflections

The canonical position of the book of Ruth is varied in the textual traditions, and each unique placement may offer its own theological perspectives for interpretation (see table 1).[22]

Table 1: The Canonical Position of Ruth

Hebrew Canon	JPS	Song of Songs	Ruth	Lamentations
	BHS	Proverbs	Ruth	Song of Songs
Greek Canon		Judges	Ruth	1–2 Samuel

In the Hebrew canon Ruth is placed in the Writings (Ketuvim) and is grouped with the five festal scrolls (Megilloth). There is a talmudic tradition that places Ruth first in the Writings (i.e., before Psalms),[23] but modern Jewish Bibles (e.g., the JPS translation) have Ruth following Song of Songs because this corresponds with the sequence in the Jewish liturgical calendar (Song of Songs for Passover, Ruth for Weeks, Lamentations for Ninth of Ab, Ecclesiastes for Tabernacles, and Esther for Purim). Most Hebrew Bibles, like *Biblia Hebraica Stuttgartensia* (*BHS*), have Ruth as the first book of the Megilloth (ordered as Ruth, Song of Songs, Ecclesiastes, Lamentations, Esther) and have Ruth following the book of Proverbs.[24] This latter arrangement may capitalize on the phrase "woman of noble character," appearing only in Proverbs (12:4; 31:10) and in Ruth (3:11), and it suggests that Ruth can be read as a story about wisdom.

The Greek canon (LXX), placing Ruth between Judges and 1–2 Samuel, exhibits the canonical order that is most familiar to Christians today. The order in the Greek canon appears to be based on the historical setting in the days of the judges (see Ruth 1:1) and on chronological sequencing (i.e., the transition from judges to monarchy; see 4:22). Younger points out that this juxtaposition may also account for the thematic connections with the closing chapters of Judges, which serve as a striking contrast to Ruth (consider common themes such as Bethlehem of Judah, marriages, foreigners, sojourners, valiant fighters, etc.).[25] It is also possible that the book of Ruth "occupies the center and focal point of a second 'Pentateuch,'" composed of Joshua–Kings in the Greek canon.[26]

Methodology

As with the book of Judges, it is essential to maintain a theocentric focus and to avoid role modeling of human characters in applying the book of Ruth. This principle can be challenging when encountering such exceptional personalities as Ruth and Boaz, especially when their character is explicitly commended in the story (see 2:1 and 3:11). But the status of this book as Scripture (i.e., God's self-revelation) means that this story is not primarily about Ruth, Boaz, or even Naomi. The human protagonists are not to be viewed as heroes or heroines for emulation. Rather, they are merely the "bit players" in God's story.[27] The main focus is on what God is doing in and through these characters. If God is "the primary actor in the drama,"[28] then

Introduction to Ruth

his presence, actions, and plans must serve as the foundation for applying and teaching the text of Ruth.

An important first step for teaching the book of Ruth is to help people acquire a sense of the whole story before expounding the individual chapters. It may be beneficial, for example, to encourage people to read the book in its entirety—preferably in one sitting—before engaging in a closer, slower read. One might also present the whole story orally in as little as twenty minutes or over the course of one worship service by performing it dramatically with multiple roles or readers.[29]

Historical Setting and Composition

The book of Ruth is historical narrative, although some have attempted to identify the genre more restrictively as novella, short story, idyll, comedy, or folktale.[30] Whatever literary designation is preferred, the essential historicity of the story should be maintained, especially if the opening and closing verses are taken seriously. Many commentators have also noted the highly unlikely scenario of inventing such a scandalous story about King David's foreign lineage.[31] It is more probable that the story was composed in order to provide theological perspective on the real, but potentially problematic, family history of David, which would have been preserved through oral tradition.

The composer's identity is ultimately unknown, and a female is not out of the question.[32] Jewish tradition maintains the prophet Samuel as the composer (as it also does for the books of Judges and Samuel).[33] It is obvious from the opening verse (1:1), the parenthetical remark about a former custom (4:7), and the closing verses (4:17–22, mentioning David) that some distance existed between the historical setting of Ruth and the time(s) of its composition. Composition could have been as early as the reign of David (tenth century BC) or as late as the postexilic period (late sixth–fifth centuries BC). It is also possible that the story was composed even earlier but that the present form represents an updated and expanded version from as late as the postexilic period. Linguistic features are somewhat inconclusive as a basis for early or late compositional dating.[34]

The historical setting of the story is clearly indicated by the opening verse: "In the days when the judges ruled" (1:1). This period spans roughly from the death of Joshua to the coronation of King Saul, although the precise date of the exodus-conquest is a still a matter of some debate (see the introduction to Judges). The maximum span of time for the setting of Ruth is from the early fourteenth century to the late eleventh century BC. In archaeological terms this period extends from Late Bronze Age II (ca. 1400–1200 BC) to Iron Age I (ca. 1200–1000 BC). At the end of the Bronze Age, Canaan was overshadowed by the mighty Egyptian Nineteenth Dynasty, but the early Iron Age was characterized by Egyptian withdrawal and a power vacuum in which many people groups (including Moabites and Israelites) were vying for survival.

The historical setting might be pinpointed with higher precision if famines (1:1, 6) were not so common or if Moabite-Judahite geopolitics were better understood (1:1–7). Furthermore, the ten-name genealogy might offer some historical guidance if it does in fact preserve a comprehensive family record. That is, if Boaz's parents were Salmah/Salmon and Rahab (Ruth 4:20–21; 1 Chron. 2:11; Matt. 1:5; Luke 3:32), and if Rahab is the same person mentioned in Joshua 2, then the setting of Ruth could be one or two generations after Joshua. However, it is well known that ancient genealogical lists can be selective and schematic.[35] Therefore, one must be content with the very general time frame given in 1:1 and resist the temptation to locate the Ruth story more precisely in relation to the events recounted in the books of Joshua and Judges.[36]

Synopsis of Contents in the Book of Ruth

The Widows Return after a Bitter Past (1:1–22): After the bitterness of famine, relocation, and loss of her husband and sons, Naomi departs with her loyal daughters-in-law, sends Orpah back to Moab, and arrives in Bethlehem, where she experiences God's provision through the harvest and through Ruth's extraordinary acts of faithfulness.

Ruth's Initiative and the Character of Boaz (2:1–23): In order to survive and provide for Naomi, Ruth sets out to glean and providentially happens upon the field of Boaz, who magnanimously supplies her with food, protection, encouragement, and honor and who happens to be both a close relative and an instrument of God's kindness.

Naomi's Initiative and the Character of Ruth (3:1–18): In order to provide for Ruth, Naomi initiates a plan that Ruth secretively present herself to Boaz for the purpose of marriage; Ruth obeys but also advocates for redemption on Naomi's behalf, and Boaz acquiesces with blessing, integrity, propriety, generosity, and alacrity.

Redemption and Marriage for a Blessed Future (4:1–22): Through the charitable initiatives of Boaz, involving legal negotiations for land and for widows at the town gate, God answers prayers and gives Ruth and Boaz a son, who serves as the heir to Elimelek's estate, the provider for Naomi, and the grandfather of King David.

The Widows Return after a Bitter Past

Big Idea

God is present in his provision and care for his people, even when they experience suffering.

Key Themes

- The light of loyalty shines brightly during the dark age of the judges.
- God graciously provides for his people and cares for their needs.
- God is present with his suffering people even when his justice seems obscure.
- God's faithfulness can be expressed through the faithfulness of others.
- God cares for the vulnerable people of society.

Understanding the Text

The Text in Context

The first chapter of Ruth has two literary components that correspond in chiastic structure to the two literary components of chapter 4 (see the introduction to Ruth). The family history in 1:1–5 recounts past deaths, whereas the family history in 4:18–22 recounts future births, and both of these sections employ groups of ten (note the total number of proper nouns in each section).[1] The story of widows and childlessness in 1:6–22 parallels the story of marriage and descendants in 4:1–17, and both of these sections stress the Lord's gifts (1:6; 4:11–13), the husband's house (1:9; 4:11–12), bearing sons (1:12; 4:12–13, 15–17), name calling (1:20–21; 4:11, 14, 17), and speeches of the local women (1:19; 4:14–15, 17).

Historical and Cultural Background

"When the judges ruled" (1:1) is a temporal clause providing the historical setting of the story, which is obviously some distance from the time of composition. The setting is most likely during the Iron Age I (1200–1000

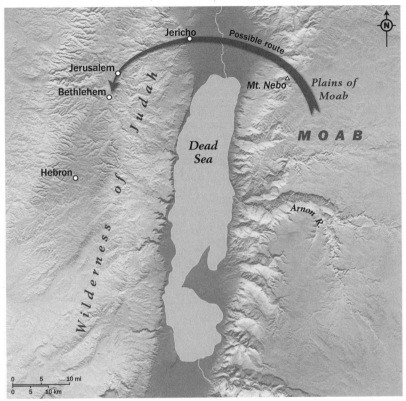

Ruth and Naomi leave Moab for Bethlehem.

BC), although an earlier date is possible (see the introductions to Judges and Ruth). The time of the judges is also called Israel's "settlement period" because it precedes the advent of centralization and monarchy. This transitional period was a kind of "dark age,"[2] when Israel spiraled downward in their cycles of sin-oppression-deliverance to the extent that they became indistinguishable from their surroundings (i.e., "Canaanization") and they incurred God's judgment.

The phrase "country of Moab" (1:1; cf. 1:2, 6) likely refers to the plains north of the Arnon River, a region previously allotted to the tribe of Reuben, in the Transjordan. Moabite territory extended some sixty miles on the east side of the Dead Sea from these plains in the north to the Zered River in the south. The Moabites and Ammonites were descendants of Lot (Gen. 19:30–38) and were banned from entering the assembly of Yahweh because of their hostile track record toward Israel (see Deut. 23:3–6; cf. Num. 21–24; Deut. 2:26–30). For more background information on Moab, see the sidebar "Moab" in the unit on Judges 3:12–30.

Interpretive Insights

1:1 *famine.* Flight to a foreign neighboring land due to famine was a relatively common phenomenon in the biblical world (cf. Gen. 12:10; 26:1; 41:57; 42:5; 47:4; etc.). But given the assumption that God provides rain/produce (see Deut. 28:1–14) and given the context of apostasy during the time of the judges, one might be justified to interpret this reference to famine as divine judgment. In fact, famine is specifically listed as an outcome for breaking covenant (see Deut. 11:13–17; 28:23–24, 48; 32:24).

Bethlehem in Judah. The name Bethlehem, meaning "(Store)house of Bread," ironically identifies a town lacking food. This Bethlehem, located about five miles south of Jerusalem, is distinguished from the northern Bethlehem (Beit Lahm) mentioned in Joshua 19:15 and Judges 12:8, 10.[3] Although archaeological finds are meager at Bethlehem due to modern occupation of the site, the name Bethlehem occurs in paleo-Hebrew on a recently excavated seal impression from Jerusalem dating to the late eighth or seventh century BC.[4] The phrase "Bethlehem of Judah" is found elsewhere only in Judges 17:7–9; 19:1–2, 18; and 1 Samuel 17:12, and this may partly explain the canonical placement of Ruth between Judges and Samuel as preserved in the Septuagint (see the introduction to Ruth). While the Judges epilogue associates Bethlehem with unfaithfulness and "no king," the story of Ruth contrastively associates Bethlehem with faithfulness and the birth of King David. First Samuel 16–17 then picks up where the book of Ruth leaves off by commencing the story of David's rise.

1:2 *Ephrathites.* The term "Ephrath" (and its various forms) is an early name for Bethlehem (Gen. 35:16, 19; 48:7) that could refer to "a geographical district or a clan ancestor."[5] In Ruth the term may also connote a higher socio-economic status or reputation within Bethlehem (1:2; 4:11; cf. 1 Sam. 17:12; Ps. 132:6; Mic. 5:2), which is implicit in the town's humming and women's buzzing (1:19) and in Naomi's lament about her former fullness (1:20–21).[6]

1:7 *the road that would take them back.* The route from the plains of Moab to Bethlehem probably included the so-called Jerusalem–Jericho road. The entire trip of seventy to one hundred miles could have taken them as long as a week by foot.[7] Their "return" (a key word in this chapter)[8] is technically Naomi's, but it may anticipate Ruth's "new destiny" (cf. 1:19, 22).[9]

1:8 *mother's home.* While the more common phrase "father's house" was associated with legal protection for women, the "mother's house" was associated with marriage matters (cf. Gen. 24:28; Song 3:4; 8:2).[10] By turning back, Orpah and Ruth may still have an opportunity to "find rest in the home of another husband" (1:9). Based on typical marriage traditions in the ancient Near East, Manor estimates that, at this point in the story, "Naomi is likely in her mid-forties and Ruth and Orpah in their mid-to-upper twenties."[11]

1:13 *the LORD's hand.* The imagery of God's hand can be positive or negative in the Bible. In some contexts, it signifies blessing, guidance, or protection (cf. Ezra 7:6, 9, 28; 8:18, 22, 31; Neh. 2:8, 18; Acts 11:21). In other contexts, and here in Naomi's mouth, it signifies curse, discipline, or judgment (cf. Exod. 9:3; Deut. 2:15; Judg. 2:15; 1 Sam. 5:9; 12:15; Acts 13:11).

1:15 *her people and her gods.* Orpah's "people" are clearly Moabites (1:4), but her "gods" are undefined. While Chemosh was ostensibly the national deity of Moab (see the comments on Judg. 11:24), he was presumably "beyond the reach" of common people, who would likely relate to the lesser deities of the pantheon.[12] Since women often retained allegiances to their native deities even after marrying into a foreign family (cf. Gen. 31:19; 1 Kings 11:8; 16:31), Orpah's return to her people and gods is all that Naomi can expect. From a literary perspective, however, Orpah's presence in the narrative may serve as a foil to Ruth so that the former is merely a good daughter-in-law (cf. 1:8) while the latter is a great daughter-in-law.[13]

1:16 *your God my God.* Ruth's extraordinary speech to Naomi rings with biblical "cadences of covenant and contract."[14] Her expression of commitment is primarily to Naomi (cf. 2:11); it is not necessarily a confession of mono-theistic theology.[15] When she previously married Mahlon, she married the people and the God of Mahlon. Here she solemnly commits, at a minimum, to continuing the same "package deal"[16] by assuming the role of Naomi's daughter even though she is not obligated to do so. Given Ruth's foreign background, her remarkable loyalty shines brightly during the dark age of the judges, when the trend was toward syncretism and self-interest. The account of her faithful actions (like those of the foreigners Caleb, Rahab, Othniel, and Jael) could be viewed as an indictment against ethnic Israel, who was better equipped to act faithfully.[17] Ruth's response to Naomi in verses 16–17 is foundational to the rest of the narrative and serves as her first recorded act of faithfulness through which God shows his own faithfulness to his people.

1:17 *if even death separates.* The NIV and NRSV nicely capture the con-textual sense of Ruth's oath: "if even death separates," rather than the more common rendering "anything but death" (cf. ESV, HCSB, NASB, NJPS, NKJV, NLT).[18] Addressing the typical concerns of childless widows, Ruth commits to care for Naomi in her old age, death, and burial, and perhaps even beyond the grave, since Ruth would be buried in the same plot. By invoking the Lord's curse, Ruth effectively ends the deliberations and silences Naomi (1:18). Im-plicit in Ruth's commitment is her selfless choice to risk jeopardizing her own future as she would likely be alone in her own old age, death, and burial.[19]

1:20 *the Almighty.* Naomi's title for Yahweh in verses 20–21 is "Shaddai." Although it is often translated "Almighty," the term probably identifies God as lord of the mountain/steppe.[20] The divine title occurs prominently in the books of Genesis and Job, and it is also associated with the Transjordanian Balaam traditions in Numbers 24:4, 16 and the Deir 'Alla Plaster Texts.[21] Perhaps Naomi's word choice represents the dialect of Moab.[22]

1:22 *barley harvest.* See the sidebar "The Agricultural Calendar" in the unit on Ruth 2:1–23.

Theological Insights

God is present in this chapter both as a judge and as a provider, and Naomi experiences God's presence in both her hurts and her helps. God's judgment is implicit in 1:1–5, where dark themes like drought, disease, and death dominate the scene. Since "deity played the most important role in cause and effect, both in history and in nature,"[23] Naomi naturally accepts that her bitter situation is from "the LORD's hand" (1:13; cf., 1:20–21). It is important, however, to notice that even though Naomi is afflicted (1:20, "the Almighty has made my life very bitter") and destitute (1:21, "the LORD has brought me back empty"), she is not necessarily bitter or contemptuous *toward God*, nor does she adamantly claim personal innocence or accuse God of injustice.[24] The text is silent about whether her circumstances are a consequence of her own sin, Elimelek's sin, the corporate sins of her people, or something else. Regardless of this ambiguity about the cause of God's (possible) judgment in her life, Naomi is also experiencing God's provision in a number of tangible ways.

God's presence in the wake of tragedy is explicitly expressed by bringing an end to the famine: the Lord has visited his people "by providing food for them" (1:6; notice the beautiful assonance and alliteration in the Hebrew: *latet lahem lahem*). This gracious gift from God—presumably based on his compassion and his commitment to his covenant people—provides the setting for the rest of the story as the two widows arrive in Bethlehem when "the barley harvest was beginning" (1:22). God's provisions are also implied in the ways God cares for Naomi's personal needs. In her prayer for God's kindness (*hesed*) toward her daughters-in-law, Naomi acknowledges that Orpah and Ruth have already been serving as agents of kindness (*hesed*) toward herself (1:8). Then, in Ruth's extraordinary speech, it is implied that God will continue to take care of Naomi's needs through Ruth's continued presence and actions (1:16–17).

Teaching the Text

The most important principle in teaching narratives like Ruth is to remember that the story is primarily revelation of God, not revelation of the human characters.[25] It would be inappropriate, for example, to make Ruth's response

(1:16–17) into a blueprint for religious conversion or to interpret Ruth as a typological representation of the gentile church.[26] Likewise, the relationship of Ruth and Naomi is not intended as a model for in-law relationships or wedding ceremonies today. There is also no reason to condemn Orpah for returning to Moab or to evaluate and diagnose Naomi's psychological disposition. A better approach is to ask what is learned about God through this story of Naomi and Ruth. Three big themes readily emerge: God is the gracious provider, God cares deeply for the disadvantaged, and God is the sovereign Judge.

First, God's provision for his people is expressed directly by his giving them a harvest of barley (1:6, 22) and indirectly by the past faithful acts of Orpah and Ruth (1:8) and the future faithful acts of Ruth (1:16–17). God's provision does not always come in the form or time frame one might expect or select, but God knows the needs of his people (cf. Heb. 4:15–16), and he delights in giving them "good gifts" (Matt. 7:11). Importantly, God often provides his love through the loving actions of his people toward each other (cf. John 13:35; 1 John 4:12).

Second, the torah reveals God as the great King who "defends the cause of the fatherless and the widow, and loves the foreigner residing among you, giving them food and clothing" (Deut. 10:18), and these attributes are certainly on dispay in this chapter as God protects and preserves disadvantaged women. God cares deeply for these disenfranchised women (cf. Luke 18:7–8), and he expects his people to follow his lead so that his community can be a place of safety and thriving for those who are socially disadvantaged.[27]

Third, God is the perfect Judge, but he usually does not disclose why he administers justice the way he does. It is generally true that suffering (like that referenced in 1:1–5, 13, 20–21) is a consequence of sin in the world, but the specific offense or offender is usually unknown to the sufferer. God's people in every age will inevitably wrestle to understand the causes of their crises, and they may be tempted to question God's justice. But the wise approach to suffering is to seek the Lord and to put trust and hope in him because he has purposes that are far better than we can understand (see John 9:1–3).[28] Furthermore, God remains present with his suffering people (see Pss. 23:4; 139:7–12).

Illustrating the Text

Acts of faithfulness and loyalty stand out all the brighter in times of great darkness.

Literature: Writers are familiar with the power of a foil—a character or situation introduced by the author to create a contrast that reveals the main character's qualities. Famous author Charles Dickens wrote about the power of contrast: "There are dark shadows on the earth, but its lights are stronger in the contrast."[29] The Author and Perfector of our faith is also the main character in his own story. He likes to place a person like Ruth against the backdrop of a time like the era of the judges in order to reveal his own best qualities to the world.

Nature: Show a picture of a night sky full of amazing stars, planets, and galaxies. Invite your listeners to reflect on times they have seen the stars in full definition. Chances are, it was in a remote place with no "city glow" (ambient light from sources on the ground) to detract from the display of grandeur, and possibly even a high-altitude location with few atmospheric particles to reflect light from terrestrial sources. Invite your listeners to reflect on the idea that the stars are there *all* the time, even in the daylight. The only time they can be seen in all their glory is when all competing sources of light here on earth are extinguished. In the same way, we often get our best glimpses of God's majesty when the rarified air of lonely places and the dark absence of any terrestrial helps reveal him.

Sometimes outsiders can show faith in ways that challenge insiders.

Bible: **The Parable of the Good Samaritan.** Luke 10:25–37 provides a New Testament parallel to Ruth, in that it depicts an outsider who embraces and embodies the faith and teachings of the torah more faithfully than insiders, who have been formally trained to do so.

Applying the Text: Invite your listeners to think together about the people like Ruth in their lives—people who may not even know Jesus, but whose character shows some godly qualities. Ask them if there is any part of their life in which they are being shown to be less spiritually mature or less behaviorally acceptable than those outside their church context. Invite them to be humbled, to bring such complacency to the foot of the cross, and to repent in order to show godliness to outsiders.

Poverty somehow reveals providence better than plenty.

Bible: **The Parable of the Rich Fool.** In Luke 12:13–21, Jesus reveals that when we have too much provision that comes to us too easily, we quickly become focused on ourselves and imagine that we are self-sufficient. In contrast, Ruth and Naomi show how times of material struggle can actually deepen our understanding of God's provision and make us even more thankful for the little blessings we have.

Testimony: This would be a great time to use a testimony of someone in your congregation who has experienced God's providence in a time of poverty. The person needs to avoid the pitfalls of glorifying poverty itself or of playing the victim. This needs to be a word of encouragement from someone who has met God and grown close to him in a time of loss or affliction. They also need to have come out of this tough time sweetened and joy filled. Have them detail how they relate to Naomi at this point in the narrative and whether God has sent them any Ruths along the way.

Ruth's Initiative
and the Character of Boaz

Big Idea

God is present and active when his people take initiative and seek the welfare of others.

Key Themes

- God orchestrates events in the lives of his people.
- God blesses those who bless others.
- God protects and cares for the vulnerable.
- God's faithfulness may come through human expressions of faithfulness.

Understanding the Text

The Text in Context

Naomi is the main character at the beginning and end of the book of Ruth, but the focus is primarily on Ruth and Boaz in chapters 2 and 3. These central chapters are understood respectively as C and C′ in the story's chiastic structure (see the introduction to Ruth). The two chapters are complementary in that they each employ the term *hayil* ("worthy"; ESV) to describe the main characters (2:1 and 3:11) and they each have the same sequence of episodes: Ruth/Naomi initiating plans (2:1–3; 3:1–5), Boaz favoring Ruth (2:4–17; 3:6–15), and Ruth deliberating with Naomi (2:18–23; 3:16–18).

Historical and Cultural Background

The practice of gleaning dominates the social scene in this chapter (2:2–3, 7–8, 15–19, 23). Gleaning was a way for widows, orphans, and sojourners in ancient Israel to retain their dignity by having to work hard for their own sustenance.[1] It required that the reapers intentionally neglect some of the produce on the edges of their fields. Although this welfare system is stipulated in the torah (Lev. 19:9–10; 23:22; Deut. 24:19), one could not assume that everyone upheld the practice, especially during the time of the judges (cf. Ruth 2:9, 15,

22). Ruth therefore politely makes a request to glean and hopes for a favorable answer from a generous landowner (2:2, 7). While gleaning provisions are not attested in extrabiblical legal collections, the practice of gleaning appears along with a widespread concern for the poor in a number of ancient Near Eastern texts.[2] While some ancient Near Eastern peoples would leave a portion of their crops unharvested as an offering to local fertility deities,[3] the Israelites would do so as an expression of loving their neighbor (Lev. 19:18) and "treating the vulnerable with justice"[4] (Deut. 24:17–25:19) in order that God may bless their work (Deut. 24:19).

Interpretive Insights

2:1 *man of standing.* The narrator uses this phrase to describe Boaz as a person of wealth, prominence, and influence (cf., e.g., Judg. 6:12; 11:1; 1 Sam. 9:1; 16:18; see the comments on Judg. 11:1; see also *hayil* in Ruth 3:11; 4:11). He resembles the husband of Proverbs 31:23, who is "respected at the city gate, where he takes his seat among the elders of the land." This bodes well for the disenfranchised widows.

2:3 *As it turned out.* Since Ruth knows nothing about Boaz, the location of his field, or whether he might appear and show her favor, the narrator uses this phrase to subtly indicate that God is orchestrating these events for the benefit of his people (see "Theological Insights," below). Although it may sound like a reference to chance, the narrator is "underplaying for effect" so that what looks accidental from the characters' perspectives is actually planned by God in light of "the tenor of the whole story."[5]

2:9 *drink from the water jars.* This water is presumably drawn from the same local well to which David refers (2 Sam. 23:15–16 // 1 Chron. 11:17–18), although its location is presently unknown.

2:10 *you notice me—a foreigner.* In the next two verses, Boaz will identify this ethnic outsider as an Israelite insider based on her faithful actions, which "amply serve in place of a genealogy,"[6] and on her coming to God's people and to the refuge of his wings (cf. 1:8, 16; 2:11–12). Furthermore, by bringing blessing and generosity to Naomi (see also 2:18; 3:10, 17; 4:11, 15), Ruth proves exceptional to the stereotype of Moabites as miserly people who curse Israelites (see Num. 22; Deut. 23:4).[7]

2:11 *how you left.* This key statement by Boaz may employ two allusions to passages in Genesis (see the sidebar "Intertextuality" in the unit on Judges 19:1–30). First, Ruth's "leaving" (2:11) and "cleaving" (1:14; 2:8, 21, 23) activity in this story may echo the description of marriage in Genesis 2:24.[8] Second, Ruth's leaving of her family and land is reminiscent of Abraham's faithful actions in Genesis 12:1, except that Ruth does so without any summons or assurances from God.[9]

2:12 *wings.* The imagery of protection and care under divine wings is common not only in Scripture (see "Teaching the Text," below) but also in ancient Near Eastern iconography. In Syria winged goddesses are portrayed nursing and protecting individuals. In Egypt the deity Horus hovers behind Pharaoh in the form of a falcon, and Osiris is depicted between the wings of the goddess Isis.[10]

2:17 *about an ephah.* This dry measurement in the preexilic period varies in capacity from ten to twenty liters (= 2.64–5.28 US gallons).[11] It is the same amount that David brings to his three brothers on the battlefield (1 Sam. 17:17), and it could probably last the two women for more than a week (given the typical food ration of one liter of barley per day for male workers).[12] If Ruth collected an ephah every day for the entire seven weeks of harvest (cf. 2:21, 23), she would gather enough barley and wheat to sustain them for eight to twelve months.[13] The massive proportion of Boaz's provision for these widows is a detail that would not be lost on the ancient audience of this account—it reveals Boaz's generosity as well as Ruth's industry.[14]

2:20 *He has not stopped showing.* The verb used here (*ʿzb*), also translated "abandoned" or "forsaken," may be a pun on the name Boaz (*Boʿaz*).[15] Although Boaz is the most likely grammatical subject of this action (see the following remark), the verb is used elsewhere for God as the one who does not abandon his people (cf. Gen. 24:27; 28:15; Deut. 31:6, 8).

kindness. The rich meaning of this Hebrew term (*hesed*) is difficult to capture in a single English word. It can be rendered as "loyalty," "faithfulness," "devotion," "love," or any combination of these nuances. Usually in Scripture it refers to God's actions toward people (especially in a covenant relationship), but it can also refer to the actions of people in relationship to one another.[16] In the book of Ruth the term appears only three times, though the theme of *hesed* is found throughout. In 1:8 Naomi prays for God's future *hesed* toward Ruth and Orpah while acknowledging Ruth and Orpah's prior *hesed* toward herself. In 3:10 Boaz refers to Ruth's present and previous acts of *hesed*. Here in 2:20, a verse completing the first half of the Hebrew text of Ruth,[17] Naomi refers somewhat ambiguously to the *hesed* shown to both the two living widows and the three dead men. While the syntax indicates that Boaz is the one expressing this *hesed* (see the close parallel in 2 Sam. 2:5),[18] the literary and theological contexts indicate that God is simultaneously at work. Boaz's *hesed* to the widows in chapter 2 is an implicit answer to the prayers expressed by Naomi (for God's *hesed* to her daughters-in-law; 1:8) and by Boaz (for God's reward to Ruth; 2:12).

guardian-redeemers. See the comments on Ruth 3:9 for an explanation of this term.

2:22 *you might be harmed.* Naomi's remark is a reminder that the setting is not safe for women, especially young, widowed, poor foreigners like Ruth

The Agricultural Calendar[a]

The seasonal setting in the story of Ruth is very specific. The two widows arrive in Bethlehem at the beginning of barley harvest (1:22), commemorated by the Feasts of Passover and Unleavened Bread. The barley harvest occurs in mid to late April, and although it is not the preferred grain for eating, barley comes first in the harvest cycle and therefore serves as a firstfruits offering (Lev. 23:9–14) and as an indicator of prosperity for the coming year. Ruth gleans through the barley harvest and continues until the end of the wheat harvest (2:23), commemorated by the Feast of Weeks/Pentecost. While wheat and barley are sown at the same time (in November-December), wheat matures about a month later than barley. The duration of Ruth's gleaning is somewhere around seven weeks, from mid-April to early June (i.e., Ziv/Iyyar-Sivan; cf. Deut. 16:9–12). The agricultural cycle of ancient Israel is documented in a short ditty preserved on a small stone tablet (from ca. 900 BC) recovered from Gezer over a century ago. Lines 4–5 of the Gezer Calendar read: "Month of barley harvest; month of [wheat] harvest and measuring." Appropriately, the scroll of Ruth is read in its entirety each year during the liturgy of the Feast of Weeks/Pentecost (Shavuot), and Jewish tradition maintains that this is the time when God revealed the torah at Sinai.[b]

[a] See Borowski, *Agriculture in Iron Age Israel*, 31–44, 57–62, 88–92; Borowski, *Daily Life in Biblical Times*, 27–28; Manor, "Ruth," 2:249, 251, 256.
[b] See Eskenazi and Frymer-Kensky, *Ruth*, xxvi.

(cf. 2:9, 15). Boaz is exceptional in this period when many men were exploiting and violating the women around them (cf. Judg. 5:30; 11:30–40; 15:6; 19:16–30; 20:48; 21:10–23). He worked hard to create and maintain a safe environment for the widows to flourish.

2:23 *barley and wheat harvests.* See the sidebar.

Theological Insights

Ruth 2:3 reveals an important perspective on how people of faith may experience God's sovereignty in their everyday lives. After taking personal responsibility to care for Naomi's needs and her own, Ruth "happens" upon the part of the field belonging to Boaz, who, Ruth learns later, is Elimelek's close relative (2:1, 3, 20). While the phraseology in 2:3 ("her happening happened upon"; author's translation) may sound like it describes a random coincidence or a stroke of luck, it should not be viewed from the modern secular perspective about fate or chance.[19] Since the narrator explicitly asserts elsewhere that God furnishes food and controls conception (1:6; 4:13), this phrase must be understood as a subtle hint that God specially orchestrates this encounter, albeit in a "hidden" manner.[20] While Ruth certainly makes her own free choices here, God superintends her steps according to his own perfect plan and knowledge.[21]

This perspective on the providential relationship between God and people may also help to explain the ambiguity of Naomi's statement about the one "who has not forsaken His kindness to the living and the dead" (2:20 NKJV). Does this refer to Yahweh or to Boaz? While Boaz is the most probable antecedent of the pronoun "who" (see above), the wider narrative context suggests that God is also showing kindness to the living and the dead *through* the faithful deeds of Boaz. Boaz rightly acknowledges that Ruth has come under the protection and care of God (2:12), but Boaz himself also begins to serve as God's primary means of blessing to the widows. This powerfully illustrates how God is faithful to those who show faithfulness (Ps. 18:25).[22]

Teaching the Text

Because the moral character of Ruth and Boaz is so commendable in this chapter, when teaching this text it may prove challenging to maintain a focus on God and what he is doing. The narrator calls Boaz a "man of standing" (2:1), and Boaz appears to embody the teachings of the torah in his words and actions. Ruth is commended for her acts of kindness and commitment to Naomi, and she is compared to Father Abraham (such as saying today that someone "walks on water"). However, the character traits of Ruth and Boaz are ultimately a reflection of God, and this story is primarily intended as his revelation. When teaching this pericope, one can highlight at least three theocentric principles pertaining to practical providence.

First, God is a benevolent parent who provides for and protects his people. This image is powerfully communicated through Boaz's metaphor about God's maternal "wings" (2:12), which appears frequently in Scripture (see Pss. 17:8; 57:1; 61:4; 63:7; 91:4; Matt. 23:37; Luke 13:34; cf. Gen. 1:2; Isa. 34:15)[23] and is celebrated by the psalmist: "How priceless is your unfailing love, O God! People take refuge in the shadow of your wings" (Ps. 36:7). Trusting that God has a good plan and does what is best for his people (Rom. 8:28) is foundational for living godly lives under his care.

Second, God is orchestrating events according to his own plan even though Ruth is taking initiative (2:2–3). Human responsibility to choose and act wisely is not neutralized by divine sovereignty. The apostle Paul likewise exhorts: "Continue to work out your salvation with fear and trembling, for it is God who works in you to will and to act in order to fulfill his good purpose" (Phil. 2:12–13). Even in uncertain or risky circumstances, responsible human initiatives may be the very means of God's sovereign provision for his people. In other words, providence should not paralyze but energize godly action.

Third, God's faithfulness is expressed through Boaz's benevolent actions toward Ruth (2:20). Selfless and generous actions, like bearing "each other's burdens" and doing "good to all people, especially to . . . believers" (Gal. 6:2, 9–10), are often the tangible means of God's presence in other people's lives. Acts of love toward one another are how Christians can reflect God's character (John 13:34–35; 1 John 4:12), and God may bless his people as they are a blessing to each other (see 2 Sam. 2:5–6; Ps. 18:25).

Illustrating the Text

God is the one providing, even when the provision comes through people.

Bible: The Bible refers to God as the provider in numerous ways, especially when it speaks of his *hesed* (faithful love). For one example of a meditation on God's *hesed* toward his people, see Psalm 136.

Human Experience: Invite your listeners to think about a time when they gave or received gifts as a "secret Santa" or a "secret admirer." Perhaps you have a story of your own to share on the topic. The point of sharing the story is to explore the dynamic of giving and receiving gifts from behind a veil of mystery. There are times when the recipient guesses wrong about who is behind the gifts, and there are times when the giver must conceal his or her identity by using helpers to deliver the gift. In a similar way, since God sends his provision to us from behind a veil of mystery, we can sometimes make the mistake of thinking other givers or providers have been the source. In the end, however, every good and perfect gift comes to us not by chance but from him, no matter which courier he may use.

Hymn: Both "God of the Ages" and "He Leadeth Me" offer some inspiring lyrics about God's providential orchestration in everyday life.[24]

God, in his providence, does not undermine faith-filled initiative; he underwrites it!

Humor: Recount for your listeners the old joke in which a man waits on top of his roof, praying for salvation from a raging and rising flood. A number of people in boats, helicopters, rafts, and so on offer to help. The man refuses them all, insisting that he is waiting for God to save him so God alone can have the glory. Eventually, he drowns and in heaven asks why God did not save him. God explains that he sent a boat, a helicopter, a raft, and so on, but that the man was too foolish to accept. Admit that the story is an oversimplification, but ask if your listeners have ever been foolishly passive in their lives. We please God neither by recklessness nor by cowardice; once we have sought him for a responsible and faithful course, he underwrites courage and blesses boldness.

Passing God's provision on is a life-giving privilege.

Testimony: Have a very generous (not necessarily wealthy) giver in your congregation write out an *anonymous* testimony about what it has meant to them to tithe, give offerings, and share assistance with those in need. (Anonymity ought to allow the giver to speak boldly without boasting. Be sure to remove any detail that could identify the giver.) In particular, ask them to state how they think about their possessions and why God has given them. Point out that Boaz and the person writing the testimony have both discovered that their possessions are not just for them but for the joy of sharing with others and for giving life and flourishing to others.

Quote: Rabbi Ze'ira. This rabbi comments on acts of faithfulness: "This scroll [of Ruth] tells us nothing either of cleanliness or of uncleanliness, either of prohibition or permission. For what purpose then was it written? To teach how great is the reward of those who do deeds of kindness."[25]

Naomi's Initiative and the Character of Ruth

Big Idea
God's blessings are often realized through audacious acts of love that inspire others to similar behavior.

Key Themes
- God may bring blessing through selfless actions toward one another.
- Ruth takes personal risks for Naomi's benefit.
- Kindness is contagious.
- God's wisdom and order are illustrated in everyday life.
- God may answer prayers for others through the one who prays.

Understanding the Text

The Text in Context

Chapters 2 and 3, centered on Ruth and Boaz during the barley harvest, are understood, respectively, as C and C′ in the chiastic structure of the narrative (see the introduction to Ruth). These chapters each present a trifold sequence in which plans are initiated (2:1–3; 3:1–5), favor is expressed (2:4–17; 3:6–15), and the women deliberate (2:18–23; 3:16–18). Additionally, Ruth and Boaz are each uniquely described with the term *hayil* in these chapters (2:1; 3:11), and they each employ the term "wing" (*kanap*) in key conversations with each other (2:12; 3:9).

Historical and Cultural Background

The primary setting for this chapter is a threshing floor in the vicinity of Bethlehem (3:2, 3, 6, 14).[1] Threshing floors were often located outside the city gates[2] and were typically in open areas of exposed, polished bedrock where workers could exploit the breeze in the late afternoon. Stalks of barley or wheat were initially brought there for threshing, which might employ animal hooves and a wooden sledge or cart pulled by draft animals in order to separate the grains from the stalks (cf. Deut. 25:4; Isa. 28:28; 41:15; Mic. 4:13). Threshing was followed by winnowing, which required pitchforks for tossing the threshed grain into the air so that the lighter chaff blew away and the heavier grain fell to the ground (Ruth 3:2; cf. Jer. 15:7; Hosea 13:3). Festivities would often follow the communal work, and some owners or caretakers would stay with the grain overnight (cf. Ruth 3:7), presumably to guard it from thieves until it was sold or transported for storage on the following day.

Interpretive Insights

3:3 *get dressed.* Naomi's directives may signify a transition of Ruth's social identity from a widow in mourning to one who resumes normal life (cf. 2 Sam. 12:20). Such a change in Ruth's appearance would send the proper signal to Boaz about her marital eligibility and interests.[3]

3:4 *uncover his feet.* The term used here for "feet" actually refers to the whole lower half of the body from hips to toes, that is, the "legs" (cf. Dan. 10:6). Some references to "feet" in the Old Testament are used euphemistically to refer to genitalia (cf. Exod. 4:25; Isa. 6:2; 7:20; etc.), but in the present context there appears to be "intentional ambiguity about just how much of Boaz was uncovered."[4] It is possible that Naomi's plan is for Ruth to seduce Boaz so that he might feel inclined to marry her.[5] While her precise intentions remain unclear, it is at least clear that Naomi's plan is extremely risky because the desired outcome of marriage is not guaranteed (Boaz was not legally obligated), and Ruth's reputation could become ruined in the process.

3:5 *I will do whatever you say.* Ruth's compliant words are reminiscent of Israel's responses to the Lord's covenant in Exodus 19:8; 24:3, 7. In Ruth 3:11, Boaz uses these same words in his response to Ruth, indicating that Boaz and Ruth are complementary in character and that they each act loyally for the benefit of another.

3:7 *at the far end of the grain pile.* The narrator likely notes this detail as a subtle reminder that the events are unfolding according to plan (see 3:4) and that God is orchestrating this encounter (cf. 2:3).[6] God's providential activity in these events may also be indicated by the narrator's use of the term "behold" in 3:8 (cf. 2:4; 4:1)[7] and Naomi's final remark about "what happens" in 3:18.[8]

3:9 *your servant.* Previously Ruth self-identifies as a mere "foreigner" (*nokriyyah*; 2:10) who receives the gracious distinction of laborer (*shiphah*; 2:13), but here Ruth audaciously presents herself as a handmaid (*'amah*) who could be Boaz's wife.[9] Boaz then responds by promoting her to "a woman [or wife] of noble character" (3:11), that is, a primary wife with status equal to his own (cf. 2:1).[10]

the corner of your garment. This is a contextually sensitive translation of the term "your wing [*kanap*]," which Ruth cleverly borrows from the vocabulary of Boaz in 2:12. But here, Ruth employs the term in a slightly different phrase that proposes marriage to Boaz (see Ezek. 16:8; cf. Deut. 22:30; 27:20; Mal. 2:16).[11] This is an unexpected development in the scene and in the cultural context. Instead of letting Boaz tell her what to do (see Ruth 3:4), Ruth speaks and tells Boaz what to do. Essentially she says, "Marry me as an act of redemption!" This is not merely a marriage proposal for Ruth's sake (note 3:10, "You have not run after the younger men"), but it is for the sake of Naomi and her family, and that is precisely how Boaz understands her offer (cf. 3:10–13). By speaking up, Ruth also presents Boaz with the opportunity to think (before acting quickly in the heat of the moment) so that he is presented with a choice and is then able to respond in a proper and dignified manner.[12] While Boaz might have responded by cursing Ruth for attempting to seduce and manipulate him, instead he blesses her (3:10) for this selfless expression of loyalty to Naomi, which he views as greater than her previous demonstration (1:8, 16–17; cf. 2:11).

guardian-redeemer. The Hebrew word *go'el* is translated in various ways: "covenant redeemer" (MSG), "family redeemer" (HCSB, NLT), "guardian-redeemer of our family" (NIV), and "redeeming kinsman" (NJPS), but the best renderings in Old Testament (i.e., non-soteriological) contexts are "benefactor"[13] or "guardian of the family interests" (NET). While God is the ultimate *go'el* of his people (e.g., Exod. 6:6; 15:13), which is a major theme in Psalms, Isaiah, and the New Testament, God's people may also function in the same capacity for the benefit of each other. Human applications often occur in legal contexts such as release from debt slavery, avenging murder, purchasing

Ruth as a Wisdom Story

The position of the book of Ruth between the historical books of Judges and Samuel provides a familiar canonical context for interpreting the story. However, Ruth is positioned among the Writings in the Hebrew canonical traditions (see the introduction to Ruth), where it is usually sandwiched between the wisdom books of Proverbs and Song of Songs. These three books (Proverbs, Ruth, and Song of Songs) share some common themes, such as female perspectives on marriage, family, and sexuality. Strikingly, Proverbs and Ruth are the only two books in the Bible that employ the phrase "woman of noble character" (Prov. 12:4; 31:10; Ruth 3:11). When the book of Ruth is juxtaposed with Proverbs, one can easily appreciate the many ways that the narrative presentation of Ruth and Boaz is similar to the poetic portrait expressed in Proverbs 31:10–31. Both the Proverbs 31 poem and the story of Ruth can be viewed as inspiring illustrations of God's wisdom and order in the contexts of daily life.[a]

[a] Perhaps even the language of "acquiring [*qnh*] a wife," which is unique to Ruth 4 (see vv. 5, 10), is also intended as an allusion to the acquisition of wisdom (see Prov. 4:5, 7; 16:16; 17:16; 23:23; cf. 18:15).

land, or even marrying a relative's widow. The common denominator in all these situations is "to recover losses and to salvage the dignity of the one who has suffered loss."[14]

3:11 *woman of noble character.* Boaz here ascribes to Ruth the same status that the narrator previously has ascribed to him (cf. "man of standing"; 2:1). For the significance of this phrase (employing the term *hayil*), see the sidebar; see also the comments on Ruth 2:1.

3:12 *another who is more closely related than I.* This disclosure of Boaz and his desire to defer to this other redeemer (3:13) reveals the improbability that Boaz and Ruth had sexual intercourse. While the scenario of a woman stealthily uncovering and lying beside a man at night is brimming with sexual possibilities, the narrator presents this as a chaste encounter by describing how Ruth modifies Naomi's plan (3:9) and how Boaz responds to Ruth with the longest speech in the book (3:10–13). Furthermore, the narrator demonstrates in the following chapter that he is perfectly capable of making explicit statements about sex ("he made love to her"; 4:13), yet the verbs used in this chapter for "staying" and "lying down" (3:4, 7–8, 13–14) do not require sexual activity.

3:15 *six measures of barley.* Boaz's gift is a "symbolic action of promise" that is parallel to his previous provisions for the widows in 2:14–18.[15] The precise amount of barley placed in Ruth's shawl is unspecified, but the idea is "that she receives as much as she can carry."[16]

3:17 *empty-handed.* The term "empty," used only twice in the story (here and in 1:21), anticipates Naomi's reversal of fortunes. These last words of Ruth, like her first words (1:16–17), "express her commitment to Naomi and Naomi's well-being."[17]

Theological Insights

In the Ruth story, God's blessings often come through human expressions of selfless love. That is, God grants blessings to Naomi, Ruth, and Boaz as they each act in *hesed* toward one another (see 1:8; 2:20; 3:10; cf. 4:14).[18] Naomi proposes her plan out of a concern for Ruth's welfare and "rest" (3:1 ESV; cf. 1:9) rather than a concern for her own redemption (she mentions here only that Boaz is a "relative"; 3:2).[19] Ruth demonstrates concern for Naomi's needs when she loyally responds at great personal risk (3:5) and specifically reminds Boaz that he is a "guardian-redeemer" (3:9)—possibly supplementing Naomi's plan. Boaz also seeks Ruth's welfare by invoking God's blessing (3:10), identifying her as his equal (3:11; cf. 2:1), responding with integrity and alacrity (3:12–13), and sharing his barley (3:15, 17).

Interestingly, the actions of Naomi and Boaz in this chapter become answers to each of their prayers on Ruth's behalf. Naomi previously prayed that her daughters-in-law would find "rest" in a husband's house (1:9), and here she apparently recognizes God's orchestration of events (cf. 2:20) and personally seeks out "rest" (3:1) for Ruth by initiating her own plan (3:2–4). Boaz previously prayed for Ruth's reward and protection under Yahweh's "wings" (2:12), and here he shows the intention to act personally as God's "wing" (3:9) and thereby help to reward and protect Ruth.

Teaching the Text

Teachers must carefully handle the account of Ruth and Boaz at the threshing floor because of the common tendency to sensationalize it as a romance story. "If this is a love story, it is primarily the love between Ruth and Naomi,"[20] not Ruth and Boaz. Ruth's "kindness" (*hesed*) to Naomi is precisely what impresses Boaz and motivates him to action in 3:10–11. Ruth's *hesed* is not a "sentimental love"[21] but a godly love in which Ruth's concerns for Naomi are more important than her own interests. Also, the nighttime encounter is not a scandalous sex scene, as some have intimated.[22] Even if Naomi's plan allowed for sexual entrapment,[23] the narrator indicates that Ruth presents Boaz with a choice and that Boaz does *not* do what one might expect him to do during the time of the judges, when men were accustomed to exploiting vulnerable women (cf. Judg. 19–21). The significance of the story comes, not from such romantic and racy readings, but from observations about the nature of *hesed* as it is expressed in the narrative.

First, God's love may be expressed through human acts of love. Indeed, God's blessings come to the main characters as they bring blessings to one another (see 3:10; cf. 1:8; 2:4, 12, 19, 20; 4:14–15). The psalmist likewise proclaims, "To the faithful you show yourself faithful" (Ps. 18:25), and the apostle John explains, "If we love one another, God lives in us and his love is made complete in us" (1 John 4:12). Another way to frame this principle is that God takes care of those who put others first (cf. Matt. 6:33). Ruth's initial words to Boaz at the threshing floor (about redemption; Ruth 3:9) reveal that she is concerned mainly for Naomi's family, yet God later provides for both widows through Boaz (see 4:13–15).

Second, God may lead those who pray for others to act personally on behalf of others. That is, a prayer for a needy person may be answered through the actions of the one who prays. This is how God provides for Ruth in this chapter (1:9; 2:12; 3:1–4, 9–11), and it is also how God may provide for "a brother or sister in need" (1 John 3:17; cf. James 2:15–16).

Third, this story powerfully demonstrates how kindness is contagious. That is, selfless actions stimulate others to act selflessly. Ruth's "earlier" acts of *hesed* toward Naomi (1:8; 2:11; 3:10) inspire both Naomi and Boaz to seek Ruth's welfare (1:8–15; 2:8–16, 22; 3:1), and Ruth's "greater" act of *hesed* to Naomi (3:10) inspires Boaz toward even further action on behalf of the widows (3:10–15). In the same way, God's people must consider how to "spur one another on toward love and good deeds" (Heb. 10:24). Of course, the ultimate impetus for God's people to express *hesed* to one another—even if they have not received it from other people—is that God is "abounding in love and faithfulness" (Exod. 34:6–7; cf. 15:13; 20:6) and that "Jesus Christ laid down his life for us" (1 John 3:16; cf. John 13:34; 15:12–13; 1 John 4:11, 19).

Illustrating the Text

God takes care of those who put others first.

Popular Saying: Many will be familiar with the popular saying, "God helps those who help themselves." Point out that the book of Ruth seems to say the opposite, and so does Jesus. By putting God and his kingdom first and the interests of others before our own, we accept the posture in which we can best receive God himself, along with all his benefits.

Mnemonic: Remind your listeners about the old Sunday school mnemonic given by the acronym JOY. Explain that the letters help us remember the proper ordering of a Christian's priorities: J is for putting Jesus and his kingdom first; O is for putting others next; and Y is for putting yourself last.

Bible: Philippians 2. The servant song in Philippians 2 makes it abundantly clear that Jesus poured himself out for us and is now exalted by the Father to the highest place. Our best example of God taking care of a selfless servant is the glory and honor he bestows on his own Son, who died for us. Invite your listeners to receive this gift of selfless service and to follow Christ's example by serving others.

Be willing to join God in answering your prayers for other people.

Bible: Matthew 9–10. Point out that after Jesus instructs his disciples to pray that God would send out laborers into the harvest (Matt. 9:35–38), he immediately sends them out in mission, two by two (Matt. 10). He instructs them to pray for workers and then commissions them as workers!

Evangelism: Point out that many people have been reached with the gospel because someone prayed for their salvation. Also, the ones who prayed such prayers have often been used to share the gospel with such persons. Point your listeners toward resources that can increase their effectiveness in seeking the salvation of others and preparing to back it up with evangelistic actions. (Some possibilities include resources from the organization Moms in Prayer International [formerly Moms in Touch] and the prayer booklet *Paths of Gold*.)[24]

Kindness is contagious.

Literature: *A Christmas Carol,* **by Charles Dickens.** In Dickens's *A Christmas Carol,* Ebenezer Scrooge goes through a night of harrowing self-examination and is given a chance at repentance. His joy the next day (Christmas Day) is one of the most delightful examples of contagious kindness in literature; God's kindness to him erupts in kindness to others. There are lots of cinematic depictions of Scrooge's delight in becoming generous and kind; consider showing one.

Health: Talk about the way in which certain diseases are more contagious than others. Some require direct contact, while others can be passed on through the air. This is due to the biological design of each virus, bacteria, or amoeba, combined with the weaknesses of the immune systems in the animals they affect. Similarly, there are certain designs built into behaviors that God has placed there to teach and build up the hearts of the people who practice them. Kindness is designed by God to have a liberating and life-giving effect on the hearts of humans. Kindness has the power to disarm, bless, nurture, free, and heal, not only for those who show or receive it but even for others around them who observe it.

Film: *Pay It Forward.* In this 2000 film a young boy proposes a way to make the world a better place based on the idea that acts of kindness can inspire more acts of kindness, forming a branching tree of good deeds. "Pay it forward" can describe the outward ripples of blessing that can cascade from a single act of selflessness or service.

Kindness is often risky.

Quote: *Love Kindness,* **by Barry H. Corey.**

> The way of kindness comes with risks. The way of kindness is vulnerable and unsafe. The way of kindness should not expect a thank-you and may even receive a rebuke. Living this way means taking initiative and sometimes stepping into a pile of rejection. The way of kindness is others-centered and not me-centered, which is the hardest place of all for many of us. . . . The way of kindness is always selfless and often awkward.[25]

Redemption and Marriage for a Blessed Future

Big Idea

God's blessings are often realized through the faithful actions and prayers of his people.

Key Themes

- God graciously provides for his people and cares for their needs.
- God answers prayers in his own time and in his own ways.
- God's blessings can come through unexpected means.
- God has long-term plans to bless his people.
- David is descended from faithful people.

Understanding the Text

The Text in Context

The Ruth story opens with death and emptiness, but it closes with life and fullness (1:3–5, 21; 4:13–17).[1] The last chapter of the book brings the story full circle from a bitter situation to a blessed one (1:20–21; 4:11–15).[2] Ruth 4 has two literary components that correspond in reverse order to the two literary components of chapter 1 (see the introduction to Ruth). The family history in 4:18–22 recounts future births, whereas the family history in 1:1–5 recounts past deaths, and each of these sections lists a total of ten proper nouns. The story of marriage and descendants in 4:1–17 parallels the story of widows and childlessness in 1:6–22, and both of these sections stress the Lord's gifts (1:6; 4:11–13), the husband's house (1:9; 4:11–12), bearing sons (1:12; 4:12–13, 15–17), name calling (1:20–21; 4:11, 14, 17), and speeches of the local women (1:19; 4:14–15, 17).

Historical and Cultural Background

The gate of Bethlehem, presently unidentified in the archaeology, serves as one of the primary settings in the story of Ruth (3:11; 4:1, 10, 11).[3] Bethlehem's gate is associated with a well (2 Sam. 23:15–16 // 1 Chron. 11:17–18), and the threshing floor is presumably located just outside it. The gate with its adjacent square is the socioeconomic "center" of town because it is the bottleneck through which everyone enters or exits to go about their daily business. Its diverse functions may relate to military security, market activity, legal transactions, administrative matters, ceremonial gatherings, and religious rituals. In the Bible and in the ancient Near East the gate is supposed to be a place where justice is maintained.[4] Gates often include meeting spaces (inside or outside) with seating to settle situations like the one described in Ruth 4, where Boaz sits down with the closer kinsman and ten elders[5] of the town (4:1–2), a scene that is reminiscent of Proverbs 31:23.

Interpretive Insights

4:1 *friend.* The Hebrew term translated as "friend" here (*peloni 'almoni*) is a farrago, that is, "a (rhyming) medley of words that gains meaning through context."[6] If it is understood as a reference to the closer kinsman (thus translated "So-and-so"; cf. NJPS), then it is "a particularly pointed refusal to name this character."[7] But recent suggestions about this phrase point out that it more likely refers to an indeterminate place (cf. 1 Sam. 21:2 [Heb. v. 3]; 2 Kings 6:8); thus, Boaz says, "Sit here at such and such spot."[8] Nevertheless, the closer kinsman still remains unnamed in this story, perhaps because he refuses "to maintain the *name* of the dead" (4:5), and he therefore serves as an effective literary foil for the frequently named Boaz, who becomes "famous in Bethlehem" (4:11).[9]

4:3 *our relative Elimelek.* Boaz and the unnamed kinsman are probably not literal "brothers" of Elimelek because "they would have inherited the field on this basis," making redemption unnecessary.[10] Instead, it is more likely that they are Elimelek's cousins. The precise relationships of the two redeemers to Naomi or to Elimelek are ultimately uncertain, although Jewish traditions offer some interesting speculations.[11]

4:4 *But if you will not.* Based on some text-critical variants, the subject of the verb in this clause could be either second person (cf. many medieval Hebrew manuscripts, LXX, Vulgate, modern English translations) or third person ("But if he will not"; MT). The former reading makes best sense contextually (where the second person dominates), and the latter reading may indicate that Boaz is briefly turning his attention from the kinsman to the elders.[12]

4:5 *you also acquire Ruth.* There are also some text-critical questions about the Hebrew in this verse because the subject of the verb could be either second person (Qere, consistent with a few medieval Hebrew manuscripts, LXX, Vulgate, modern English translations) or first person ("I acquire"; Kethib).[13]

In either case, regardless of who might marry Ruth, Boaz asserts that "the child legally belongs to the other family line,"[14] and that is the bottom line in this negotiation.

4:6 *endanger my own estate.* In light of the condition that Boaz explains in the previous verse, the kinsman realizes that he "has little or nothing to gain and a great deal to lose."[15] Essentially, he would be "disinherited through his own actions"[16] because "the deceased's property is transferred to [Ruth's] children rather than reverting back to his family of origin. . . . The only incentive . . . is a sense of fraternal or familial obligation."[17] Perhaps one might compare this closer kinsman to Onan, who "knew that the child would not be his" (Gen. 38:9).[18] The kinsman appears to act out of self-interest by deeming the acquisition as a poor financial investment, whereas Boaz appears to act out of loyalty to his family by taking a risk for others' benefit.

4:7 *took off his sandal.* The narrator's parenthetical mention of earlier customs here demonstrates that the time of composition (or editing) is somewhat removed from the setting of the historical events (see the introduction

Levirate Marriage[a]

The Israelite practice of levirate marriage, described in Deuteronomy 25:5–10, consists of a brother-in-law marrying his widowed sister-in-law in order to produce an heir for the deceased brother's estate. The practice is also illustrated in Genesis 38—a narrative that is unmistakably echoed in Ruth 4:12—and throughout ancient and modern world cultures.[b] The scenario in the book of Ruth in which Boaz or the unnamed relative could marry the widow may not be technically levirate marriage (at least according to Deut. 25) because Mahlon has no living brothers—a reality acknowledged by Naomi in 1:11–13. However, the fact that Boaz marries Ruth "in order to maintain the name of the dead with his property" (4:5, 10; cf. Deut. 25:7) indicates that the redemption scenario in this story is a levirate-like situation carried out by the closest willing relative. Thus Boaz is portrayed in Ruth 4 as upholding not the letter but the spirit of torah by "doing justice"[c] both for the widows and for the estate of Mahlon, although Boaz is under no obligation to do so. The narrator "construes his plot in such a way that, what in terms of the Deuteronomic law could not be a levirate union, becomes just that in the story. In this way the story can 'work' and display the virtue of *hesed*."[d]

[a] See Eskenazi and Frymer-Kensky, *Ruth*, xxxi–xxxviii, 76–78; Greengus, *Laws in the Bible*, 14–26, 108; Lau, *Identity and Ethics in the Book of Ruth*, 4–5, 69–74, 87–89, 173–74, 191–95; Levine, "In Praise of the Israelite *Mišpāḥâ*"; Weisberg, *Levirate Marriage*; Younger, *Judges, Ruth*, 401–3, 476–78.
[b] E.g., see Hittite Laws §193 (*COS* 2.19:118) and Middle Assyrian Laws A §30 (*COS* 2.132:356–58).
[c] Walton, "Decalogue Structure of the Deuteronomic Law," 113. Note that Boaz may uphold the spirit of the ninth commandment (pertaining to the integrity of the justice system; cf. Deut. 5:20; 24:17–25:19) through just treatment of the vulnerable, whether living or dead.
[d] Loader, "Of Barley, Bulls, Land and Levirate," 130.

to Ruth). Footwear like sandals was symbolic for ownership and dominion in the biblical world (cf. Deut. 25:9–10; Pss. 60:8; 108:9).[19] By removing and passing his sandal to Boaz in 4:7–8, the kinsman legally relinquishes his right to tread on the designated piece of land.[20]

4:13 *So Boaz took Ruth.* Seven times prior to this point Ruth has been called "the Moabite" (1:4, 22; 2:2, 6, 21; 4:5, 10), but here in this final reference—as well as in 2:8, 22—the narrator just calls her Ruth, with no ethnic identifier.[21] Glover suggests that "Ruth's name is used without the Moabite tag whenever her re-situation within Israel has been recognized,"[22] and this may show that "biological descent is not always necessary for ethnic belonging."[23]

4:18 *family line of Perez.* This linear genealogy employs a phrase that is used ten times in Genesis to mean "These are the generations,"[24] and it preserves ten generations like the genealogies in Genesis 5 and 11. Also as in Genesis, the emphasis is here placed on the seventh and tenth positions (Boaz and David, respectively).[25] Verses 18–22 are by no means an appendix or secondary addition to the story of Ruth. Rather, the genealogy serves as a "coda"[26] or an integrated conclusion to a story that opens with past family deaths and recounts God's blessing and providence toward his faithful people. It can show that "common people [like Boaz] achieve uncommon ends when they act unselfishly toward each other."[27] The last word of the Hebrew text ("David") shows that Israel's ideal king emerges from righteous stock and that the "fragile thread"[28] leading to David (and ultimately to Jesus) is forged through acts of faithfulness initiated by a foreign woman. Most important, the genealogy shows that by blessing Naomi's family, God brings blessings to the whole nation (and ultimately to the whole world).

Theological Insights

The final chapter of Ruth emphasizes God's gracious provision for his people. This theme is made explicit by the three uses of the verb "to give" (*ntn*) with the Lord as subject. The witnesses at the gate bless the marriage twice with "May the Lord give"—first, that Ruth may be a matriarch like Rachel and Leah (4:11), and second, that Boaz may be a patriarch like Judah "through the offspring [Heb., *zera'*] the LORD gives" through Ruth (4:12). The third instance is expressed in the very next verse, where the narrator reports: "The LORD gave her conception, and she bore a son" (4:13 ESV). The connections with Genesis[29] are unmistakable in these verses as God's gifts are expressed in terms of his covenant relationship with his people. God not only creates new life in Ruth's (presumably) barren womb, but he also orchestrates the redemption of land and widows (4:9–10, 14) and eventually blesses his people with a faithful human king who will make the way for the divine King (4:17, 22).

The final chapter of Ruth also emphasizes answered prayer.[30] The short story of Ruth is packed with prayers of blessing that are spoken on behalf of others, and all of these prayers are answered in chapter 4. Naomi's prayers for the widows (1:8–9) are answered—at least for Ruth—in 4:10–13. Boaz's prayers for Ruth (2:12; 3:10) are answered in 4:10–11, 13, 15, 21. Naomi's prayers for Boaz (2:19–20) are answered in 4:11–13, 21. Finally, the witnesses' prayers for Ruth and Boaz (4:11–12) are answered in 4:13, 15, 21–22, and the women's prayer for Obed (4:14) is answered in 4:17, 21–22.[31] In this summary it is evident that God is predisposed to answering selfless prayers, that selfless prayers can inspire others toward selfless prayer, and that faithful petitioners can also participate in God's answers to their prayers (e.g., Naomi takes action for Ruth's benefit in 3:1, and Boaz takes action for the widows' benefit in 3:11–13; 4:9–10).

Teaching the Text

When teaching Ruth 4, one must be careful not to misconstrue the meaning. It would be a mistake, for example, to approach Boaz and Ruth typologically so that their marriage prefigures Christ's relationship to his gentile bride, the church.[32] The problem with this interpretation, found in neither Testament, is that it tends to circumvent the relevance of the story for the ancient Israelite audience. The best approach to applying the book of Ruth is to keep in mind that the objective is not necessarily to be like Boaz or Ruth but rather to model God's character. Granted, the characters in this story are exceptional examples of what godliness (or wisdom) might look like in a particular context. But they are not intended as perfect examples or as prescriptive models for all God's people in every time and place. The point is to let this story be a catalyst for inspiring torah living in the present context.

Be a torah person. Because God is just and faithful, his followers must be the same—people who love others by seeking their flourishing and taking measures both to maintain equity and to mitigate exploitive abuses of power. This is what it means to uphold the spirit of torah (cf. Lev. 19:9–18; Deut. 16:19–20; Hosea 6:6; Mic. 6:8; James 1:27; etc.). The specific applications of torah living may take various forms, but selflessness is a key virtue. A selfless individual can serve as an agent of redemption for others, maintain justice in his/her sphere of influence, and leave a legacy of loyalty (*hesed*) by being like Jesus, who perfectly fulfills the torah and urges his followers to do the same (see Matt. 5:17–20). The story of Ruth, which features everyday people in various stations of life, shows that anyone can be a torah person and that "God can use common folk (Ruth) as the foundation for major stages in his plan (David)."[33]

Pray for others. One specific way that anyone can embody the torah is by praying for God's blessings in the lives of other people. This selfless and loving act is displayed in every chapter of the book of Ruth (see "Theological Insights," above). Amazingly in the story, prayers for others may inspire others' prayers for others. Prayers for others may also inspire personal initiatives on behalf of others so that people "act to fulfill the blessings that they bestow on one another in the name of God."[34] It is evident in Ruth 4 that God delights in fulfilling selfless requests and that his answers may go way beyond what petitioners ever expect or imagine.[35]

Illustrating the Text

If you like the story of Ruth and Boaz, then imitate their God.

Human Experience: Childhood costumes are a common experience that highlights our desire to literally put on the admirable traits we see in a hero or famous character. Share about a time you dressed up in a costume and how you thought or felt. (If you have a picture from your childhood, it might be fun to show it.) Perhaps you even imagined you would become the person you dressed like. Tell people that if hero costumes were licensed from the Bible for marketing, there would be a very limited line of outfits—all character costumes for biblical heroes and heroines would look identical: they would all be modeled after Jesus, since he is the true hero behind all the characters. Every character in the Bible reveals God—he is the only real hero in the book. Ruth's and Boaz's good examples came from imitating God—that same way of living, serving, and loving is just as available to us right now.

Believers are called to embody the spirit of the law by imitating the one who gave it.

Quote: Daniel I. Block. Biblical scholar Daniel Block writes, "The instructions in Deuteronomy should not be viewed as providing final boundaries for covenant righteousness (Moses could not possibly provide legislation for every eventuality); rather, they present minimal requirements, presenting a moral compass and an ethical trajectory for the community of faith."[36]

Human Experience: There are odd or outdated laws on the books in many states and municipalities. For instance, in Missouri it is illegal to drive down the road with an uncaged bear. In Salem, West Virginia, you can't eat candy less than an hour and a half before a church service. In Illinois it is against the law to give a lighted cigar to a pet.[37] Share some amusing laws with your listeners, and invite them to help you discern the difference between the *letter* of the law and the *spirit* of the law. This could be quite funny, especially as you try to rationalize the spirit behind capricious or outdated laws. Point out that each of God's laws has both a prohibitive aspect and a life-giving intent. We do not keep them just by avoiding the prohibited activities—we keep them by using the space created by the prohibition to pursue the life-giving intent.

God delights in fulfilling selfless prayers.

Testimony: Invite someone to share a short story about how they were blessed by someone praying for them . . . and that prayer being answered. If possible, have both the one who prayed and the one for whom he or she prayed present to share their experiences.

Applying the Text: Allow time in the service for people to pray silently for others. Guide them through three or four themes that would be meaningful for your congregation. Consider a special prayer service or event aimed at selfless prayers of blessing. Remind others that the most selfless prayer of all is the prayer of blessing over one's enemies (Matt. 5:43–48).

Notes

Introduction to Judges

1. "Classification and Rating Rules," Motion Picture Association of America, Inc., and National Association of Theatre Owners, Inc., January 1, 2010, http://filmratings.com/downloads/ratingrules .pdf. For further discussion comparing Judges with R-rated movies, see Lapsley, *Whispering the Word*, 35–36.

2. See Younger, *Judges, Ruth*, 30.

3. See Gooding, "Composition of the Book of Judges."

4. Ibid.

5. See Douglas, *Thinking in Circles*.

6. See Douglas, *In the Wilderness*, esp. 118; cf. Douglas, *Thinking in Circles*, 43–71.

7. For an expanded presentation of this view, see Way, "Literary Structure of Judges Revisited."

8. Douglas, *Thinking in Circles*, 36.

9. Ibid.

10. See Stone, "Judges, Book of," 592, 601.

11. Douglas, *Thinking in Circles*, 36.

12. Ibid., 36–37.

13. Ibid., 37.

14. Ibid.

15. E.g., see Dorsey, *Literary Structure*, 105–20.

16. Douglas, *Thinking in Circles*, 37–38.

17. See Chisholm, "Role of Women."

18. Younger, *Judges, Ruth*, 37. See also Globe, "'Enemies Round About,'" 235.

19. This designation is proposed by Kitchen, *Reliability of the Old Testament*, 203–4. See also the description in Stone, "Eglon's Belly," 656–57.

20. Block, *Judges, Ruth*, 58, 73, 75, 143–44, 473.

21. Cf. Butler, *Judges*, lvii–lxiv.

22. The selection of seven stories (i.e., the two triads plus the central Gideon narrative) may be related to the sevenfold judgment of God in Lev. 26:18, 21, 24, 28; cf. Deut. 28:25 (see Block, *Judges, Ruth*, 145).

23. The two middle occurrences are also modestly chiastic: *'en melek* versus *melek 'en* (see Fokkelman, "Structural Remarks on Judges 9 and 19," 43).

24. For a stimulating discussion on "the increasingly ambiguous role of the deity" in Judges, see Exum, "Centre Cannot Hold."

25. See Greenspahn, "Theology of the Framework of Judges," 386, 393–96.

26. See Hill and Walton, *Survey*, 241.

27. Ibid., 251–52.

28. See Fee and Stuart, *How to Read the Bible for All Its Worth*, 98, 106.

29. For further discussion, see Walton, Bailey, and Williford, "Bible-Based Curricula"; see also Walton, "Inspired Subjectivity," 73–74; Walton and Hill, *Old Testament Today*, 141, 181, 184–87; Walton and Walton, *Bible Story Handbook*, 13–30, 129, 131, 135, 140.

30. For a helpful survey of the relevant data, see Walton, "Exodus, Date of." For recent discussion in *JETS*, see articles by B. G. Wood, R. K. Hawkins, J. K. Hoffmeier, R. C. Young, and R. Dalman in vols. 48–51 (2005–8).

31. For a helpful data chart, see Provan, Long, and Longman, *Biblical History of Israel*, 163. Alternatively, the total is 420 years based on the numbers in the Septuagint (reading fifty in 3:11).

32. Of course, this literary reading of Judges does not preclude the historicity of the accounts.

33. See Fouts, "Defense of the Hyperbolic Interpretation"; Fouts, "Numbers, Large Numbers"; Hoffmeier, "What Is the Biblical Date for

the Exodus?"; Hoffmeier, "Rameses of the Exodus Narratives."

34. For further references on the Late Bronze Age II and Iron Age I, see the essays by A. Leonard and R. W. Younker, respectively, in Richard, *Near Eastern Archaeology*, 351–56, 367–74.

35. See *b. Baba Bathra* 14b in Epstein, *Seder Nezikin*, 2:71.

36. See, e.g., the views of T. C. Butler and W. J. Dumbrell, respectively (Butler, *Judges*, lxxiv; Dumbrell, "In Those Days," 29–32).

37. For helpful discussion on the composition of Judges, see Stone, "Judges, Book of"; see also Amit, "Book of Judges." For a general introduction to compositional theory, see Römer, *So-Called Deuteronomistic History*.

Judges 1:1–2:5

1. See Younger, *Ancient Conquest Accounts*, 246, 252–53.

2. "Cisjordanian" refers to the region west of the Jordan River.

3. For literary analysis, see O'Connell, *Rhetoric of the Book of Judges*, 59–72; Webb, *Book of the Judges: An Integrated Reading*, 81–105; Younger, *Judges, Ruth*, 61–75.

4. *COS* 2.6:41; cf. Rainey and Notley, *Sacred Bridge*, 99.

5. See Hasel, "Merneptah's Reference to Israel."

6. See, e.g., Judg. 16:21; 1 Sam. 11:2; 2 Sam. 4:12; Ezek. 23:25; *COS* 2.113:262; 2.115:280.

7. See Lemos, "Shame and Mutilation of Enemies."

8. See Judg. 8:30; 9:2, 5, 18, 24, 56; 12:14; 2 Kings 10:1, 6–7; cf. *COS* 1.86:262; 2.35:155(?); 2.37:158; 2.39:161(?).

9. Hess, *Joshua*, 30.

10. See Cantrell, *Horsemen of Israel*, 63n8; Millard, "Back to the Iron Bed," 193–95.

11. See Block, *Judges, Ruth*, 91.

12. See Webb, *Book of the Judges: An Integrated Reading*, 101.

13. See Walton, *Covenant*.

14. Cf. Younger, *Judges, Ruth*, 79.

Judges 2:6–3:6

1. See Walton, *Ancient Near Eastern Thought*, 222–23.

2. E.g., see Kitchen, *Reliability of the Old Testament*, 217–18.

3. See Block, *Gods of the Nations*, 127–29; cf. Brinkman, "Through a Glass Darkly," 35–42.

4. This refrain is employed with the same meaning in Num. 32:13; Deut. 4:25; 9:18; 17:2; 31:29; 1 Sam. 12:17; 15:19; 2 Sam. 12:9; 1 Kings 11:6; 14:22; 15:26, 34; 16:7, 19, 25, 30; 21:20, 25; 22:52; 2 Kings 3:2; 8:18, 27; 13:2, 11; 14:24; 15:9, 18, 24, 28; 17:2, 17; 21:2, 6, 16, 20; 23:32, 37; 24:9, 19. Note that the refrain of "doing what is *right* in the eyes of the

Lord" (Exod. 15:26; Deut. 6:18; 12:25, 28; 13:18; 21:9; 1 Kings 11:33, 38; 14:8; 15:5, 11; 22:43; 2 Kings 10:30; 12:2; 14:3; 15:3, 34; 16:2; 18:3; 22:2) means the exact opposite, that is, obedience to the covenant.

5. For the first view, see *IVPBBCOT*, 246; for the second view, see Fox, "Concepts of God," 333–34, 337.

6. For the first view, see *IVPBBCOT*, 246; for the second view, see Fox, "Concepts of God," 334, 337.

7. For additional references, see Wyatt, "Astarte," *DDD*, 109–14; Cornelius, *Many Faces of the Goddess*, esp. 93–94.

8. Mafico, *Yahweh's Emergence*, 1, 6, 113–22. On the function of bringing justice for Israel, see Hill and Walton, *Survey*, 236, 242, 243; cf. Heb. 11:33 ("administered justice").

9. See Hitchcock and Maeir, "Yo-ho, Yo-ho, A *Seren*'s Life for Me!," 12.

10. See Sweeney, "Davidic Polemic in the Book of Judges," 523.

11. See Hoffman, "Concept of 'Other Gods.'"

12. See Block, *Judges, Ruth*, 136–37.

13. Cf. Lev. 26:14–39; Deut. 4:25–27; 6:14–15; 8:19; 28:15–68; 31:16–21, 29; Josh. 23:13, 15–16.

14. Cf. Gen. 22:1; Exod. 15:25; 16:4; 20:20; Deut. 8:2, 16; 13:3.

15. For further exposition, see Hutchison, *Thinking Right When Things Go Wrong*, 27–70, 215–18.

16. Cf. Num. 15:39–40; Deut. 4:9, 23; 6:12; 8:2, 11, 14, 18–19; Josh. 1:13; Ps. 78:7, 11, 42.

17. See Younger, *Judges, Ruth*, 45, 95–98.

18. See Block, *Judges, Ruth*, 141.

19. Cf. Deut. 4:9; 6:2, 7, 20–25; Josh. 4:6, 21; Ps. 78:5–8.

20. Boda, *A Severe Mercy*, 523.

21. Plantinga, *Not the Way*, 53.

22. Statistics gleaned from "Plague (disease)," *Wikipedia*, http://en.wikipedia.org/wiki/Plague (disease).

Additional Insights, pp. 26–27

1. For additional references, see Way, "Giants in the Land."

2. *COS* 3.2:13.

3. *COS* 1.32:51.

4. *COS* 1.32:51–52; Rainey and Notley, *Sacred Bridge*, 58.

5. *COS* 2.2:9, 19; Rainey and Notley, *Sacred Bridge*, 72–74.

6. *COS* 3.92:238–39, 241–42; Rainey and Notley, *Sacred Bridge*, 79.

7. *COS* 3.2:12, 14; Rainey and Notley, *Sacred Bridge*, 101–2.

8. *COS* 3.45:94; Rainey and Notley, *Sacred Bridge*, 101.

9. For additional references, see Herrmann, "Baal," *DDD*, 132–39; Cornelius, *Iconography of the Canaanite Gods Reshef and Ba'al*.

10. See 2 Kings 17:16; Jer. 2:8, 23; 7:9; 9:14–16; 11:13, 17; 12:16; 19:5; 23:13, 27; 32:29, 35; Hosea 2:8, 13, 17; 13:1; Zeph. 1:4.

Judges 3:7–11

1. The selection of seven stories may be related to God's sevenfold judgment in Lev. 26:18, 21, 24, 28; cf. Deut. 28:25; see Block, *Judges, Ruth*, 145.
2. See Olson, "Buber, Kingship, and the Book of Judges," 206.
3. See Brettler, "Book of Judges," 404; Brettler, *Book of Judges*, 4, 27.
4. See Block, "Judges," 2:126; Younger, *Judges, Ruth*, 106–7.
5. See COS 2.1:7; 2.2C:19.
6. See the comments on Judg. 2:11, 13, above; cf. Fox, "Concepts of God," 337.
7. See Wyatt, "Asherah," *DDD*, 99–105.
8. See Hess, *Israelite Religions*, 12–14, 67, 283–90; cf. COS 2.47A–B:171–72; 2.52:179. For additional reference on Asherah, see "Historical and Cultural Background" in the unit on Judg. 6:1–32.
9. Brettler, "Book of Judges," 404–5; Brettler, *Book of Judges*, 4, 27.
10. See Brettler, *Book of Judges*, 4, 27; Hallo, "Scurrilous Etymologies," 773, 776.
11. For "judge/govern" (NIV: "lead"), see Judg. 3:10; 4:4; 10:2–3; 12:7–9, 11, 13–14; 15:20; 16:31; for "deliver/save," see 3:9, 31; 6:14–15; 8:22; 10:1; 13:5.
12. See Mafico, *Yahweh's Emergence*, 97–99, 102; cf. Block, *Judges, Ruth*, 23, 145.
13. See Sasson, "Coherence and Fragments," 364n6, 367.
14. Hess, "Israelite Identity," 33.
15. See Younger, *Judges, Ruth*, 66–67n17.
16. Cf. Block, *Judges, Ruth*, 150n15.
17. See Lindars, *Judges 1–5*, 22, 27, 28, 128, 134.
18. See Younger, *Judges, Ruth*, 100, 105, 106, 108.
19. See Mullen, "Judges 1.1–36," 48.
20. Cf. Greenspahn, "Theology of the Framework of Judges," 386, 391, 394–96.
21. See Walton, "Inspired Subjectivity," 67–69, 72; cf. Klein, Blomberg, and Hubbard, *Introduction to Biblical Interpretation*, 11–12.
22. *Simon Birch*, directed by Mark Steven Johnson (Burbank, CA: Hollywood Pictures Home Entertainment, 1999), DVD.
23. Philip Yancey, *What's So Amazing about Grace?* (Grand Rapids: Zondervan, 1997), 280.
24. Corrie ten Boom, *The Hiding Place*, with Elizabeth and John Sherrill, 35th anniversary ed. (Grand Rapids: Chosen, 2006), 44.

Judges 3:12–30

1. Between the extremes of these two events (and precisely at the literary center of the book), the Ephraimites both cooperate and clash with Gideon (Judg. 7:24–8:3). For an insightful analysis of these

three Ephraimite episodes, see Jobling, "Structuralist Criticism," 107–11.
2. See Amit, *Book of Judges*, 171–98; Dorsey, *Literary Structure*, 108–9; Mobley, *Empty Men*, 77–79, 86–93; O'Connell, *Rhetoric of the Book of Judges*, 84–100; Younger, *Judges, Ruth*, 112–21.
3. See Halpern, *First Historians*, 46–55, 59, 67.
4. See King and Stager, *Life in Biblical Israel*, 31–33; Sasson, "Ethically Cultured Interpretations," 583–84; Stager, "Key Passages."
5. Rainey and Notley, *Sacred Bridge*, 137.
6. See Stone, "Eglon's Belly," 655.
7. Hess, "Israelite Identity," 34.
8. See Halpern, *First Historians*, 40–43; Walton and Walton, *Bible Story Handbook*, 128–29.
9. See Stone, "Eglon's Belly," 661.
10. Ibid., 661–62.
11. See Sasson, "Ethically Cultured Interpretations," 574–76, 587–92; Stone, "Eglon's Belly," 649–57, 663.
12. Alter, *Art of Biblical Narrative*, 39.
13. I owe this observation to Michael Sanborn.
14. Stone, "Eglon's Belly," 659.
15. See Sasson, "Ethically Cultured Interpretations," 584–86, 590.
16. See Amit, *Book of Judges*, 171–73, 178, 181, 194–98.
17. See Hill and Walton, *Survey*, 243, 247.

Judges 4:1–24

1. The terms "self-interest" and "communal interest" are borrowed from Assis, *Self-Interest or Communal Interest*.
2. For helpful structural analysis, see Dorsey, *Literary Structure*, 109; Stek, "The Bee and the Mountain Goat," 54–59.
3. See Ben-Tor, "Hazor."
4. See Polzin, *Moses and the Deuteronomist*, 177.
5. See Hess, "Israelite Identity," 30; Zertal, *Sisera's Secret*, 124–25, 226–27, 230–35, 317–18; Zertal, "Philistine Kin Found in Early Israel," 31, 60.
6. See Rainey and Notley, *Sacred Bridge*, 137–38, 150–51, 353.
7. See Zertal, *Sisera's Secret*, 231, 235, 246, 249, 255, 261, 269, 276, 308; Zertal, "Philistine Kin Found in Early Israel," 60.
8. See Hess, "Israelite Identity," 26.
9. Cf. Exod. 15:20; 2 Kings 22:14; 2 Chron. 34:22; Neh. 6:14; Isa. 8:3. On prophetesses in the ancient Near East, see Malamat, *Mari and the Bible*, 73–74, 95, 125.
10. See Hess, "Israelite Identity," 33–34. Sasson similarly suggests that Deborah may be described as a "wielder of flames" (*Judges 1–12*, 102, 255, 273).
11. Cf. Mafico, *Yahweh's Emergence*, 117–18.
12. Contra Block, *Judges, Ruth*, 193–97; Block, "Deborah among the Judges."
13. See Rainey and Notley, *Sacred Bridge*, 138.

14. See Hoffmeier, *Immigration Crisis*, 99–100.

15. See Amit, *Book of Judges*, 199, 203–4, 209–10, 213–20.

16. See Block, *Judges, Ruth*, 196, 197, 246; cf. 2 Chron. 15:3.

17. See Amit, *Book of Judges*, 199, 202–4, 206–18.

18. See ibid., 214–18.

19. When the Hebrew infinitive absolute is used *before* a cognate finite verb, the action is qualified with respect to the preceeding context (S. A. Kaufman, personal communication). Thus Deborah surprisingly answers: "I will in fact go with you." See also Wang, "Use of the Infinitive Absolute," chap. 2 ("The Prepositive Paranomastic Infinitive Absolute").

20. This scenario is only one speculative possibility. It is also possible that Jael and Heber are unified in a "double agent role" so that they can help the cause of Israel (J. H. Walton, personal communication).

21. Tedd Tripp, *Shepherding a Child's Heart* (Wapwallopen, PA: Shepherd, 1995), 139.

Judges 5:1–31

1. Fokkelman, "Song of Deborah and Barak," 596.

2. See Younger, "Heads! Tails! Or the Whole Coin?!"; Younger, *Judges, Ruth*, 137, 147, 157–58; cf. Brenner, "A Triangle and a Rhombus in Narrative Structure."

3. See Fokkelman, "Song of Deborah and Barak," 595–96; Younger, *Judges, Ruth*, 147–48.

4. Cf. Younger, *Judges, Ruth*, 148, 161.

5. See Hess, "Israelite Identity"; Hess, "Name Game."

6. See a review of the discussion in Echols, *"Tell Me, O Muse,"* 44–63.

7. For the former text, see *COS* 2.5A:32–38; for the latter see Chavalas, *Ancient Near East*, 145–52.

8. On all these texts, see Younger, "Heads! Tails! Or the Whole Coin?!"

9. See Smith, *Memoirs of God*, 24; Smith and Pitard, *Ugaritic Baal Cycle*, 2:373, 648, 651, 694–95; cf. *COS* 1.163:532n11; Num. 6:5; Deut. 32:42; Judg. 13:5; 16:17; Amos 2:11.

10. Cf. Deut. 33:2; Ps. 68:7–8; Hab. 3:3; see Hoffmeier, *Ancient Israel in Sinai*, 129–30, 237.

11. Cf. Judg. 1:4; 3:29; 4:6, 10, 14; 7:3; 8:10; 12:6; 15:11, 15, 16; 16:27; 20:2–46; 21:10. See Fouts, "Numbers, Large Numbers"; Hoffmeier, *Ancient Israel in Sinai*, 153–59; *IVPBBCOT*, 215, 220, 250, 274, 275.

12. See Rainey and Notley, *Sacred Bridge*, 138, 151.

13. For an Egyptian example, see *COS* 2.2B:14, 17; for a Mesopotamian example, see Westenholz, *Legends of the Kings of Akkade*, 71.

14. See *COS* 1.86:251; Smith and Pitard, *Ugaritic Baal Cycle*, 2:128, 133, 137, 192. For additional discussion on 5:20, see Cooley, *Poetic Astronomy in the Ancient Near East*, 298–303, 326.

15. See Younger, *Judges, Ruth*, 155.

16. For additional discussion on this motif, see Ackerman, *Warrior, Dancer, Seductress, Queen*, 155–62.

17. See Chisholm, "Yahweh versus the Canaanite Gods," 166–70.

18. It is also possible that the prophetess Deborah functioned as the angel/messenger of the Lord (see Judg. 4:8 in LXX); cf. Block, *Judges, Ruth*, 198, 214, 238.

19. For further discussion on panic, see Mobley, *Empty Men*, 61–63.

20. See Stager, "Song of Deborah," 62–64; Stager, "Archaeology, Ecology, and Social History."

21. See Foster, *Celebration of Discipline*, 190–201; Willard, *Spirit of the Disciplines*, 179–81.

22. See Hellerman, *When the Church Was a Family*, esp. 111.

Additional Insights, pp. 56–57

1. For additional references, see Ackerman, *Warrior, Dancer, Seductress, Queen*; Block, "Unspeakable Crimes"; Chisholm, "Role of Women"; Klein, "Spectrum of Female Characters"; O'Connor, "Women in the Book of Judges."

Judges 6:1–32

1. See Hawkins, *Iron Age I Structure on Mt. Ebal*; Hess, *Israelite Religions*, 216–21, 234, 236; Mazar, "Bronze Bull Found in Israelite 'High Place'"; Mazar, "'Bull Site.'"

2. See Zevit, *Religions of Ancient Israel*, 217–18, 263. For additional references on Asherah, see the comments on Judg. 3:7, above.

3. Many scholars regard the uninterrupted transition from verse 6 to verse 11 in the Qumran version (4QJudg[a]) as evidence for an earlier literary form of the book that predates a "Deuteronomistic" editing (see Abegg, Flint, and Ulrich, *Dead Sea Scrolls Bible*, 208, 209).

4. See Butler, *Judges*, xli, 185; Hess, "Dead Sea Scrolls and Higher Criticism."

5. See Bluedorn, *Yahweh versus Baalism*, 73–74, 89.

6. See Rainey and Notley, *Sacred Bridge*, 139–40.

7. *IVPBBCOT*, 253.

8. See, e.g., Younger's interpretation (*Judges, Ruth*, 167, 173, 177, 179, 181).

9. See Bluedorn, *Yahweh versus Baalism*, 96; Garsiel, "Homiletic Name-Derivations," 305–6.

10. See Chisholm, "Yahweh versus the Canaanite Gods," 172.

11. E.g., Lev. 10:1–3; 1 Sam. 5:1–12; 6:19; 2 Sam. 6:7.

12. See Wong, "Gideon," 543; cf. Block, *Judges, Ruth*, 267.

13. See Beale, *Temple and the Church's Mission*, 259–63.

14. See Walton, "Interpreting the Bible," 305–9.

Judges 6:33–7:25

1. For additional thematic parallels between Judges 7 and 20, see Exum, "Centre Cannot Hold," 430.

2. See Schmitz, "Deity and Royalty in Dedicatory Formulae."

3. See LXX, Vulgate, NLT, NRSV; cf. 1 Chron. 12:18 (Heb. v. 19); 2 Chron. 24:20; Luke 24:49 (*endyō*).

4. See Waldman, "Imagery of Clothing, Covering, and Overpowering."

5. See Walton, *Ancient Near Eastern Thought*, 259.

6. Cf. 1 Kings 17:1; Job 38:28; Prov. 3:20; Hag. 1:10; Zech. 8:12; see Chisholm, "Yahweh versus the Canaanite Gods," 171–72; Woods, *Water and Storm Polemics*, 67–69. For Baal's relationship to the dew, see COS 1.103:351; 1.86:250–51.

7. See *IVPBBCOT*, 255.

8. See T. L. Brensinger, "נסח (*nsh*)," *NIDOTTE* 3:111–13 (#5814).

9. See Gen. 22:1; Exod. 15:25; 16:4; 20:20; Deut. 8:2, 16; 13:3 (Heb. v. 4); 2 Chron. 32:31.

10. See Exod. 17:2, 7; Num. 14:22–23; Deut. 6:16; 9:22; 33:8; Pss. 78:18, 41, 56; 95:8–11; 106:14–15; cf. 1 Cor. 10:9.

11. See helpful background discussion in Sasson, "Oracle Inquiries in Judges"; Cooley, "Story of Saul's Election (1 Sam. 9–10)"; Walton, *Ancient Near Eastern Thought*, 253.

12. See Block, "Judges," 2:161.

13. Cf. Judg. 4:14–15, 23; 5:4–5, 11, 20–21; Ps. 83:9–10.

14. See Assis, *Self-Interest or Communal Interest*, 76–77, 80, 118–25.

15. See J. H. Walton and A. E. Hill, *Old Testament Today: A Journey from Original Meaning to Contemporary Significance* (Grand Rapids: Zondervan, 2004), 217 (this discussion is not included in the 2013 edition of the book).

16. Note that I usually employ the term "torah" (rather than "law") throughout this commentary as a generic reference to God's authoritative instructions that are revealed to Israel.

17. See Walton and Walton, *Bible Story Handbook*, 27–28; cf. Walton, Bailey, and Williford, "Bible-Based Curricula," 86.

18. See Smith-Christopher, "Gideon at Thermopylae?"

19. See Walton and Walton, *Bible Story Handbook*, 134.

20. For additional references, see Huffman, *How Then Should We Choose?*; Willard, *Hearing God*.

21. Henry Blackaby, *Experiencing God* (Nashville: Broadman & Holman, 1998), 22.

22. *Rocky*, directed by John G. Avildsen (1976; Santa Monica, CA: MGM, 2004), DVD.

Judges 8:1–32

1. See Exum, "Centre Cannot Hold," 412–13, 418, 425, 426, 428; cf. Claassens, "Character of God in Judges 6–8," 58, 62–71.

2. Cf. Assis, *Self-Interest or Communal Interest*, 127–29.

3. These names, respectively, mean "raven" and "wolf"; "sacrifice" and "statue/image" (see Hess, "Israelite Identity," 32–35; Garsiel, "Homiletic Name-Derivations," 308).

4. See Wong, *Compositional Strategy*, 129.

5. See Rainey and Notley, *Sacred Bridge*, 139.

6. See COS 2.1:5–7; Bietak, "Archaeology of the 'Gold of Valour.'"

7. John and Kim Walton explain: "Since Gideon had been 'successful' in gaining an oracle from God by means of the fleece, it would seem that he decided to exploit this success as he set up this oracular device so that he could serve as mediator of God's communication to the people. If the fleece showed a weakness, as we have suggested, the ephod institutionalizes that weakness" (Walton and Walton, *Bible Story Handbook*, 133).

8. See Fox, "Holy Piercing?" (summarized by Block, "Judges," 2:165–66).

9. See Ilan, *Image and Artifact*, 34–39, 56–59.

10. See *ANEP*, plates 351 (register A-3), 353 (register C-1), 355 (register A-3 detail).

11. See Ortlund, *God's Unfaithful Wife*.

12. Klein, *Triumph of Irony*, 65.

13. Cf. Judg. 9:22; 10:2–3; 12:7, 9, 11, 14; 16:31.

14. See Younger, *Judges, Ruth*, 209.

15. See ibid., 197, 201.

16. See Assis, *Self-Interest or Communal Interest*, 127–30.

17. See Exum, "Centre Cannot Hold," 411, 412–13, 418, 427, 431.

18. Note the pattern in Judg. 5:15b–17; 8:1–3; 12:1–6; 15:9–13; 19:1–21:25.

19. See Davies, "Judges VIII 22–23," 154–57; Heffelfinger, "'My Father Is King,'" 285–87; Olson, "Buber, Kingship, and the Book of Judges," 210–12, 216.

20. A shekel is here computed as equal to 11.5 grams.

21. See Josephus, *Antiquities* 5.6.6 (Thackeray and Marcus, *Josephus*, 105).

22. See Younger, *Judges, Ruth*, 197, 201, 204.

23. This tends to be a royal idiom (see COS 2.31:150); cf. Neh. 9:7. See Buber, *Kingship of God*, 74.

24. Cf. Ps. 115:1; 1 Cor. 1:31; 2 Cor. 10:17; 1 Pet. 4:11.

25. Cf. Matt. 20:25–28; 23:11; 1 Pet. 4:10.

26. Cf. Matt. 23:12; Phil. 2:3–8; 1 Pet. 5:5–6.
27. Cf. Heb. 4:14–5:10; 7:23–8:7; 10:19–22.
28. Foster, *Challenge of the Disciplined Life*, 175 and 196 respectively.

Additional Insights, pp. 79–80

1. See Greene, *Role of the Messenger and Message*; López, "Identifying the 'Angel of the Lord'"; MacDonald, "Christology and 'The Angel of the Lord'"; Meier, "Angel I" and "Angel of Yahweh," *DDD*, 45–50, 53–59; Meier, *Messenger in the Ancient Semitic World*; Walton, *Genesis*, 462–66.
2. For additional references, see Block, *Judges, Ruth*, 70; Block, "Will the Real Gideon Please Stand Up?," 358–59, 362, 365; Walton, "Inspired Subjectivity"; Walton and Hill, *Old Testament Today*, 181, 184–87; Walton and Walton, *Bible Story Handbook*, 21, 129; Way, "Handling 'Heroes' in Hebrews 11," 39; Younger, *Judges, Ruth*, 326–27.
3. Walton, "Inspired Subjectivity," 76.

Judges 8:33–9:57

1. See Stager, "Fortress-Temple at Shechem"; Stager, "Shechem Temple."
2. Stager, "Shechem Temple," 68.
3. See Lewis, "Identity and Function of El/Baal Berith," 416, 423; Wright, *Shechem*, 136.
4. See Cross, *Canaanite Myth*, 39; Lewis, "Identity and Function of El/Baal Berith," 408, 416.
5. On this deity, see Herrmann, "El," *DDD*, 274–80.
6. For these bronze statuettes, see Lewis, "Identity and Function of El/Baal Berith," 416–23; Stager, "Shechem Temple," 34, 66.
7. Mobley, *Empty Men*, 2, 36, 37; cf. Doak, "'Some Worthless and Reckless Fellows.'"
8. See *COS* 2.37:158. The Panamuwa inscription is written in Samalian Aramaic.
9. See Schipper, *Parables and Conflict*, 14, 25, 29, 37.
10. E.g., see *ANET* 410–11, 427–30, 592–93; *COS* 1.178:571–73; 1.180–83:575–88.
11. *IVPBBCOT*, 259.
12. See Tatu, "Jotham's Fable," 108.
13. See Block, "Empowered by the Spirit of God," 47–52, 59, 61. The phrase "spirit of disaster" also occurs in 1 Sam. 16:13–23; 18:10–12; 19:9–10; cf. 1 Kings 22:19–23; 2 Kings 19:7.
14. See Hess, "Israelite Identity," 34.
15. See Way, *Donkeys in the Biblical World*, 175–76.
16. Ibid., 3, 8–9, 12, 157, 173–76, 180–81, 196, 201–2.
17. Ibid., 117–18, 155, 175, 201.
18. Cf. Deut. 29:23; Ps. 107:34; Jer. 17:6; Zeph. 2:9.
19. See Block, "Judges," 2:174; *COS* 2.82:214; 3.89:219; cf. 1.72:83 (sowing cress).
20. See Stager, "Fortress-Temple at Shechem," 243–45; Stager, "Shechem Temple," 32.

21. See Herr and Boyd, "Watermelon Named Abimelech," 34–37, 62.
22. See Block, *Judges, Ruth*, 308–9, 335, 336.
23. See helpful discussion in Exum, "Centre Cannot Hold," 419–20.
24. See Malamat, *History of Biblical Israel*, 168.
25. Block, *Judges, Ruth*, 335.
26. Ibid., 321, 336; cf. Webb, *Book of the Judges: An Integrated Reading*, 159.
27. Cf. Judg. 1:7; 2:2–3, 20–21; 5:23; 9:24, 56–57; Prov. 26:27; Matt. 26:52; 2 Thess. 1:6.
28. Block, *Judges, Ruth*, 308–9; Block, "Judges," 2:169. Compare the political situation in Canaan that is portrayed in the Amarna letters (*COS* 3.92A–G); cf. Doak, "'Some Worthless and Reckless Fellows'"; Rainey and Notley, *Sacred Bridge*, 139–40.
29. Plantinga, *Not the Way*, 54–55.
30. "Lord Acton Quote Archive," Acton Institute, http://www.acton.org/research/lord-acton-quote-archive.

Judges 10:6–16

1. See Polzin, *Moses and the Deuteronomist*, 177–80; cf. Webb, *Book of the Judges: An Integrated Reading*, 41–78.
2. On self-interest, see Assis, *Self-Interest or Communal Interest*, 197–99, 208, 212, 215–37.
3. See Provan, Long, and Longman, *Biblical History of Israel*, 164–65.
4. See O'Connell, *Rhetoric of the Book of Judges*, 179.
5. See Provan, Long, and Longman, *Biblical History of Israel*, 161–62; cf. Globe, "'Enemies Round About,'" 236, 248; Younger, *Judges, Ruth*, 24, 25, 34–35, 242n3.
6. See Younger, *Judges, Ruth*, 243.
7. Endris, "Yahweh versus Baal," 189.
8. See Berman, *Narrative Analogy in the Hebrew Bible*, 102–14.
9. See ibid., 93–95; Block, *Judges, Ruth*, 348–49; Haak, "Study and New Interpretation of *QSR NPŠ*"; Janzen, "Why the Deuteronomist Told," 346–47; Mullen, "'Minor Judges,'" 198; Polzin, *Moses and the Deuteronomist*, 177–78; Webb, *Book of the Judges: An Integrated Reading*, 44–48.
10. See Exum, "Centre Cannot Hold," 412, 421–22.
11. See Galli, *Jesus Mean and Wild*.
12. Plantinga, *Not the Way*, 147.
13. Ibid., 133.
14. Ibid.
15. Galli, *Jesus Mean and Wild*, 171.
16. C. S. Lewis, *The Chronicles of Narnia: The Lion, the Witch and the Wardrobe* (New York: HarperCollins, 1950), chap. 8.

Judges 10:17–11:28

1. For all of these sites, see B. MacDonald, "Ammonite Territory and Sites," in MacDonald and

Younker, *Ancient Ammon*, 30–56 (esp. 30–39, 46); Rainey and Notley, *Sacred Bridge*, 140–41.

2. Rainey and Notley, *Sacred Bridge*, 140.

3. See Younger, *Judges, Ruth*, 248n14.

4. I must thank Michael Sanborn for this term.

5. See Exum, *Tragedy and Biblical Narrative*, 48, 53, 60–65; Garsiel, *Biblical Names*, 105–6.

6. See Mobley, *Empty Men*, 35, 38.

7. Rainey and Notley, *Sacred Bridge*, 140.

8. See *COS* 1.148:479; Doak, "'Some Worthless and Reckless Fellows,'" 23–24.

9. See Garland and Garland, *Flawed Families of the Bible*, 179–92, 204–6; Smith, "Jephthah"; Smith, "Samson."

10. See Willis, "Nature of Jephthah's Authority," 34–36, 40–44; Younger, *Judges, Ruth*, 250–51.

11. Block, *Judges, Ruth*, 356.

12. See *COS* 2.23:137–38; 2.72:201.

13. For the former option, see Younger, *Judges, Ruth*, 256–57; for the latter option, see Block, *Judges, Ruth*, 362, 363.

14. See Burney, *Book of Judges*, 314–15; Younger, *Judges, Ruth*, 256–57, 259.

15. Klein, Blomberg, and Hubbard, *Introduction to Biblical Interpretation*, 69.

16. For additional discussion, see Chisholm, "Chronology of the Book of Judges," 253–55; Kitchen, *Reliability of the Old Testament*, 209.

17. *COS* 2.23:137.

18. Younger, *Judges, Ruth*, 259; cf. Boling, *Judges*, 205.

19. Younger, *Judges, Ruth*, 252; cf. O'Connell, *Rhetoric of the Book of Judges*, 191.

20. See Assis, *Self-Interest or Communal Interest*, 197–99.

21. Block, *Judges, Ruth*, 356.

22. See Feldman, *Studies in Josephus' Rewritten Bible*, 177–92.

23. Galli, *Jesus Mean and Wild*, 168.

24. Ibid., 169. See also 2 Chron. 15:2–3; Prov. 15:29.

25. Galli, *Jesus Mean and Wild*, 170.

26. Ibid., 171.

27. For example, in the Torah/Pentateuch (Gen. 16:5; 18:25; 30:6; 31:53; Exod. 5:21; Deut. 1:17; 10:17–18; 32:4, 36), the Prophets (1 Sam. 3:13; 24:12, 15; 2 Sam. 18:19, 31; Isa. 2:4; 11:3–5; 33:22; 51:5; Jer. 11:20; Ezek. 34:22; Mic. 4:3), the Writings (Pss. 7:8, 11; 50:4, 6; 67:4; 75:7; 94:2; 96:12–13; 99:4; 111:7), and, of course, the New Testament (John 5:22; 8:50; Acts 10:42; 17:31; Rom. 2:16; 3:6; 2 Tim. 4:1, 8; Heb. 10:30; 12:23; 13:4; James 4:12; 5:9; 1 Pet. 1:7; 2:23; 4:5; Rev. 16:5; 19:11). On the justice of Yahweh, see Block, *Deuteronomy*, 66, 273; Walton, *Ancient Near Eastern Thought*, 106–8; Wright, *Old Testament Ethics for the People of God*, 253–80.

28. S. M. Hooks, "Jephthah," *NIDOTTE* 4:751.

Judges 11:29–12:7

1. John Walton (personal communication); cf. Sasson, "Jephthah," 411, 414.

2. For a dissenting (i.e., nonsacrificial) interpretation of this story, see Archer, *Encyclopedia of Bible Difficulties*, 164–65; Marcus, *Jephthah and His Vow*; cf. Walton, *Chronological and Background Charts*, 104.

3. See Cartledge, *Vows in the Hebrew Bible*, 178–79; Steinberg, "Problem of Human Sacrifice in War," 123.

4. See Mullen, "'Minor Judges,'" 199n36, 201; Smith, "Jephthah," 282–83, 287–90, 296, 297.

5. This point is made in *Targum Jonathan*; see Smelik, *Targum of Judges*, 554–57.

6. See Mullen, "'Minor Judges,'" 199.

7. See Block, "Judges," 2:183–84; Hendel, "Sibilants"; Kaufman, "Classification of the North West Semitic Dialects," 56; Rainey and Notley, *Sacred Bridge*, 141.

8. See O'Connell, *Rhetoric of the Book of Judges*, 181–83.

9. Ibid., 192.

10. See Gane, *God's Faulty Heroes*, 94; Janzen, "Why the Deuteronomist Told," 345–46, 355.

11. See Trible, *Texts of Terror*, 93–116. For further references, see Thompson, "Preaching Texts of Terror."

12. The same question could, of course, be posed for the deaths of Gideon's sons, the Timnite woman, Samson, the Levite's concubine, and so on.

13. For additional discussion, see Chisholm, "Ethical Challenge"; Copan, *Is God a Moral Monster?*, 97–99.

14. See Thorn, *Note to Self*, 121–22.

15. See Wilson, *Hurt People Hurt People*.

16. Augustine of Hippo (d. 430), in Franke, *Joshua, Judges, Ruth, 1–2 Samuel*, 138.

17. John Chrysostom (d. 407), in Franke, *Joshua, Judges, Ruth, 1–2 Samuel*, 139.

18. Martin Luther King Jr., *Strength to Love* (1963; repr., Minneapolis: Fortress, 2010), 47.

Judges 3:31; 10:1–5; 12:8–15

1. Cf. Judg. 10:8, 17–18; 11:1–11, 29, 40; 12:4–7.

2. Note the contrast with childless Jephthah (Judg. 11:34).

3. Word counts are computed in Bible Works software (based on the Hebrew text: search version WTM).

4. See Hess, "Israelite Identity," 29; Hess, "Judges 1–5," 148–49.

5. Block, *Judges, Ruth*, 175; cf. Younger, *Judges, Ruth*, 130–31.

6. See Hess, "Israelite Identity," 26, 28; Hess, "Judges 1–5," 148; Shupak, "New Light on Shamgar ben 'Anath," 523–24.

7. E.g., see *COS* 2.84:221; cf. Hess, "Israelite Identity," 26, 28.

8. For additional references, see Day, "Anat," *DDD*, 36–43; Cornelius, *Many Faces of the Goddess*, esp. 92–93.

9. See Block, "Judges," 2:133.

10. See Mobley, *Empty Men*, 56–59.

11. See Nelson, "Ideology," 358–59; Stager, "Shemer's Estate," 103–4.

12. See Way, "Donkey Domain," 106, 110–11, 113.

13. Cf. Beem, "Minor Judges," 152, 158; Nelson, "Ideology," 355.

14. The Hebrew wordplay is also preserved in the Septuagint, employing *pōlos* ("young animal") and *polis* ("city").

15. Hess, "Israelite Identity," 37–39; Hess, "Arrowheads from Iron Age I," 125.

16. See Globe, "'Enemies Round About,'" 243; Sasson, "Coherence and Fragments," 367, 368–69.

17. Younger, *Judges, Ruth*, 278.

18. See Alt's *Essays on Old Testament History and Religion*, 130–31.

19. See Exum, "Centre Cannot Hold," 411–12, 421, 431.

20. Notice that the Qal stem is used here rather than the Hiphil.

21. Cf. 1 Cor. 11:3; Eph. 1:22; 4:15; 5:23; Col. 2:19.

22. See Pritchard, *He's God and We're Not*, esp. 9–31.

23. Cf. Zech. 14:9; Matt. 6:10; Luke 11:2; 1 Cor. 15:24–28; Heb. 1:8; Rev. 15:3.

24. See Walton and Hill, *Old Testament Today*, 18.

25. Cf. 1 Cor. 3:16–17; 6:19; Eph. 2:21–22; 1 Pet. 2:5, 9.

26. "William Ernest Henley, "Invictus," Poetry Foundation website, accessed January 15, 2016, http://www.poetryfoundation.org/poem/182194.

Judges 13:1–25

1. See especially Judg. 13:5; 14:4; 15:11, 20.

2. See Olson, "Buber, Kingship, and the Book of Judges," 206.

3. See Exum, "Aspects of Symmetry," 3, 4, 9–10, 12, 16–18, 21; cf. Amit, *Book of Judges*, 267–68, 274–75; Block, *Judges, Ruth*, 393, 421; Younger, *Judges, Ruth*, 281–82.

4. See Gen. 11:30; 16:1; 21:2; 25:21; 29:31; 30:22; 1 Sam. 1:2, 6, 20; Matt. 1:18–25; Luke 1:7, 15, 26–38, 57.

5. Perhaps "the reader's frustration at Samson's failure to live up to his great expectations in some way mirrors YHWH's frustration [cf. 10:10–16] at Israel's failure to live up to their great expectations" (Johnson, "What Type of Son is Samson?," 284n86). For this type-scene, see also Alter, *Art of Biblical Narrative*, 51–56, 181, 188.

6. See Emmrich, "Symbolism of the Lion and the Bees," 68, 74.

7. Younger, *Judges, Ruth*, 288; cf. Alter, *Art of Biblical Narrative*, 101.

8. See also Judg. 2:23; 3:1; 6:18, 20; 16:26; 20:43.

9. Block, *Judges, Ruth*, 397. I must thank my colleague Daniel E. Kim for his remarks on this paragraph (personal communication, fall 2011).

10. See Taylor, *Yahweh and the Sun*, 93–95. Sun deities are variously named Shemesh, Shamash, Shapshu, and so on.

11. Ibid., 95–96.

12. See Amit, *Book of Judges*, 278–79.

13. See Kelm and Mazar, *Timnah*, 93–95; Rainey and Notley, *Sacred Bridge*, 16, 141, 151.

14. Younger, *Judges, Ruth*, 293.

15. Davis, *Such a Great Salvation*, 167.

16. Ibid., 159.

17. Ibid., 167.

18. Block, *Judges, Ruth*, 420; cf. Younger, *Judges, Ruth*, 295.

Judges 14:1–20

1. See Judg. 1:12–15; 3:9, 11; 14:1–3, 7, 10, 14; 15:1, 10–11; 16:1, 4, 30.

2. See Strawn, *What Is Stronger Than a Lion?*, 54–58, 174–84, 268–70.

3. See Dick, "Neo-Assyrian Royal Lion Hunt."

4. See Mobley, "Wild Man in the Bible and the Ancient Near East," 229.

5. Cf. 1 Kings 13:24–26; 20:36; 2 Kings 17:25–26; Dan. 6:16–24.

6. Cf. Gen. 49:9; Deut. 33:22; Judg. 14:5; 18:7, 14, 27, 29; Ezek. 19:2–9; Rev. 5:5. See also the "Historical and Cultural Background" in the unit on Judg. 18:1–31.

7. See Borowski, *Every Living Thing*, 199–200, 226–27.

8. See Kelm and Mazar, *Timnah*, 91–104.

9. See Strawn, "*kĕpîr 'ărāyôt* in Judges 14:5."

10. Ibid., 158.

11. See Exod. 3:8, 17; 13:5; 33:3; Lev. 20:24; Num. 13:27; 14:8; 16:13–14; Deut. 6:3; 11:9; 26:9, 15; 27:3; 31:20; Josh. 5:6; Jer. 11:5; 32:22; Ezek. 20:6, 15.

12. That is, Iron IIA (Stratum V; mid tenth–early ninth centuries BC). See Mazar and Panitz-Cohen, "It Is the Land of Honey."

13. See Dayagi-Mendels, *Drink and Be Merry*, 122–24.

14. See Num. 12:8; 1 Kings 10:1; 2 Chron. 9:1; Pss. 49:4 (Heb. v. 5); 78:2; Prov. 1:6; Ezek. 17:2; Dan. 8:23; Hab. 2:6.

15. See Yadin, "Samson's ḤÎDÂ."

16. See Stager, Schloen, and Master, *Ashkelon 1*, 217.

17. On the animals as divine agents, see Emmrich, "Symbolism of the Lion and the Bees," 69; Way, "Animals in the Prophetic World," 57–58.

18. See Davis, *Such a Great Salvation*, 176.

19. Cf. Exod. 34:15–16; Deut. 7:3–4; Josh. 23:12; Judg. 3:6.

20. See Willard, *Renovation of the Heart*, 138, 142–44, 219, 253.

21. See Judg. 14:6, 19; 15:14; cf. 1 Sam. 10:6, 10; 11:6; 16:13; 18:10.
22. Cf. Jer. 9:23–24; Zech. 4:6–7; 1 Cor. 1:31.

Judges 15:1–20

1. For these and other similarities, see Exum, "Aspects of Symmetry," 12, 16–17, 21.
2. Yadin, "Samson's ḤÎDÂ," 417.
3. Ibid., 418.
4. See Borowski, *Every Living Thing*, 203–4; Kogan, "Animal Names in Biblical Hebrew," 275.
5. See Amit, *Book of Judges*, 279.
6. See Chisholm, "Yahweh versus the Canaanite Gods," 175–76.
7. See Younger, *Judges, Ruth*, 307n61.
8. See Way, *Donkeys in the Biblical World*, 59–60, 165–66. In addition to the bibliography cited in Way, see Exum, "Aspects of Symmetry," 7; Segert, "Paranomasia in the Samson Narrative," 456–57.
9. See, e.g., Judg. 1:2, 4; 2:16, 18; 3:9–10, 15, 28; 4:14–15; 6:36–37; 7:9, 15, 22; 10:12–14; 11:9, 32; 12:3.
10. See Exum, "Theological Dimension," 39, 41, 42; cf. Exum, "Apects of Symmetry," 24.
11. Cf. Lev. 19:18; Deut. 32:35–36, 41, 43; Ps. 94:1–2, 23; Prov. 24:29; Jer. 11:20; Nah. 1:2.
12. See Foster, *Challenge of the Disciplined Life*, 179–80; Willard, *Spirit of the Disciplines*, 184–86.
13. "Carl's Jr. and Hardee's Offer No B.S. and That's Just the Way It Is," Carl's Jr. press release, April 27, 2011, http://www.carlsjr.com/company /releases/carls-jr-and-hardees-offer-no-bs-and-thats -just-the-way-it-is.

Judges 16:1–31

1. For some of these (and additional) parallels, see Broida, "Closure in Samson," 25, 26, 28–31; Exum, "Aspects of Symmetry," 4, 10.
2. See Exum, "Centre Cannot Hold," 412, 423, 425.
3. See Maeir, "Insights on the Philistine Culture," 365–66.
4. See Ovadiah, "Gaza."
5. Bierling, *Giving Goliath His Due*, 112.
6. It is also possible that she is ethnically an Israelite (see Walton and Walton, *Bible Story Handbook*, 141) who identifies with Philistia and betrays her own people for an irresistibly large amount of money. If so, then she is an example of Canaanization (or in this case, "Philistinization").
7. Block, "Judges," 2:200. A shekel is here computed as equal to 11.5 grams.
8. Sasson, "Who Cut Samson's Hair?," 338.
9. See Niditch, *"My Brother Esau Is a Hairy Man,"* 69–70.
10. See Olyan, "What Do Shaving Rites Accomplish?," 615, 621.

11. See Younger, *Judges, Ruth*, 316–17, 322; cf. *IVPBBCOT*, 269–70.
12. See Hoffner, "Slavery and Slave Laws," 133–34; van der Toorn, "Judges XVI 21."
13. Cf. Exod. 11:5; Judg. 9:53; Jer. 52:11 (LXX); Lam. 5:13.
14. Cf. 1 Sam. 11:2; 2 Kings 25:7; Isa. 42:7; Jer. 39:7; 52:11.
15. E.g., Asherah, Ashtaroth, Baal, Baal-zebub, Pythogayah; see Judg. 10:6; 1 Sam. 31:10; 2 Kings 1:2–3, 6, 16; *COS* 2.42:164. For additional background on Dagon, see Feliu, *God Dagan in Bronze Age Syria*.
16. See Ellingworth and Mojola, "Translating Euphemisms in the Bible."
17. See Exum, "Centre Cannot Hold," 425.
18. See Crenshaw, *Samson*, 29; cf. Block, *Judges, Ruth*, 469.
19. See Exum, *Tragedy and Biblical Narrative*, 43; cf. Exum, "Centre Cannot Hold," 424.
20. Cf. Lev. 19:18; Deut. 32:35–36, 41, 43; Prov. 24:29; Rom. 12:19; Heb. 10:30.
21. See Greenberg, *Biblical Prose Prayer*, 13.

Judges 17:1–13

1. Douglas, *Thinking in Circles*, 37.
2. Examples from archaeology are found at sites such as Ai/Et-Tell, Mount Ebal, Shechem, and the so-called "Bull site" near Dothan (see Hawkins, *Iron Age I Structure on Mt. Ebal*; Hess, *Israelite Religions*, 216–21, 235–38).
3. See *IVPBBCOT*, 270. For more on the shekel, see the comments on Judg. 16:5, above.
4. See Klein, "Book of Judges," 66–67.
5. See Exod. 20:4, 23; 34:17; Lev. 19:4; 26:1; Deut. 4:16, 23, 25; 5:8; 7:5, 25; 12:3; 27:15.
6. See, e.g., Exod. 32:1–4; Judg. 3:19; 1 Kings 12:28; Isa. 40:19–20; Hosea 8:4–6.
7. See Block, "Judges," 2:206.
8. See, e.g., Exod. 15:26; Deut. 6:18; 12:25, 28; 13:18; 21:9.
9. For his unmarried status, see King and Stager, *Life in Biblical Israel*, 9, 12, 15.
10. See Block, *Judges, Ruth*, 321; Walton and Hill, *Old Testament Today*, 173; Walton, Strauss, and Cooper, *Essential Bible Companion*, 31.
11. Note especially the positive assessments of Hezekiah and Josiah in 2 Kings 18:3–6; 22:2; 23:24–25.
12. Unless the "shrine/house of God" in Judg. 17:5 is interpreted as a "house of gods."
13. Cf., 1 Sam. 2:2; Ps. 113:5; Isa. 40:18–20, 25; 46:5–9; Mic. 7:18.
14. See Walton, "Interpreting the Bible," 308.

Judges 18:1–31

1. Exum, "Centre Cannot Hold," 426.
2. For additional discussion, see Sharon, "Echoes of Gideon's Ephod," 99–100.

3. See Block, *Judges, Ruth*, 66, 513.

4. See Rainey and Notley, *Sacred Bridge*, 126.

5. See Biran, *Biblical Dan*, 21, 90; Rainey and Notley, *Sacred Bridge*, 58, 72.

6. See Finkelstein, *Shiloh*, 388–89.

7. Bauer, "Judges 18 as an Anti-Spy Story," 42.

8. See Block, "Judges," 2:139, 209; cf. Sasson, "Oracle Inquiries in Judges," 1:158.

9. Biran, *Biblical Dan*, 125.

10. Block, "Judges," 2:210; cf. Biran, *Biblical Dan*, 120–21.

11. The term "rest-disturber" is from my colleague Daniel E. Kim (personal communication, fall 2012). See now D. E. Kim, "From Rest to Rest."

12. See Bauer, "Metaphorical Etiology in Judges 18:12," section 5.4.

13. See Biran, *Biblical Dan*, 135–42.

14. See ibid., 165.

15. See Garsiel, *Biblical Names*, 137–38.

16. Marcos, *Judges*, 53, 104*–105*; Rainey and Notley, *Sacred Bridge*, 142, 151; Wegner, *Student's Guide*, 75–76. The reading "Manasseh" derives from the Masoretic Text (with suspended *nun*).

17. Finkelstein, *Shiloh*, 385.

18. Ibid., 7.

19. See Wilson, "As You Like It," 73, 84.

20. See Block, *Judges, Ruth*, 490, 509.

21. A. W. Tozer, *Knowledge of the Holy* (New York: Harper & Row, 1961), 12.

Judges 19:1-30

1. Cf. Younger, *Judges, Ruth*, 34, 36, 37, 43, 70.

2. See Schneider, "Achsah, the Raped *Pîlegeš*, and the Book of Judges."

3. See Fokkelman, "Structural Remarks on Judges 9 and 19," 40–45; Younger, *Judges, Ruth*, 351–52, 354.

4. See Mazar, *Palace of King David*, 36–42. On the Jebusites, see Hostetter, *Nations Mightier and More Numerous*, 76–80.

5. See Rainey and Notley, *Sacred Bridge*, 142.

6. Cf. Exum, "Centre Cannot Hold," 427.

7. See Block, "Judges," 2:168.

8. Boling, *Judges*, 274. For further discussion, see Block, *Judges, Ruth*, 522–23; Butler, *Judges*, 418–20; Marcos, *Judges*, 105*.

9. In fact, there may be another root, *znh* II, meaning "to be angry" (see *DCH* 3:123).

10. It is also possible that this "house of the Lord" is at Bethel (cf. Judg. 20:18, 26; 21:2).

11. See Tov, *Textual Criticism of the Hebrew Bible*, 238. In favor of the MT, see Butler, *Judges*, 408–9, 423; Marcos, *Judges*, 108*.

12. See Webb, *Book of Judges*, 466.

13. Block, *Deuteronomy*, 334; cf. Deut. 13:13.

14. See Marcos, *Judges*, 109*–110*.

15. See the discussion in Freedman, *Nine Commandments*, 114–18.

16. That is, *ARM* 2.48; see Block, "Judges," 2:215.

17. Cf. Block, *Judges, Ruth*, 519; Exum, "Centre Cannot Hold," 428; Schulte and Schneider, "Absence of the Deity in Rape Scenes."

18. Trible, *Texts of Terror*, 65.

19. For further reference on this issue, see Taylor, "Bible and Homosexuality."

20. That is, the men of Gibeah were possibly guilty of adultery by raping a married woman.

21. See Trible, *Texts of Terror*, 64–91.

22. See Erickson, *Christian Theology*, 1242–43, 1247, 1248; Lewis, *Problem of Pain*, 122–23, 127–28, 152–53; cf. Matt. 25:41–46.

23. See the helpful discussion in Younger, *Judges, Ruth*, 360–63, 384.

24. See Younger, *Judges, Ruth*, 357.

25. For an excellent study on Christian acts of rescue, see Gushee, *Righteous Gentiles of the Holocaust*.

26. See Trible, *Texts of Terror*, 84–85.

27. Pastor Ed Morsey, Granada Height Friends Church, La Mirada, September 2011.

Judges 20:1-48

1. See Wong, *Compositional Strategy*, 129–30.

2. Rainey and Notley, *Sacred Bridge*, 116–18. While it is possible that some of the references to Bethel in chapters 20–21 refer to a generic "shrine," rather than the place name (see Boling, *Judges*, 285), the literary context suggests otherwise (see Judg. 20:26–28, 31; 21:2–4, 19).

3. See Rainey and Notley, *Sacred Bridge*, 143.

4. Webb, *Book of Judges*, 478; cf. Younger, *Judges, Ruth*, 375.

5. See Lapsley, *Whispering the Word*, 51.

6. See 1 Sam. 17:40, 50; 25:29; 2 Kings 3:25; 1 Chron. 12:2; 2 Chron. 26:14; Prov. 26:8; Jer. 10:18; Zech. 9:15.

7. See Sasson, "Oracle Inquiries in Judges," 1:159.

8. Stone, "Judges," 467. See also Judg. 21:4.

9. See Block, "Judges," 2:218–19; cf. Num. 10:35; 2 Sam. 11:11.

10. For further references, see Copan, *Is God a Moral Monster?*; Lamb, *God Behaving Badly*.

11. See also Josh. 22:17, 20; Ps. 78:30–31, 34, 62–64; Isa. 63:10. For further references on this theme, see Trimm, "*YHWH Fights for Them!*," 44, 236–38.

12. For "Christian" involvement in the Holocaust, see Gushee, *Righteous Gentiles of the Holocaust*, 12–16, 197–203.

13. See Rom. 12:12; 15:4; Eph. 6:18; 1 Thess. 5:17; 1 Tim. 4:13; 2 Tim. 3:14–17.

14. Thomas Merton, *Opening the Bible* (Collegeville, MN: Liturgical Press; Philadelphia: Fortress, 1970), 11.

15. A. W. Pink, *The Attributes of God* (Grand Rapids: Baker, 1975), 85.

Judges 21:1–25

1. Notice how the Kenizzite Caleb swears to give his daughter in marriage (Judg. 1:12), while the collective Israelites swear the exact opposite (21:1).

2. See Webb, *Book of Judges*, 507; Webb, *Book of the Judges: An Integrated Reading*, 196.

3. Although I have modified the details slightly, this basic structure is also adopted by Younger (*Judges, Ruth*, 347, 383) and Stone ("Judges," 483).

4. Younger, *Judges, Ruth*, 384.

5. See Rasmussen, *Zondervan Atlas of the Bible*, 287.

6. Webb, *Book of the Judges: An Integrated Reading*, 195; cf. Webb, *Book of Judges*, 498, 500, 508.

7. The term "Canaan(ite)" occurs seventeen times in the prologue (Judg. 1:1, 3–5, 9–10, 17, 27–30, 32–33; 3:1, 3, 5); cf. Stone, "Judges," 479.

8. G. T. K. Wong's suggestion that Judg. 21:15b is "Israel's perspective rather than the narrator's" (*Compositional Strategy*, 217; cf. Block, *Judges, Ruth*, 573; Lapsley, *Whispering the Word*, 60–61) is unlikely in light of how the narrator has presented God's actions in the previous chapter (esp. in 20:35).

9. See Younger, *Judges, Ruth*, 381, 383, 384.

10. See Block, "Judges," 2:220–21.

11. Younger, *Judges, Ruth*, 382.

12. See Smith, "Jephthah," 282, 284.

13. Davis, *Such a Great Salvation*, 227; cf. Neh. 9:31.

14. See Block, *Judges, Ruth*, 515–16.

15. For these imagined lands in children's literature, see Blyton, *Magic Faraway Tree*.

16. See Lapsley, *Whispering the Word*, 64–67.

17. Block, "Unspeakable Crimes," 54.

18. Lapsley, *Whispering the Word*, 64.

19. See ibid., 64–65, 124n91.

Introduction to Ruth

1. Likewise, Eskenazi eloquently remarks: "The story traces a journey from Bethlehem and back, a journey from famine to fullness, from futility to fertility" (Eskenazi and Frymer-Kensky, *Ruth*, xv).

2. See Hill and Walton, *Survey*, 249, 251–52; Walton and Hill, *Old Testament Today*, 203; Walton and Walton, *Bible Story Handbook*, 143, 144.

3. Alter, *Art of Biblical Narrative*, 58; cf. Wilson, *Divine Symmetries*, 137–38.

4. The storyteller's sensitivity to dialect and register is especially evident in the quotations of Naomi and Boaz (S. A. Kaufman, personal communication); cf. Eskenazi and Frymer-Kensky, *Ruth*, 34; Holmstedt, *Ruth*, 41–49.

5. See Hals, *Theology of the Book of Ruth*, 12–13, 16–17.

6. Depending on how one does the computation, anywhere from 52 percent to 69 percent of the book is dialogue; for these figures, see Block (*Judges, Ruth*, 588) and Chisholm (*Judges and Ruth*, 581), respectively.

7. Sasson, "Ruth," 320.

8. E.g., see Globe, "Folktale Form," 129–31.

9. On the role of the central core in ring compositions, see Douglas, *Thinking in Circles*, 32, 37; Globe, "Folktale Form," 129, 132. This ring feature is epitomized in the structure of the book of Judges (see the introduction to Judges; Way, "Literary Structure of Judges Revisited," 254, 256), but I am unconvinced that it is present in Ruth as argued by Globe.

10. See Bertman, "Symmetrical Design"; cf. Hongisto, "Literary Structure and Theology in the Book of Ruth"; Korpel, *Structure of the Book of Ruth*; Luter and Davis, *God behind the Seen*, 20–22, 63–64, 73–74, 80–81; Luter and Rigsby, "Adjusted Symmetrical Structuring"; Porten, "Scroll of Ruth," 23, 48n1; Radday, "Chiasmus in Hebrew Biblical Narrative," 71, 73, 74; Wilson, *Divine Symmetries*, 140; Younger, *Judges, Ruth*, 392–93, 397–99, 405, 472–73, 481–82, 484. Dorsey favors a seven-part chiastic structure for Ruth, but he acknowledges that Bertman's six-part analysis is a "legitimate alternative" (*Literary Structure*, 128).

11. This detail, especially in Ruth 2:1, is underappreciated by Bertman ("Symmetrical Design," 167), probably due to his slavish adherence to symmetry as he has understood it.

12. Wilson, *Divine Symmetries*, 23, 27–28. Wilson explains that "*Series episodes* are 'wired' in series like parallel strands linked in the middle (ABCD—A'B'C'D')" (*Divine Symmetries*, 28).

13. For simple trifold analyses of the series episodes in chapters 2–3, see Chisholm, *Judges and Ruth*, 558, 648; Porten, "Scroll of Ruth," 23, 32–42; Radday, "Chiasmus in Hebrew Biblical Narrative," 72–74; Wendland, "Structural Symmetry," 32; Younger, *Judges, Ruth*, 397–98, 438–39, 457. For a fivefold analysis, see Bertman, "Symmetrical Design," 165, 167. For a tenfold analysis, see Wilson, *Divine Symmetries*, 140.

14. Homiletic division by chapter is also the approach taken in Chisholm, *Judges and Ruth*, 569–72.

15. See Deut. 10:18–19; cf. Pss. 68:5; 146:9; Isa. 1:17, 23; 10:2; 54:1–10; Jer. 7:6; 49:11; Mal. 3:5; Matt. 25:31–46; Mark 12:40; Luke 20:47.

16. For an excellent analysis of the direct and indirect references to God in the story, see Hals, *Theology of the Book of Ruth*, 3–19.

17. Porten, "Theme and Historiosophic Background," 69.

18. See Alter, *World of Biblical Literature*, 52.

19. Walton and Hill, *Old Testament Today*, 204; Walton, Strauss, and Cooper, *Essential Bible Companion*, 29.

20. See a concise survey of views in Gow, "Ruth."

21. Individuals such as Caleb, Rahab, Othniel, Jael, and Ruth are examples of faithful foreigners who are probably included in the covenant community by faith rather than ethnicity (see Adamcik, "Who Are 'The People of YHWH'?").

22. Here my interest is in the interpretive *effects* of Ruth's placement rather than in ascertaining the *original* placement or the *priority* of a particular canon, matters that are presently obscure (see Goswell, "Order of the Books," 460–62, 465); cf. Childs, *Introduction to the Old Testament as Scripture*, 564.

23. Apparently, "the rationale" for the talmudic order is "that David's birth (Ruth 4:17–22) precedes the Psalms attributed to him" (Eskenazi and Frymer-Kensky, *Ruth*, xx); see *b. Baba Bathra* 14b in Epstein, *Seder Nezikin*, 2:70–71.

24. This is the order of the MT as preserved in both the Leningrad and Aleppo codices. This order is presumably chronological in that Ruth is correlated with David, Song of Songs with early Solomon, Ecclesiastes with late Solomon, Lamentations with Jeremiah, and Esther with the Persian period (see Eskenazi and Frymer-Kensky, *Ruth*, xx–xxi).

25. See Younger, *Judges, Ruth*, 391–92.

26. See Leder, "Paradise Lost," 20.

27. See Walton and Hill, *Old Testament Today*, 32, 184, 185; Walton and Walton, *Bible Story Handbook*, 21, 146.

28. Campbell, *Ruth*, 29.

29. For a suggested script adapted for five individuals and four acts, see Block, "'That They May Hear,'" 24–34.

30. For novella (or *novelle*), see Campbell, *Ruth*, 3–4; for short story, see Hubbard, *Book of Ruth*, 47; for idyll, see Würthwein, *Die Fünf Megilloth*, 3–6; for comedy, see Trible, *God and the Rhetoric of Sexuality*, 195–96; for folktale, see Sasson, *Ruth*, 214–16.

31. See Hubbard, *Book of Ruth*, 34, 48; Slotki, "Ruth," 37. Note that David's kinship ties with the Moabites may also be implied in 1 Sam. 22:3–4.

32. See discussion in Campbell, *Ruth*, 22–23; Hubbard, *Book of Ruth*, 24; Tischler, "Ruth," 153–64.

33. See *b. Baba Bathra* 14b in Epstein, *Seder Nezikin*, 2:71.

34. See extensive discussion in Bush, *Ruth, Esther*, 20–30; Holmstedt, *Ruth*, 17–39.

35. See Chisholm, *Judges and Ruth*, 684–85; Kitchen, *Reliability of the Old Testament*, 308, 357; Walton, "Genealogies"; Younger, *Judges, Ruth*, 403–4.

36. For example, the rabbis go too far by identifying Boaz with the minor judge Ibzan and suggesting a setting corresponding with Judg. 12:8–10 (see Beattie, *Targum of Ruth*, 18, 19, 32; *b. Baba Bathra* 91a in Epstein, *Seder Nezikin*, 2:375). Although Ibzan hails from Bethlehem, the city is probably not the same as "Bethlehem of Judah" (see the comments on Judg. 12:8–10; Ruth 1:1).

Ruth 1:1–22

1. See Globe, "Folktale Form," 131. Note also that "ten" is the approximate number of years spent in Moab (Ruth 1:4).

2. It is during this dark age of the judges that the "light of loyalty" shines brightly (Hill and Walton, *Survey*, 249).

3. See Rainey and Notley, *Sacred Bridge*, 139, 141, 184, 231.

4. See Reich, "Fiscal Bulla," 200–205.

5. *IVPBBCOT*, 277; cf. Eskenazi and Frymer-Kensky, *Ruth*, 6, 84; but note a few problematic passages: Judg. 12:5; 1 Sam. 1:1; 1 Kings 11:26.

6. See Cundall and Morris, *Judges and Ruth*, 249–50. Note that the rabbis interpreted Ephrathites as "courtiers" or "aristocrats" (Rabinowitz, *Ruth*, 29 [2.5]); cf. "lords" in Beattie, *Targum of Ruth*, 18.

7. See *IVPBBCOT*, 277.

8. See Ruth 1:6, 7, 8, 10, 11, 12, 15, 16, 21, 22; cf. 2:6; 4:3, 15.

9. Alter, *Art of Biblical Narrative*, 59; cf. Block, *Judges, Ruth*, 650.

10. See *IVPBBCOT*, 277.

11. Manor, "Ruth," 2:247; cf. Sakenfeld, *Ruth*, 27.

12. See Manor, "Ruth," 2:248.

13. See Chisholm, *Judges and Ruth*, 605; Weisberg, "Character Development," 217–18.

14. Frymer-Kensky, *Reading the Women of the Bible*, 241; cf. Smith, "'Your People Shall Be My People.'" See similar language in Exod. 6:7; 1 Kings 22:4; 2 Kings 3:7; 2 Chron. 18:3; Jer. 31:33; 32:38; cf. 1 Sam. 20:42; 2 Sam. 15:21.

15. See *IVPBBCOT*, 278; Walton and Walton, *Bible Story Handbook*, 143–45.

16. Walton and Walton, *Bible Story Handbook*, 143.

17. See Walton and Hill, *Old Testament Today*, 204.

18. See Campbell, *Ruth*, 74–75; Hubbard, *Book of Ruth*, 119–20. For the opposite opinion, see Conklin, *Oath Formulas in Biblical Hebrew*, 1–2, 7, 49.

19. See Walton and Walton, *Bible Story Handbook*, 144, 145.

20. See Knauf, "Shadday," *DDD*, 749–53.

21. See *COS* 2.27:142.

22. I must thank S. A. Kaufman for this insight (personal communication).

23. *IVPBBCOT*, 277.

24. See ibid., 278. Chisholm takes an opposing view, arguing that Naomi has a faulty perception of God (*Judges and Ruth*, 559, 569, 609–14, 616).

25. See Walton and Walton, *Bible Story Handbook*, 25. See also "Methodology" in the introduction to Ruth, above.

26. The rabbis had a great deal to say about Ruth and conversion (see Beattie, *Targum of Ruth*, 20–21, 23, 24, 27; Rabinowitz, *Ruth*, 35, 39–40 [2.12,

22]; etc.), and the church fathers had a great deal to say about Ruth and the church (see Franke, *Joshua, Judges, Ruth, 1–2 Samuel*, 182, 183, 191, 192; Irwin, "Ruth 3," 696).

27. See Exod. 22:21–24; Deut. 10:19; 24:17–22; 26:12–13; 27:19; Matt. 25:31–46; Acts 6:1; 1 Tim. 5:3–16; James 1:27.

28. For further discussion, see Walton, *Job*, 47–48, 428.

29. Charles Dickens, *The Posthumous Papers of the Pickwick Club* (London: Chapman and Hall, 1838), 607; final chapter (LVI).

Ruth 2:1–23

1. See *IVPBBCOT*, 278.

2. See examples in Egyptian (*COS* 1.47:121), Sumerian (*COS* 1.181:579, 580), and Old Aramaic (*COS* 2.34:154). For additional examples and discussion, see Baker, *Tight Fists or Open Hands?*, 232–39.

3. See Baker, *Tight Fists or Open Hands?*, 238; *IVPBBCOT*, 133, 199.

4. Walton, "Decalogue Structure of the Deuteronomic Law," 113.

5. Hals, *Theology of the Book of Ruth*, 12; cf. Chisholm, *Judges and Ruth*, 629.

6. Alter, *Art of Biblical Narrative*, 59.

7. See Glover, "Your People, My People," 303–5.

8. See Trible, *God and the Rhetoric of Sexuality*, 197n13.

9. See Alter, *Art of Biblical Narrative*, 59; Alter, *World of Biblical Literature*, 51–52; Trible, *God and the Rhetoric of Sexuality*, 173, 177.

10. For these examples and others, see *ANEP* 377, 544, 829; Keel, *Symbolism of the Biblical World*, 173, 190–92; LeMon, *Yahweh's Winged Form in the Psalms*; Manor, "Ruth," 2:255.

11. See Younger, *Judges, Ruth*, 448; Younger, "Two Comparative Notes," 121–25. Younger points out that the NIV footnote ("about 30 pounds or about 13 kilograms") is "too high in light of recent research" (*Judges, Ruth*, 448n36).

12. Younger, *Judges, Ruth*, 448.

13. Ibid.

14. See Hubbard, *Book of Ruth*, 179.

15. See Garsiel, *Biblical Names*, 252; Porten, "Scroll of Ruth," 36; Sasson, "Ruth," 325.

16. For helpful studies on *hesed*, see Clark, *Word Hesed in the Hebrew Bible*; Glueck, *Hesed in the Bible*; Sakenfeld, *Meaning of Hesed in the Hebrew Bible*; Sakenfeld, *Faithfulness in Action*; Sakenfeld, *Ruth*, 11–16.

17. See the marginal Masoretic note in any modern edition of the Hebrew Bible (e.g., *Biblia Hebraica Stuttgartensia*).

18. See Rebera, "Yahweh or Boaz?"; cf. Chisholm, *Judges and Ruth*, 564, 634–39.

19. Cf. Younger, *Judges, Ruth*, 451–52.

20. See Hals, *Theology of the Book of Ruth*, 11–12, 16, 18–19.

21. Ibid., 18.

22. See Chisholm, *Judges and Ruth*, 564.

23. See Ryken, Wilhoit, and Longman, *Dictionary of Biblical Imagery*, 954–55.

24. See D. P. Hustad, ed., *The Worshiping Church: A Hymnal* (Carol Stream, IL: Hope Publishing Company, 1990), nos. 363 and 635.

25. Rabinowitz, *Ruth*, 35 (2.14).

Ruth 3:1–18

1. For further references on threshing and winnowing, see Borowski, *Agriculture in Iron Age Israel*, 62–69; Manor, "Ruth," 2:256–57.

2. E.g., see 1 Kings 22:10; Jer. 15:7; *COS* 1.103:346.

3. See Bush, *Ruth, Esther*, 152.

4. Campbell, *Ruth*, 131.

5. See Glover, "Your People, My People," 304; Halton, "Indecent Proposal." This view was initially expressed by Josephus in *Antiquities* 5.9.3 (see Irwin, "Ruth 3," 694; Thackeray and Marcus, *Josephus*, 147).

6. See Trible, *God and the Rhetoric of Sexuality*, 183.

7. See Berlin, *Poetics and Interpretation of Biblical Narrative*, 91–95; cf. Younger, *Judges, Ruth*, 442, 473.

8. See Trible, *God and the Rhetoric of Sexuality*, 187.

9. See Berlin, *Poetics and Interpretation of Biblical Narrative*, 88–89, 152n5; Younger, *Judges, Ruth*, 445–46, 461; cf. 1 Sam. 25:41, where Abigail reduces herself from handmaid to laborer.

10. See Sasson, "Ruth," 326.

11. See van der Toorn, "Significance of the Veil," 334–35.

12. Halton, "Indecent Proposal," 36, 39.

13. Chisholm, *Judges and Ruth*, 624n34, 639–40, 645, 646n22, 656–58, 665–69, 673.

14. Walton, *Job*, 218. For additional references on the *go'el*, see Eskenazi and Frymer-Kensky, *Ruth*, liii–lv, 44, 60; King and Stager, *Life in Biblical Israel*, 38–39, 56; Younger, *Judges, Ruth*, 399–401, 462–63.

15. Younger, *Judges, Ruth*, 465.

16. Nielsen, *Ruth*, 79.

17. Eskenazi and Frymer-Kensky, *Ruth*, 18; cf. Trible, *God and the Rhetoric of Sexuality*, 187.

18. On the relationship between human *hesed* and divine blessing in Ruth, see Halton, "Indecent Proposal," 37–38.

19. See Bush, *Ruth, Esther*, 148.

20. Tischler, "Ruth," 155.

21. Ibid., 164.

22. See, e.g., the interpretation of Ephrem (fourth century AD; in Jensen, "Ruth according to Ephrem the Syrian"). Beattie asserts that Boaz slept with Ruth the night before his negotiations at the city gate (Beattie, "Kethibh and Qere in Ruth IV 5," 493). Also, others suggest that Ruth uncovers herself at the feet of Boaz (Nielsen, *Ruth*, 66–70, 74, 80;

van Wolde, "Texts in Dialogue with Texts," 20), but Bush and Chisholm each offer compelling counter-arguments (Bush, *Ruth, Esther*, 153; Chisholm, *Judges and Ruth*, 651–52).

23. See Halton, "Indecent Proposal."

24. http://www.momsinprayer.org; Terry Gooding, *Paths of Gold: Praying the Way to Christ for Lost Friends and Family* (Colorado Springs: NavPress, 2002).

25. B. H. Corey, *Love Kindness: Discover the Power of a Forgotten Christian Virtue* (Carol Stream, IL: Tyndale, 2016), 187.

Ruth 4:1–22

1. Cf. Bush, *Ruth, Esther*, 252, 264–65.

2. Note the inclusio in Ruth 1:21 and 4:15 ("brought me back" and "renew," respectively)—the only places in Ruth where *shub* is employed in the Hiphil (see Bush, *Ruth, Esther*, 257, 264).

3. For further references on gates, see King and Stager, *Life in Biblical Israel*, 234–36; Manor, "Ruth," 2:258, 260.

4. E.g., see COS 1.103:346, 351; 2.19:118; Deut. 21:19; 22:15; Prov. 22:22; Isa. 29:21; Amos 5:10, 12, 15.

5. For the office of "elder, senior official," see Fox, *In the Service of the King*, 63.

6. Sasson, "Farewell to 'Mr So and So' (Ruth 4.1)," 252; cf. "mish-mash" in Gen. 1:2 (Sasson, "Farewell to 'Mr So and So' (Ruth 4.1)," 252n1).

7. Glover, "Your People, My People," 300n18.

8. Sasson, "Farewell to 'Mr So and So' (Ruth 4.1)," 255; cf. Knight and Levine, *Meaning of the Bible*, 115.

9. Cf. Berlin, *Poetics and Interpretation of Biblical Narrative*, 85–86; Glover, "Your People, My People," 300; Trible, *God and the Rhetoric of Sexuality*, 188, 190, 191; Weisberg, "Character Development," 218.

10. Levine, "In Praise of the Israelite *Mišpāḥâ*," 102.

11. See *b. Baba Bathra* 91a (in Epstein, *Seder Nezikin*, 2:376); Rabinowitz, *Ruth*, 76 (6.3); cf. Beattie, *Jewish Exegesis of the Book of Ruth*, 188–89, 193–94, 199–200.

12. See de Waard, "Ruth," 55*; Sasson, *Ruth*, 103, 118; Wegner, *Student's Guide*, 126.

13. The Kethiv is the consonantal or written tradition, whereas the Qere is the vocalization or reading tradition.

14. Holmstedt, *Ruth*, 194 (see also 192); cf. Frymer-Kensky, *Reading the Women of the Bible*, 251–52.

15. Weisberg, *Levirate Marriage*, 27.

16. Ibid.

17. Ibid., 121 (see also 32, 97, 100).

18. Younger remarks, "Greed for property was thus Onan's motivation" (*Judges, Ruth*, 402).

19. See analogies from Egyptian, Hittite, and Hurrian texts in COS 1.85:226; Manor, "Ruth," 2:259; Niehaus, *Ancient Near Eastern Themes*, 67–68.

20. For further references on sandals, treading, and land ownership, see King and Stager, *Life in Biblical Israel*, 272–73; cf. Gen. 13:17; Deut. 11:24–25; Josh. 1:3.

21. See Glover, "Your People, My People," 294, 302.

22. Ibid., 302.

23. Ibid., 293 (see also 311); cf. Adamcik, "Who Are 'The People of YHWH'?"; Block, "Ruth 1," 685.

24. See Gen. 2:4; 6:9; 10:1; 11:10; 11:27; 25:12, 19; 36:1, 9; 37:2.

25. Boaz is therefore placed in the same position as Enoch, and David is placed in the same position as Noah and Abram (see Porten, "Theme and Historiosophic Background," 72).

26. See Berlin, *Poetics and Interpretation of Biblical Narrative*, 107–10.

27. Sasson, "Ruth," 321.

28. Walton and Walton, *Bible Story Handbook*, 146 (see also 144).

29. For further references on the relationship between Ruth and Genesis, see "Covenant Themes" in the introduction to Ruth; see also Alter, *Art of Biblical Narrative*, 58–60; Alter, *World of Biblical Literature*, 51–52; Porten, "Theme and Historiosophic Background," 69–72.

30. See a survey of this theme in Chisholm, *Judges and Ruth*, 564–66, 572, 685–86; Gow, "Ruth," 106.

31. Additionally, the corporate prayers for Ruth, Boaz, and Obed (in Ruth 4:11–12, 14) are answered in 1 Chron. 2:12; Matt. 1:5; Luke 3:32.

32. E.g., see Franke, *Joshua, Judges, Ruth, 1–2 Samuel*, 182–84, 190–92; Irwin, "Ruth 3," 696–97.

33. Walton and Walton, *Bible Story Handbook*, 143.

34. Frymer-Kensky, *Reading the Women of the Bible*, 245.

35. Cf. Chisholm, *Judges and Ruth*, 564, 567, 571–72, 683, 686.

36. Block, "Ruth 1," 685.

37. Stephanie Morrow, "Top Craziest Laws Still on the Books," LegalZoom.com, October 2009, https://www.legalzoom.com/articles/top-craziest-laws-still-on-the-books.

Bibliography

Recommended Resources

Block, D. I. "Judges." In *Zondervan Illustrated Bible Backgrounds Commentary*, edited by J. H. Walton, 2:94–241. Grand Rapids: Zondervan, 2009.

———. *Judges, Ruth*. New American Commentary. Nashville: Broadman & Holman, 1999.

Chisholm, R. B. *A Commentary on Judges and Ruth*. Grand Rapids: Kregel, 2013.

Exum, J. C. "The Centre Cannot Hold: Thematic and Textual Instabilities in Judges." *Catholic Biblical Quarterly* 52 (1990): 410–31.

Gooding, D. W. "The Composition of the Book of Judges." *Eretz-Israel* 16 (1982): 70*–79*.

Manor, D. W. "Ruth." In *Zondervan Illustrated Bible Backgrounds Commentary*, edited by J. H. Walton, 2:242–65. Grand Rapids: Zondervan, 2009.

Way, K. C. "The Literary Structure of Judges Revisited: Judges as a Ring Composition." In *Windows to the Ancient World of the Hebrew Bible: Essays in Honor of Samuel Greengus*, edited by B. T. Arnold, N. L. Erickson, and J. H. Walton, 247–60. Winona Lake, IN: Eisenbrauns, 2014.

Webb, B. G. *The Book of Judges*. New International Commentary on the Old Testament. Grand Rapids: Eerdmans, 2012.

Younger, K. L. *Judges, Ruth*. NIV Application Commentary. Grand Rapids: Zondervan, 2002.

Other Works

Abegg, M., P. Flint, and E. Ulrich. *The Dead Sea Scrolls Bible*. New York: HarperCollins, 1999.

Ackerman, S. *Warrior, Dancer, Seductress, Queen: Women in Judges and Biblical Israel*. New York: Doubleday, 1998.

Adamcik, Stephen. "Who Are 'The People of YHWH'? The Extra-Ethnic Dimension of Early Israelite Identity." MA thesis, Talbot School of Theology, Biola University, 2014.

Ahituv, S. *Echoes from the Past: Hebrew and Cognate Inscriptions from the Biblical Period*. Jerusalem: Carta, 2008.

Alexander, T. D., and D. W. Baker, eds. *Dictionary of the Old Testament: Pentateuch*. Downers Grove, IL: InterVarsity, 2003.

Alt, A. *Essays on Old Testament History and Religion*. Garden City, NY: Doubleday, 1968.

Alter, R. *The Art of Biblical Narrative*. New York: Basic Books, 1981.

———. *The World of Biblical Literature*. New York: Basic Books, 1992.

Amit, Y. *The Book of Judges: The Art of Editing*. Leiden: Brill, 1999.

———. "The Book of Judges—Dating and Meaning." In *Homeland and Exile: Biblical and Ancient Near Eastern Studies in Honour of Bustenay Oded*, edited by G. Galil, M. Geller, and A. Millard, 297–322. Leiden: Brill, 2009.

Archer, G. L. *Encyclopedia of Bible Difficulties*. Grand Rapids: Zondervan, 1982.

Arnold, B. T., and H. G. M. Williamson, eds. *Dictionary of the Old Testament: Historical Books*. Downers Grove, IL: InterVarsity, 2005.

Arnold, P. M. *Gibeah: The Search for a Biblical City*. Sheffield: JSOT Press, 1990.

Ashmon, S. A. "Sampson and Christ, Type and Antitype." *Lutheran Forum* (Fall 2008): 15–17.

Assis, E. *Self-Interest or Communal Interest: An Ideology of Leadership in the Gideon, Abimelech and Jephthah Narratives (Judg. 6–12)*. Leiden: Brill, 2005.

Averbeck, R. E. "The Holy Spirit in the Hebrew Bible and Its Connections to the New Testament." In *Who's Afraid of the Holy Spirit?*, edited by M. J. Sawyer and D. B. Wallace, 15–36. Dallas: Biblical Studies Press, 2005.

Baker, D. L. *Tight Fists or Open Hands? Wealth and Poverty in Old Testament Law*. Grand Rapids: Eerdmans, 2009.

Barrios, Eric. "The Ḥērem and Israel's Sacred Space and Status." ThM thesis, Talbot School of Theology, Biola University, 2014.

Bauer, U. F. W. "Judges 18 as an Anti-Spy Story in the Context of an Anti-Conquest Story: The Creative Usage of Literary Genres." *Journal for the Study of the Old Testament* 88 (2000): 37–47.

———. "A Metaphorical Etiology in Judges 18:12." *Journal of Hebrew Scriptures* 3 (2001). doi:10.5508/jhs.2001.v3.a5.

Beale, G. K. *The Temple and the Church's Mission*. Downers Grove, IL: InterVarsity, 2004.

Beattie, D. R. G. *Jewish Exegesis of the Book of Ruth*. Sheffield: JSOT Press, 1977.

———. "Kethibh and Qere in Ruth IV 5." *Vetus Testamentum* 21 (1971): 490–94.

———. *The Targum of Ruth*. In *The Targum of Ruth; The Targum of Chronicles*, by D. R. G. Beattie and J. S. McIvor. Collegeville, MN: Liturgical Press, 1994.

Beem, B. "The Minor Judges: A Literary Reading of Some Very Short Stories." In *The Biblical Canon in Comparative Perspective: Scripture in Context IV*, edited by K. L. Younger Jr., W. W. Hallo, and B. Batto, 147–72. Lewiston, NY: Mellen, 1991.

Ben-Shlomo, D. *Philistine Iconography: A Wealth of Style and Symbolism*. Fribourg: Academic Press; Göttingen: Vandenhoeck & Ruprecht, 2010.

Ben-Tor, A. "Hazor." In *The New Encyclopedia of Archaeological Excavations in the Holy Land*, edited by E. Stern et al., 5:1769–76. Jerusalem: Israel Exploration Society, 2008.

Berlin, A. *Poetics and Interpretation of Biblical Narrative*. Winona Lake, IN: Eisenbrauns, 1994.

Berman, J. A. *Narrative Analogy in the Hebrew Bible: Battle Stories and Their Equivalent Non-battle Narratives*. Leiden: Brill, 2004.

Bertman, S. "Symmetrical Design in the Book of Ruth." *Journal of Biblical Literature* 84 (1965): 165–68.

Bierling, N. *Giving Goliath His Due: New Archaeological Light on the Philistines*. Grand Rapids: Baker, 1992.

Bietak, M. "The Archaeology of the 'Gold of Valour.'" *Egyptian Archaeology* 40 (Spring 2012): 32–33.

Biran, A. *Biblical Dan*. Jerusalem: Israel Exploration Society, 1994.

Block, D. I. "Bny 'mwn: The Sons of Ammon." *Andrews University Seminary Studies* 22 (1984): 197–212.

———. "Deborah among the Judges: The Perspective of the Hebrew Historian." In *Faith, Tradition, and History: Old Testament Historiography in Its Near Eastern Context*, edited by A. R. Millard, J. K. Hoffmeier, and D. W. Baker, 229–53. Winona Lake, IN: Eisenbrauns, 1994.

———. *Deuteronomy*. NIV Application Commentary. Grand Rapids: Zondervan, 2012.

———. "Echo Narrative Technique in Hebrew Literature: A Study in Judges 19." *Westminster Theological Journal* 52 (1990): 325–41.

———. "Empowered by the Spirit of God: The Holy Spirit in the Historiographic Writings of the Old Testament." *Southern Baptist Journal of Theology* 1 (1997): 42–61.

———. *The Gods of the Nations: Studies in Ancient Near Eastern National Theology*. Grand Rapids: Baker Academic, 2000.

———. "Ruth 1: Book of." In *Dictionary of the Old Testament: Wisdom, Poetry & Writings*, edited by T. Longman III and P. Enns, 672–87. Downers Grove, IL: InterVarsity, 2008.

———. "'That They May Hear': Biblical Foundations for the Oral Reading of Scripture in Worship." *Journal of Spiritual Formation & Soul Care* 5 (2012): 5–34.

———. "Unspeakable Crimes: The Abuse of Women in the Book of Judges." *The Southern Baptist Journal of Theology* 2/3 (Fall 1998): 46–55.

———. "Will the Real Gideon Please Stand Up? Narrative Style and Intention in Judges 6–9." *Journal of the Evangelical Theological Society* 40.3 (1997): 353–66.

Bluedorn, W. *Yahweh versus Baalism: A Theological Reading of the Gideon-Abimelech Narrative*. Sheffield: Sheffield Academic Press, 2001.

Blyton, E. *The Magic Faraway Tree*. London: Newnes, 1943.

Boda, Mark J. *A Severe Mercy: Sin and Its Remedy in the Old Testament*. Winona Lake, IN: Eisenbrauns, 2009.

Boling, R. G. *Judges*. Anchor Bible. Garden City: Doubleday, 1975.

Borowski, O. *Agriculture in Iron Age Israel*. Winona Lake, IN: Eisenbrauns, 1987.

———. *Daily Life in Biblical Times*. Atlanta: Society of Biblical Literature, 2003.

———. *Every Living Thing: Daily Use of Animals in Ancient Israel*. Walnut Creek, CA: AltaMira, 1998.

Bray, J. S. *Sacred Dan: Religious Traditions and Cultic Practice in Judges 17–18*. New York: T&T Clark, 2006.

Brenner, A., ed. *A Feminist Companion to Judges*. Sheffield: Sheffield Academic Press, 1993.

———. "A Triangle and a Rhombus in Narrative Structure: A Proposed Integrative Reading of Judges 4 and 5." In *A Feminist Companion to Judges*, edited by A. Brenner, 98–109. Sheffield: Sheffield Academic Press, 1993.

Brettler, M. Z. *The Book of Judges*. London: Routledge, 2002.

———. "The Book of Judges: Literature as Politics." *Journal of Biblical Literature* 108 (1989): 395–418.

Brinkman, J. A. "Through a Glass Darkly: Esarhaddon's Retrospects on the Downfall of Babylon." *Journal of the American Oriental Society* 103 (1983): 35–42.

Broida, M. "Closure in Samson." *Journal of Hebrew Scriptures* 10 (2010): 2–34. doi:10.5508/jhs.2010.v10.a2.

Buber, M. *Kingship of God*. New York: Harper & Row, 1967.

Burney, C. F. *The Book of Judges*. London: Rivingtons, 1920.

Bush, F. *Ruth, Esther*. Word Biblical Commentary. Dallas: Word, 1996.

Butler, T. *Judges*. Word Biblical Commentary. Nashville: Nelson, 2009.

Campbell, E. F. *Ruth*. Anchor Bible. New York: Doubleday, 1975.

Cantrell, D. O. *The Horsemen of Israel: Horses and Chariotry in Monarchic Israel (Ninth–Eighth Centuries B.C.E.)*. Winona Lake, IN: Eisenbrauns, 2011.

Cartledge, T. W. *Vows in the Hebrew Bible and the Ancient Near East*. Sheffield: Sheffield Academic Press, 1992.

Chavalas, M. W. *The Ancient Near East: Historical Sources in Translation*. Oxford: Blackwell, 2006.

Childs, B. S. *Introduction to the Old Testament as Scripture*. Philadelphia: Fortress, 1979.

Chisholm, R. B. "The Chronology of the Book of Judges: A Linguistic Clue to Solving a Pesky Problem." *Journal of the Evangelical Theological Society* 52 (2009): 247–55.

———. "The Ethical Challenge of Jephthah's Fulfilled Vow." *Bibliotheca Sacra* 167 (Oct–Dec 2010): 404–22.

———. "The Role of Women in the Rhetorical Strategy of the Book of Judges." In *Integrity of Heart, Skillfulness of Hands: Biblical and Leadership Studies in Honor of Donald K. Campbell*, edited by C. G. Dyer and R. B. Zuck, 34–49. Grand Rapids: Baker, 1994.

———. "What's Wrong with This Picture? Stylistic Variation as a Rhetorical Technique in Judges." *Journal for the Study of the Old Testament* 34 (2009): 171–82.

———. "Yahweh versus the Canaanite Gods: Polemic in Judges and 1 Samuel 1–7." *Bibliotheca Sacra* 164 (2007): 165–80.

Claassens, L. J. M. "The Character of God in Judges 6–8: The Gideon Narrative as Theological and Moral Resource." *Horizons in Biblical Theology* 23 (2001): 51–71.

Clark, G. R. *The Word Hesed in the Hebrew Bible*. Sheffield: Sheffield Academic Press, 1993.

Conklin, B. *Oath Formulas in Biblical Hebrew*. Winona Lake, IN: Eisenbrauns, 2011.

Cooley, J. L. "Etymology, Assyriology, Philology and the Hebrew Bible: Toward an Understanding of Judean Onomastic Hermeneutics." Paper presented at the Annual Meeting of the Society of Biblical Literature, Baltimore, MD, November 2013.

———. *Poetic Astronomy in the Ancient Near East: The Reflexes of Celestial Science in Ancient Mesopotamian, Ugaritic, and Israelite Narrative*. Winona Lake, IN: Eisenbrauns, 2013.

———. "The Story of Saul's Election (1 Sam. 9–10) in the Light of Mantic Practice in Ancient Iraq." *Journal of Biblical Literature* 130 (2011): 247–61.

Copan, P. *Is God a Moral Monster? Making Sense of the Old Testament God*. Grand Rapids: Baker Books, 2011.

Copan, P., and M. Flannagan. *Did God Really Command Genocide? Coming to Terms with the Justice of God.* Grand Rapids: Baker Books, 2014.

Cornelius, I. *The Iconography of the Canaanite Gods Reshef and Ba'al: Late Bronze and Iron I Periods (c 1500–1000 BCE).* Fribourg: University Press, 1994.

———. *The Many Faces of the Goddess: The Iconography of the Syro-Palestinian Goddesses Anat, Astarte, Qedeshet, and Asherah c. 1500–1000 BCE.* Fribourg: Academic Press, 2008.

Cowles, C. S., E. H. Merrill, D. L. Gard, and T. Longman III. *Show Them No Mercy: Four Views on God and Canaanite Genocide.* Grand Rapids: Zondervan, 2003.

Cox, B. D., and S. Ackerman. "Micah's Teraphim." *Journal of Hebrew Scriptures* 12 (2012): 1–37. doi:10.5508/jhs.2012.v12.a11.

Crenshaw, J. L. *Samson: A Secret Betrayed, A Vow Ignored.* Atlanta: John Knox, 1978.

Cross, F. M. *Canaanite Myth and Hebrew Epic.* Cambridge: Harvard University Press, 1973.

Cryer, F. H. *Divination in Ancient Israel and Its Near Eastern Environment.* Sheffield: Sheffield Academic Press, 1994.

Cundall, A. E., and L. Morris. *Judges and Ruth.* Tyndale Old Testament Commentaries. London: Tyndale, 1968.

Davies, G. H. "Judges VIII 22–23." *Vetus Testamentum* 13 (1963): 151–57.

Davis, D. R. *Such a Great Salvation: Expositions of the Book of Judges.* Grand Rapids: Baker, 1990.

Dayagi-Mendels, M. *Drink and Be Merry: Wine and Beer in Ancient Times.* Jerusalem: The Israel Museum, 1999.

Dearman, J. A. "Moab, Moabites." In *Dictionary of the Old Testament: Historical Books*, edited by B. T. Arnold and H. G. M. Williamson, 705–7. Downers Grove, IL: InterVarsity, 2005.

de Waard, J. "Commentaries on the Critical Apparatus: Ruth." In *Biblica Hebraica Quinta, Fasicle 18: General Introduction and Megilloth*, 51*–56*. Stuttgart: Deutsche Bibelgesellschaft, 2004.

Dick, M. B. "The Neo-Assyrian Royal Lion Hunt and Yahweh's Answer to Job." *Journal of Biblical Literature* 125 (2006): 243–70.

Doak, B. R. "'Some Worthless and Reckless Fellows': Landlessness and Parasocial Leadership in Judges." *Journal of Hebrew Scriptures* 11 (2011): 2–29. doi:10.5508/jhs.2011.v11.a2.

Dorsey, D. A. *The Literary Structure of the Old Testament: A Commentary on Genesis–Malachi.* Grand Rapids: Baker, 1999.

Douglas, M. *In the Wilderness: The Doctrine of Defilement in the Book of Numbers.* Sheffield: Sheffield Academic Press, 1993.

———. *Thinking in Circles: An Essay on Ring Composition.* New Haven: Yale University Press, 2007.

Dumbrell, W. J. "'In Those Days There Was No King in Israel; Every Man Did What Was Right in His Own Eyes': The Purpose of the Book of Judges Reconsidered." *Journal for the Study of the Old Testament* 25 (1983): 23–33.

Echols, C. L. *"Tell Me, O Muse": The Song of Deborah (Judges 5) in the Light of Heroic Poetry.* New York: T&T Clark, 2008.

Ehrlich, C. S. "Philistines." In *Dictionary of the Old Testament: Historical Books*, edited by B. T. Arnold and H. G. M. Williamson, 782–92. Downers Grove, IL: InterVarsity, 2005.

Ellingworth, P., and A. Mojola. "Translating Euphemisms in the Bible." *Bible Translator* 37 (1986): 139–43.

Emmrich, M. "The Symbolism of the Lion and the Bees: Another Ironic Twist in the Samson Cycle." *Journal of the Evangelical Theological Society* 44 (2001): 67–74.

Endris, V. "Yahweh versus Baal: A Narrative-Critical Reading of the Gideon/Abimelech Narrative." *Journal for the Study of the Old Testament* 33 (2008): 173–95.

Epstein, I., ed. *The Babylonian Talmud: Seder Nezikin.* Vol. 2. London: Socino, 1935.

Erickson, M. J. *Christian Theology.* 2nd ed. Grand Rapids: Baker, 1998.

Eskenazi, T. C., and T. Frymer-Kensky. *Ruth.* JPS Bible Commentary. Philadelphia: Jewish Publication Society, 2011.

Exum, J. C. "Aspects of Symmetry and Balance in the Samson Saga." *Journal for the Study of the Old Testament* 19 (1981): 3–29.

———. "The Theological Dimension of the Samson Saga." *Vetus Testamentum* 33 (1983): 30–45.

———. *Tragedy and Biblical Narrative: Arrows of the Almighty.* Cambridge: Cambridge University Press, 1992.

Faraone, C. A., B. Garnand, and C. López-Ruiz. "Micah's Mother (Judg. 17:1–4) and a Curse from Carthage (*KAI* 89): Canaanite Precedents for Greek and Latin Curses Against Thieves?" *Journal of Near Eastern Studies* 64 (2005): 161–86.

Fee, G. D., and D. Stuart. *How to Read the Bible for All Its Worth*. Grand Rapids: Zondervan, 2003.

Feldman, L. H. *Studies in Josephus' Rewritten Bible*. Leiden: Brill, 1998.

Feliu, L. *The God Dagan in Bronze Age Syria*. Leiden: Brill, 2003.

Finkelstein, I., ed. *Shiloh: The Archaeology of a Biblical Site*. Tel Aviv: Tel Aviv University, Institute of Archaeology, 1993.

Finsterbusch, K., A. Lange, and K. F. D. Römheld, eds. *Human Sacrifice in Jewish and Christian Tradition*. Leiden: Brill, 2007.

Fishbane, M. *Biblical Interpretation in Ancient Israel*. Oxford: Clarendon, 1985.

Fokkelman, J. P. "The Song of Deborah and Barak: Its Prosodic Levels and Structure." In *Pomegranates and Golden Bells: Studies in Biblical, Jewish, and Near Eastern Ritual, Law, and Literature in Honor of Jacob Milgrom*, edited by D. P. Wright, D. N. Freedman, and A. Hurvitz, 595–628. Winona Lake, IN: Eisenbrauns, 1995.

———. "Structural Remarks on Judges 9 and 19." In *"Sha'arei Talmon": Studies in the Bible, Qumran, and the Ancient Near East Presented to Shemaryahu Talmon*, edited by M. Fishbane, E. Tov, and W. W. Fields, 33–45. Winona Lake, IN: Eisenbrauns, 1992.

Foster, R. J. *Celebration of Discipline: The Path to Spiritual Growth*. Rev. ed. San Francisco: HarperSanFrancisco, 1988.

———. *The Challenge of the Disciplined Life: Christian Reflections on Money, Sex & Power*. New York: HarperCollins, 1985.

Fouts, D. M. "A Defense of the Hyperbolic Interpretation of Large Numbers in the Old Testament." *Journal of the Evangelical Theological Society* 40 (1997): 377–87.

———. "Numbers, Large Numbers." In *Dictionary of the Old Testament: Historical Books*, edited by B. T. Arnold and H. G. M. Williamson, 750–54. Downers Grove, IL: InterVarsity, 2005.

Fox, N. S. "Concepts of God in Israel and the Question of Monotheism." In *Text, Artifact, and Image*, edited by G. Beckman and T. J. Lewis, 326–45. Providence: Brown University, 2006.

———. "Holy Piercing? The Connection between Earrings and Cult Images." Paper presented at the Annual Meeting of the American Schools of Oriental Research, San Antonio, TX, November 2004.

———. *In the Service of the King: Officialdom in Ancient Israel and Judah*. Cincinnati: Hebrew Union College Press, 2000.

Franke, J. R., ed. *Joshua, Judges, Ruth, 1–2 Samuel*. Ancient Christian Commentary on Scripture. Downers Grove, IL: InterVarsity, 2005.

Freedman, D. N. *The Nine Commandments: Uncovering a Hidden Pattern of Crime and Punishment in the Hebrew Bible*. New York: Doubleday, 2000.

Frymer-Kensky, T. *Reading the Women of the Bible*. New York: Schocken, 2002.

Galli, M. *Jesus Mean and Wild: The Unexpected Love of an Untamable God*. Grand Rapids: Baker Books, 2006.

Gane, R. *God's Faulty Heroes*. Hagerstown, MD: Review and Herald, 1996.

Garland, D. E., and D. R. Garland. *Flawed Families of the Bible: How God's Grace Works through Imperfect Relationships*. Grand Rapids: Brazos, 2007.

Garsiel, M. *Biblical Names*. Ramat Gan: Bar-Ilan University, 1991.

———. "Homiletic Name-Derivations as a Literary Device in the Gideon Narrative: Judges VI–VIII." *Vetus Testamentum* 43 (1993): 302–17.

Giorgetti, A. D. "The Nature of the Biblical Teraphim: An Inductive Study of the Ancient Israelite Cultic Paraphernalia." MA thesis, Talbot School of Theology, Biola University, 2010.

Globe, A. "'Enemies Round About': Disintegrative Structure in the Book of Judges." In *Mappings of the Biblical Terrain: The Bible as Text*, edited by V. L. Tollers and J. Maier, 233–51. Lewisburg, PA: Bucknell University Press, 1990.

———. "Folktale Form and National Theme, with Particular Reference to Ruth." In *Approaches to Teaching the Hebrew Bible as Literature in Translation*, edited by B. N. Olshen and Y. S. Feldman, 127–32. New York: Modern Language Association of America, 1989.

Glover, N. "Your People, My People: An Exploration of Ethnicity in Ruth." *Journal for the Study of the Old Testament* 33 (2009): 293–313.

Glueck, N. Hesed *in the Bible*. New York: Ktav, 1975.

Goswell, G. "The Order of the Books in the Greek Old Testament." *Journal of the Evangelical Theological Society* 52 (2009): 449–66.

Gow, M. D. "Ruth." In *Theological Interpretation of the Old Testament: A Book by Book Survey*, edited by K. J. Vanhoozer, 102–10. Grand Rapids: Baker Academic, 2008.

Greenberg, M. *Biblical Prose Prayer*. Berkeley: University of California Press, 1983.

Greene, J. T. *The Role of the Messenger and Message in the Ancient Near East*. Atlanta: Scholars Press, 1989.

Greengus, S. *Laws in the Bible and in Early Rabbinic Collections: The Legal Legacy of the Ancient Near East*. Eugene, OR: Cascade, 2011.

Greenspahn, F. E. "The Theology of the Framework of Judges." *Vetus Testamentum* 36 (1986): 385–96.

Gushee, D. P. *Righteous Gentiles of the Holocaust: Genocide and Moral Obligation*. St. Paul: Paragon House, 2003.

Haak, R. D. "A Study and New Interpretation of QṢR NPŠ." *Journal of Biblical Literature* 101 (1982): 161–67.

Hallo, W. W. "Ancient Near Eastern Texts and Their Relevance for Biblical Exegesis." In *The Context of Scripture: Canonical Compositions from the Biblical World*, edited by W. W. Hallo and K. L. Younger Jr., 1:xxiii–xxviii. Leiden: Brill, 1997.

———. "Scurrilous Etymologies." In *Pomegranates and Golden Bells: Studies in Biblical, Jewish, and Near Eastern Ritual, Law, and Literature in Honor of Jacob Milgrom*, edited by D. P. Wright, D. N. Freedman, and A. Hurvitz, 767–74. Winona Lake, IN: Eisenbrauns, 1995.

Halpern, B. *The First Historians: The Hebrew Bible and History*. San Francisco: Harper & Row, 1988.

Hals, R. M. *The Theology of the Book of Ruth*. Philadelphia: Fortress, 1969.

Halton, C. "An Indecent Proposal: The Theological Core of the Book of Ruth." *Scandinavian Journal of the Old Testament* 26 (2012): 30–43.

Hasel, M. G. "Merneptah's Reference to Israel: Critical Issues for the Origin of Israel." In *Critical Issues in Early Israelite History*, edited by R. S. Hess, G. A. Klingbeil, and P. J. Ray Jr., 47–59. Winona Lake, IN: Eisenbrauns, 2008.

Hawkins, Ralph K. "The Date of the Exodus-Conquest is Still an Open Question: A Response to Roger Young and Bryant Wood." *Journal of the Evangelical Theological Society* 51 (2008): 245–66.

———. *The Iron Age I Structure on Mt. Ebal: Excavation and Interpretation*. Bulletin for Biblical Research Supplements 6. Winona Lake, IN: Eisenbrauns, 2012.

———. "Propositions for Evangelical Acceptance of a Late-Date Exodus-Conquest: Biblical Data and the Royal Scarabs from Mt. Ebal." *Journal of the Evangelical Theological Society* 50 (2007): 31–46.

Heffelfinger, K. M. "'My Father Is King': Chiefly Politics and the Rise and Fall of Abimelech." *Journal for the Study of the Old Testament* 33 (2009): 277–92.

Hellerman, J. H. *When the Church Was a Family*. Nashville: Broadman & Holman, 2009.

Hendel, R. S. "Sibilants and *šibbōlet* (Judges 12:6)." *Bulletin of the American Schools for Oriental Research* 301 (1996): 69–75.

Hennessy, J. B. "Thirteenth Century B.C. Temple of Human Sacrifice at Amman." In *Phoenicia and Its Neighbours*, edited by E. Gubel and E. Lipinski, 85–104. Studia Phoenicia 3. Leuven: Peeters, 1985.

Herr, D. D., and M. P. Boyd. "A Watermelon Named Abimelech." *Biblical Archaeology Review* 28 (January/February 2002): 34–37, 62.

Hess, R. S. "Arrowheads from Iron Age I: Personal Names and Authenticity." In *Ugarit at Seventy-Five*, edited by K. L. Younger Jr., 113–29. Winona Lake, IN: Eisenbrauns, 2007.

———. "The Dead Sea Scrolls and Higher Criticism of the Hebrew Bible: The Case of 4QJudgᵃ." In *The Scrolls and the Scriptures: Qumran Fifty Years After*, edited by S. E. Porter and C. A. Evans, 122–28. Sheffield: Sheffield Academic Press, 1997.

———. "Israelite Identity and Personal Names from the Book of Judges." *Hebrew Studies* 44 (2003): 25–39.

———. *Israelite Religions*. Grand Rapids: Baker Academic, 2007.

———. *Joshua*. Tyndale Old Testament Commentaries. Downers Grove, IL: InterVarsity, 1996.

———. "Judges 1–5 and Its Translation." In *Translating the Bible: Problems and Prospects*, edited by S. E. Porter and R. S. Hess, 142–60. Sheffield: Sheffield Academic Press, 1999.

———. "The Name Game: Dating the Book of Judges." *Biblical Archaeology Review* 30 (November/December 2004): 38–41.

———. "Non-Israelite Personal Names in the Book of Joshua." *Catholic Biblical Quarterly* 58 (1996): 205–14.

Hildebrandt, W. *An Old Testament Theology of the Spirit of God*. Peabody, MA: Hendrickson, 1995.

Hill, A. E., and J. H. Walton. *A Survey of the Old Testament*. Grand Rapids: Zondervan, 2009.

Hitchcock, L. A., and A. M. Maeir. "Yo-ho, Yo-ho, A *Seren*'s Life for Me!" *World Archaeology* 46 (2014): 1–17.

Hoffman, Y. "The Concept of 'Other Gods' in the Deuteronomistic Literature." In *Politics and Theopolitics in the Bible and Postbiblical Literature*, edited by H. G. Reventlow et al., 66–84. Sheffield: Sheffield Academic Press, 1994.

Hoffmeier, J. K. *Ancient Israel in Sinai*. Oxford: Oxford University Press, 2005.

———. *The Immigration Crisis*. Wheaton: Crossway, 2009.

———. "Rameses of the Exodus Narratives Is the 13th Century B.C. Royal Ramesside Residence." *Trinity Journal* 28 NS (2007): 281–89.

———. "What Is the Biblical Date for the Exodus? A Response to Bryant Wood." *Journal of the Evangelical Theological Society* 50 (2007): 235–39.

Hoffner, H. A., Jr. *Hittite Myths*. 2nd ed. Atlanta: Scholars Press, 1998.

———. "Slavery and Slave Laws in Ancient Hatti and Israel." In *Israel: Ancient Kingdom or Late Invention?*, edited by D. I. Block, 130–55. Nashville: Broadman & Holman, 2008.

Holmstedt, R. D. *Ruth: A Handbook on the Hebrew Text*. Waco: Baylor University Press, 2010.

Hongisto, L. "Literary Structure and Theology in the Book of Ruth." *Andrews University Seminary Studies* 23 (1985): 19–28.

Horowitz, W., T. Oshima, and S. L. Sanders. *Cuneiform in Canaan*. Jerusalem: Israel Exploration Society, 2006.

Hostetter, E. C. *Nations Mightier and More Numerous: The Biblical View of Palestine's Pre-Israelite Peoples*. N. Richland Hills, TX: BIBAL Press, 1995.

Hubbard, R. L. *The Book of Ruth*. New International Commentary on the Old Testament. Grand Rapids: Eerdmans, 1988.

Huffman, D. S. *How Then Should We Choose? Three Views on God's Will and Decision Making*. Grand Rapids: Kregel, 2009.

Hutchison, J. C. *Thinking Right When Things Go Wrong*. Grand Rapids: Kregel, 2005.

Ilan, O. *Image and Artifact: Treasures of the Rockefeller Museum*. Jerusalem: The Israel Museum, 2000.

Irwin, B. P. "Ruth 3: History of Interpretation." In *Dictionary of the Old Testament: Wisdom, Poetry & Writings*, edited by T. Longman III

and P. Enns, 693–700. Downers Grove, IL: InterVarsity, 2008.

Janzen, J. G. "Why the Deuteronomist Told about the Sacrifice of Jephthah's Daughter." *Journal for the Study of the Old Testament* 29 (2005): 339–57.

Jensen, J. R. "Ruth according to Ephrem the Syrian." In *A Feminist Companion to Ruth*, edited by A. Brenner, 170–76. Sheffield: Sheffield Academic Press, 1993.

Jobling, D. "Structuralist Criticism: The Text's World of Meaning." In *Judges and Method: New Approaches in Biblical Studies*, edited by G. A. Yee, 90–114. 2nd ed. Minneapolis: Fortress, 2007.

Johnson, B. J. M. "What Type of Son is Samson? Reading Judges 13 as a Biblical Type Scene." *Journal of the Evangelical Theological Society* 53 (2010): 269–86.

Kaufman, S. A. "The Classification of the North West Semitic Dialects of the Biblical Period and Some Implications Thereof." In *Proceedings of the Ninth World Congress of Jewish Studies*, 41–57. Jerusalem: Magnes Press / Hebrew University, 1988.

———. "The Phoenician Inscription of the Incirli Trilingual: A Tentative Reconstruction and Translation." *Maarav* 14 (2007): 7–26.

Keel, O. *The Symbolism of the Biblical World: Ancient Near Eastern Iconography and the Book of Psalms*. Winona Lake, IN: Eisenbrauns, 1997.

Kelm, G. L., and A. Mazar. *Timnah: A Biblical City in the Sorek Valley*. Winona Lake, IN: Eisenbrauns, 1995.

Killebrew, A. E. *Biblical Peoples and Ethnicity: An Archaeological Study of Egyptians, Canaanites, Philistines, and Early Israel, 1300–1100 B.C.E.* Atlanta: Society of Biblical Literature, 2005.

Kim, D. E. "From Rest to Rest: A Comparative Study of the Concept of Rest in Mesopotamian and Israelite Literature." PhD diss., University of Aberdeen, Scotland, UK, 2014.

King, P., and L. Stager. *Life in Biblical Israel*. Louisville: Westminster John Knox, 2001.

Kitchen, K. A. *On the Reliability of the Old Testament*. Grand Rapids: Eerdmans, 2003.

Klein, L. R. "The Book of Judges: Paradigm and Deviation in Images of Women." In *A Feminist Companion to Judges*, edited by A. Brenner, 55–71. Sheffield: Sheffield Academic Press, 1993.

———. "A Spectrum of Female Characters in the Book of Judges." In *A Feminist Companion* to *Judges*, edited by A. Brenner, 24–33. Sheffield: Sheffield Academic Press, 1993.

———. *The Triumph of Irony in the Book of Judges*. Sheffield: Almond, 1988.

Klein, W. W., C. L. Blomberg, and R. L. Hubbard. *Introduction to Biblical Interpretation*. Nashville: Nelson, 2004.

Knight, D. A., and A.-J. Levine. *The Meaning of the Bible: What the Jewish Scriptures and Christian Old Testament Can Teach Us*. New York: HarperCollins, 2011.

Kogan, L. "Animal Names in Biblical Hebrew: An Etymological Overview." *Babel und Bibel* 3 (2006): 257–320.

Korpel, M. C. A. *The Structure of the Book of Ruth*. Assen: Van Gorcum, 2001.

Lamb, D. T. *God Behaving Badly: Is the God of the Old Testament Angry, Sexist and Racist?* Downers Grove, IL: InterVarsity, 2011.

Lapp, N. "Ful, Tell el-." In *The New Encyclopedia of Archaeological Excavations in the Holy Land*, edited by E. Stern et al., 2:445–48. Jerusalem: Israel Exploration Society and Carta; New York: Simon & Schuster, 1993.

Lapsley, J. E. *Whispering the Word: Hearing Women's Stories in the Old Testament*. Louisville: Westminster John Knox, 2005.

Lau, P. H. W. *Identity and Ethics in the Book of Ruth: A Social Identity Approach*. Beihefte zur Zeitschrift für die alttestamentliche Wissenschaft 416. Berlin: de Gruyter, 2011.

Leder, A. C. "Paradise Lost: Reading the Former Prophets by the Rivers of Babylon." *Calvin Theological Journal* 37 (2002): 9–27.

LeMon, J. M. *Yahweh's Winged Form in the Psalms: Exploring Congruent Iconography and Texts*. Fribourg: Academic Press; Göttingen: Vandenhoeck & Ruprecht, 2010.

Lemos, T. M. "Shame and Mutilation of Enemies in the Hebrew Bible." *Journal of Biblical Literature* 125 (2006): 225–41.

Levine, B. A. "In Praise of the Israelite *Mišpāḥâ*: Legal Themes in the Book of Ruth." In *The Quest for the Kingdom of God: Studies in Honor of George E. Mendenhall*, edited by H. B. Huffman, F. A. Spina, and A. R. W. Green, 95–106. Winona Lake, IN: Eisenbrauns, 1983.

Lewis, C. S. *The Problem of Pain*. New York: Macmillan, 1962.

Lewis, T. J. "The Identity and Function of El/Baal Berith." *Journal of Biblical Literature* 115 (1996): 401–23.

Lindars, B. *Judges 1–5*. Edinburgh: T&T Clark, 1995.

Loader, J. A. "Of Barley, Bulls, Land and Levirate." In *Studies in Deuteronomy in Honour of C. J. Labuschagne on the Occasion of his 65th Birthday*, edited by F. G. Martínez, A. Hilhorst, J. T. A. G. M. van Ruiten, and A. S. van der Woude, 123–38. Leiden: Brill, 1994.

López, R. A. "Identifying the 'Angel of the Lord' in the Book of Judges: A Model for Reconsidering the Referent in Other Old Testament Loci." *Bulletin for Biblical Research* 20 (2010): 1–18.

Luter, A. B., and B. C. Davis. *God behind the Seen: Expositions of the Books of Ruth and Esther*. Grand Rapids: Baker, 1995.

Luter, A. B., and R. O. Rigsby. "An Adjusted Symmetrical Structuring of Ruth." *Journal of the Evangelical Theological Society* 39 (1996): 15–28.

MacDonald, B., and R. W. Younker, eds. *Ancient Ammon*. Leiden: Brill, 1999.

MacDonald, W. G. "Christology and 'The Angel of the Lord.'" In *Current Issues in Biblical and Patristic Interpretation: Studies in Honor of Merrill C. Tenney Presented by His Former Students*, edited by G. F. Hawthorne, 324–35. Grand Rapids: Eerdmans, 1975.

Maeir, A. M. "Insights on the Philistine Culture and Related Issues: An Overview of 15 Years of Work at Tell es-Safi/Gath." In *The Ancient Near East in the 12th–10th Centuries BCE: Culture and History; Proceedings of the International Conference Held at the University of Haifa, 2–5 May, 2010*, edited by G. Galil, A. Gilboa, A. M. Maeir, and D. Kahn, 345–404. Münster: Ugarit-Verlag, 2012.

Mafico, T. L. J. *Yahweh's Emergence as "Judge" among the Gods: A Study of the Hebrew Root Špt*. Lewiston, NY: Mellen, 2006.

Malamat, A. *History of Biblical Israel: Major Problems and Minor Issues*. Leiden: Brill, 2001.

———. *Mari and the Bible*. Leiden: Brill, 1998.

———. "The Period of the Judges." In *The World History of the Jewish People*, edited by B. Mazar, 3:129–63, 314–23. New Brunswick, NJ: Rutgers University / Jewish History Publications, 1971.

Marcos, N. Fernández. *Judges*. Biblia Hebraica Quinta 7. Stuttgart: Deutsche Bibelgesellschaft, 2011.

Marcus, D. *Jephthah and His Vow*. Lubbock: Texas Tech Press, 1986.

Mattingly, G. L. "Moabites." In *Peoples of the Old Testament World*, edited by A. J. Hoerth,

G. L. Mattingly, and E. M. Yamauchi, 317–33. Grand Rapids: Baker, 1994.

———. "Who Were Israel's Transjordanian Neighbors and How Did They Differ?" In *Israel: Ancient Kingdom or Late Invention?*, edited by D. I. Block, 201–24. Nashville: Broadman & Holman, 2008.

Mazar, A. "Bronze Bull Found in Israelite 'High Place' from the Time of the Judges." *Biblical Archaeology Review* 9 (September/October 1983): 34–40.

———. "The 'Bull Site'—An Iron Age I Open Cult Place." *Bulletin of the American Schools for Oriental Research* 247 (1982): 27–42.

Mazar, A., and N. Panitz-Cohen. "It Is the Land of Honey: Beekeeping at Tel Rehov." *Near Eastern Archaeology* 70 (2007): 202–19.

Mazar, E. *The Palace of King David: Excavations at the Summit of the City of David; Preliminary Report of Seasons 2005–2007.* Jerusalem: Shoham Academic Research and Publication, 2009.

Meier, S. A. *The Messenger in the Ancient Semitic World.* Atlanta: Scholars Press, 1988.

Millard, A. R. "Back to the Iron Bed: Og's or Procrustes'?" In *Congress Volume: Paris 1992*, edited J. A. Emerton, 193–203. Leiden: Brill, 1995.

Mobley, G. *The Empty Men: The Heroic Tradition of Ancient Israel.* New York: Doubleday, 2005.

———. "The Wild Man in the Bible and the Ancient Near East." *Journal of Biblical Literature* 116 (1997): 217–33.

Mullen, E. T. "Judges 1.1–36: The Deuteronomistic Reintroduction of the Book of Judges." *Harvard Theological Review* 77 (1984): 33–54.

———. "The 'Minor Judges': Some Literary and Historical Considerations." *Catholic Biblical Quarterly* 44 (1982): 185–201.

Nelson, R. D. "Ideology, Geography, and the List of Minor Judges." *Journal for the Study of the Old Testament* 31 (2007): 347–64.

Niditch, S. *"My Brother Esau Is a Hairy Man": Hair and Identity in Ancient Israel.* New York: Oxford University Press, 2008.

Niehaus, J. J. *Ancient Near Eastern Themes in Biblical Theology.* Grand Rapids: Kregel, 2008.

Nielsen, K. *Ruth: A Commentary.* Old Testament Library. Louisville: Westminster John Knox, 1997.

O'Connell, R. H. *The Rhetoric of the Book of Judges.* Leiden: Brill, 1996.

O'Connor, M. "The Women in the Book of Judges." *Hebrew Annual Review* 10 (1986): 277–93.

Olson, D. T. "Buber, Kingship, and the Book of Judges: A Study of Judges 6–9 and 17–21." In *David and Zion: Biblical Studies in Honor of J. J. M. Roberts*, edited by B. F. Batto and K. L. Roberts, 199–218. Winona Lake, IN: Eisenbrauns, 2004.

Olyan, S. M. "What Do Shaving Rites Accomplish and What Do They Signal in Biblical Ritual Contexts?" *Journal of Biblical Literature* 117 (1998): 611–22.

Oppenheim, A. L. "The Golden Garments of the Gods." *Journal of Near Eastern Studies* 8 (1949): 172–93.

Oren, E. D., ed. *The Sea Peoples and Their World: A Reassessment.* Philadelphia: University of Pennsylvania Museum, 2000.

Ortlund, R. C., Jr. *God's Unfaithful Wife: A Biblical Theology of Spiritual Adultery.* Downers Grove, IL: InterVarsity, 2002.

Ovadiah, A. "Gaza." In *The New Encyclopedia of Archaeological Excavations in the Holy Land*, edited by E. Stern et al., 2:464–67. Jerusalem: Israel Exploration Society and Carta; New York: Simon & Schuster, 1993.

Plantinga, C. *Not the Way It's Supposed to Be: A Breviary of Sin.* Grand Rapids: Eerdmans, 1995.

Polzin, R. *Moses and the Deuteronomist: A Literary Study of the Deuteronomic History.* Part 1: *Deuteronomy, Joshua, Judges.* Bloomington: Indiana University Press, 1980.

Porten, B. "The Scroll of Ruth: A Rhetorical Study." *Gratz College Annual of Jewish Studies* 7 (1978): 23–49.

———. "Theme and Historiosophic Background of the Scroll of Ruth." *Gratz College Annual of Jewish Studies* 6 (1977): 69–78.

Pritchard, R. *He's God and We're Not: The Seven Laws of the Spiritual Life.* Nashville: Broadman & Holman, 2003.

Provan, I., V. P. Long, and T. Longman III. *A Biblical History of Israel.* Louisville: Westminster John Knox, 2003.

Rabinowitz, L. *Ruth.* In *Midrash Rabbah*, edited by H. Freedman and M. Simon, 1–94. London: Soncino, 1939.

Radday, Y. T. "Chiasmus in Hebrew Biblical Narrative." In *Chiasmus in Antiquity: Structures, Analyses, Exegesis*, edited by J. W. Welch, 50–117. Hildesheim: Gerstenberg, 1981.

Rainey, A. F., and R. S. Notley. *The Sacred Bridge: Carta's Atlas of the Biblical World.* Jerusalem: Carta, 2006.

Rasmussen, C. G. *Zondervan Atlas of the Bible*. Rev. ed. Grand Rapids: Zondervan, 2010.

Rebera, B. A. "Yahweh or Boaz? Ruth 2.20 Reconsidered." *Bible Translator* 36 (1985): 317–27.

Reich, R. "A Fiscal Bulla from the City of David, Jerusalem." *Israel Exploration Journal* 62 (2012): 200–205.

Richard, S., ed. *Near Eastern Archaeology: A Reader*. Winona Lake, IN: Eisenbrauns, 2003.

Römer, T. C. *The So-Called Deuteronomistic History: A Sociological, Historical and Literary Introduction*. New York: T&T Clark, 2007.

Routledge, B. *Moab in the Iron Age*. Philadelphia: University of Pennsylvania Press, 2004.

Ryken, L., J. C. Wilhoit, and T. Longman III. *Dictionary of Biblical Imagery*. Downers Grove, IL: InterVarsity, 1998.

Sakenfeld, K. D. *Faithfulness in Action*. 1985. Reprint, Eugene, OR: Wipf and Stock, 2001.

———. *The Meaning of* Hesed *in the Hebrew Bible: A New Inquiry*. Missoula, MT: Scholars Press, 1978.

———. *Ruth*. Interpretation. Louisville: John Knox, 1999.

Sasson, J. M. "Coherence and Fragments: Reflections on the *SKL* and the *Book of Judges*." In *Opening the Tablet Box: Near Eastern Studies in Honor of Benjamin R. Foster*, edited by S. C. Melville and A. L. Slotsky, 361–73. Leiden: Brill, 2010.

———. "Ethically Cultured Interpretations: The Case of Eglon's Murder (Judges 3)." In *Homeland and Exile: Biblical and Ancient Near Eastern Studies in Honour of Bustenay Oded*, edited by G. Galil, M. Geller, and A. Millard, 571–95. Leiden: Brill, 2009.

———. "Farewell to 'Mr So and So' (Ruth 4.1)." In *Making a Difference: Essays on the Bible and Judaism in Honor of Tamara Cohn Eskenazi*, edited by D. J. A. Clines, K. H. Richards, and J. L. Wright, 251–56. Sheffield: Phoenix, 2012.

———. "Jephthah: Chutzpah and Overreach in a Hebrew Judge." In *Literature as Politics, Politics as Literature: Essays on the Ancient Near East in Honor of Peter Machinist*, edited by D. S. Vanderhooft and A. Winitzer, 405–20. Winona Lake, IN: Eisenbrauns, 2013.

———. *Judges 1–12*. New Haven: Yale University Press, 2014.

———. "Oracle Inquiries in Judges." In *Birkat Shalom: Studies in the Bible, Ancient Near Eastern Literature, and Postbiblical Judaism Presented to Shalom M. Paul on the Occasion of His Seventieth Birthday*, edited by C. Cohen, V. A. Hurowitz, A. Hurvitz, Y. Muffs, B. J. Schwartz, and J. Tigay, 1:149–68. Winona Lake, IN: Eisenbrauns, 2008.

———. "Ruth." In *The Literary Guide to the Bible*, edited by R. Alter and F. Kermode, 320–28. Cambridge: Harvard University Press, 1987.

———. *Ruth: A New Translation with a Philological Commentary and a Formalist-Folklorist Interpretation*. 2nd ed. Sheffield: Sheffield Academic Press, 1995.

———. "Who Cut Samson's Hair? (And Other Trifling Issues Raised by Judges 16)." *Prooftexts* 8 (1988): 333–39.

Schipper, J. *Parables and Conflict in the Hebrew Bible*. New York: Cambridge University Press, 2009.

Schmitz, P. C. "Deity and Royalty in Dedicatory Formulae: The Ekron Store-Jar Inscription Viewed in the Light of Judges 7:18, 20 and the Inscribed Gold Medalion from the Douïmès Necropolis at Carthage (*KAI* 73)." *Maarav* 15 (2008): 165–73.

Schneider, T. J. "Achsah, the Raped *Pîlegeš*, and the Book of Judges." In *Women in the Biblical World: A Survey of Old and New Testament Perspectives*, edited by E. A. McCabe, 43–57. Lanham, MD: University Press of America, 2009.

Schniedewind, W. M. "The Search for Gibeah: Notes on the Historical Geography of Central Benjamin." In *"I Will Speak the Riddles of Ancient Times": Archaeological and Historical Studies in Honor of Amihai Mazar on the Occasion of His Sixtieth Birthday*, edited by A. M. Maeir and P. de Miroschedji, 2:711–22. Winona Lake, IN: Eisenbrauns, 2006.

Schnittjer, G. E. "The Narrative Multiverse within the Universe of the Bible: The Question of 'Borderlines' and 'Intertextuality.'" *Westminster Theological Journal* 64 (2002): 231–52.

Schulte, L. R., and T. J. Schneider. "The Absence of the Deity in Rape Scenes of the Hebrew Bible." In *The Presence and Absence of God: Claremont Studies in the Philosophy of Religion, Conference 2008*, edited by I. U. Dalferth, 21–33. Tübingen: Mohr Siebeck, 2009.

Segert, S. "Paronomasia in the Samson Narrative in Judges XIII–XVI." *Vetus Testamentum* 34 (1984): 454–61.

Sharon, D. M. "Echoes of Gideon's Ephod: An Intertextual Reading." *Journal of the*

Ancient Near Eastern Society 30 (2006): 89–102.

Shupak, N. "New Light on Shamgar ben 'Anath." *Biblica* 70 (1989): 517–25.

Slotki, J. J. "Ruth." In *The Five Megilloth*, edited by A .Cohen, 34–65. London: Soncino, 1961.

Smelik, W. F. *The Targum of Judges*. Leiden: Brill, 1995.

Smith, M. J. "The Failure of the Family in Judges, Part 1: Jephthah." *Bibliotheca Sacra* 162 (2005): 279–98.

———. "The Failure of the Family in Judges, Part 2: Samson." *Bibliotheca Sacra* 162 (2005): 424–36.

Smith, M. S. *The Early History of God: Yahweh and the Other Deities in Ancient Israel*. Grand Rapids: Eerdmans, 2002.

———. *The Memoirs of God*. Minneapolis: Fortress, 2004.

———. "'Your People Shall Be My People': Family and Covenant in Ruth 1:16–17." *Catholic Biblical Quarterly* 69 (2007): 242–58.

Smith, M. S., and W. T. Pitard. *The Ugaritic Baal Cycle*. Vol. 2. Leiden: Brill, 2009.

Smith, P. "Infants Sacrificed? The Tale Teeth Tell." *Biblical Archaeology Review* 40 (July/August 2014): 54–56, 68.

Smith-Christopher, D. L. "Gideon at Thermopylae? On the Militarization of Miracle in Biblical Narrative and 'Battle Maps.'" In *Writing and Reading War: Rhetoric, Gender, and Ethics in Biblical and Modern Contexts*, edited by B. E. Kelle and F. R. Ames, 197–212. Atlanta: Society of Biblical Literature, 2008.

Stager, L. E. "Archaeology, Ecology, and Social History: Background Themes to the Song of Deborah." In *Congress Volume: Jerusalem, 1986*, edited by J. A. Emerton, 221–34. Leiden: Brill, 1988.

———. "Biblical Philistines: A Hellenistic Literary Creation?" In *"I Will Speak the Riddles of Ancient Times": Archaeological and Historical Studies in Honor of Amihai Mazar on the Occasion of His Sixtieth Birthday*, edited by A. M. Maeir and P. de Miroschedji, 1:375–84. Winona Lake, IN: Eisenbrauns, 2006.

———. "The Fortress-Temple at Shechem and the 'House of El, Lord of the Covenant.'" In *Realia Dei: Essays in Archaeology and Biblical Interpretation in Honor of Edward F. Campbell, Jr. at His Retirement*, edited by P. H. Williams Jr. and T. Hiebert, 228–49. Atlanta: Scholars Press, 1999.

———. "Key Passages." *Eretz-Israel* 27 (2003): 240*–45*.

———. "The Shechem Temple: Where Abimelech Massacred a Thousand." *Biblical Archaeology Review* 29 (July/August 2003): 26–35, 66, 68–69.

———. "Shemer's Estate." *Bulletin of the American Schools for Oriental Research* 277/278 (1990): 93–107.

———. "The Song of Deborah: Why Some Tribes Answered the Call and Others Did Not." *Biblical Archaeology Review* 15 (January/February 1989): 51–64.

Stager, L. E., J. D. Schloen, and D. M. Master, eds. *Ashkelon 1: Introduction and Overview (1985–2006)*. Winona Lake, IN: Eisenbrauns, 2008.

Stavrakopoulou, F. *King Manasseh and Child Sacrifice: Biblical Distortions of Historical Realities*. Berlin: de Gruyter, 2004.

Steinberg, N. "The Problem of Human Sacrifice in War: An Analysis of Judges 11." In *On the Way to Nineveh: Studies in Honor of George M. Landes*, edited by S. L. Cook and S. C. Winter, 114–35. Atlanta: Scholars Press, 1999.

Stek, J. H. "The Bee and the Mountain Goat: A Literary Reading of Judges 4." In *A Tribute to Gleason Archer*, edited by W. C. Kaiser and R. F. Youngblood, 53–86. Chicago: Moody, 1986.

Stern, E., et al., eds. *The New Encyclopedia of Archaeological Excavations in the Holy Land*. 4 vols. Jerusalem: Israel Exploration Society and Carta; New York: Simon & Schuster, 1993.

———, et al., eds. *The New Encyclopedia of Archaeological Excavations in the Holy Land*. Vol. 5: Supplementary Volume. Jerusalem: Israel Exploration Society, 2008.

Stone, L. G. "Eglon's Belly and Ehud's Blade: A Reconsideration." *Journal of Biblical Literature* 128 (2009): 649–63.

———. "Judges." In *Cornerstone Biblical Commentary*, edited by P. W. Comfort, 3:185–494. Carol Stream, IL: Tyndale, 2012.

———. "Judges, Book of." In *Dictionary of the Old Testament: Historical Books*, edited by B. T. Arnold and H. G. M. Williamson, 592–606. Downers Grove, IL: InterVarsity, 2005.

Strawn, B. A. "*kĕpîr 'ărāyôt* in Judges 14:5." *Vetus Testamentum* 59 (2009): 150–58.

———. *What Is Stronger Than a Lion? Leonine Image and Metaphor in the Hebrew Bible and the Ancient Near East*. Fribourg: Academic Press; Göttingen: Vandenhoeck & Ruprecht, 2005.

Sweeney, M. A. "Davidic Polemic in the Book of Judges." *Vetus Testamentum* 47 (1997): 517–29.

Tatlock, J. "The Place of Human Sacrifice in the Israelite Cult." In *Ritual and Metaphor: Sacrifice in the Bible*, edited by C. A. Eberhart, 33–48. Atlanta: Society of Biblical Literature, 2011.

Tatu, S. "Jotham's Fable and the *Crux Interpretum* in Judges IX." *Vetus Testamentum* 56 (2006): 105–24.

Taylor, J. G. "The Bible and Homosexuality." *Themelios* 21 (1995): 4–9.

———. *Yahweh and the Sun: Biblical and Archaeological Evidence for Sun Worship in Ancient Israel.* Sheffield: JSOT Press, 1993.

Thackeray, H. St. J., and R. Marcus. *Josephus.* Cambridge: Harvard University Press, 1966.

Thompson, J. L. "Preaching Texts of Terror in the Book of Judges: How Does the History of Interpretation Help?" *Calvin Theological Journal* 37 (2002): 49–61.

Thorn, J. *Note to Self: The Discipline of Preaching to Yourself.* Wheaton: Crossway, 2011.

Tischler, N. M. "Ruth." In *A Complete Literary Guide to the Bible*, edited by L. Ryken and T. Longman III, 151–64. Grand Rapids: Zondervan, 1993.

Tov, E. *Textual Criticism of the Hebrew Bible.* 3rd ed. Minneapolis: Fortress, 2012.

Tracy, E. "Why the Levite Lied: Solving the Mystery of Judges 19 and 20." Paper presented at the Annual Meeting of the Society of Biblical Literature, San Francisco, CA, November 2011.

Trible, P. *God and the Rhetoric of Sexuality.* Philadelphia: Fortress, 1978.

———. *Texts of Terror: Literary-Feminist Readings of Biblical Narratives.* Philadelphia: Fortress, 1984.

Trimm, C. "Recent Research on Warfare in the Old Testament." *Currents in Biblical Research* 10 (2012): 1–46.

———. *"YHWH Fights for Them!" The Divine Warrior in the Exodus Narrative.* Piscataway, NJ: Gorgias, 2014.

Tsevat, M. "Two Old Testament Stories and Their Hittite Analogues." *Journal of the American Oriental Society* 103 (1983): 321–26.

van der Toorn, K. "Judges XVI 21 in the Light of the Akkadian Sources." *Vetus Testamentum* 36 (1986): 248–53.

———. "The Nature of the Biblical Teraphim in the Light of the Cuneiform Evidence." *Catholic Biblical Quarterly* 52 (1990): 203–22.

———. "The Significance of the Veil in the Ancient Near East." In *Pomegranates and Golden Bells: Studies in Biblical, Jewish, and Near Eastern Ritual, Law, and Literature in Honor of Jacob Milgrom*, edited by D. P. Wright, D. N. Freedman, and A. Hurvitz, 327–39. Winona Lake, IN: Eisenbrauns, 1995.

van Wolde, E. "Texts in Dialogue with Texts: Intertextuality in the Ruth and Tamar Narratives." *Biblical Interpretation* 5 (1997): 1–28.

Waldman, N. M. "The Imagery of Clothing, Covering, and Overpowering." *Journal of the Ancient Near Eastern Society* 19 (1989): 161–70.

Walton, J. H. "The Ancient Near Eastern Background of the Spirit of the Lord in the Old Testament." In *Presence, Power and Promise*, edited by D. G. Firth and P. D. Wegner, 38–67. Downers Grove, IL: InterVarsity, 2011.

———. *Ancient Near Eastern Thought and the Old Testament.* Grand Rapids: Baker Academic, 2006.

———. *Chronological and Background Charts of the Old Testament.* Grand Rapids: Zondervan, 1994.

———. *Covenant: God's Purpose, God's Plan.* Grand Rapids: Zondervan, 1994.

———. "The Decalogue Structure of the Deuteronomic Law." In *Interpreting Deuteronomy: Issues and Approaches*, edited by D. G. Firth and P. S. Johnston, 93–117. Downers Grove, IL: InterVarsity, 2012.

———. "Exodus, Date of." In *Dictionary of the Old Testament: Pentateuch*, edited by T. D. Alexander and D. W. Baker, 258–72. Downers Grove, IL: InterVarsity, 2003.

———. "Genealogies." In *Dictionary of the Old Testament: Historical Books*, edited by B. T. Arnold and H. G. M. Williamson, 309–16. Downers Grove, IL: InterVarsity, 2005.

———. *Genesis.* NIV Application Commentary. Grand Rapids: Zondervan, 2001.

———. "Inspired Subjectivity and Hermeneutical Objectivity." *The Master's Seminary Journal* 13 (Spring 2002): 65–77.

———. "Interpreting the Bible as an Ancient Near Eastern Document." In *Israel: Ancient Kingdom or Late Invention?*, edited by D. I. Block, 298–327. Nashville: Broadman & Holman, 2008.

———. *Job.* NIV Application Commentary. Grand Rapids: Zondervan, 2012.

Walton, J. H., L. D. Bailey, and C. Williford. "Bible-Based Curricula and the Crisis of Scriptural Authority." *Christian Education Journal* 13 (Spring 1993): 83–94.

Walton, J. H., and A. E. Hill. *Old Testament Today: A Journey from Ancient Context to Contemporary Relevance*. 2nd ed. Grand Rapids: Zondervan, 2013.

Walton, J. H., M. L. Strauss, and T. Cooper. *The Essential Bible Companion*. Grand Rapids: Zondervan, 2006.

Walton, J. H., and K. E. Walton. *The Bible Story Handbook: A Resource for Teaching 175 Stories from the Bible*. Wheaton: Crossway, 2010.

Wang, T. "The Use of the Infinitive Absolute in the Hebrew Bible and the Septuagint." PhD diss., Hebrew Union College, 2003.

Way, K. C. "Animals in the Prophetic World: Literary Reflections on Numbers 22 and 1 Kings 13." *Journal for the Study of the Old Testament* 34 (2009): 47–62.

———. "Assessing Sacred Asses: Bronze Age Donkey Burials in the Near East." *Levant* 42 (2010): 210–25.

———. "Donkey Domain: Zechariah 9:9 and Lexical Semantics." *Journal of Biblical Literature* 129 (2010): 105–14.

———. *Donkeys in the Biblical World: Ceremony and Symbol*. Winona Lake, IN: Eisenbrauns, 2011.

———. "Giants in the Land: A Textual and Semantic Study of Giants in the Bible and the Ancient Near East." MA thesis, Trinity Evangelical Divinity School, 2000.

———. "Handling 'Heroes' in Hebrews 11." *Biola Magazine* (Fall 2011): 39.

Webb, B. G. *The Book of the Judges: An Integrated Reading*. Sheffield: Sheffield Academic Press, 1987.

Wegner, P. D. *A Student's Guide to Textual Criticism of the Bible*. Downers Grove, IL: InterVarsity, 2006.

Weisberg, D. B. "Character Development in the Book of Ruth." In *Leaders and Legacies in Assyriology and Bible: The Collected Essays of David B. Weisberg*, 217–20. Winona Lake, IN: Eisenbrauns, 2012.

Weisberg, D. E. *Levirate Marriage and the Family in Ancient Judaism*. Waltham, MA: Brandeis University Press, 2009.

Wendland, E. R. "Structural Symmetry and Its Significance in the Book of Ruth." In *Issues in Bible Translation*, edited by P. C. Stine, 30–63. London: United Bible Societies, 1988.

Westenholz, J. G. *Legends of the Kings of Akkade*. Winona Lake, IN: Eisenbrauns, 1997.

Willard, D. *Hearing God: Developing a Conversational Relationship with God*. Downers Grove, IL: InterVarsity, 1999.

———. *Renovation of the Heart: Putting on the Character of Christ*. Colorado Springs: NavPress, 2002.

———. *The Spirit of the Disciplines: Understanding How God Changes Lives*. New York: HarperCollins, 1988.

Willis, T. M. "The Nature of Jephthah's Authority." *Catholic Biblical Quarterly* 59 (1997): 33–44.

Wilson, M. K. "'As You Like It': The Idolatry of Micah and the Danites (Judges 17–18)." *Reformed Theological Review* 54 (1995): 73–85.

Wilson, S. D. *Hurt People Hurt People: Hope and Healing for Yourself and Your Relationships*. Nashville: Nelson, 1993.

Wilson, V. M. *Divine Symmetries: The Art of Biblical Rhetoric*. Lanham, MD: University Press of America, 1997.

Wong, G. T. K. *Compositional Strategy of the Book of Judges: An Inductive, Rhetorical Study*. Leiden: Brill, 2006.

———. "Gideon: A New Moses?" In *Reflection and Refraction: Studies in Biblical Historiography in Honour of A. Graeme Auld*, edited by R. Rezetko, T. H. Lim, and W. B. Auker, 529–45. Leiden: Brill, 2007.

Wood, B. G. "The Biblical Date for the Exodus is 1446 BC: A Response to James Hoffmeier." *Journal of the Evangelical Theological Society* 50 (2007): 249–58.

———. "The Rise and Fall of the 13th-Century Exodus-Conquest Theory." *Journal of the Evangelical Theological Society* 48 (2005): 475–89.

Woods, F. E. *Water and Storm Polemics against Baalism in the Deuteronomistic History*. New York: Peter Lang, 1994.

Wright, C. J. H. *Old Testament Ethics for the People of God*. Downers Grove, IL: InterVarsity, 2004.

Wright, G. E. *Shechem: The Biography of a Biblical City*. New York: McGraw-Hill, 1964.

Würthwein, E. *Die Fünf Megilloth*. Tübingen: Mohr Siebeck, 1969.

Yadin, A. "Samson's ḤÎDÂ." *Vetus Testamentum* 52 (2002): 407–26.

Yasur-Landau, A. *The Philistines and Aegean Migration at the End of the Late Bronze Age*. Cambridge: Cambridge University Press, 2010.

Yee, G. E., ed. *Judges and Method: New Approaches in Biblical Studies*. 2nd ed. Minneapolis: Fortress, 2007.

Young, R. C., and B. G. Wood, "A Critical Analysis of the Evidence from Ralph Hawkins for a Late-Date Exodus-Conquest." *Journal* of the *Evangelical Theological Society* 51 (2008): 225–43.

Younger, K. L. *Ancient Conquest Accounts: A Study in Ancient Near Eastern and Biblical History Writing.* Sheffield: Sheffield Academic Press, 1990.

———. "Heads! Tails! Or the Whole Coin?! Contextual Method & Intertextual Analysis: Judges 4 and 5." In *The Biblical Canon in Perspective: Scripture in Context IV*, edited by K. L. Younger, W. W. Hallo, and B. F. Batto, 109–46. Lewiston, NY: Mellen, 1991.

———. "Some Recent Discussion on the *Ḥērem*." In *Far from Minimal: Celebrating the Work and Influence of Philip R. Davies*, edited by D. Burns and J. W. Rogerson, 505–22. London: T&T Clark, 2012.

———. "Two Comparative Notes on the Book of Ruth." *Journal of the Ancient Near Eastern Society* 26 (1998): 121–32.

Younker, R. W. "Ammon, Ammonites." In *Dictionary of the Old Testament: Historical Books*, edited by B. T. Arnold and H. G. M. Williamson, 23–26. Downers Grove, IL: InterVarsity, 2005.

Zertal, A. "Philistine Kin Found in Early Israel." *Biblical Archaeology Review* 28 (May/June 2002): 18–31, 60–61.

———. *Sisera's Secret: A Journey Following the Sea Peoples and the Song of Deborah* [in Hebrew]. Tel Aviv: Dvir, 2010.

Zevit, Z. *The Religions of Ancient Israel.* London: Continuum, 2001.

Contributors

General Editors
Mark. L. Strauss
John H. Walton

Associate Editors, Illustrating the Text
Kevin and Sherry Harney

Contributing Author, Illustrating the Text
Joshua Blunt

Series Development
Jack Kuhatschek
Brian Vos

Project Editor
James Korsmo

Interior Design
Brian Brunsting
William Overbeeke

Cover Direction
Paula Gibson
Michael Cook

Index

Caiaphas, 40
Caleb, 30–31
Canaan, 44
Canaanites, 17
  as quiet, 153
  religion of, 27, 145, 148
Canaanization, 6, 57, 58, 80, 86, 102, 103, 111,
    161, 165, 168, 169, 173, 175, 176, 179, 187
canon, 8–9
celebration, 55
celestial omens, 51
central loading (ring structure), 4
chaos, 162
chariots, 16
Chemosh, 97, 189
chiasm
  in Judges, 2
  in Ruth, 181
Christophanies, 79
Chrysostom, John, 107
church, mirrored in Judges, 9
church discipline, 25, 163
City of Palms, 16, 36
civil war, 101, 103, 104, 165, 176
closure at two levels (ring structure), 4
commemoration, 53
communal interest, 42, 217
concubines, 75, 160
confession of sin, 91, 92
conquest, 13
  failure to follow through on, 38
  reversal of, 6, 175
contingents, 51, 173
Corey, Barry H., 207
corporal dismemberment, 158
corporate responsibility, 112–13
corpse, 124, 125, 131
covenant
  breaking, 7, 23, 118, 188
  renewal, at Shechem, 82
Crusades, 169
Cummings, E. E., 127–28
curses and blessings, 146
Cushan-Rishathaim, 29
Cyrus, 40

Dagon, 130, 139, 140
Dan, 53, 115, 116, 118, 123, 166
Danite migration, 12, 151–56
darkness and light, 191–92
daughter of Jephthah, 34, 36, 56, 101–4
daughters of Shiloh, 175
David, 18, 182, 185, 188, 211
Davis, D. R., 119
day and night, 137
death, 189

Deborah, 108
  poetic account of, 11, 49–54
  as prophetess, 46, 56
  prose account of, 11, 41–47
decision making, 69–70
defecation, 37
Delilah, 56, 137–38, 145
deliverance, 102, 111, 163
  through Samson, 118–19, 126
deliverers, 29–30
depravity, 162–63
dew, 66
dialectical diversity, 103, 153
Dickens, Charles, 192, 207
dietary prohibitions, 118
dismembered body, 161, 166
disobedience, 19, 149
disorder, 161
divination, 146, 149–50, 153
divine manipulation, 105
divine sovereignty and human responsibility,
    198
divorce, 160
donkey, 158
donkey riders, 110
double-edged sword, 36
double epilogue, 20
double prologue, 20
Douglas, Mary, 2–5
downward spiral of sin. See sin: downward
    spiral of
dream omen, 67, 68

Edom, 51
Edud, 101
Eglon, 34, 35–39, 44, 90, 101
Egyptians, 91
Ehud, 11, 34–39, 52, 108
El-Berith, 82
elders of the assembly, 174
eleven hundred shekels, 137, 138, 145
Elimelek, 209
Elizabeth, 117
Elon, 108
Emites, 26
emotions, 127
ephah, 196
ephod, 66, 74, 77, 144, 146, 151, 153
Ephraim, 34, 53, 75, 101, 145, 152, 159, 160,
    166
Ephrathites, 188
Esarhaddon, 21
Eshtaol, 116, 118, 136, 152
"evil in the eyes of the LORD," 6–7, 21, 23, 85,
    123
exile, 155

exodus, dating of, 9–10
exposition (ring structure), 2
Exum, J. C., 140–41

faith, 46–47
false worship, 87
family, breakdown of, 96, 106
famines, 188
fasting, 167
fat, as health and prosperity, 36
father (title), 147
father and priest, 147, 253
fear, 67
Feast of Unleavened Bread, 197
Feast of Weeks/Pentecost, 197
feeling, 127
"festival of the LORD," 174–75
fleece, 66, 69, 219
Fokkelman, J. P., 159
foolishness, 125
foreigners, 181
forty (number), 10
forty years of oppression, 29, 115, 118
forty years of tranquility, 29, 31, 41, 115
Foster, Richard J., 78
foxes, 130
Francis of Assisi, 135

Gaal, 84
Galli, Mark, 94, 99
Gaza, 137
genealogical lists, 185
genitalia, 202
genocide, 105, 174, 175, 176
gentile inclusion, 182
Gershom, 154
giants, in the Old Testament, 26
Gibeah, 159, 162, 166
Gideon, 56, 79, 96, 108
    aspirations of kingship, 67, 76
    battle of, 11, 65–70
    demise of, 11, 72–77
    feeble faith of, 68–69
    idolatry of, 144
    rise of, 11, 58–63
    slaughter of Israelites, 165
    testing of God, 66, 69
Gilead, 53, 101, 108, 166
Gilgal, 37, 38
Gilgamesh, 122
gleaning, 194–95, 197
God
    absence of, 98–99, 137, 140, 158
    anger of, 93
    authority of, 149, 154, 155
    care for needy, 181

compassion of, 31, 93
covenant promises of, 174
as deliverer, 119–20, 126, 132
exclusivity of, 61–63, 148
faithfulness of, 7–8, 9, 23, 141, 199
as gracious, 120, 163
as hero in Samson narrative, 140
hmm warfare of, 52–53
holiness of, 174
as Israel's enemy, 169, 175
as Judge, 86, 97, 99, 102, 103, 169, 190
judgment of, 156, 174
justice of, 99, 168–69
kingship of, 8, 52, 76–77, 111, 146, 154, 155
    not recognized as king, 175
omnipresence of, 99
passivity of, 103, 105, 156
patience of, 68, 69, 156
presence of, 61–62, 63
provision of, 190–91, 199, 211
retribution of, 86
sovereignty of, 32, 38, 52, 134, 197
tests his people, 23, 24, 66
uses unworthy agents to accomplish plans, 133
    See also Holy Spirit; Spirit of the Lord
godliness, 212
gold earrings, 73
golden calf incidents, 148
Goliath, 26
Gooding, D. W., 2
good Samaritan, parable of, 192
good works, 32
governor, 22
grace, 32, 33, 133, 134–35, 176
grinding grain, 138
guardian-redeemer, 196, 203, 204

Hamor, 84
hands, of slain foes, 73
Hannah, 117, 163
hayil, 180, 181, 194, 195, 201, 204
Hazor, 46
heart, following of, 126–27
Heber the Kenite, 42, 43
Hebron, 137
Heracles, 122
herem, 174. *See also* ban
hesed, 182, 190, 196, 199, 204–6, 212
Hess, R. S., 50
holiness, 113, 142–43
Holocaust, 169
Holy Spirit, 30, 32. *See also* Spirit of the Lord
honey, 124, 125
horoscopes, 149
Horus, 196

Hosea, 162
household gods, 147, 148
"house of the LORD," 160, 175
human kingship, 111
human sacrifice, 34, 97, 103–5, 107
hyperbole, 97

Ibzan, 108, 109, 112, 226
idolatry, 20, 58, 93, 112, 156, 157
Ilan, David, 152
images, 146
incarnation, 79
indicators to mark individual sections (ring
    structure), 3–4
infidelity, 106
intermarriage, with Canaanites, 22, 23, 28, 56,
    75, 112, 56, 123, 126
intertextuality, 161, 182
Iron Age I, 10, 50, 59
Israel
    apostasy of, 11, 42, 46, 53, 85, 90, 91, 118,
        141
    breach in tribes, 174, 175
    Canaanization of, 6, 57, 58, 80, 86, 102, 103,
        111, 161, 165, 168, 169, 173, 175, 176, 179,
        187
    civil war, 101, 103, 104, 165, 176
    dark age, 175, 187, 189
    dismembering of, 166–67
    disobedience of, 8
    failures of, 6, 11, 13–19, 141
    had no king, 146, 148
    idolatry of, 20, 151
    not to test God, 66
    unfaithfulness of, 7, 9, 23, 73, 179
    unity of tribes, 167, 168
    worse than Canaanites, 162
Issachar, 53

Jabesh Gilead, 173
Jabin, 42, 45
Jael, 44, 46–47, 52
Jair, 108, 109
jawbone of a donkey, 131–32
Jephthah, 56, 79, 89–92
    fall of, 12, 101–7
    rise of, 12, 95–99
    vow of, 102–3, 107, 173
Jephthah, daughter of. See daughter of
    Jephthah
Jericho, 16, 36, 38
Jerub-Baal, 61
Jerusalem, 16, 158
Jesus Christ
    as head of the church, 112
    as one mediator, 77

sacrifice of, 104
    as suffering servant, 120
jewelry, 73
Jezreel Valley, 67
Joash, 62
Jonathan (son of Gershom), 154, 155–56
Josephus, 76, 98
Joshua (book), 13
Joshua, death of, 20
Jotham, 49, 81, 83, 85
JOY (acronym), 206
Judah, tribe of, 18, 28, 31, 32, 53, 115, 123, 129
Judges (book of)
    in canon, 8–9
    composition of, 10–11
    dating of, 9–10
    illicit behavior in, 1
    literary structure of, 2–6
    as mirror for the church, 9
judges (office)
    as administrators or governors, 21–22, 30
    as role models, 79–80
judgment, 84, 156, 169
justice, 133, 169, 191

Karkor, 73
Kenaz, 30
Kenizzites, 43
Kilion, 180
kindness, 196, 205–6, 207
kingdom building, 112, 113
King, Martin Luther, Jr., 107
kingship, 85, 148
Kiriath Jearim, 152
Kishon, 43

Laish, 152, 153
land, 182
Leah, 182
leaving and cleaving, 195
left-handed, 36
legalism, 173
levirate marriage, 210
Levite of Micah's house, 147, 148–49
Levites, corruption of, 144, 151, 160, 162
Levite's concubine, 12, 56, 96, 158–62
Lewis, C. S., 94
lions, 122–23
"LORD's hand," 189
love, for neighbor, 195
loyalty, 212

Mahaneh Dan, 118, 152
Mahlon, 180, 189
maintaining the family, 106
"major" judges, 31

Index

revelation, 149

revenge, of Samson. *See* Samson: revenge of

rich fool, parable of, 192

riddle, 124

"right in one's own eyes," 7, 137, 146–147, 176–77

"right in the eyes of the LORD," 147, 176–77, 216

Rimmon, 166

ring compositions, 2–6, 144

"ring within a ring," 4, 144, 159

Ruth (book of), 163
  in canon, 7–8, 182–83
  composer of, 184
  dating of, 184–85
  genre of, 184
  introduction to, 179–85
  as microcosm of Genesis, 182
  as wisdom story, 203

Ruth (person)
  character of, 163, 185, 198, 204
  as foreigner, 202
  as handmaid, 202
  industry of, 196
  name, 180
  oath to Naomi, 189
  proposes marriage to Boaz, 202–3

salt, 84

Samson, 79, 91, 96
  as agent of God's justice, 141
  beginning of, 12, 115–20
  end of, 12, 136–44
  final prayer of, 140–41
  hair of, 138
  illicit relationships with women, 56
  marriage of, 12, 28, 39, 122–27
  miraculous nature of birth, 117
  as quasi deliverer, 117
  revenge of, 12, 129–34, 140
  selfishness of, 123, 126, 132–34, 140
  strength of, 127, 128, 136, 138, 140
  tenure as judge, 132
  as type of Christ, 117, 141
  vices of, 38, 140
  weakness of, 124–25

Samuel, as composer of Ruth, 184

sanctification, 179

sandal, removal of, 210–11

Sasson, Jack, 138

secret/divine word, 37, 52

Seir, 51

self-destruction, 87

self-inflicted consequences, 106

self-interest, 75, 86, 89, 93, 104, 106, 132, 177, 189, 210, 217

selfishness, 133, 141, 156, 170

selflessness, 104, 212, 214

Sellin, Ernst, 82

servants, 155

seven deities, 90

seventy (number), 75, 110

seventy brothers, 83

sexual intercourse, 204

Shaddai, 189

Shamgar, 41, 108–9, 111, 131

Shamir, 109

Shechem, 81–83, 86

Shephelah, 116

shibboleth, 103

Shiloh, 145, 152, 154, 156, 173

Shiloh, daughters of, 175

Simeon, 53

sin
  downward spiral of, 5, 23, 24, 58, 105, 106, 107, 141, 162, 169
  generational patterns of, 86
  potential of, 155
  trajectory of, 162

sin offering, 167

Sisera, 42–43, 44, 46, 52, 56

sling, 167

snare, 74

sojourners, 194

song of Deborah and Barak, 11, 49–54, 81

Song of the Sea, 50

Sorek Valley, 116, 137–38

southern geographical orientation, 28, 109, 115, 136

southern tribes, 53–54

spies, 153

"spirit of disaster," 83–84

Spirit of the Lord, 30, 32, 45
  absence of, 153
  upon Gideon, 66, 68
  upon Jephthah, 101–2
  upon Samson, 118, 127, 129–30

spiritual apathy, 126

Stager, L. E., 82

Stone, L. G., 167

stone images, 37

stronghold, 84

subjective hermeneutic, 79–80

success, measured on God's terms, 19

suffering, 191

Sukkoth, 73, 75

sword, 36

syncretism, 74, 86, 103, 105, 144, 148–49, 154–55

tabernacle, 154

Tale of Zaipa, 110

Tamar, 182

Tel Dan, 152, 153–54
ten Boom, Corrie, 33
teraphim, 66, 147, 153
testing God, 66, 69
"texts of terror," 105, 162, 176
Thebez, 83
theocracy, 8, 67, 76, 148, 149, 155
theology, importance of, 105
theophanies, 79
threshing floor, 201–2, 205, 209
Timnah, 116, 123, 138
Timnite woman, 122–23, 132
Tirzah, 83
Tola, 108, 111
torah, ignorance of, 97
torah person, 212–13
tower of Shechem, 82
Tozer, A. W., 157
Transjordan, 73, 75, 101, 109
trees, 83
Trible, P., 161
Tripp, Ted, 47–48
"Trust and Obey" (hymn), 70
typology, 141

unclean, 131
upper millstone, 84
Urim and Thummim, 66, 74

vengeance, 141
verbiage, in literary units, 5

victimization, 56–57, 176
victory song, 50
violence, 106, 169, 176
vow, of Jephthah. *See* Jephthah: vow of

Walton, J. H., 80
water, miracle of, 132
Webb, B. G., 172–73
wheat harvest, 197
wicked men, 160
widows, 181, 185, 191, 194
wild animals, 130
window, 52
wings, 196, 198, 205
wisdom books, 203
women
    abduction of, 175
    in book of Judges, 56–57
    exploitation of, 162, 176, 197
world, alliances with, 112, 113
worldly sorrow, 94
worship, as exclusive, 63–64
worthless fellows, 160

Yadin, A., 130
Younger, K. L., 5–6, 49, 97, 159

Zamzummites, 26
Zebulun, 53
Ze'ira, Rabbi, 200
Zorah, 116, 118, 136, 152

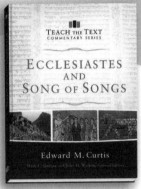

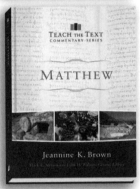